W9-BPM-297

The Old Farmer's Almanac

CALCULATED ON A NEW AND IMPROVED PLAN FOR THE YEAR OF OUR LORD

2007

BEING 3RD AFTER LEAP YEAR AND (UNTIL JULY 4) 231ST YEAR OF AMERICAN INDEPENDENCE

Fitted for Boston and the New England states, with special corrections and calculations to answer for all the United States.

Containing, besides the large number of Astronomical Calculations and the Farmer's Calendar for every month in the year, a variety of

NEW, USEFUL, & ENTERTAINING MATTER.

Established in 1792 by Robert B. Thomas

So the little minutes, humble though they be, make the mighty ages of eternity.
—Julie A. Carney, American poet (1823–1908)

Cover T.M. registered in U.S. Patent Office

Copyright © 2006 by Yankee Publishing Incorporated
ISSN 0078-4516

Library of Congress Card No. 56-29681

Original wood engraving by Randy Miller

Address all editorial correspondence to: THE OLD FARMER'S ALMANAC, DUBLIN, NH 03444

Contents

The Old Farmer's Almanac • 2007

continued on page 4

Contents · continued from page 2

The fads,

fashions, and

farsighted

ideas that

define our life

and times.

compiled by

Anastasia

Kusterbeck

How We Live

INTEREST IN SOLAR ENERGY ON THE RISE

Environmentally conscious home owners are clamoring to power their homes with the Sun's rays. The number of houses getting electricity from the Sun (currently about 200,000) is expected to grow 35 percent this year. "In 2007, demand will again exceed supply," says Ronal Larson, chair of the American Solar Energy Society.

Today's solar panels aren't the conspicuous bulky ones of yesteryear—some are discreetly integrated into roofing tiles. "Photovoltaic" paints and windows are also on the rise.

Not all energy savers are going high tech; some are returning to woodstoves—especially those that burn wood pellets.

NATURE, THE FIRST ARCHITECT

The most cutting-edge design tool these days isn't a computer—it's Mother Nature, with engineers using biological organisms as models for all kinds of inventions. Expect to see . . .

■ **Plywoods and synthetic glues based on mussels' naturally secreted "superglue," which enables them to adhere so well to rocks**

■ **Smoke detectors that mimic jewel beetles' ability to detect freshly burned trees, where they then lay their eggs**

■ **Shatterproof tiles with the strength of abalone shells**

■ **Computer screens that reflect ambient light, using microstructures similar to those found on butterfly wings and peacock feathers**

"If you have a design problem, there is probably an organism that's solved it already," says Janine Benyus, author of *Biologist at the Design Table.*

WE'RE GA-GA OVER GARAGES

Our full-to-overflowing closets have driven sales of home organization products to more than $6 billion annually. So what's a professional organizer to do? How about zeroing in on the new frontier for storing stuff—the garage?

"The average two-car garage has become a no-car garage because it is crammed full of clutter," says Barry J. Izsak, president of the National Association of Professional Organizers. "It is the most unsightly, poorly utilized, neglected room of the house."

In the works: garage-organizing books, garage consultants, and stores devoted to garage organization.

TOUGH-AS-NAILS DÉCOR

New fabrics will be "practically indestructible," says Kenneth Brown, a Los Angeles–based interior designer. We'll see rugs, sofas, and chairs with plastics woven into the fabrics—but they'll feel soft as cotton.

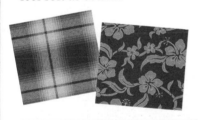

PEOPLE ARE TALKING ABOUT . . .

- Specialized entryway mats designed to remove dirt from shoes as you walk across them
- Kit homes designed by computer and consisting of 1,100 pieces of laser-cut plywood held together with stainless steel fasteners—no posts, beams, or nails
- "Smart" windows that become opaque on summer days to block heat
- Solar-powered backpacks to recharge cell phones
- Customized home furnishings (e.g., monogrammed curtains; the ability to choose the number of drawers in your nightstand)

On the Farm

FARM-FRESH AT YOUR FINGERTIPS

More farmers are selling frozen meat, cheeses, and fruits via

the Web. "People in urban areas don't realize that they can buy a quarter of a cow," says Corinne Alexander, agricultural professor at Purdue University. "There is a huge untapped market out there."

Other offerings include niche items such as soaps, goat's milk, and free-range Thanksgiving turkeys selected by customers as the birds are growing.

On the horizon: regional databases to connect farmers with their hungry customers. To find a farm near you, go to www.local harvest.org.

(c o n t i n u e d)

PEOPLE ARE TALKING ABOUT . . .

■ **Tractors with automatic steering.** Less seed and fertilizer are used, since the ground is covered with more precision.

■ **Agritourism.** "In years past, if folks wanted to go out to the country, they would head out to Grandma's place, but many people have lost ties to farms," says Bruce J. Erickson, an agricultural economics professor at Purdue. Farmers' new cash crop is city folk, to whom they cater with overnight stays, gift shops, theme parks with haunted barns, and guided tours through apple orchards. It's all driven, says Kelly Fuerstenberg, spokesperson for the North American Farmers' Direct Marketing Association, by the public's urge to get back to the farm and the source of their food. To find farms near you, go to www.agritourismworld.com or www.farmstop.com.

A LITTLE BIT COUNTRY

If you've been looking for love in all the wrong places, perhaps you can find it through an online dating service for rural folks. All 15,000 current members are looking for a special someone who is "honest, religious, and family-oriented," according to the site's founder, Jerry Miller (www.farmersonly.com). "You don't need to be a farmer, but you do need to have old-fashioned values." Indeed: Many of the site's users are nonfarm people yearning for a simpler way of life.

In the Garden

PLOTS, NOT PLAYGROUNDS

By growing their own vegetables, children in 3,000 California schools are learning about how food gets on the table. "The results are magical," says Delaine Eastin, founder of

A Garden in Every School. "Even those children who claimed to have hated vegetables in the past have become avid gardeners and partakers of the fruits of their labors." Researchers agree, with studies showing that children change their eating habits as a result of tending a garden.

Great expectations: The National Gardening Association aims to put a garden in every public school. To find a school garden near you, go to www.kidsgardening.com or www.edibleschoolyard.org.

GOING FOR THE GREEN

■ **On the ground:** "Green maps" are now essential tools for thousands of gardeners, tourists, and others who use them to pinpoint botanic gardens, farmer's markets, scenic trails, and the like. "For 2007, we'll be seeing theme-oriented maps for healthy food, energy conservation, water quality, and indigenous culture," says Wendy Brawer, founder of Green Map System, which currently publishes maps for 225 areas. For more information, go to www.greenmap.org.

■ **On the roof:** Grasses, perennials, and herbs on rooftops? High time, some would say. Chicago currently has the most "green roofs" in the United States, amounting to 2 million square feet, but other cities are catching up. "Small

pieces on individual buildings will add up to the effect of big parks," says Diana Balmori, a New York City–based landscape architect. "I expect the most forward-looking of big cities to be full of

Rooftop garden on Chicago's City Hall.

them. They are overlooked real estate and climate and air improvers."

(continued)

■ Permeable paving surfaces to improve driveway drainage

■ Rubber "mulch" made from recycled truck tires that lasts a decade

■ Seed-starters using fibers from recycled coconut shells instead of peat moss

■ Replacing lawns with low-maintenance, chemical-free meadows of native grasses and wildflowers

ADVERTISEMENT

Hot Collectibles

WHY WE BUY

Pieces take us to other time periods. That is the power of stuff," says Tim Luke, a Stuart, Florida–based appraiser and co-owner of TreasureQuest Auction Galleries.

COOLING OFF:

- High-maintenance goods. "People don't have time to polish anymore," says Luke. "You can't give away silver-plated items."

- Contemporary comic books and baseball cards

- Ornate Victorian and Asian black lacquer furniture

GETTING HOT:

- Plastic dolls (e.g., "Blythe" by Kenner and any by Madame Alexander)

- Simple, classic designs (e.g., Danish modern furniture, circa the 1950s; coffee tables and couches, circa the 1970s)

- Vintage (post–World War II) kitchen stoves

- Bell-bottom jeans, circa the 1970s

- Disposables and trinkets (e.g., cereal boxes, gum machine charms, Cracker Jack prizes)

- Signatures of American historical figures (e.g., Amelia Earhart, Charles Lindbergh, presidents). "If you find a signature of Button Gwinnett, a signer of the Declaration of Independence, it's worth half a million dollars," says Luke.

The Way We Look

NATURAL IS IN

People accepted a balance between nature and technology in 2006, but the equilibrium has shifted in nature's favor. We have a greater need for soothing calm and simplicity," says Charles Smith, president of Color Marketing Group.

COLORS TO COUNT ON

Leatrice Eiseman, a spokesperson for Pantone (a firm recognized internationally as the authority on color), predicts big things for these shades:

- Sage and other greens. "There is a larger social movement of sustainability, and green is the color that represents that movement."

- Pastels. "These colors aren't sugary sweet—they're much more sophisticated. Quieter colors are used when people feel the need for comfort."

■ **New neutrals.** "They're not your mother's neutrals—these are colors with subtle nuances, such as when you're not sure if it's blue or gray."

WHAT WOMEN WANT . . .

■ Unique, handcrafted clothing. "The more detail work, the better," says *Vogue* editor Sally Singer. "Women are no longer willing to spend a lot of money on a designer T-shirt. They want something that looks like it was made properly and feels like someone designed it."

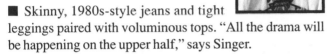

■ Skinny, 1980s-style jeans and tight leggings paired with voluminous tops. "All the drama will be happening on the upper half," says Singer.

■ "Ethical" clothing brands, with apparel makers using recycled fabrics and family-run factories instead of sweatshops.

■ A cleaner, finished look; no more "destroyed" denim

(c o n t i n u e d)

PEOPLE ARE TALKING ABOUT . . .

■ Down-filled skirts developed by a Toronto woman as unisex attire for those times when temperatures plummet. Featuring a Teflon shell for wind protection, a zipper front, and a pocket for holding a disposable heating pouch to warm the wearer's lower back, the full-length garments are fittingly manufactured by a company called Toast.

■ Small, boutique designers. "Consumers are no longer equating hipness with big names and logos. They want little names. People are rooting for the underdogs," Singer observes.

IN MENSWEAR . . .

■ "Unexpected use of fabrics is something we'll notice," says Keith Pollock, fashion editor of men.style.com. "We'll see tuxedos made from sweatshirt material, rain-proof shirting, and neckties filled with down."

■ Formfitting suits, for a tailored rather than mass-produced look

■ Self-designed clothes. "Just as people customize the interiors of their cars, they will do it with clothing," says Pollock. Customized choices will include thread and embroidery on jeans, suit linings, and sneaker sole colors—plus labels bearing the wearer's name.

PEOPLE ARE TALKING ABOUT . . .

■ Automated telephone alerts that tell you when the space shuttle flies over your home or when to expect northern lights activity (http://spaceweather phone.com)

■ "StarSeeker" chairs with mounted binoculars, allowing gazers to look skyward for hours in comfort

Science and Technology

HERE A METEORITE, THERE A METEORITE . . .

The discovery of four new meteorites made 2005 a record-setting year for recovering rocks from outer space in eastern Manitoba. Locals are over the Moon: The area may now rival Antarctica as a new "dumping ground" for space rocks left behind after the last Ice Age.

ANTS 'R' US

A donation of as little as $1,500 will buy the privilege of naming one of 600 new ant species found in Madagascar by Dr. Brian Fisher, an entomologist at the California Academy of Sciences (www.antweb.org). Fisher's goal is to create a database to identify ants anywhere in the world.

THE REALLY BIG PICTURE

The biggest telescopes ever created are coming. They're called Giant Magellan, James Webb, and Very Large Optical Telescope, and are expected to reveal the origin of the universe, thanks to their improved light-gathering capability and sharper images.

MANNING THE MELTDOWN

As ice cover thins, glaciers retreat, and permafrost thaws, scientists are embarking on the International Polar Year 2007–08, a global campaign to study the effects. Researchers will explore the Arctic and Antarctic with high-power computers, unmanned observatories, satellite-based remote sensing, and autonomous underwater vehicles. Watch for traveling educational events such as lectures and interactive exhibits to come to many communities.

How We Work and Play

TOOLS OF THE TRADE

A growing number of midlife workers are swapping their briefcases for tool belts, choosing to climb real ladders instead of corporate ones—and young people are also turning to the trades instead of college. "Many of them don't want to get stuck behind a desk, and they love the ability to physically point to the fruits of their labor at the end of a hard day," says Matt Walker, producer of the DIY network's *Trade School* series.

QUIET, PLEASE!

■ **Research is showing that input overload—from messages via phones, computers, and other high-tech gizmos—is affecting workers more than ever. Instead of resulting in super-efficiency, this information flood makes us unfocused, impulsive, and hasty. It also makes us feel guilty and inadequate. To reduce distractions in general, some bosses are asking employees to wear black baseball caps to signal a need for quiet. Others recommend "Do Not Disturb" signs.**

(c o n t i n u e d)

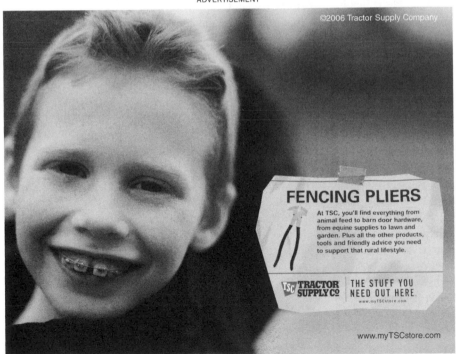

PEOPLE ARE TALKING ABOUT . . .

- **Simplified schedules.** "Time is the new currency, and it is a badge to have—or purport to have—time," says Ron Rentel of Consumer Eyes.

- **In-flight foreign language classes**

- **Retired couples, college grads, and singles forsaking high rents on land to be "live-aboards"—tenants on houseboats at marinas**

THE DNA DIET

- **Cutting calories won't cut it anymore.** Really motivated dieters are now having their DNA checked and tailoring their diets to the results. Adherents aim to modify what they eat based on their genetic risk factors in order to ward off afflictions such as diabetes or bone loss.

PEDESTRIAN PERKS

What's the latest executive status symbol? An office with a walking track instead of conference table and a treadmill instead of a desk chair. "By walking at 1 mile an hour, you don't break a sweat and can type completely normally," says James Levine, an endocrinologist at the Mayo Clinic who designed the work/workout stations to combat rising obesity levels.

NERDY NO MORE

More kids are hanging out in alleys—bowling alleys, that is. Bowling is the fastest-growing varsity sport in 16 states, with more expected to shift the activity from club to competition level. Students love the team spirit, the challenge, and the social scene.

What We Eat

FRUIT LOVERS, UNITE

On the rise in Canada are "exotic" fruits, as vegetable eaters are dwindling, according to a report from Statistics Canada. The increase may be due in part to research showing that pomegranates may prevent prostate cancer, while kiwis thin the blood.

Not so exotic but even more tempting is the apple. Studies show that apples can reduce the risk of asthma and lung cancer, as well as lower cholesterol.

WE'RE HUNGRY FOR INFORMATION

It's not enough today for a product to taste good or be good—we want to know what happens to food before it reaches the store shelf or cooler. "Today's consumer wants to know how the raw materials for the product were grown and processed. They want to know if the farmer received fair compensation for his goods. They want to know that meat, poultry, or fish were treated fairly," says Tom Verhile, director of ProductScan.

MAKE MINE LOCAL

Local food is better food, say a growing number of

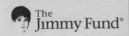

Americans looking for less processed, fresher flavors. College students are calling for school cafeterias to buy local—and others are pushing the "democratization" of local food.

There's also an upsurge in start-up "artisanal" food businesses selling cured meats, cheeses, and jams from treasured family recipes.

HEY, GET YOUR TOFU HERE!

Healthy foods are making headway into the last bastions of junk food: museum restaurants, national parks, and sports and entertainment arenas. Expect to hear vendors hawking organic hamburgers and Polish sausages, as well as tofu burgers with sprouts.

To Our Health

BRAINS, BETTER WITH AGE

A growing body of evidence says that aging brains are more finely tuned than younger brains—a biological basis for what we call wisdom. Scientists now say that older minds are more balanced, after spending decades "upgrading" themselves—a process that isn't completed until midlife.

NOT ENOUGH SHUT-EYE

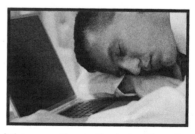

One in seven Canadians has trouble getting enough sleep, with many saying that they are lucky to get even five hours of shut-eye a night, according to Statistics Canada. The U.S. population is equally sleep-deprived, according to the National Sleep Foundation. That's not good. "Sleeping is as important as exercise, drinking, and eating," says Dr. Meir Kryger, director of the Sleep Disorders Center at St. Boniface Hospital in Winnipeg.

(c o n t i n u e d)

SMILE, ROVER

■ When researchers played recordings of dog "laughter" (a breathy exhalation made by pooches), barking and pacing canines at an animal shelter calmed down instantly. "The dogs . . . seem to be happy, not stressed," says animal behaviorist Patricia Simonet. To hear the sound, go to www.laughing-dog.org.

TOP CATS

■ Five percent of cat owners hold a birthday party for their kitties, according to the American Pet Products Manufacturers Association. They also spend more than other pet owners for gifts—$30 per year, on average.

WHERE THERE'S A WILL . . . THERE'S A LESSON

■ More people are leaving behind "ethical wills," which convey life lessons. A new survey says that nonfinancial "gifts"—such as morality, faith, and religion—are more important than money to some benefactors. "Think of it as a love letter to family and friends," says Andrew Weil, author of *Healthy Aging*. "This makes you take stock of your life experiences and distill from it the values and wisdom that you have gained."

Watch for Web sites, books, and consultants to teach us how.

Signs of the Times

LADIES FIRST

Comfortable" is how 79 percent of Americans would feel with a woman as president, according to a poll by Roper Public Affairs. "This is going to be the decade when women are going to lead," says Marie Wilson of the White House Project, a New York City–based nonprofit group supporting future female leaders.

PLUTONIUM PARK?

Innovative cleanup programs are creating controversy as polluted areas such as former landfills and chemical warfare weapons plants are reclaimed for public use. Some examples: Denver's Rocky Flats Wildlife Refuge (formerly a plutonium factory) and California's Orange County Park (previously the El Toro Marine Corps Air Station).

NOISE TOYS

■ Got a loud neighbor? The CD *Revenge* features earsplitting tracks such as "Drill," "Garbage Truck," and "Unhappy Dog"—and comes complete with earplugs.

■ Trapped on the phone with a telemarketer or annoying relative? Use the "Get Off the Phone Excuse" machine, to make it sound as though you have to answer the doorbell or sign for a package.

(c o n t i n u e d)

PEOPLE ARE INVESTING IN . . .

- Alternative energy solutions that rely on the Sun, wind, hydrogen, and biofuels

- American businesses. "While everyone is looking for foreign stocks to be the big winners, there will be a stealth rally in the stocks of the biggest U.S. companies," says *SmartMoney* magazine editor Jack Otter. Referring to mutual funds that can be traded like stocks, Otter adds: "The hot product will be exchange-traded funds, as billions of dollars pour into them."

- Companies owned by or targeting Latinos. Hispanic purchasing power is expected to reach $1 trillion in 2010 (up from $700 billion in 2004), and an increasing number of private equity firms are targeting promising Latino businesses to capitalize on their future success by capitalizing their new endeavors.

Money Matters

SHIFTING PRIORITIES

A quarter of Americans say that getting out of debt is their number one New Year's resolution, trumping losing weight and exercising more, according to a poll taken by the Cambridge Consumer Credit Index. Our debt has more than doubled in the past decade: It's currently $1.98 trillion (or $18,700 per household, on average).

Financial planners are reaping the benefits, with their ranks nearly doubling in the past five years.

DOUBLE YOUR MONEY

A new study says that married couples who stay together end up almost twice as wealthy—per person—as singles. Given child-rearing expenses, the finding is especially surprising. Divorced couples ended up worse off.

"Staying happily married is a wonderful way to increase wealth—but getting married with the idea that it will make you rich is a terrible idea," says researcher Jay Zagorsky of The Ohio State University. The moral? Marry for love, not for money.

THE NEW NEST

The number of single female home owners is surging: Bachelorettes bought 1.5 million houses in 2005, more than double the number purchased by single men.

SOCIAL INSECURITY

The golden years are losing their luster. The responsibility for retirement savings will be all ours—not the government's or our employers'. "People will be given more choices, but less help," says *Fortune* editor Eric Gelman. "The basic message: Start saving now!" □ □

SO, WHAT ELSE IS NEW?

For more statistics, data, and colorful details about our life and times, go to **Almanac.com/extras**.

Better Sleep Better Health Better Bed

The Weightless Comfort™ of Tempur-Pedic!

In a recent survey, 92% of our enthusiastic owners report sleeping better and waking more refreshed! Our sleep technology is recognized by NASA and raved about by the media. And ours is the <u>only</u> mattress recommended worldwide by more than 25,000 medical professionals.

Yet this miracle has to be <u>felt</u> to be believed.

While the thick, ornate pads that cover most mattresses are necessary to keep the hard steel springs inside, they create a hammock effect outside—and can actually *cause* pressure points. Inside *our* bed, billions of microscopic cells work in perfect harmo-

ny to contour precisely to your every curve.

Our scientists used NASA's early anti-G-force research to invent TEMPUR® pressure-relieving material—a remarkable new kind of viscoelastic bedding that *reacts* to body mass and temperature. It *automatically adjusts* to your exact shape and weight. And it's the reason why millions are falling in love with the first *really* new bed in 75 years: our high-tech Weightless Sleep™ marvel.

No wonder, 9 out of 10 of our happy owners go out of their way to recommend our Swedish Sleep System® to friends and family. Call toll-free, without obligation, for your FREE DEMONSTRATION KIT!

TEMPUR-PEDIC®
PRESSURE RELIEVING
SWEDISH MATTRESSES AND PILLOWS

Changing the way the world sleeps!®

© Copyright 2006 by Tempur-Pedic Direct Response, Inc. All Rights Reserved. Furniture components not included.

FREE VIDEO/FREE SAMPLE/FREE INFO

888-702-8557

Call today or send fax 866-795-9367

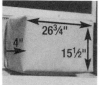

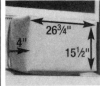

Daisy, Daisy . . .

America's Most Loved (and Misunderstood) Flower

BY CYNTHIA VAN HAZINGA

Buttercups and daisies,
Oh, the pretty flowers;
Coming ere the Springtime,
To tell of sunny hours.
—Mary Howitt (1799–1888)

Everybody loves daisies! A daisy is the first flower a child draws. With its unpretentious air and sunny face, the daisy is a blossom that beams at us. Indeed, in the Victorian language of flowers, the daisy speaks of innocence.

We find daisies and daisy looka-likes in fields and along road-sides—everywhere. Daisies bloom all summer to give us an available and immediate jolt of joy. They embody simple pleasure and have become shorthand for all flowers. In fact, the term "daisy" is often used to refer to different members of the daisy family, the Asteraceae.

All the members of this largest of all plant families bear a strong resemblance to one another.

continued

Most daisies grow 1 to 3 feet tall and have alternate, elongated, lobed leaves. Members of the daisy family include sunflowers, coreopsis, coneflowers, chrysanthemums, asters, cosmos, marigolds, zinnias, and many other familiar flowers.

The daisy's name comes from the old English *daegeseage,* or "day's eye," because it closes at night. The name probably goes back to the Norse god Odin, who had only one eye (he sacrificed the other in order to drink from the well of wisdom).

Common, or ox-eye, daisy is also known as marguerite, from the Greek *margaretes,* or "pearl," perhaps for its pearly color. Others believe that the name may come from Margaret of Anjou, the ruthless, ambitious wife of Henry VI who had daisies embroidered on her personal banners.

To botanists, the ox-eye daisy is *Leucanthemum vulgare,* from the Greek *leukos* for "white" and *anthemum* for "flower." Tall *L. vulgare* is usually alone on its tough stem. It overwinters with a dark-green, basal rosette of hardy leaves and spreads ambitiously (in Zones 3 to 8), via rhizomes as well as seeds, from coast to coast in fields and along roadsides.

The "little," or English, daisy is *Bellis perennis,* Robert Burns's "wee, modest, crimson-tippit flower." It is not wild in North America and is a bit tricky to grow, but it will bloom in a mowed lawn (in Zones 4 to 8). On a cloudy day, these don't open at all. In cultivar form, *B. perennis* often has no golden center.

More Than Meets the Ox-Eye

■ Although we associate the daisy with simplicity, its structure is complicated. Simply speaking, each bloom has a yellow center, or head, surrounded by 15 to 30 narrow, white petals, making a blossom about 1 to 2 inches wide.

LUCKY CHARM
Stepping on the season's first daisy brings good luck.

Right: Ox-eye daisy
'May Queen'
Below: English daisy

—top: Johnny's Selected Seeds; bottom: Park Seed Company

c o n t i n u e d

"A relaxing bath is something we all have a right to."

Walk-In Bath Tubs from Premier

Ed McMahon

Getting older shouldn't get in the way of enjoying your bathroom. Premier's extensive range of Walk-in Tubs have helped improve the lives of thousands of people. Low entry, built in seat and temperature control are some of the benefits our tubs offer. Call or send for a FREE brochure.

Premier BATHROOMS

Please send me a FREE color brochure featuring the Premier range of walk-in tubs

Name _____

Telephone _____

Address _____

City _____

State _____

Zip _____

Send to: Premier Bathrooms Inc, 2330 S. Nova Rd, S. Daytona, Florida 32119 [CODE 53017]

CALL NOW • TOLL FREE
1-800-578-2899
SOURCE CODE 53017

A closer inspection reveals the daisy's composite nature. Each of the white petals is actually a separate flower, known as a ray-flower, or ray. The tightly packed yellow center is made up of the hundreds of true flowers, or tubular florets. If you look very closely with the naked eye, you can see the little tubes. Each one is a complete and perfect flower, called a disk-flower.

One native daisy is fleabane *(Erigeron philadelphicus)*, a biennial; another is gaillardia, or blanketflower. Many of the *Tanacetum* genus, including feverfew, or *T. parthenium*, are daisy lookalikes, as is the 'Susanna Mitchell' marguerite daisy *(Anthemis tinctoria)*.

Relatively new on the scene and very popular with gardeners are daisies from South Africa: the bright-color African or Transvaal daisy *(Osteospermum)* in red, yellow, and orange as well as white (see page 30); brilliant, variously colored gazanias; and the low-growing grassleaf mat daisy *(Hirpicium)*.

Perhaps the quintessential plants are hybrid Shasta daisies (*Leucanthemum* x *superbum*). A gardener's delight, they have strong, straight stems about 3 feet tall and large heads (as much as 5 to 6 inches across) of showy white rays around a golden eye. They form a low, basal rosette of dark-green leaves that are nearly evergreen and can be staked. Stunning Shasta cultivars (perennial from Zones 5 to 8) include 'Snowcap', 'Snow Lady', 'Alaska', 'Little Silver Princess', and 'Crazy Daisy'.

Then there is *L.* 'Becky'. Facing down stiff competition, it was named perennial plant of the year in 2003. 'Becky' popped up in a private garden in Atlanta, Georgia, in the 1960s, a

Right: Shasta daisy 'Becky'

The Master of the Shasta

■ Californian Luther Burbank first grew the hybrid Shasta daisy in 1901; it was the crowning success of his 17-year search for the perfect cut flower. He bred the winning hybrid with a triple cross: The wild ox-eye daisy gave the hybrid cold hardiness; a cross with the English daisy promised a neater clumping habit and large flowers. He

Luther Burbank

crossed the progeny of this marriage with an obscure Japanese chrysanthemum chosen for its sparkling white flowers. Magnificent Mount Shasta rises in the northern part of his home state of California, hence the name.

DesCar
JEWELRY DESIGNS, LTD.

Hundreds of charms,
available in 14kt
White or Yellow Gold,
or Sterling Silver.

www.alkrisdiamonds.com a subsidiary of *DesCar*

49 River Street
Watham, MA 02453

866-253-7610
www.descar.com

at home in nature™

From seaside getaways to mountain retreats, the Pacific Yurt goes where you want to be.

Call today for a brochure:
1.800.944.0240
www.yurts.com

pacific **yurts** inc.
WORLD'S LEADING MANUFACTURER

MAINTAIN YOUR COUNTRY DRIVEWAY WITH THE DR® POWER GRADER!

PROFESSIONAL POWER FOR HOMEOWNERS

WORKS WITH YOUR RIDING MOWER, ATV, OR TRACTOR!

- **PATENTED DESIGN**
  enables you to loosen and regrade enormous amounts of materials with minimal power.

- **POWERED ACTUATOR**
  allows you to control how deeply you remove and regrade material with the push of a button.

- **CARBIDE SCARIFYING TEETH**
  loosen the hardest composite surfaces.

- **FILLS IN POTHOLES AND WASH-OUTS**, and smooths washboard on gravel, limestone, dirt, or sand roads without hauling in new material, shoveling, or raking.

Call for your FREE Catalog and DVD TODAY!

1-800-835-9511

☑ **YES!** Please send me your free information package all about the revolutionary **DR® POWER GRADER**, including factory-direct prices, and details of your 6-month risk-free trial!

Name _____
Address _____ OFA
City _____ State ____ ZIP _____
E-mail _____
DR® POWER EQUIPMENT, Dept. 54293X
127 Meigs Road, Vergennes, VT 05491
www.DRpowergrader.com
© 2006 CHP, Inc.

self-selected hybrid. For years, this dazzling Shasta daisy was passed from gardener to gardener, until it appeared in the Wayside Gardens catalog under the name 'Becky', in honor of Becky Stewart, one gardener who had nurtured the plant. This long-blooming sun-lover is hardy to Zone 4, provided it is grown away from excess moisture and wet soils in winter.

GIVE ME YOUR ANSWER, DO . . .

To learn how to make a daisy chain and how to use (and not use) daisies in the kitchen, plus see the complete lyrics to "Bicycle Built for Two," go to **Almanac.com/extras.**

Growing your own daisies is easy. They thrive in full sun and rich soil with a bit of lime and good drainage, but they readily tolerate poorer soils and partial shade. To keep them blooming, deadhead regularly.

Divide clumps every few years and replant rooted stems at least a foot apart. Insects and diseases seldom bother daisies.

African daisies: 'Kalanga' *(above)*; 'Elena' *(below)*

Friends or Foes?

A little Cyclops, with one eye,
Staring to threaten and defy . . .
–William Wordsworth, English poet (1770–1850)

■ Daisies can be charming, yes, but they also have a dark side, as William Wordsworth warns. To some people, the naturalized, ox-eye daisy is a noxious weed. Sale of its seed is prohibited in many agricultural states, including Ohio, Colorado, Wyoming, Montana, and Washington, and in Canada. Farmers hate it because it spreads aggressively in pastures, choking out more nutritious plants. It tempts cows and then lends an off-flavor to the milk of those that eat it. Thus it is no small wonder that this is sometimes called white weed, poverty weed, or poor-land flower.

–both photos: www.osteospermum.com

Cynthia Van Hazinga, who gardens in New Hampshire, is a master daisy-chainer and welcomes daisies into her gardens.

continued

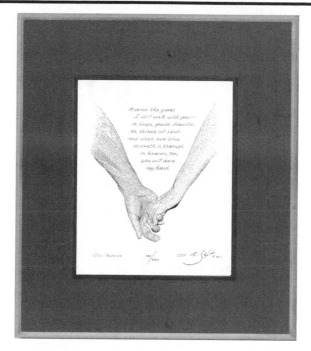

WHAT WOULD WE DO WITHOUT THEM?

Daisies' influence on our culture is just as widespread as the plant itself:

■

Celts considered daisies to be the spirits of children who died at birth.

■

In Christian legend, daisies represent the tears of Mary Magdalene; each tear she shed in repentance became a daisy upon touching the earth.

■

In British tradition, daisies are the flower of April.

■

Juliette Gordon Low, founder of the Girl Scouts, was nicknamed Daisy, which inspired the name for pre-Brownie groups of Scouts, ages 5 and 6, who meet to earn Participation Patches or Learning Petals.

Oops! Ups! What's-a-Daisy?

■ "Upsidaisy" is a nonsense word that exists in a wide variety of forms and spellings; it dates to 1862. "Up-a-dazy" is older, from around 1711. Just as today, the original word represented an exclamation by someone playfully picking up a child. Other variants include "oops-a-daisy" and "whoops-a-daisy."

□ □

☞ *Use the Outdoor Planting Table to find the most favorable planting dates.*

32

Food Emporium

33

Belgian endive. Brussels sprouts. Chinese cabbage. Jerusalem artichoke. Have you ever wondered how these plants got their names? Some varieties of these vegetables have interesting stories to tell about their origin and migration (some, for example, are unrelated to the place whose name they bear) and most—though they have roots in other parts of the world—will thrive in your soil. By growing some international favorites, you can travel the globe without ever leaving your garden.

HARVEST

'AMERICAN GREEN' CELERY has its roots in ancient history. In 628 B.C., the city of Selinus, located on the south coast of Sicily, was considered the celery capital of the world. (*Selino* is the Greek word for celery.) At that time, celery was used as a flavoring and medicinal herb (not as a vegetable) and was so highly valued that coins were embossed with its leaves. Ancient Romans thought that wearing a crown of celery leaves would keep them from getting a hangover, and medieval magicians believed that putting celery seeds inside their shoes

–Park Seed Company

SAVED, SMUGGLED, SOWN

Through the centuries, the seeds of exotic vegetables have been transported around the globe by immigrants, slaves, refugees, missionaries, soldiers, and explorers, who often resorted to ingenious ways to smuggle them: sewn into a hem, stashed inside the lining of a suitcase, hidden under a hatband or in a hollow cane, or concealed under a postage stamp. By whatever means necessary, travelers wanted to maintain their familiar diet and a connection to their homeland.

A WORLD OF FLAVORS

BY ROBIN SWEETSER

would enable them to fly! The city of Kalamazoo, Michigan, was once considered to be the "Celeryville" of the United States because of its large-scale celery growing.

GROWING TIP

Ninety-five percent water, celery grows best in damp, marshy areas. Traditionally, the sweetest celery comes from blanching the stalks—that is, by piling soil around them as they grow. Most new varieties are self-blanching. Look for 'Full White', 'Daybreak', 'Tango', or the heirloom variety 'Golden Self-Blanching'.

BELGIAN ENDIVE, OR WITLOOF CHICORY, was grown during the late 1700s for its root, which was dried, ground, and added to coffee grounds for flavoring and to "stretch" the coffee supply. A Belgian farmer discovered that

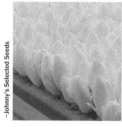

-Johnny's Selected Seeds

the foliage was not only edible but delectable: the paler the leaf, the less bitter the taste, with white leaves having the best flavor (*witloof* is Flemish for "white leaf"). Today, these tender, torpedo-shape heads, called chicons, are a gourmet delicacy that can be eaten raw or cooked.

BLACK SPANISH RADISH was known in ancient Egypt, where it was prized as both food and a remedy for coughs and digestive ailments. It was probably brought to Spain by the Moors during their occupation, from 711 to 1492, and is so named because plants commonly grown on the Iberian Peninsula were generally known as "Spanish." In American colonial times, radishes were often eaten at mealtime and were traditionally planted in the fall for an early spring crop. Along with parsnips, they were one of the first vegetables available to colonists after a long winter. Black radish fell out of favor with the general public over the years, but it is still used for its antibacterial, diuretic, and antioxidant properties.

-seedsofchange.com

BRUSSELS SPROUTS were grown in Flanders (present-day Belgium) during the Middle Ages, when they were known as *spruyten.* Our modern brussels sprouts were first noted in 1752; they spread rapidly throughout Europe in the early 19th century. The Germans called them *rosenkohl,* meaning "rose cabbage,"

-W. Atlee Burpee & Co.

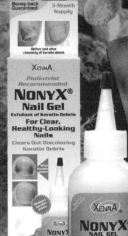
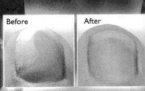

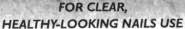

because they resemble rosebuds. Thomas Jefferson introduced the sprouts to the United States in 1812.

GROWING TIP

Brussels sprouts have a distinctly sweet, nutty flavor. For an early crop, try 'Oliver', which matures in just 90 days. It can also be sown late and still produce sprouts.

CHINESE, OR NAPA, CABBAGE has been cultivated for centuries in China. During the 18th century, returning missionaries brought seeds to Europe. There are many varieties that use the name Chinese cabbage, some originally coming from Thailand.

This is a cool-weather crop more closely related to turnip than to cabbage. 'Michihli', widely grown in the Orient and in the United States, has tall heads of pale-green, crinkly leaves and wide white ribs that look so much like fat celery that the plant is sometimes called celery cabbage. The plant is sensitive to day length and cold night temperatures.

PLANTING TIP

Plant in August for a late fall crop. Direct-seed or use peat pots, as it does not like to be transplanted.

—W. Atlee Burpee & Co.

The **JERUSALEM ARTICHOKE** has nothing to do with the Israeli city; the plant is native to North America. The name comes from a corruption of its Italian name, *girasole articiocco,* meaning "sunflower artichoke"—but it isn't even an artichoke! It is related to the sunflower and, like it, turns its blossoms toward the Sun. Today, it is often called sunchoke. On a trip to the New World in 1615, French explorer Samuel de Champlain noticed the 6- to 10-foot-tall perennial being grown by the Hurons. He collected samples and brought the plant to France, where it was a hit at first bite.

—Johnny's Selected Seeds

COOKING TIP

The tubers have a distinctive nutty taste and can be eaten raw, baked, or boiled. For the best flavor, harvest after the first frost. (Beware: The sunchoke is an invasive perennial; once you plant it, you'll always have it.)

NEW ZEALAND SPINACH isn't true spinach, but it is indeed from that island nation. Sir Joseph Banks discovered the plant growing on the shores of Queen Charlotte's Sound during Captain Cook's 1770 voyage. It proved to be a valuable source of vitamin C for the sailors and was introduced in North America soon after.

The plant's Latin name is *Tetragonia expansa,* though it is sometimes called summer spinach. The small, triangular-shape leaf does not look like spinach,

Gardening

but it has a similar taste. Unlike spinach, it thrives in the summer heat and is free of pests, but it is sensitive to cold.

> **PLANTING TIP** — To speed germination, soak seeds overnight in warm water before sowing.

–Seed Savers Exchange

POTATOES originated in South America. Today, we have more than 400 international varieties—one for almost every ethnic group, including 'Russian Banana', 'Swedish Peanut' (shown below), 'Irish Cobbler', 'Rose Finn Apple', and 'Purple Peruvian'. The German 'Lady Finger' potato, a pale-brown, 4- to 5-inch-long spud also called a fingerling, was brought to North America by immigrants.

> **PLANTING TIP** — When cutting a seed potato, be sure to keep plenty of flesh around the eyes; this is the food that the plant will need during its initial growth period.

–W. Atlee Burpee & Co.

'PALAWA' GARLIC is named for an island in the Philippines, not a part of the world usually associated with the plant. Garlic is believed to have originated in the mountains of Central Asia.

> **PLANTING TIP** — This soft-neck variety is prized for its mild taste and long storage life. Plant in the fall for a summer harvest.

–Territorial Seed Company

'POLISH LINGUISA' TOMATO is an heirloom variety that was brought by an immigrant family to New York in the late 1800s. The sweet, sausage-shape fruits have a tender skin and are good raw or in sauces.

> **GROWING TIP** — In about 75 days, this vigorous and highly productive plant bears mature 7- to 10-ounce fruit packed with vitamins, fiber, and potassium.

'ROMANIAN ANTOHI' PEPPER is named for Jan Antohi, a Romanian acrobat who defected to the United States while touring in the early 1980s. Following the subsequent overthrow of dictator Nicolae Ceaucescu in 1989, Antohi went back to his

GET GROWING

For advice on preparing soil, starting seeds, and transplanting sets, go to **Almanac.com/extras.**

homeland to visit his family. They gave him seeds from their favorite pepper, a Romanian heirloom dating from before 1920, to take back to the United States when he returned in 1991.

–Johnny's Selected Seeds

The Antohi is a mildly hot, 4-inch-long tapered pepper that is yellow when it first appears and turns red over its 70-day maturation period. It is best cooked the Romanian way—fried in a hot skillet to bring out the full flavor.

SWISS CHARD originated in Sicily. (Even though there is a variety called 'Swiss chard of Geneva' that may have originated in Switzerland, the plant itself is not from there.) The Swiss reference was meant to distinguish it from French cardoon, "chard" being a corruption of the French word *chardon,* for cardoon. The variety 'Lucullus' was named after the Roman general Lucius Lucullus, who was famous for his sumptuous banquets.

–Johnny's Selected Seeds

☞ *Find the most favorable planting dates in the Outdoor Planting Table.*

Bred for its tasty leaves, chard is a cultivated form of the sea beet. It is easy to grow as a cut-and-come-again crop by harvesting the outer leaves and allowing the center to keep growing. It will keep producing until the first hard frost.

The WEST INDIAN GHERKIN sounds Jamaican but is African in origin, having been carried from Algeria in the slave trade. In 1793, merchant Minton Collins of Richmond, Virginia, brought it to the United States, where it enjoyed great popularity throughout the 19th century. Today, this cucumber is widely grown from Brazil to the Caribbean.

–Pinetree Garden Seeds

This gherkin has large, vigorous vines; its foliage resembles watermelon leaves. It is best when small—under 1½ inches long—and used for pickling. If allowed to mature, it becomes spiny, seedy, and bitter. Legend has it that the success of any cucumber depends on the virility of the planter!

Robin Sweetser, who lives in New Hampshire, grows a multicultural garden that includes Asian eggplants, French beans, Greek basil, Czech tomatoes, and Italian broccoli.

TheElegantCane
...*a fashionable alternative*

A full palette of hand-painted canes are available in a variety of colors and designs.

Call Toll Free:
888-244-2020

On-Line at:
TheElegantCane.com

MEN'S WIDE SHOES
EEE-EEEEEE
SIZES 5-15

FREE catalog
200 styles

HITCHCOCK SHOES,INC.
Dept. FA2 Hingham, MA 02043
1-800-992-WIDE   *www.wideshoes.com*

STEAM MODELS
Over 150 Working Steam Toys, Stirling Hot Air Engines and Collectible Tin Toys.
Kits or Assembled From $74.21
43 PAGE COLORED CATALOG $6.95
CATALOG IS REFUNDABLE WITH ORDER
YESTERYEAR TOYS & BOOKS INC.
DEPT. OF7 • BOX 537, ALEXANDRIA BAY, NY 13607
1-800-481-1353   www.yesteryeartoys.com

ADDRESS LABELS by FAMILY LABELS®
THE MILLER FAMILY
13785 Woodcliff Drive • Orlando, FL 32835

Michael   Rhonda   Brandon   Tina   Salty   Brandy

Visit us on the web: www.familylabels.com
Call for a free brochure: 1-800-441-2945

Glide Upstairs on a Stannah Stairlift!

- A family business since 1862
- Buy direct from the world's largest stairlift manufacturer
- Ideal for narrow stairs with tight turns
- FREE in-home evaluation
- New or reconditioned, buy or rent
- We service all Stannah Stairlifts and offer a guaranteed buy-back
- Visit our showroom!

www.stannah.com

Call for FREE information NOW!
1-800-877-8247 x 166

101 CONSTITUTION BLVD., SUITE C, FRANKLIN, MA 02038

45 KNOLLWOOD RD, ELMSFORD NY 10523
LOCAL TEL 914-345-8484

CARVING CUES from a PUMPKIN PRO

by Jeff Baker

Michael Valladao saw his first giant pumpkins at California's Half Moon Bay Pumpkin Festival in 1984. The event's biggest entry weighed 612 pounds and was (at the time) the world's largest pumpkin. Valladao left the festival determined to grow his own field of great pumpkins at his San Jose home. He contacted a grower for seeds, planted and tended them, and by the next year had produced gargantuan specimens of 'Atlantic Giant'. His neighbors were impressed, but he was left wondering, What do you do with pumpkins that weigh three times as much as you do? "That's when I pulled out the carving chisels and started

Whether your prospective jack-o'-lantern weighs five pounds or 500, the tips on the next pages will help you make it special.

"Farmer Mike" Valladao and friend

–photography: Susan Valladao

to work on the pumpkins," he says.

The first public showing of two of Valladao's pumpkins—one a "Man in the Moon" face and the other a head atop another pumpkin that served as the body, complete with arms of pumpkin rind—took place at a local country club in 1985. Word of his talent spread, and the following year he returned to the Half Moon Bay festival, but not as an observer. He was named the event's "official" pumpkin carver and has held the position ever since, becoming a main attraction.

Valladao believes that every pumpkin has a personality waiting to be revealed. Where others see only gnarls and bumps on the orange-color rinds, he imagines facial features such as rippled chins, toothy or "dopey" grins, bulbous noses, deep-set eyes, and odd wrinkles. Within three

hours, on average, using mainly a common pocketknife (he discarded the chisels long ago), he can bring out these features, creating a fantastic character. His secret is a self-taught method he calls "pumpkin carving in the round," a reference to the three-dimensional aspect of his carvings. He carves the rind all around the pumpkin (sometimes including ears) instead of just the face on the front.

Today, Valladao is better known as "Farmer Mike," and he continues to grow 'Atlantic Giant' pumpkins, usually ranging in size from 150 to 1,000 pounds. He carves 30 to 40 pumpkins every autumn, often in front of audiences at malls, casinos, and state fairs. He says that one of the first questions from onlookers is always, "Are they real?"

CARVING TIPS

"The whole concept here is to have fun," Valladao says. **"The only thing that you really need to carve a pumpkin is imagination."**

HOW TO PICK A GOOD PUMPKIN FOR CARVING: Look for one that is a little misshapen. Inspect it for soft spots (especially the end opposite the stem). Reject a pumpkin that has soft spots; they will cause it to deteriorate quickly. Remember, your pumpkin doesn't have to sit on its base; in fact, that's often its weakest spot.

Let the pumpkin guide the shape of the face: An elongated pumpkin should have an elongated face. A fat and happy pumpkin should have a fat and happy face.

HOLLOW OR WHOLE? There are two reasons for hollowing: (1) If the inside is going to be exposed (through the mouth, etc.), it looks better if it is hollowed neatly. (2) If you plan to light the pumpkin from the inside, it must be

Where others see only gnarls and bumps on the orange-color rinds, Valladao imagines facial features such as rippled chins, toothy or "dopey" grins, bulbous noses, deep-set eyes, and odd wrinkles.

hollow. You can hollow it out from a hole in the back instead of the top, so that the look of the face isn't affected. If you're illuminating with a candle, you need to hollow from the top to allow the heat and smoke to escape.

THE TOOLS: Use a water-based marker to outline the face that you want to carve. First, draw a line down the center to establish symmetry. Then sketch the nose, the approximate center of the face. Once you're satisfied with the details, trace over the lines using a permanent marker. For carving, basic kitchen implements, such as a paring knife or a steak knife with a standard—not serrated—blade that's not going to bend, work well. You can also use a standard jigsaw blade. Otherwise, improvise: Use a melon-ball cutter to make circles, for example.

CARVE WITH CARE. Use two hands at all times: one to control the blade and the other to control the pressure with which you cut (and thus the depth). Take care not to jab the blade into the pumpkin; you don't want to cut all the way through the rind—except to determine its depth. The thickness of the rind will vary, not only from pumpkin to pumpkin, but also within one pumpkin. To determine your pumpkin's average depth, cut a core sample where you want an eye or a nostril to be. Keep that piece nearby as a reminder of how deep you can safely cut.

MAKE A FACE. To achieve a three-dimensional appearance, carve the entire pumpkin. Exaggerate the features.

(continued)

(If you aren't sure what teeth really look like or how the gum line works, smile and look in the mirror.) If the pumpkin is frowning, carve wrinkles under the mouth. To add character, carve a lot of "crow's feet" lines around the eyes.

Consider using the stem as the nose and inserts such as radishes for the eyes, or cut eyeballs from the back of the pumpkin and hold them in place with toothpicks.

ENJOY IT WHILE IT LASTS. Pumpkins, which are actually a fruit, not a vegetable, are 90 percent water, so after carving they usually last only three days to a week. A jack-o'-lantern with a surface carving will last longer than one that is cut all the way through. Putting a candle or other light inside will shorten its life span, as the heat that results can "cook" the pumpkin and reduce its longevity to a matter of hours.

For a bright, shiny finish, spray Armor All on the pumpkin and rub it in. Paint will not preserve a pumpkin. However, if you decide to paint your pumpkin for decoration, use a water-based latex paint and wait at least an hour after carving so that the cuts you have made in the pumpkin have a chance to dry. □ □

Jeff Baker writes from the Pacific Northwest. He is a self-proclaimed expert at carving into pumpkin pies.

FIELD REPORT

People love pumpkins.

☞ U.S. growers produced 998 million pounds of pumpkins in 2004; that's up from 815 million pounds in 2003. The top pumpkin-producing states are (in millions of pounds):

Illinois	.457
Pennsylvania	.136
Ohio	.112
California	.110
Michigan	.101

–courtesy U.S. Dept. of Agriculture National Agricultural Statistics Survey, 2005

☞ Between 1986 and 2001, Canadian farmers more than doubled the area planted with pumpkins. Over 5,700 hectares were planted, including . . .

■ 2,024 hectares in southern Ontario

■ 828 hectares in the Montérégie region of Quebec

■ 376 hectares in lower mainland/southwestern British Columbia

–courtesy Statistics Canada

GROW A GREAT PUMPKIN

For advice on how to grow a giant pumpkin (or just an average-size one), go to **Almanac.com/extras.**

Do You Need Pea and Bean Shelling Equipment?

Whether you're a small gardener or a professional grower, the famous "Little Sheller" or one of our commercial hullers will take the work out of your pea and bean shelling. These machines are efficient, smooth running, and easy to operate.

FOR FREE BROCHURE WRITE:

TAYLOR MANUFACTURING CO., INC. OFA07
128 Talmadge Dr., Moultrie, GA 31768   (800) 985-5445   www.peasheller.com

Home of the "Little Sheller" for over 42 years

THE AMAZING
TWENTY
POUND

MANTIS
TILLER

One Year RISK-FREE Home Trial!

The *Mantis*ller/Cultivator

- Tills up to 10" deep
- Cultivates in narrow rows
- Patented serpentine tines

Call for FREE Info and Video

1-800-366-6268

send coupon or visit www.emantis.com

To: Mantis, 1028 Street Rd., Dept. **MT8009**
Southampton, PA 18966

☑ YES! Please rush me **FREE INFORMATION** and a **FREE VIDEO** about the amazing Mantis Tiller/Cultivator!

Name_____

Street _____

City_____

State _____ Zip_____

©2005 Mantis Div. of Schiller-Pfeiffer, Inc.

SUNPORCH®
SUNROOM / SCREENROOM

COMPLETE KIT
READY-TO-ASSEMBLE
ON YOUR DECK OR PATIO

BUILD AND PRICE ONLINE

- Build it in a weekend!
- Converts from screens to windows in minutes!
- Factory direct pricing, delivered to your door.
- Standard & custom sizes.
- Meets codes for snow & wind loads.

FOR CATALOG, SIZES & PRICES

- **www.sunporch.com**
  Promo Code: OFA

- **1-203-557-2569**
  Extension: OFA
  Mon-Fri 8AM-5PM EST

SunPorch®
Our 32nd Year

The Commonsense Apple Orchard

A hedge between keeps friendship green.

Ever wish you could have an apple orchard in your backyard? You can—in the space of a single tree—if you plant a hedge of dwarf apple trees or an apple espalier. What's more, such plantings are bountiful: The trees send up aromatic blossoms in spring, serve as a green screen through the summer, and yield a harvest in fall.

Before you get out your shovel, do some planning. An apple

'Egremont Russet' apples thrive in an espalier supported by a fence.

by Tim Hensley

hedge invites interaction, so you'll want it to be conveniently located. Choose a site that allows the hedge to thrive—that is, where it will get plenty of sunlight and sufficient airflow. If your hedge is visible from your kitchen window, so much the better: You can keep an eye out for apple-pecking jays and starlings.

The best exposure for apples is a north- or east-facing slope. Apples on a south or west face tend to bloom early, making them susceptible to late frosts. They also drop fruit during extended periods of hot, dry weather. One exception is worth noting: If you live north of the Mason-Dixon Line and want to grow apples that ripen late—'Arkansas Black' or 'Ralls Genet', for example—plant on a south-facing slope to extend the growing season as much as possible.

Dwarf apple trees are notoriously prone to uprooting under the weight of a heavy crop, so you must provide a support system for your hedge. There are a number of ways to do this. You can grow your trees against a fence. (Almost any kind will do: board, rail, even chain link.) You can plant them next to buildings. Or you can provide freestanding support in the form of a trellis.

For a more formal look, create an apple espalier. Espaliered trees require tight spacing. Five or six feet is the standard for high-density, commercial plantings. Two-foot centers are adequate to grow lots of different apples in a small space. Dwarf rootstock can be planted as close as one foot apart. Close spacing necessitates pruning the trees to a very specific form. An "oblique fan" apple espalier is easy to maintain (just

prune to two dimensions); it is also a little more artistic than a simple straight-up planting. Other forms to consider include tiered, oblique cordon, and Belgian fence.

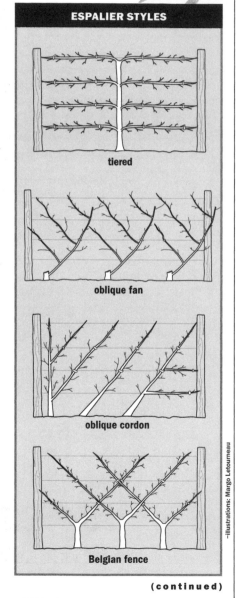

ESPALIER STYLES

tiered

oblique fan

oblique cordon

Belgian fence

—Illustrations: Margo Letourneau

(continued)

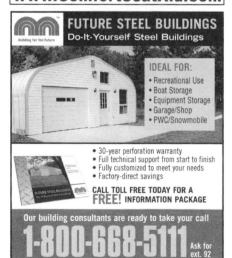
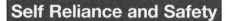

From the Bottom Up: Rootstocks and Pruning

*T*he most technical aspect of planting a home orchard is choosing the foundation for your trees, or what is known as the rootstock. For an apple espalier, this means a full-dwarf root, of which there are many options. Consult a specialty nursery for full-dwarf apple trees; don't risk purchasing a semi-dwarf root from a general retailer. Here are some rootstocks to consider:

M9/EMLA 111: a double graft that produces a vigorous, freestanding, 12- to 15-foot-tall tree; often more expensive because of the labor involved in a double graft.

BUD 9: a Russian rootstock that makes a hardy, 10-foot-tall tree; even growth makes this easy to train.

M9: probably the most widely planted dwarf rootstock; produces a tree that grows to about 10 feet; susceptible to fire blight, a serious bacterial infection.

CG16: new from Cornell University; similar in size to M9; resists fire blight.

'Newtown Pippin'

–Rob Crassweller/Penn State University

56

(continued)

New England style

$\mathcal{C}$ountry Carpenters introduces Early New England Homes.

Our 1750s style cape home building system boasts beautiful timbered ceilings, a center chimney, wide board floors and many custom, handmade features. This home reflects all the charm of early New England life with the convenience and efficiency of a new home. Our model is open Monday-Friday, 8-4:30 and Saturdays, 9-3.

Come see how the timeless traditions of an Early New England Home can improve your lifestyle today!

Early New England HOMES™
by country carpenters, inc.

26 West Street (Route 85) Bolton, CT 860.643.1148
www.EarlyNewEnglandHomes.com

The Secret to Successful Pollination

Some people believe that you have to plant two trees of every variety to get good pollination. Others say that pollination is not a problem as long as you have a crab apple within a few hundred yards.

The truth is somewhere in the middle. On one hand, if you plant three or four different trees, it's not likely that you'll have a problem setting fruit. But if you want to plant only one or two varieties, you could end up with no fruit at all. Some trees, such as 'Arkansas Black', 'Mutsu', and 'Stayman Winesap', are infertile; their pollen is sterile. If you plant these trees together, none of them will produce a single apple.

For best results, include a 'Grimes Golden', 'Golden Delicious', 'Red Delicious', or 'Winter Banana' in your planting. These varieties are known pollinators, and their midseason bloom covers just about any tree you could name.

A pollination chart also comes in handy. Available in nursery catalogs and books on apple culture, these charts tell you which trees need pollen, which ones provide pollen, and which ones are self-fruitful.

Choosing Varieties

A young dwarf tree produces about 1½ bushels of fruit—and even less when the tree is part of an apple hedge. So, if you're interested in baking lots of 'Cox's Orange Pippin' apple pies, you'll need to plant several trees of that variety to get enough fruit. If you have no particular culinary goal, try planting one each of different varieties that ripen over the entire harvest season. (See below and page 62 for some suggestions.) This will allow you to enjoy regular apple tastings and still have enough fruit on hand for a "mess" of cooked apples.

The Apples of My Eye

■ 'Yellow Transparent', also known as the June apple, is a yellow, thin-skinned sort that cooks up to make a superb sauce.

■ 'Summer Rambo' ripens in late August/early September and has a light, sprightly flesh. It makes delicious apple butter.

–Rob Crassweller/Penn State University

'York'

–Adams County Nursery

'Jonagold'

(continued)

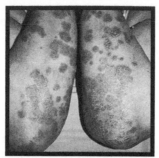
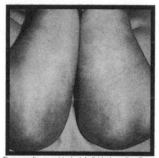

■ 'York' stays crisp and fresh late into the winter. It is an excellent choice for making cider.

■ 'Virginia Beauty' has a mild, sweet flavor with hints of cherry and vanilla. It is most delicious eaten right off the tree.

Final words of advice: Not every apple will do well in all parts of the country. Seek out the advice of local orchardists about varieties that will do well in your area. Do the bulk of your planning from an easy chair, with a half-dozen nursery catalogs in your lap—and expect to order more trees than you need. You'll discover, over time, that there is more work in an orchard than you imagined. Still, taking care of an apple hedge or espalier is the kind of work that makes for some truly glorious rewards, all season long.

Tim Hensley, whose home sits on a 50x150-foot urban lot in Virginia, maintains a 24-tree espalier. It occupies roughly 120 square feet—less than half the area used by a single semi-dwarf tree at maturity.

'Cox's Orange Pippin'

(continued)

1-12 Stone Mother's Basket

Born from the tradition of the Nantucket Lightship Basket, we present the **Original Mother's Basket** with each flower representing your child's birth month. Handcrafted 14K gold pendant, synthetic stones, and 14K gold chain. *$200-$312* (based on number of stones)

Cranberry Jewelers
554 Rte. 28, Harwich Port, Cape Cod, MA 02646
Toll free **1-866-286-5036**
www.cranberryjewelers.net

Real Cedar Hot Tubs
• *Electric, gas or wood fired models*
• *Basic soaking tubs, exercise tubs, or full-featured spas.*
• *Natural cedar or bonded fiberglass interiors*

Maine Cedar Hot Tubs, Inc.
P.O. Box 689
Skowhegan, ME 04976
207.474.0953
Email: dewinc@prexar.com
www.mainecedartubs.com

NEW Long 'N Strong Extra
Grows Longer, Thicker, Hair In Just 5-7 Days!!!

IMAGINE YOUR HAIR WAIST LENGTH! Not a false hair extension but your own hair... grown naturally with the remarkable fast-acting formulation - **New Long 'N Strong Extra**. This amazing "Hair Raising" formulation "nourishes" your hair right down to the root. You simply won't believe your eyes... Longer, Thicker, Stronger - - Radiantly Alive Hair in just 5 - 7 days!!!

"Serving The Public Since 1977"

Long 'N Strong Extra conditions from within without messy buildup. Helps restore natural moisture balance as it repairs damage caused by chemicals, rich in hair building proteins, vitamin B5 (Panthenol) polymers and sunscreen block. Non-sticky, 100% safe, even for colored, tinted, or processed hair. **Long 'N Strong Extra** with Polyquaternium-II..... adds EXTRA THICKNESS to thinning hair.

Developed by a world-renowned pharmaceutical co. and now brought to you in this exclusive formulation. *See the following clinical photos.*

 BEFORE: Ends are splitting, breaking off.

AFTER: See how split ends have been corrected. Goodbye to weak, brittle, straw-like hair that breaks in bunches.

 THICKENS HAIR
BEFORE
AFTER

FOR ALL TYPES OF HAIR

Rush Industries ©2004 06/01/04   **30 DAY MONEY BACK GUARANTEE** (less S&H)

Send to: Rush Ind., Inc.™ Dept. KRE223GA
263 Horton Hwy., Mineola, NY 11501
Yes, I wish to keep my hair growing longer, thicker, stronger every-day! Please send:
❏ 30 Day Supply **LONG 'N STRONG Extra**
  Only $14.95 + $2.95 Ship. + Handling
❏ **Save $5** 60 Day Supply Only $24.90 + $3.95 Ship. + Handling
❏ **Save $10** 90 Day Supply Only $34.85 + $4.95 Ship. + Handling
❏ **Express service add $5.00 per order**

Enclosed is $_____ Or Charge It!
❏ Visa ❏ MC ❏ Amex ❏ Dscvr Exp. Date_____
Acct.# _____
Name_____
Address_____
City_____
State_____Zip_____
Credit Card Buyers • Order By Phone! Call (516) 741-0346

Order By Phone! Call (516) 741-0346 or at www.rushindustries.com

A Few Good Apples

Apple	Characteristics	Taste	Best Use	Harvest Season	Hardiness Zones
'Arkansas Black' (orig. in Benton County, Arkansas, c. 1870)	Medium to large; waxy skin, dark red to nearly black; yellow flesh; keeps well	Mildly sweet	Sauces, cider	Late October–November	5–8
'Cox's Orange Pippin' (the most popular English apple)	Dull, orange-red skin	Exquisite flavor and aroma	Pies, fresh eating	September–October; keeps into January	5–8
'Duchess of Oldenburg' (orig. in Russia; brought to North America from England, 1835)	Flatly rectangular fruit; thick, pale-yellow skin with crimson stripes and splashes	Tart	Pies, sauces	August–September	4–8
'Early Harvest' (one of the finest early apples)	Medium; yellow skin	Rich, sprightly, sweet-tart	Pies, sauces	June–August	2–7
'Grimes Golden' (orig. in West Virginia, 1775)	Medium to large	Sweet, rich, spicy	Juice, cider, fresh eating	October; keeps into January	5–7
'Jonagold' (a cross of 'Jonathan' and 'Golden Delicious', 1968)	Hardy, productive tree; coloring varies with season	Full, sweet-tart	Baking, sauces	September–October	5–8
'Newtown Pippin' (also known as 'Yellow Newtown')	Medium, squatty fruit, with greenish-yellow skin	Rich, crisp	Baking, cider	October–November; with proper storage, will keep until March	5–8
'Spigold' (a cross of 'Northern Spy' and 'Golden Delicious')	Red stripes over green	Juicy, sweet, distinctive	All purposes	October	4–8
'Sweet Sixteen' (a cross of 'Malinda' and 'Northern Spy')	Late-blooming, good for frost pockets; red stripes	Faint nutty flavor	Pies, sauces	September–October	3–6
'Wolf River' (orig. in Wisconsin, 1875)	Vigorous, productive tree; large, dull-red over yellow fruit	Juicy, subacid	Baking, pies, or apple butter	September–October	2–8

CORE CONSIDERATIONS

Get tips on building a trellis and find out how the author would have done his differently at **Almanac.com/extras**.

To Patrons

Beginnings, Ends, and Trends

This Almanac regularly observes others' anniversaries. This year, we note a few of our own.

***

First, 2007 marks the 175th anniversary of the word "Old" in our title. How did this come to be?

In 1792, "farmer's almanacs" were ubiquitous—for good reason. Most people lived on farms and grew at least a portion of their food. They sought practical, reliable advice on a variety of daily matters. Among almanac makers, the competition for readers was fierce and, as a result, nobody had a majority of market share.

Until 1793. That was the first issue year of this Almanac by Robert B. Thomas. By name, this was like all the others, called simply *The Farmer's Almanac,* but its contents apparently better served the public. The first edition outsold all of its competitors. The second, at triple the print run of the first, was also a best-seller. Ensuing editions similarly enjoyed an increasing readership.

Fast-forward to 1831. Although Thomas's Almanac had by then outsold and outlasted countless others, it was not yet officially "Old." Perhaps, though, at 66, Thomas felt that way. In the next edition, he added "Old" to the title (hence the anniversary) and penned this observation: "Time, which brings all things to a conclusion, will soon terminate our labors."

Fortunately, Thomas's labors did not "terminate." Four years later, having apparently regained some pep and optimism, he struck "Old" from the title of his Almanac, without comment. He continued calculating and publishing *The Farmer's Almanac* until the age of 80, when he died reading proofs of the 1847 edition. By then, his was unquestionably the oldest almanac in the country, so his successor, John H. Jenks, returned "Old" to the title of the next edition, forever distinguishing it from any competition.

***

Another man who had a lasting impact on this Almanac was Dr. Richard M. Head, who died in January 2006. Dr. Head was a weather scientist— a renowned authority on sunspot and solar flare activity and their influence on Earth's atmosphere. He spent much of his illustrious career at NASA, where, among other things, he forecast the safest "windows" in which to launch Apollo space missions. Later, he was named NASA's first chief scientist. In 1970, at the invitation of this Almanac's then-editor Robb Sagendorph, Head began making what would be a quarter-century of weather predictions on these pages. In keeping with tradition, he assumed the pseudonym "Abe Weatherwise," but before long, this editorial veil was lifted by Sagendorph to reveal Head's real name. This cast light on Head's consid-

Dr. Richard M. Head

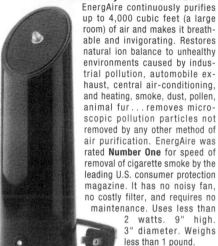

erable expertise and—not coincidentally—the Almanac's credibility.

Today, we have Head to thank for the formats both of our forecasts and of our regional weather maps. Most important, however, we thank him for bringing state-of-the-art science to our predictions—and for his career-average 87 percent accuracy rate regarding sunspot activity.

***

We are also grateful for the contributions of George Greenstein, a professor of astronomy at Amherst College, who 30 years ago—using punched cards and an IBM mainframe computer—worked with several assistants for weeks to produce for our 1978 edition his first rendition of our astronomical events. These were then mailed to our offices and typed up by editors. Today, he supervises the computer generation of this information, which is delivered via e-mail.

***

Finally, in noting another trend of the old toward the new, we call your attention to Almanac.com/podcast, where you can find audio versions of our Farmer's Calendar. Each month's essay is read by the author himself, Castle Freeman Jr., whom we now thank for providing 25 years of captivating natural observations. Without his insights each year, *The "Old" Farmer's Almanac* would not be the same. J. S., June 2006

However, it is by our works and not our words that we would be judged. These, we hope, will sustain us in the humble though proud station we have so long held in the name of

Your obedient servant,

2007   THE OLD FARMER'S ALMANAC   67

THE 2007 EDITION OF

The Old Farmer's Almanac

Established in 1792 and published every year thereafter

ROBERT B. THOMAS (1766–1846), *Founder*

YANKEE PUBLISHING INC.

EDITORIAL AND PUBLISHING OFFICES
P.O. Box 520, 1121 Main Street, Dublin, NH 03444
Phone: 603-563-8111 • Fax: 603-563-8252

EDITOR *(13th since 1792):* Janice Stillman
ART DIRECTOR: Margo Letourneau
SENIOR/INTERNET EDITOR: Mare-Anne Jarvela
COPY EDITOR: Jack Burnett
SENIOR ASSOCIATE EDITOR: Heidi Stonehill
RESEARCH EDITOR: Martie Majoros
ASSISTANT EDITOR: Sarah Perreault
WEATHER GRAPHICS AND CONSULTATION:
AccuWeather, Inc.

PRODUCTION DIRECTOR: Susan Gross
PRODUCTION MANAGER: David Ziarnowski
SENIOR PRODUCTION ARTISTS: Lucille Rines,
Rachel Kipka, Nathaniel Stout

WEB SITE: ALMANAC.COM
NEW MEDIA DIRECTOR: Paul Belliveau
DESIGN COORDINATOR: Lisa Traffie
DESIGNER: Stephen O. Muskie
PROGRAMMER: Peter Rukavina

CONTACT US
We welcome your questions and comments about articles in and topics for this Almanac. Mail all editorial correspondence to Editor, The Old Farmer's Almanac, P.O. Box 520, Dublin, NH 03444-0520; fax us at 603-563-8252; or send e-mail to us at almanac@ yankeepub.com. *The Old Farmer's Almanac* can not accept responsibility for unsolicited manuscripts and will not acknowledge any hard-copy queries or manuscripts that do not include a stamped and addressed return envelope.

The newsprint in this edition of *The Old Farmer's Almanac* consists of 23 percent recycled content. All printing inks used are soy-based. This product is recyclable. Consult local recycling regulations for the right way to do it.

Thank you for buying this Almanac!
We hope you find it new, useful, and entertaining.
Thanks, too, to everyone who had a hand in it, including advertisers, distributors, printers, and sales and delivery people.

OUR CONTRIBUTORS

Bob Berman, our astronomy editor, is the director of Overlook Observatory in Woodstock and Storm King Observatory in Cornwall, both in New York. In 1976, he founded the Catskill Astronomical Society. Bob will go a long way for a good look at the sky: He has led many aurora and eclipse expeditions, venturing as far as the Arctic and Antarctic.

Castle Freeman Jr., who lives in southern Vermont, has been writing the Almanac's Farmer's Calendar essays for 25 years. The essays come out of his longtime interest in wildlife and the outdoors, gardening, history, and the life of rural New England. His most recent book is *My Life and Adventures* (St. Martin's Press, 2002).

George Greenstein, Ph.D., who has been the Almanac's astronomer for 30 years, is the Sidney Dillon Professor of Astronomy at Amherst College in Amherst, Massachusetts. His research has centered on cosmology, pulsars, and other areas of theoretical astrophysics, and on the mysteries of quantum mechanics. He has written three books and many magazine articles on science for the general public.

Celeste Longacre, our astrologer, often refers to astrology as "the world's second-oldest profession." A New Hampshire native, she has been a practicing astrologer for more than 25 years: "It is a study of timing, and timing is everything." Her book, *Love Signs* (Sweet Fern Publications, 1999), is available on her Web site, www.yourlovesigns.com.

Michael Steinberg, our meteorologist, has been forecasting weather for the Almanac since 1996. In addition to having college degrees in atmospheric science and meteorology, he brings a lifetime of experience to the task: He began making weather predictions when he attended the only high school in the world with weather Teletypes and radar.

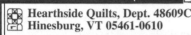

Advertising deadline for *The 2008 Old Farmer's Almanac* is May 9, 2007.

THE 2007 EDITION OF

The Old Farmer's Almanac

Established in 1792 and published every year thereafter

ROBERT B. THOMAS (1766–1846), *Founder*

YANKEE PUBLISHING INC.
P.O. Box 520, 1121 Main Street, Dublin, NH 03444
Phone: 603-563-8111 • Fax: 603-563-8252

GROUP PUBLISHER: John Pierce
PUBLISHER *(23rd since 1792):* Sherin Wight
EDITOR IN CHIEF: Judson D. Hale Sr.
DIRECT RETAIL SALES MANAGER: Cindy Schlosser
DIRECT RETAIL SALES ASSISTANT: Stacey Korpi

ADVERTISING
90 Canal Street, Suite 301, Boston, MA 02114-2022

FOR ADVERTISING RATES AND INFORMATION
800-736-1100 • Almanac.com/advertising
ADVERTISING SYSTEMS MANAGER: Rebecca DiFalco
PRODUCTION ARTIST: Janet Calhoun

ADDITIONAL ADVERTISING REPRESENTATION
Classified: Gallagher Group • 203-263-7171
Northeast & West: Robert Bernbach • 914-769-0051
Midwest & South: Gallagher Group • 203-263-7171

FOR RETAIL SALES
Contact Cindy Schlosser, 800-729-9265, ext. 126,
or Stacey Korpi, ext. 160.

The Old Farmer's Almanac publications are available at special discounts for bulk purchases for sales promotions or premiums. Contact MeadWestvaco, 800-333-1125.

SUBSCRIBE TO THIS ALMANAC
Subscription: 3 years, $15 (plus $4.95 s/h)
Call 800-256-2622 to subscribe.

Jamie Trowbridge, *President;* Judson D. Hale Sr., John Pierce, *Senior Vice Presidents;* Jody Bugbee, Judson D. Hale Jr., Sherin Wight, *Vice Presidents.*

Vinegar Can Be Used For WHAT?

We're looking for people to—

Write Children's Books

By Kristi Holl

I f you've ever dreamed of writing for children, here's your chance to test that dream ... and find out if you have the aptitude to make it a reality. If you do, we'll teach you how to crack one of today's most rewarding markets for new writers.

The $2 billion children's market

The tremendous recent success of children's books has made the general public aware of what we've known for years: There's a huge market out there. And there's a growing need for new writers trained to create the nearly $2 billion of children's books purchased every year ... plus the stories and articles needed by more than 600 publishers of magazines for and about children and teenagers.

Who are these needed writers? They're ordinary people like you and me.

"But am I good enough?"

I was once where you may be now. My occasional thoughts of writing had been pushed down by self-doubt, and I didn't know where to turn for help. Then, on an impulse, I sent for the Institute's free writing aptitude test and it turned out to be the spark I needed. I took their course and my wonderful author-instructor helped me to discover, step-by-step, that my everyday life—probably not much different from yours—was an endless creative resource for my writing!

The promise that paid off

The Institute made the same promise to me that they'll make to you, if you demonstrate basic writing aptitude: *You will complete at least one manuscript suitable to submit to editors by the time you finish the course.*

I really didn't expect to be published before I finished the course, but

Kristi Holl, a graduate of our course, has published 24 books and more than 180 stories and articles. She is now an instructor at the Institute.

I was. I sold three stories. And I soon discovered that that was not unusual at the Institute. Now, as a graduate and a nationally published author of 24 children's books, and more than 180 stories and articles, I'm teaching: I'm passing along what I've learned to would-be writers like you.

One-on-one training with your own instructor

My fellow instructors—all of them professional writers or editors—work with their students the same way I work with mine: When you've completed an assignment on your own schedule, at your own pace, you send it to me. I read it and reread it to make sure I get everything out of it that you've put into it. Then I edit it line-by-line and send you a detailed letter explaining my edits. I point out your strengths and show you how to shore up your weaknesses. Between your pushing and my pulling, you learn how to write—and how to market what you write.

I am the living proof

What I got from my instructor at the Institute changed me from a "wannabe" into a nationally published writer. While there's no guarantee that every student will have the same success, we're showered with letters like these from current and former students.

"Since graduating from your course," says Heather Klassen, Edmonds, WA, "I've sold 125 stories to magazines for children and teenagers."

"Before this, I didn't know if my work was typical or bland, or if there was even a spark of life in it," writes Kate Spanks, Maple Ridge, BC. "I now have over 30 articles published...."

"... a little bird ... has just been given freedom"

This course has helped me more than I can say," says Jody Drueding, Boston, MA. "It's as if a little bird that was locked up inside of me has just been given the freedom of the garden."

"... I was attracted by the fact that you require an aptitude test," says Nikki Arko, Raton, NM. "Other schools sign you up as long as you have the money to pay, regardless of talent or potential."

"I'd take the course again in a heartbeat!"

"My most recent success has been the publication of the novel I started for my last Institute assignment," writes Jennifer Jones, Homer, NY. "Thank you for giving me the life I longed for."

"I'd take the course again in a heartbeat!", says Tonya Tingey, Woodruff, UT. "It made my dream a reality."

Don't let your dream die— send for your free test today!

If life as a successful writer is your dream, here's your chance to test that dream. We've developed a revealing aptitude test based on our 37 years of experience. Just fill out and mail the coupon below to receive your free test and a 32-page introduction to our course, *Writing for Children and Teenagers,* and 80 of our instructors. *There is no obligation.*

Get both free

Institute of Children's Literature
93 Long Ridge Road
West Redding, CT 06896-0812

Yes, please send me your free Writing Aptitude Test and illustrated brochure. I understand I'm under no obligation, and no salesperson will visit me.

Please circle one and print name clearly:
Mr. Mrs. Ms. Miss   F8352

Name

Street

City

State   Zip

Recommended for college credits by the Connecticut Board for State Academic Awards and approved by the Connecticut Commissioner of Higher Education.

THE LAST LOFTY

See it now—and then not again for nearly 20 years.

We all observe (and many of us plan around) the changing phases of the Moon, but have you ever tracked its path across the sky? That, too, changes. During some years, the Moon's nocturnal motion mimics the Sun's daytime route. In others, it doesn't ascend as high as the Sun. Then there are years when the Moon rises much higher in the sky than the Sun—a phenomenon that fascinated ancient civilizations. Modern astronomers call this the "precession of the lunar orbit's inclination"; casual observers refer to it simply as the "super-high" Moon. It occurs for a three-year period exactly every 18.61 years, and 2007 marks the end of the current period, which began in 2005.

This is all due to the wobbly lunar orbit. Think of the Moon's orbit as the edge of a dinner plate that falls on the floor. The path wobbles, and this causes its orientation in space to change constantly. Super-high Moons occur when the Moon's orbit's direction of tilt is more aligned with the direction of Earth's tilt.

THE SUPER-HIGHLIGHTS

While the timing is precise, all super-high Moon years are not equal. In the most dramatic years, this one included,

by Bob Berman

the lunar orb performs in ways that the Sun never does. For example, when the Moon is full this year, it will appear to viewers in southern states to hover directly overhead. And, in all of its phases, from all viewing points, it will rise and set far left or right of its normal haunts on the horizon.

The Moon will reach a super-high position every month in 2007. On most occasions when it is this high, it will ap-

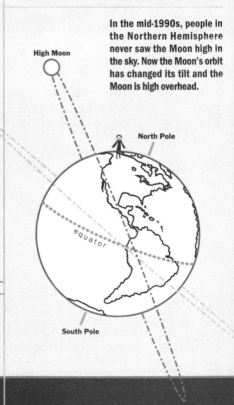

In the mid-1990s, people in the Northern Hemisphere never saw the Moon high in the sky. Now the Moon's orbit has changed its tilt and the Moon is high overhead.

High Moon

North Pole

equator

South Pole

MOON

pear to be gibbous or crescent, and sometimes this will happen during daylight hours. The dramatic super-high full Moon will occur twice this year. On one or two nights in both January and December, depending on the observer's location, the full Moon will straddle the border of the northern constellations Auriga and Gemini. Look for it at midnight, first on January 2–3, and later on December 23–24 (the year's 13th full Moon), when it will appear imperceptibly lower.

In a year that brings extreme highs, we also witness extremely low lows. This year's lowest full Moon—and lowest until the 2020s—occurs at 1:00 A.M. on June 30, several hours before its actual full Moon time of 9:49 A.M. EDT. In its "highest" position that night, it will climb barely a quarter of the way up in the sky (the exact height depends on your location in the Northern Hemisphere). From northern states and Canada, it will appear to rise no more than 18 degrees above the horizon. In far northerly places, such as Fairbanks, Alaska, it won't be seen even to clear the horizon. (That's right. No full Moon in Fairbanks in June.)

Beginning in 2008, each succeeding year's highest Moons will be two or more Moon-widths lower than those of the prior year. The Moon will reach its nadir, or low point, in 2014, when the "loftiest" Moons float 20 Moon-widths lower than those of this year. In 2016, the Moon will again begin its ascent, at the rate of two Moon-widths per year, until it reaches the next super-high year, 2023.

Ancient cultures marked such extreme lunar events with lavish ceremonies. Today, we can set our alarm clocks to signal the high times.

57 DEGREES OF SEPARATION

The difference in elevation between this year's highest and lowest full Moons is a whopping 57 degrees—nearly two-thirds of the sky from horizon to zenith—making for a dramatic viewing experience.

Winter's full Moons will be exceptionally bright due to the cold, dry air. However, summer's warm, moist air, combined with a long lunar light path, will cause full Moons during that season to have a yellow, orange, or red cast. As a result, the Moon will illuminate the sky only dimly. ☐ ☐

THE MOON AND YOU
To get the Moon rise and set times for any place in the United States or Canada, go to **Almanac.com/rise.**

SEVENTH HEAVEN

The 7th planet appears

Can you name the most astonishing astronomical discovery ever made? If you guessed black holes or quasars, you are wrong. While modern findings such as those may pique public interest, they have not caused the near hysteria that resulted on March 13, 1781, when William Herschel first sighted the seventh planet, as-yet-unnamed Uranus, from Bath, England.

−North Wind Picture Archives

Amateur astronomer William Herschel discovered the seventh planet from the Sun, Uranus, whose encircling rocky chunks are depicted in the artist's rendering at right.

Why the panic? For centuries, people took comfort in the fact that the night sky's five obvious bright planets were the only ones in the universe. (Earth, of course, was a given.) No one had theorized about other planets, nor had anyone dared to dream about others—at least not in a scientific fashion. News of this unknown world not only shattered a fundamental and profound belief, but also struck fear in the hearts and minds of the citizenry. Tongues wagged and newspapers speculated about the strange new world. Why hadn't Uranus been sighted by ancient civilizations? wondered 18th-century astronomers. Perhaps it was newly born? Perchance it had drifted into view? Being faintly visible to the naked eye and positively

brilliant against the starry background through even the smallest telescope, how, they asked themselves, had it escaped notice all that time?

This year, Uranus will again be visible and, for viewers, astonishing all over again. The following seven heavenly details will prepare you for its appearance:

1 Uranus was almost named "George"

William Herschel, who was a professional musician and amateur astronomer when he discovered the

SUN

for 7 key viewing dates in '07.

BY BOB BERMAN

–David A. Hardy/AstroArt

Mercury Venus Earth Mars Jupiter Saturn Uranus Neptune Pluto

DISTANCES NOT TO SCALE

–NASA

planet, proposed calling it Georgium Sidus ("George's Star"), after King George III. Given the turmoil in Britain at the time (the empire was sorely losing to the colonists in the struggle of the American Revolution), there was little popular support for that, but many people were willing to name it Herschel. Ultimately, tradition ruled, and the planet was given a name from mythology. Uranus, the Greek god of the heavens, was the grandfather of Jupiter and father of Saturn. The name is properly pronounced YER-eh-nus, with the accent on the first syllable, not with a long-A sound in the middle—although both ways are acceptable.

For his part, Herschel won the patronage and benevolence of the king, including an annual salary of 200 British pounds—a gift that changed his life utterly. He was able to give up music for good, build a major observatory, and go on to discover thousands of nebulas.

It's Green

For centuries, even the most powerful telescopes failed to reveal anything significant about the large planet. (At about 32,000 miles in diameter, Uranus is four times the size of Earth.) It was not until January 24, 1986, when NASA's *Voyager 2* sped by taking pictures from 50,000 miles distant, that humans got a close look at Uranus and learned the components of its atmosphere. Photos revealed uniform, featureless clouds—a gaseous fog. Onboard instruments determined the gases

to be 83 percent hydrogen, 15 percent helium, and 2 percent methane, thus explaining Uranus's distinctive greenish color. (Methane absorbs red light but reflects the Sun's other colors, causing sunlight's greens and blues to combine into the aquamarine, or cyan, tint that is the planet's trademark hue.)

It Rotates Like a Chicken on a Rotisserie

Uranus, like Venus, rotates clockwise (unlike all the other planets and the Sun, which rotate counterclockwise), and each of its days lasts 17 hours, 14 minutes. Its axis of spin is at a 98-degree angle relative to its motion through space. Think of it as spinning on its side, with the poles at the center, similar to a bull's-eye

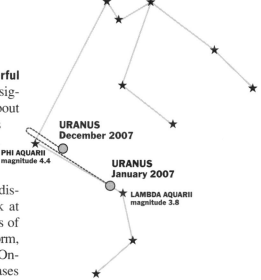

In 2007, Uranus appears in the constellation Aquarius.

PHI AQUARII
magnitude 4.4

URANUS
December 2007

URANUS
January 2007

LAMBDA AQUARII
magnitude 3.8

"If I told you that I can end a lifetime of foot pain instantly, you probably wouldn't believe me..."

"Half a million other men and women didn't either... until they tried this revolutionary European discovery that positively killed their foot pain dead!

"Don't live with foot pain a moment longer! If you're ready to recapture the vitality and energy that healthy feet provide, I'll give you 60 days to try the remarkable foot support system I discovered in Europe. You will immediately experience relief and freedom from foot ailments. I GUARANTEE IT!

"How can I make such an unprecedented guarantee? Because I personally lived in constant, agonizing foot pain for years

Harvey Rothschild,
Founder of Featherspring Int'l.

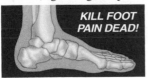

KILL FOOT PAIN DEAD!

before my exciting discovery. What started out as simple aching from corns and calluses grew into full-blown, incapacitating misery only a few other foot pain sufferers could understand.

"Believe me, I tried all the so-called remedies I could get my hands on (and feet into), but none of them really worked. It wasn't until my wife and I took a trip to Europe that I discovered a remarkable invention called Flexible Featherspring® Foot Supports. Invented in Germany, these custom-formed foot supports absorb shock as they cradle your feet as if on a cushion of air.

© FEATHERSPRING, 712 N. 34th Street, Seattle, WA 98103-8881

"Imagine my complete surprise as I slipped a pair of custom-formed Feathersprings into my shoes for the first time and began the road to no more pain. The tremendous pain and pressure I used to feel every time I took a step was gone! I could scarcely believe how great a relief I felt even after walking several hours. And after just a few days of use, my pain disappeared totally - *and has never returned.*

"Whatever your problem— corns, calluses, bunions, pain in the balls of your feet, toe cramps, fallen arches, burning nerve endings, painful ankles, back aches, or just generally sore, aching feet and legs – *my Feathersprings are guaranteed to end your foot pain or you don't pay a penny.*

"But don't just take my word for it: Experience for yourself the immediate relief and renewed energy that Feathersprings provide. Send for your FREE kit today on our no risk, 60-day trial offer!"

Visit our web site at: www.featherspring.com

Please send FREE INFORMATION KIT!

FEATHERSPRING INTERNATIONAL, INC.
712 N. 34th Street, Dept. OF017
Seattle, WA 98103-8881

Name _____

Address _____

City _____ State ____ Zip _____

Look for a **LARGE PINK ENVELOPE** containing all the details. No obligation. No salesperson will call.

target. Then, turn it sideways, because this year neither pole faces Earth. One pole is on the left and one is on the right, with the planet's equator moving vertically in the middle (imagine a chicken on a rotisserie).

The combination of Uranus's cockeyed tilt and its long orbit produces 42-year-long seasons at the poles. If you lived there or, more accurately, floated in its thick, soupy air—because Uranus has no solid surface—the Sun would shine for 42 years straight. Then, the longest nocturnal interval in the known universe would occur. After that, the cycle—at 84 years, about the duration of a human life span—would repeat.

It's Cloudy, Verrry Cold, and Windy

On Uranus, the poles receive more sunlight and thus are warmer than the areas around the equator—but the extent of this difference is slight. Uranus's only source of heat is the Sun, and sunlight there is 1/400 as strong as it is on Earth. The atmospheric temperature can vary, but generally remains at –270°F. (Unlike neighbors Jupiter, Saturn, and Neptune, the seventh planet does not have a superhot core that delivers heat to its outer layers from within.) The planet is almost always windy, with frequent gusts to 360 mph.

Its Moons Are Dramatic

Uranus is surrounded by a retinue of at least 27 moons. The outermost five, which

80

were discovered more than 50 years ago, are, at 300 to about 900 miles in diameter, relatively large. The others are tiny in comparison—chunks of icy rock about ten miles wide. They are probably asteroids or comets that were captured by the planet's strong gravity while passing by. Uranus's moons are the "highbrow" satellites of the solar system, all with names from dramas by William Shakespeare (e.g., Puck, Juliet, Oberon) or verse by Alexander Pope (e.g., Ariel, Belinda, Umbriel).

Other Planets Point to It

Uranus's tilted orbital path means that it follows the zodiacal highway more faithfully than any other planet, never wavering a single degree and averaging seven years in each constellation. However, much of that time is spent lurking in the lowest alleyways of the zodiac, in constellations that never rise very high for observers in the United States and Canada. This year, Uranus finally emerges out of horizon haze. Now floating in the faint and sprawling constellation Aquarius, it ascends halfway up the sky, a height it hasn't reached since 1972.

Better still, this year features several conjunctions between Uranus and other visible bodies, which can serve as guides to the dim green world. Best seen through binoculars, Uranus meets Venus in late evening twilight from February 7 to 9, and the Moon on May 12, October 22, and December 16, though the moonlight will subdue the planet. Uranus's easiest-to-find appearance may be its

Visit the Almanac Online Store and get instant digital access to

✿ Our famous long-range weather forecasts

✿ Astrological Moon's sign calendar and the Man of Signs

✿ Almanac replicas from 1905, 1906, and 1907

✿ 10 helpful charts

Almanac.com/instant

SUFFERING FROM
COLD SORES?
HAY FEVER?
SINUSITIS?
SKIN IRRITATION?

RELIEF

CAN BE
YOURS WITH

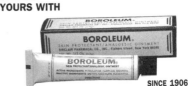

SINCE 1906

BOROLEUM®

*It's mild and
IT WORKS...all year 'round!*

SINCLAIR PHARMACAL CO., INC.
Fishers Island, N.Y. 06390

*To order, call 1-800-649-4372
Or visit our Web site: www.boroleum.com*

Interested in Advertising in
The Old Farmer's Almanac?
Call 800-736-1100

FREE: THE ESSIAC HANDBOOK

Learn about the famous Ojibway Herbal Healing Remedy

Write For a Free Copy:
**Box 278
Crestone CO 81131**

nearly two-night rendezvous with Mars. Look low in the east an hour before sunrise on April 29 and again on April 30. The bright-reddish, nearer planet will point the way, making for an easy observation with binoculars or a small portable telescope.

September Offers the Best Sightings

Viewing the giant green world is easy —that is, as easy as it ever gets, considering that it's almost two billion miles away. In practice, it's usually zealous amateur astronomers who take the trouble to observe dim Uranus, but knowing what you know now, the planet surely merits a peek. It will be faintly visible to the naked eye from July through November, and closest to Earth on September 8, when it will be at magnitude 5.8. September 8 begins a nearly moonless week and thus an excellent viewing opportunity, since normally Uranus is so dim that it can be masked by moonlight, light pollution, or haze. Face south at midnight. From rural locations, Uranus will appear as a faint, starlike dot.

Being distant and mysterious, Uranus has a role in our destiny that may lie somewhere in the future. Studies of the seventh planet remain ongoing and will keep scientists occupied throughout the 21st century. □□

Bob Berman is the Almanac's astronomy editor. His most recent books are *Strange Universe* (Henry Holt, 2003) and *Shooting for the Moon* (Lyons Press, 2007).

TURN YOUR EYES TO THE SKIES
For planet rise and set times, see page 94.

Henrietta Who?

*She has been called "one of the most important women ever to touch astronomy,"
yet most people have never heard of Henrietta Swan Leavitt.* • *by Alice Cary*

hen a telescope known as "The Great Refractor" was installed at the Harvard College Observatory in Cambridge, Massachusetts, 160 years ago, astronomers reveled. In 1847 and for years afterward, it was one of the best in the world, allowing scientists to spot Saturn's inner ring and to take the first picture of a star.

In 1876, Edward Charles Pickering became director of the Observatory. He decided that his mission would be to collect as much astronomical information as possible. The astronomers in his charge had an infinite task as their goal: to record by hand data about every star in the sky, noting color, brightness, and position. Men were not interested in this tedious, 25-cents-an-hour job, so Pickering, a detail zealot, hired women. One of his first employees was his housekeeper; eventually, another was Henrietta Swan Leavitt.

Studying pictures of stars became Leavitt's life work. Thanks to her, scientists can now explain how far away certain stars are. She found a way to measure beyond the Milky Way—at a time when many astronomers thought that the Milky Way itself comprised the entire universe.

Although we know that Leavitt was born on July 4, 1868, in Lancaster, Massachusetts, further details of her life remain as elusive as a shooting star. Biographer George Johnson, author of *Miss Leavitt's Stars* (W. W. Norton & Company, Inc., 2005), noted that "few details of her life remain, except evidence of her dedication and years of tedious toil." With thanks to Mr. Johnson, we present some additional background on this stellar stargazer:

Leavitt stumbled into her career in astronomy. Not until her last year at Radcliffe College (then called the Society for the Collegiate Instruction of Women) in Cambridge did Leavitt take an astronomy class. In the years prior, at Ohio's Oberlin College, she had focused on music (an interesting choice, as she was plagued by a hearing problem that grew worse over time and eventually approached deafness).

In 1893, a year after graduating from Radcliffe, Leavitt became a volunteer at the nearby Harvard Observatory, where she earned graduate credits. Biographer Johnson speculates that Leavitt's uncle may have helped her get the position. **(c o n t i n u e d)**

Left: Superimposed on the stars she studied so much, Henrietta Swan Leavitt is shown hard at work at the Harvard College Observatory, c. 1917.

enrietta noted that the brighter variables had the longest cycles

Her job at the Observatory was to be a computer. As one of several "human computers," Leavitt had the task (under the supervision of Pickering) of peering at photographic negatives of stars on glass plates and taking copious notes about the stars' characteristics. She and the other women were sometimes referred to as "Pickering's Harem."

Her work was spotless, but her schedule was spotty. From time to time, Leavitt took long leaves from work, sometimes to travel, sometimes because of illness, at other times to help her family. In 1896, for instance, she traveled in Europe for two years, before returning to aid family she had in Wisconsin. While she was there, Pickering offered her a full-time job (at 30 cents an hour!) if she would return to the Observatory. In Spring 1902, she accepted the offer,

but by January 1903 she was again sailing to Europe. She became sick at the end of 1908, returning to Wisconsin to recuperate until Spring 1910. Such interruptions prompted Pickering to write: "It occurs to me, when you do return, you may be able to do much of your work in your room, and thus save yourself the walk to the Observatory."

She developed the "Harvard Standard," used to measure the brightness of stars. Leavitt measured 96 stars from the North Polar Sequence, studying 299 plates from 13 different telescopes. She categorized 17 magnitudes of brightness, publishing her conclusions in a 184-page report.

"Pickering's Harem" in a paper-doll formation in front of the Harvard College Observatory, c. 1917. (Leavitt is beneath arrow.)

rightness . . . she realized that the cycles were related to the stars' magnitudes. For astronomers, this was big news.

When working, she could become fanatical. Leavitt noticed many variables (cyclical changes in stars' brightnesses) in the area of the cosmos she was studying known as the Magellanic Clouds (a neighboring galaxy, although this wasn't known at the time). This prompted another astronomer to note: "What a variable-star 'fiend' Miss Leavitt is—One can't keep up with the roll of the new discoveries."

Once, she voiced her frustrations about a variable star that was giving her trouble: "We shall never understand it until we find a way to send up a net and fetch the thing down!"

During her lifetime, Leavitt discovered 2,400 variables, about half of all those known at the time and about 10 percent of those known today. She discovered so many stars that a reporter writing in *The Washington Post* compared her to a legendary Broadway producer.

She made a monumental observation. In 1908, Leavitt published a paper called "1,777 Variables in the Magellanic Clouds" in the *Annals of the Astronomical Observatory of Harvard College*. In it, she noted that the brighter variables had the longest cycles of brightness. Since she knew that these variables in the Magellanic Clouds were about the same distance from Earth, she realized that the cycles were related to the stars' magnitudes. For astronomers, this was big news, because magnitude also allowed them to calculate the distances of stars. Her discovery became known as the Period-Luminosity Law and meant that variable stars could be used as a sort of cosmic yardstick.

Leavitt did not get to continue to work

–Harvard College Observatory

Astronomy

on her theory; Pickering directed her to other projects. Despite her achievements, her job title remained "Assistant."

Over the years, other astronomers, including Edwin Hubble, used Leavitt's law to prove that stars and galaxies did indeed lie beyond the Milky Way. In fact, her work later allowed astronomers to calculate the distances of variable stars up to 10 million light-years away.

She didn't live to see the full ramifications of her discovery. By the end of 1921, Leavitt was sick with stomach cancer. She died on December 12, leaving an estate of $315. She is buried in Cambridge Cemetery in her family plot.

One of the few personal remarks about Leavitt, who never married, comes from an obituary written by an astronomer: "She took life seriously. Her sense of duty, justice, and loyalty was strong. For light amusement she appeared to care little." He added that she was "so full of sunshine that, to her, all of life became beautiful and full of meaning."

Her spirit and reputation live on. Leavitt's desk at the Observatory was given to Cecilia Payne, who earned Harvard's first doctorate in astronomy and became a professor and department chair. Payne was aware of, but dismissed, rumors that Leavitt's ghost haunted the facility—that her lamp could sometimes be seen burning at night and that "her spirit still haunted the plate stacks." ☐☐

Alice Cary frequently writes about popular culture for the Almanac.

From *Miss Leavitt's Stars* by George Johnson. Copyright © 2005 by George Johnson. Used by permission of W. W. Norton & Company, Inc. and Atlas Books, LLC.

Enjoy Better Hearing Quickly & Easily

Introducing the EarMate-4000

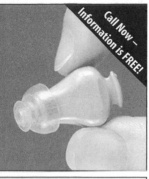

Information is FREE! Call Now –

EarMate-4000 enlarged to show detail

Are you one of the millions of Americans suffering from gradual hearing loss? You often say "What?" because it sounds to you like people are mumbling. Family members complain that you play the TV too loudly. You avoid conversations because you hear but don't understand.

Hearing loss is a natural part of aging.

U.S. Army research concluded hearing loss associated with aging is a normal, predictable process. In today's noisier world that loss occurs at younger ages. Slowly your hearing changes. You may not even be aware it's happening.

> *"I can hear things I haven't heard in years. Really makes a big difference on TV volume. Thanks."*
> C.P. - Wells, NV

There is a quick & easy solution.

The EarMate-4000 hearing aid amplifies mainly the high-frequency sounds that help you hear and understand.

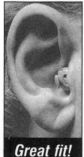

Great fit!

Select from three sizes of soft ear tips to get a comfortable, secure fit. Easy-to-use volume control locks in your preferred setting - no more fumbling!

Use your EarMate™ every day or just when you need a little help.

© Hearing Help Express, Inc™

> *"Easy to use and the fit system is great. Thank you for making a quality product and selling it for an affordable price."*
> Dr. P. Vallone, PhD – Chipley, FL

Order risk-free with 45-day home trial.

➤ **FREE Information**
➤ **Ready to use hearing aid**
➤ **FREE Shipping**
➤ **Compare to hearing aids costing $1,000 or more**
➤ **Order by mail from a family business with over 300,000 satisfied customers & 25 years selling hearing aids by mail**

Call 1-800-782-6897
ext 15-348
www.HearingHelpExpress.com/15348

Hearing Help Express, Inc.
105 North First St, Dept 15-348
DeKalb, IL 60115-0586

Free Shipping!

☑ **YES!** Please rush me free details on the ready to use EarMate™-4000. I understand there is no obligation and I get FREE shipping.

Dr/Mr/Mrs/Ms _____

Address _____

City _____

State/Zip _____

Eclipses

■ There will be four eclipses in 2007, two of the Sun and two of the Moon. Solar eclipses are visible only in certain areas and require eye protection to be viewed safely. Lunar eclipses are technically visible from the entire night side of Earth, but during a penumbral eclipse, the dimming of the Moon's illumination is slight.

MARCH 3: total eclipse of the Moon. This eclipse will be visible only in eastern North America, so the times here are in Eastern Standard Time only. The Moon will enter the penumbra at 3:16 P.M. EST and will leave the penumbra at 9:25 P.M. EST.

MARCH 18: partial eclipse of the Sun. This eclipse will be visible only from Alaska, so the times here are in Alaska Daylight Time only. The eclipse begins at 4:38 P.M. AKDT and ends at 8:25 P.M. AKDT. The time of greatest eclipse will occur at 6:32 P.M. AKDT.

AUGUST 28: total eclipse of the Moon. This eclipse will be visible throughout most of North America. The Moon will enter the penumbra at 3:52 A.M. EDT (12:52 A.M. PDT) and will leave the penumbra at 9:23 A.M. EDT (6:23 A.M. PDT).

SEPTEMBER 11: partial eclipse of the Sun. This eclipse will not be visible in North America.

Full-Moon Dates (Eastern Time)				
	2007	2008	2009	2010	2011
Jan.	3	22	10	30	19
Feb.	2	20	9	28	18
Mar.	3	21	10	29	19
Apr.	2	20	9	28	17
May	2 & 31	19	9	27	17
June	30	18	7	26	15
July	29	18	7	25	15
Aug.	28	16	5	24	13
Sept.	26	15	4	23	12
Oct.	26	14	4	22	11
Nov.	24	13	2	21	10
Dec.	23	12	2 & 31	21	10

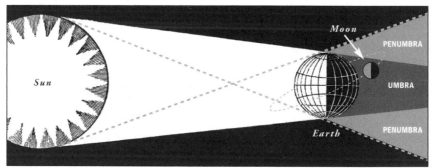

In a lunar eclipse *(above)*, Earth is between the Sun and the Moon. The umbra is the central dark part of the shadow created during an eclipse. The penumbra is the area of partial darkness surrounding the umbra. During a total lunar eclipse, the Moon passes through the umbra.

Total Solar Eclipse Dates, 2008–12	
DATE	**REGIONS WITH VISIBLE TOTALITY**
2008 August 1	Northern Canada, Greenland, Siberia, China
2009 July 22	India, China, central Pacific Ocean
2010 July 11	South Pacific Ocean, southern South America
2012 November 13	Northern Australia, South Pacific Ocean

Why wait ten months?

Now you can have rich, dark compost *in just 14 days!*

With the amazing ComposTumbler, you'll have bushels of crumbly, ready-to-use compost — *in just 14 days!* (And, in the ten months it takes to make compost the old way, your ComposTumbler can produce *hundreds of pounds* of rich food for your garden!)

Say good-bye to that messy, open compost pile (and to the flies, pests, and odors that come along with it!) Bid a happy farewell to the strain of trying to turn over heavy, wet piles with a pitchfork.

Compost the Better Way

Compost-making with the ComposTumbler is neat, quick and easy!

Gather up leaves, old weeds, kitchen scraps, lawn clippings, etc. and toss them into the roomy 18-bushel drum. Then, once each day, give the ComposTumbler's *gear-driven* handle a few easy spins.

The ComposTumbler's Magic

Inside the ComposTumbler, carefully positioned mixing fins blend materials, pushing fresh mixture to the core where the temperatures are the hottest (up to 160°) and the composting bacteria most active.

After just 14 days, open the door, and you'll find an abundance of dark, sweet-smelling "garden gold" — ready to enrich and feed your garden!

NEW SMALLER SIZE!

Now there are 2 sizes. The 18-bushel original ComposTumbler and the NEW 9.5-bushel Compact ComposTumbler. Try either size risk-free for 30 days!

See for yourself! Try the ComposTumbler risk-free with our 30-Day Home Trial!

Call Toll-Free 1-800-880-2345

NOW ON SALE— SAVE UP TO $115

ComposTumbler®

The choice of more than 250,000 gardeners

☐ YES! Please rush FREE information on the ComposTumbler, including special savings and 30-Day Home Trial.

Name _____

Address _____

City _____

State _____ ZIP _____

MAIL TO:

ComposTumbler
30 Wright Ave., Dept. 42017C
Lititz (Lancaster Co.), PA 17543

© 2006 PBM Group

Bright Stars

Transit Times

■ This table shows the time (EST or EDT) and altitude of a star as it transits the meridian (i.e., reaches its highest elevation while passing over the horizon's south point) at Boston on the dates shown. The transit time on any other date differs from that of the nearest date listed by approximately four minutes per day. To find the time of a star's transit for your location, convert its time at Boston using Key Letter C.*

Time of Transit (EST/EDT) ☞ **Bold = P.M.**
☞ Light = A.M.

Star	Constellation	Magnitude	Jan. 1	Mar. 1	May 1	July 1	Sept. 1	Nov. 1	Altitude (degrees)
Altair	Aquila	0.8	**12:50**	8:58	5:58	1:59	**9:51**	**4:51**	56.3
Deneb	Cygnus	1.3	**1:41**	9:49	6:49	2:49	**10:42**	**5:42**	92.8
Fomalhaut	Psc. Aus.	1.2	**3:56**	**12:04**	9:04	5:04	1:00	**7:57**	17.8
Algol	Perseus	2.2	**8:06**	**4:14**	**1:15**	9:15	5:11	12:11	88.5
Aldebaran	Taurus	0.9	**9:34**	**5:42**	**2:42**	10:42	6:38	1:39	64.1
Rigel	Orion	0.1	**10:12**	**6:20**	**3:20**	11:20	7:17	2:17	39.4
Capella	Auriga	0.1	**10:14**	**6:22**	**3:22**	11:22	7:18	2:19	93.6
Bellatrix	Orion	1.6	**10:23**	**6:31**	**3:31**	11:31	7:27	2:28	54.0
Betelgeuse	Orion	var. 0.4	**10:53**	**7:01**	**4:01**	**12:01**	7:57	2:58	55.0
Sirius	Can. Maj.	−1.4	**11:42**	**7:50**	**4:51**	**12:51**	8:47	3:47	31.0
Procyon	Can. Min.	0.4	12:40	**8:44**	**5:44**	**1:45**	9:41	4:41	52.9
Pollux	Gemini	1.2	12:46	**8:50**	**5:50**	**1:51**	9:47	4:47	75.7
Regulus	Leo	1.4	3:09	**11:13**	**8:13**	**4:14**	**12:10**	7:10	59.7
Spica	Virgo	var. 1.0	6:25	2:34	**11:30**	**7:30**	**3:26**	10:26	36.6
Arcturus	Boötes	−0.1	7:16	3:24	12:21	**8:21**	**4:17**	11:17	66.9
Antares	Scorpius	var. 0.9	9:29	5:37	2:37	**10:34**	**6:30**	**1:30**	21.3
Vega	Lyra	0	11:37	7:45	4:45	12:41	**8:37**	**3:37**	86.4

Rise and Set Times

■ To find the time of a star's rising at Boston on any date, subtract the interval shown at right from the star's transit time on that date; add the interval to find the star's setting time. To find the rising and setting times for your city, convert the Boston transit times above using the Key Letter* shown at right before applying the interval. The directions in which the stars rise and set, shown for Boston, are generally useful throughout the United States.

Deneb, Algol, Capella, and Vega are circumpolar stars—they never set but appear to circle the celestial north pole.

Star	Interval (h. m.)	Rising Key	Dir.	Setting Key	Dir.
Altair	6 36	B	EbN	E	WbN
Fomalhaut	3 59	E	SE	D	SW
Aldebaran	7 06	B	ENE	D	WNW
Rigel	5 33	D	EbS	B	WbS
Bellatrix	6 27	B	EbN	D	WbN
Betelgeuse	6 31	B	EbN	D	WbN
Sirius	5 00	D	ESE	B	WSW
Procyon	6 23	B	EbN	D	WbN
Pollux	8 01	A	NE	E	NW
Regulus	6 49	B	EbN	D	WbN
Spica	5 23	D	EbS	B	WbS
Arcturus	7 19	A	ENE	E	WNW
Antares	4 17	E	SEbE	A	SWbW

*The values of Key Letters are given in the Time Corrections table (page 237).

−Beth Krommes

Find more heavenly details at Almanac.com/astronomy. **2007**

TRUSTED FRIENDS FROM THE FARM.

BAG BALM® *Ointment*
A trusted friend for more than 100 years, Bag Balm is proven to help heal cuts, scrapes, chapping, galls, and hobble burns. A great sweat. At tack shops, farm, drug, and hardware stores.
If unavailable, order direct: 10 oz. can $7.99; 1 oz. can $5.50.

GREEN MOUNTAIN® *Hoof Softener*
For softening hardened, dry, pinched, or contracted hoofs and quarter cracks. At tack shops, farms and hardware stores.
If unavailable, order direct: 10 oz. can $6.30; 28 oz. can $8.70; $6.45 non-freeze liquid pint.

TACKMASTER®
Leather cleaner, conditioner, preservative. Penetrates leather thoroughly, helps restore original life with natural oils.
If unavailable, order direct: Gallon $17.50; quart $7.80; pint $5.00; 4 oz. $3.00.

Add $3.50 handling for your order. Prices subject to change without notice. To order, send check or money order to (no credit cards please):

DAIRY ASSOCIATION CO., INC.

P.O. BOX 145, DEPT. OFA07, LYNDONVILLE, VT 05851/TEL. 802-626-3610/WWW.BAGBALM.COM
WEST OF ROCKIES: SMITH SALES SERVICE, 16372 S. W. 72ND ST., PORTLAND, OR 97223

HAULS LIKE A DUMP TRUCK
YET IT HANDLES WITH EASE!

Try the **DR® POWERWAGON™** – the heavy-duty, easy-handling, self-propelled hauler for your yard, barn, woodlot or garden – for 6 months RISK-FREE!

6-MONTH RISK-FREE TRIAL!

- **HAUL** up to 800 lbs...up or down hills, over rough, even soft, wet ground!

- **UNLOAD** it like a dump truck without shoveling or tedious hand labor. Optional *powered* lift available.

- **ENJOY** the easy handling of 4 speeds, Power Reverse, Electric-Starting, and Zero-Radius-Turning!

CALL TOLL-FREE

1-800-835-9511

☑ **YES**, please send me **FREE** details of the **DR® POWERWAGON™** including how I can try one out for 6 months **RISK-FREE!**

Name_____

Address _____ OFA

City _____ State _____ ZIP _____

Email_____

DR® POWER EQUIPMENT, Dept. 54289X
127 Meigs Road, Vergennes, VT 05491
www.DRpowerwagon.com

©2006 CHP, Inc.

The Visible Planets

■ Listed here for Boston are viewing suggestions for and the rise and set times (EST/EDT) of the visible planets Venus, Mars, Jupiter, and Saturn on the 1st, 11th, and 21st of each month and December 31. The approximate times of their visible risings and settings on other days can be found by interpolation. The capital letters that appear beside the times are Key Letters and are used to convert the times for other localities **(see pages 102 and 237)**. For all planet rise and set times, visit **Almanac.com/astronomy.**

Venus

♀ **Venus begins 2007 as a low evening star that** keeps getting brighter and higher, dominating western twilight from March through early July. It reaches greatest elevation in May and June, and maximum brightness from June 29 to July 24. Venus disappears into the solar glare in early August, reaches inferior conjunction on August 18, and reappears in the predawn east a week later. It becomes a high, superb, morning star during the autumn, appearing at greatest brilliancy (magnitude –4.5) from September 12 to October 7. Although prominent through December, it is not quite as bright or high as earlier.

Jan. 1	set	**5:34**	A	Apr. 1	set	**10:18**	E	July 1	set	**10:43**	D
Jan. 11	set	**5:59**	A	Apr. 11	set	**10:42**	E	July 11	set	**10:12**	D
Jan. 21	set	**6:25**	B	Apr. 21	set	**11:04**	E	July 21	set	**9:32**	D
Feb. 1	set	**6:54**	B	May 1	set	**11:22**	E	Aug. 1	set	**8:37**	C
Feb. 11	set	**7:19**	B	May 11	set	**11:34**	E	Aug. 11	set	**7:39**	C
Feb. 21	set	**7:43**	C	May 21	set	**11:39**	E	Aug. 21	rise	5:51	B
Mar. 1	set	**8:03**	C	June 1	set	**11:36**	E	Sept. 1	rise	4:41	B
Mar. 11	set	**9:27**	D	June 11	set	**11:25**	E	Sept. 11	rise	3:54	B
Mar. 21	set	**9:51**	D	June 21	set	**11:07**	D	Sept. 21	rise	3:25	B
Oct. 1	rise	3:09	B
Oct. 11	rise	3:05	B
Oct. 21	rise	3:08	B
Nov. 1	rise	3:18	B
Nov. 11	rise	2:32	C
Nov. 21	rise	2:48	C
Dec. 1	rise	3:06	D
Dec. 11	rise	3:26	D
Dec. 21	rise	3:47	D
Dec. 31	rise	4:09	D

Mars

♂ **In 2007, the ruddy planet starts out in Ophiuchus** as a medium-bright predawn star and steadily brightens throughout the year as it speeds along the zodiac. A postmidnight object until the autumn, Mars finally rises before midnight in October, by 8:30 P.M. in mid-November, and at sunset on December 18, when it is at its nearest and brightest (magnitude –1.4) of the year. Opposition on December 24 happens a day after it rises alongside the full Moon. Although this year's meeting with Earth is not nearly as close as previous oppositions, this event finds the planet higher in the sky than at any time since 1960.

Jan. 1	rise	5:41	E	Apr. 1	rise	4:51	D	July 1	rise	1:33	B
Jan. 11	rise	5:35	E	Apr. 11	rise	4:31	D	July 11	rise	1:12	B
Jan. 21	rise	5:29	E	Apr. 21	rise	4:10	D	July 21	rise	12:51	A
Feb. 1	rise	5:19	E	May 1	rise	3:48	C	Aug. 1	rise	12:30	A
Feb. 11	rise	5:09	E	May 11	rise	3:26	C	Aug. 11	rise	12:10	A
Feb. 21	rise	4:56	E	May 21	rise	3:04	C	Aug. 21	rise	**11:52**	A
Mar. 1	rise	4:45	E	June 1	rise	2:39	B	Sept. 1	rise	**11:32**	A
Mar. 11	rise	5:29	D	June 11	rise	2:17	B	Sept. 11	rise	**11:13**	A
Mar. 21	rise	5:12	D	June 21	rise	1:54	B	Sept. 21	rise	**10:54**	A
Oct. 1	**rise**	**10:32**	A
Oct. 11	**rise**	**10:09**	A
Oct. 21	**rise**	**9:43**	A
Nov. 1	**rise**	**9:10**	A
Nov. 11	**rise**	**7:34**	A
Nov. 21	**rise**	**6:52**	A
Dec. 1	**rise**	**6:02**	A
Dec. 11	**rise**	**5:06**	A
Dec. 21	set	7:55	E
Dec. 31	set	7:00	E

☞ **Bold = P.M.** ☞ Light = A.M.

–Illustrated by Beth Krommes

Find more heavenly details at Almanac.com/astronomy. **2007**

Jupiter

♃ Jupiter enters 2007 as a predawn star in the east in Ophiuchus, visible in the morning hours until April. By mid-May, it is up in the east by 11:00 P.M.; in June, it is above the eastern horizon at nightfall. When at opposition on June 5 and closest to Earth on June 7, Jupiter is at magnitude –2.1, bested only by Venus. It floats above Antares in the summer and autumn, is a prominent evening star in early November, and vanishes behind the Sun in December.

Jan. 1	rise	4:46 E	Apr. 1	rise	12:43 E	July 1	set	3:29 A	Oct. 1	set	9:31 A
Jan. 11	rise	4:17 E	Apr. 11	rise	12:04 E	July 11	set	2:46 A	Oct. 11	set	8:57 A
Jan. 21	rise	3:46 E	Apr. 21	rise	11:23 E	July 21	set	2:04 A	Oct. 21	set	8:25 A
Feb. 1	rise	3:12 E	May 1	rise	10:41 E	Aug. 1	set	1:20 A	Nov. 1	set	7:50 A
Feb. 11	rise	2:40 E	May 11	rise	9:57 E	Aug. 11	set	12:36 A	Nov. 11	set	6:18 A
Feb. 21	rise	2:07 E	May 21	rise	9:13 E	Aug. 21	set	11:58 A	Nov. 21	set	5:48 A
Mar. 1	rise	1:40 E	June 1	rise	8:23 E	Sept. 1	set	11:17 A	Dec. 1	set	5:17 A
Mar. 11	rise	2:05 E	June 11	set	4:56 A	Sept. 11	set	10:41 A	Dec. 11	set	4:48 A
Mar. 21	rise	1:29 E	June 21	set	4:12 A	Sept. 21	set	10:05 A	Dec. 21	rise	7:16 E
									Dec. 31	rise	6:47 E

Saturn

♄ Saturn, in Leo all year, rises by 7:30 P.M. in January. At magnitude zero—only half as brilliant as in 2003 because its rings are now tilted more edgewise—Saturn is at its closest point to Earth on February 10. It then rises at sunset and is out all night. Saturn is a prominent evening star through the spring, is low in June, and has a conjunction with Venus on June 30. It vanishes during its conjunction with the Sun on August 2 but reappears in the morning sky in late September. In November, Saturn rises by 1:00 A.M.; in December, it rises by midnight.

Jan. 1	rise	7:49 B	Apr. 1	set	4:38 D	July 1	set	10:46 D	Oct. 1	rise	3:43 B
Jan. 11	rise	7:07 B	Apr. 11	set	3:58 D	July 11	set	10:10 D	Oct. 11	rise	3:09 B
Jan. 21	rise	6:24 B	Apr. 21	set	3:19 D	July 21	set	9:34 D	Oct. 21	rise	2:35 B
Feb. 1	rise	5:37 B	May 1	set	2:40 D	Aug. 1	set	8:54 D	Nov. 1	rise	1:57 B
Feb. 11	set	6:59 D	May 11	set	2:01 D	Aug. 11	rise	6:31 B	Nov. 11	rise	12:21 B
Feb. 21	set	6:18 D	May 21	set	1:23 D	Aug. 21	rise	5:58 B	Nov. 21	rise	11:41 B
Mar. 1	set	5:45 D	June 1	set	12:38 D	Sept. 1	rise	5:22 B	Dec. 1	rise	11:04 B
Mar. 11	set	6:03 D	June 11	set	12:00 D	Sept. 11	rise	4:49 B	Dec. 11	rise	10:25 B
Mar. 21	set	5:23 D	June 21	set	11:23 D	Sept. 21	rise	4:16 B	Dec. 21	rise	9:46 B
									Dec. 31	rise	9:06 B

Mercury

☿ When Mercury appears farthest from the Sun, it is easy to view for a few weeks, especially when it hovers above the sunset or sunrise point. Its brightness also increases when it is nearly fully illuminated at the far side of its orbit. In 2007, favorable conditions make it easy to view shortly after sunset from January 2 to February 12 and from May 14 to June 4. Mercury meets the crescent Moon on May 17. It is best seen in the predawn sky during the first three weeks of November.

DO NOT CONFUSE ■ *Mercury with Taurus's star Aldebaran in mid-May: Both are the same color, but Mercury is brighter.* ■ *Jupiter with Venus in June: Venus is brighter and appears in the west; Jupiter is in the east.* ■ *Saturn with Leo's star Regulus, in the first half of September: Saturn is brighter; Regulus is bluish.* ■ *Mars with Aldebaran, in the first half of September: Mars is slightly brighter and has a deeper orange tint.*

The Twilight Zone

How to determine the length of twilight and the times of dawn and dark.

■ Twilight is the time preceding sunrise and again following sunset, when the sky is partially illuminated. The three ranges of twilight are defined according to the Sun's position below the horizon. Civil twilight occurs when the Sun is between the horizon and 6 degrees below the horizon (visually, the horizon is clearly defined). Nautical twilight occurs when the Sun is between 6 and 12 degrees below the horizon (the horizon is indistinct). Astronomical twilight occurs when the Sun is between 12 and 18 degrees below the horizon (sky illumination is imperceptible). When the Sun is at 18 degrees (dawn or dark) or below, there is no illumination.

LENGTH OF TWILIGHT (hours and minutes)

LATITUDE	Jan. 1 to Apr. 10	Apr. 11 to May 2	May 3 to May 14	May 15 to May 25	May 26 to July 22	July 23 to Aug. 3	Aug. 4 to Aug. 14	Aug. 15 to Sept. 5	Sept. 6 to Dec. 31
25°N to 30°N	1 20	1 23	1 26	1 29	1 32	1 29	1 26	1 23	1 20
31°N to 36°N	1 26	1 28	1 34	1 38	1 43	1 38	1 34	1 28	1 26
37°N to 42°N	1 33	1 39	1 47	1 52	1 59	1 52	1 47	1 39	1 33
43°N to 47°N	1 42	1 51	2 02	2 13	2 27	2 13	2 02	1 51	1 42
48°N to 49°N	1 50	2 04	2 22	2 42	—	2 42	2 22	2 04	1 50

TO DETERMINE THE LENGTH OF TWILIGHT: The length of twilight changes with latitude and the time of year and is independent of time zones. Use the **Time Corrections** table, **page 237,** to find the latitude of your city or the city nearest you. Use that figure in the chart above with the appropriate date to calculate the length of twilight in your area.

TO DETERMINE WHEN DAWN OR DARK WILL OCCUR: Calculate the sunrise/sunset times for your locality, using the instructions in **How to Use This Almanac, page 102.** Subtract the length of twilight from the time of sunrise to determine when dawn breaks. Add the length of twilight to the time of sunset to determine when dark descends.

E X A M P L E :

Boston, Mass. (latitude 42°22')

Sunrise, August 1	5:37 A.M. EDT
Length of twilight	−1 52
Dawn breaks	3:45 A.M.
Sunset, August 1	8:04 P.M. EDT
Length of twilight	+1 52
Dark descends	9:56 P.M.

Principal Meteor Showers

SHOWER	BEST VIEWING	POINT OF ORIGIN	DATE OF MAXIMUM*	PEAK RATE (/HR.)**	ASSOCIATED COMET
Quadrantid	Predawn	N	Jan. 4	80	—
Lyrid	Predawn	S	Apr. 22	12	Thatcher
Eta Aquarid	Predawn	SE	May 4	20	Halley
Delta Aquarid	Predawn	S	July 30	10	—
Perseid	Predawn	NE	Aug. 11–13	75	Swift-Tuttle
Draconid	Late evening	NW	Oct. 9	6	Giacobini-Zinner
Orionid	Predawn	S	Oct. 21–22	25	Halley
Taurid	Late evening	S	Nov. 9	6	Encke
Leonid	Predawn	S	Nov. 18	20	Tempel-Tuttle
Andromedid	Late evening	S	Nov. 25–27	5	Biela
Geminid	All night	NE	Dec. 13–14	65	—
Ursid	Predawn	N	Dec. 22	12	Tuttle

*May vary by one or two days in either direction.   **Approximate.

Astronomical Glossary

Aphelion (Aph.): The point in a planet's orbit that is farthest from the Sun.

Apogee (Apo.): The point in the Moon's orbit that is farthest from Earth.

Celestial Equator (Eq.): The imaginary circle around the celestial sphere that can be thought of as the plane of Earth's equator projected out onto the sphere.

Celestial Sphere: An imaginary sphere projected into space that represents the entire sky, with an observer on Earth at its center. All celestial bodies other than Earth are imagined as being on its inside surface.

Conjunction: The time at which two or more celestial bodies appear closest in the sky. **Inferior (Inf.):** Mercury or Venus is between the Sun and Earth. **Superior (Sup.):** The Sun is between a planet and Earth. Actual dates for conjunctions are given in the **Right-Hand Calendar Pages, 107–133;** the best times for viewing the closely aligned bodies are given in the **SKY WATCH** section of the **Left-Hand Calendar Pages, 106–132.**

Declination: The celestial latitude of an object in the sky, measured in degrees north or south of the celestial equator; analogous to latitude on Earth. The Almanac gives the Sun's declination at noon.

Eclipse, Lunar: The full Moon enters the shadow of Earth, which cuts off all or part of the sunlight reflected off the Moon. **Total:** The Moon passes completely through the **umbra** (central dark part) of Earth's shadow. **Partial:** Only part of the Moon passes through the umbra. **Penumbral:** The Moon passes through only the **penumbra** (area of partial darkness surrounding the umbra). See page 90 for more eclipse information.

Eclipse, Solar: Earth enters the shadow of the new Moon, which cuts off all or part of the Sun's light. **Total:** Earth passes through the umbra (central dark part) of the Moon's shadow, resulting in totality for observers within a narrow band on Earth. **Annular:** The Moon appears silhouetted against the Sun, with a ring of sunlight showing around it. **Partial:** The Moon blocks only part of the Sun.

Ecliptic: The apparent annual path of the Sun around the celestial sphere. The plane of the ecliptic is tipped 23½° from the celestial equator.

Elongation: The difference in degrees between the celestial longitudes of a planet and the Sun. **Greatest Elongation (Gr. Elong.):** The greatest apparent distance of a planet from the Sun, as seen from Earth.

Epact: A number from 1 to 30 that indicates the Moon's age on January 1 at Greenwich, England; used for determining the date of Easter.

Equinox: When the Sun crosses the celestial equator. This event occurs two times each year: **Vernal** is around March 21 and **Autumnal** is around September 23.

Evening Star: A planet that is above the western horizon at sunset and less than 180° east of the Sun in right ascension.

Golden Number: A number in the 19-year cycle of the Moon, used for determining the date of Easter. (Approximately every 19 years, the Moon's phases occur on the same dates.) Add 1 to any given year and divide by 19; the remainder is the Golden Number. If there is no remainder, the Golden Number is 19.

Greatest Illuminated Extent (Gr. Illum. Ext.): When the maximum surface area of a planet is illuminated as seen from Earth.

Julian Period: A period of 7,980 years beginning January 1, 4713 B.C. It provides a chronological basis for the study of ancient history. To find the Julian year, add 4,713 to any year.

Midnight: Astronomical midnight is the time when the Sun is opposite its highest point in the sky (noon). Midnight is nei-

ther A.M. nor P.M., although 12-hour digital clocks typically display midnight as
12:00 A.M. On a 24-hour time cycle,
00:00, rather than 24:00, usually indicates
midnight.

Moon on Equator: The Moon is on the celestial equator.

Moon Rides High/Runs Low: The Moon is
highest above or farthest below the celestial equator.

Moonrise/Moonset: When the Moon rises
above or sets below the horizon.

Moon's Phases: The changing appearance
of the Moon, caused by the different angles at which it is illuminated by the Sun.
First Quarter: Right half of the Moon is
illuminated. **Full:** The Sun and the Moon
are in opposition; the entire disk of the
Moon is illuminated. **Last Quarter:** Left
half of the Moon is illuminated. **New:** The
Sun and the Moon are in conjunction; the
entire disk of the Moon is darkened.

Moon's Place, Astronomical: The actual
position of the Moon within the constellations on the celestial sphere. **Astrological:** The astrological position of the
Moon within the zodiac, according to
calculations made more than 2,000 years
ago. Because of precession of the
equinoxes and other factors, this is not
the Moon's actual position in the sky.

Morning Star: A planet that is above the
eastern horizon at sunrise and less than
180° west of the Sun in right ascension.

Node: Either of the two points where a celestial body's orbit intersects the ecliptic.
Ascending: When the body is moving
from south to north of the ecliptic.
Descending: When the body is moving
from north to south of the ecliptic.

Occultation (Occn.): When the Moon or a
planet eclipses a star or planet.

Opposition: The Moon or a planet appears
on the opposite side of the sky from the
Sun (elongation 180°).

Perigee (Perig.): The point in the Moon's
orbit that is closest to Earth.

Perihelion (Perih.): The point in a planet's
orbit that is closest to the Sun.

Precession: The slowly changing position
of the stars and equinoxes in the sky resulting from variations in the orientation
of Earth's axis.

Right Ascension (R.A.): The celestial longitude of an object in the sky, measured
eastward along the celestial equator in
hours of time from the vernal equinox;
analogous to longitude on Earth.

Roman Indiction: A number within a 15-
year cycle, established January 1, A.D.
313, as a fiscal term. Add 3 to any given
year in the Christian era and divide by 15;
the remainder is the Roman Indiction. If
there is no remainder, it is 15.

Solar Cycle: In the Julian calendar, a period
of 28 years, at the end of which the days
of the month return to the same days of
the week.

Solstice, Summer: The Sun reaches its
greatest declination (23½°) north of the
celestial equator, around June 21. **Winter:**
The Sun reaches its greatest declination
(23½°) south of the celestial equator,
around December 21.

Stationary (Stat.): The apparent halted
movement of a planet against the background of the stars shortly before it
appears to move backward/westward
(retrograde motion) or forward/eastward
(direct motion).

Sun Fast/Slow: When a sundial reading is
ahead of (fast) or behind (slow) clock
time.

Sunrise/Sunset: The visible rising and
setting of the upper edge of the Sun's disk
across the unobstructed horizon of an
observer whose eyes are 15 feet above
ground level.

Twilight: For definitions of civil, nautical, and
astronomical twilight, **see page 96.** □□

Hydrogen Peroxide Can Heal What?

Medical science has discovered that hydrogen peroxide is more than just a disinfectant, it's an amazing healer. Many doctors are using hydrogen peroxide to treat a wide variety of serious ailments such as: **heart problems, clogged arteries, chest pain, allergies, asthma, migraine headaches, vascular headaches, cluster headaches, yeast infections, type II diabetes, emphysema, chronic pain syndromes, and more.**

Average consumers are also discovering that hydrogen peroxide has tons of health, beauty and household uses. A new handbook called *"The Amazing Health and Household Uses of Hydrogen Peroxide"* is now available to the general public. It shows you home remedies using diluted hydrogen peroxide and how to mix it with ordinary household items like baking soda, lemon, vinegar and salt to help:
• Soothe ARTHRITIS PAIN
• Make SORE THROATS feel better
• Ease the pain of BEE STINGS and INSECT BITES
• Treat ATHLETE'S FOOT
• Ease the PAIN OF RHEUMATISM
• Clear up FUNGUS and MINOR INFECTIONS
• Help treat minor BURNS
• Treat BRUISES and RASHES
• Soothe ACHING MUSCLES, JOINTS & SORE FEET

Hydrogen peroxide is truly amazing. Scientists have found it is involved in virtually all of life's vital processes. It stimulates the immune system, helps your body fight off viruses, parasites and bacteria. It also regulates hormones and is involved in the production of energy in the body's cells. That's just a few of the amazing things it does.

It's also a great alternative to harsh toxic chemicals and cleaners around the house. *"The Amazing Health and Household Uses of Hydrogen Peroxide"* also shows you how to make easy peroxide recipes for:
• A powerful bleaching formula for formica

• A fantastic homemade scouring powder
• The perfect drain cleaner for clogged drains
• A dishwasher detergent that makes dishes gleam
• An oven cleaner that eliminates elbow grease
• A great rust remover formula
• A tile cleaner that works like magic
• A little known formula that really cleans old porous tubs
• A solution to help house and garden plants flourish
• Use this formula to clean your pets
• This spray keeps a leftover salad fresher
• Ever wonder what happens to meats and fish before you bring them home? Here's a safety-wash for meat and fish
• A spray that's great for sprouting seeds
• Here's a sanitizing vegetable soak
• A denture soak that works great
• A tooth whitener that makes teeth sparkle
• A super polish for copper and brass
• A spot lifter for coffee, tea and wine stains

You'll learn all this and more in this remarkable book. In addition, you also get an extensive list of qualified doctors across the United States and even some in Canada who regularly use hydrogen peroxide in their practices to treat serious ailments.

Right now you can receive a special press run of *"The Amazing Health and Household Uses of Hydrogen Peroxide"* for only $8.95 plus $2.00 postage and handling. You must be completely satisfied, or simply return it in 90 days for a full refund.

HERE'S HOW TO ORDER: Simply PRINT your name and address and the words "Hydrogen Peroxide" on a piece of paper and mail it along with a check or money order for only $10.95 to: THE LEADER CO., INC., Publishing Division, Dept. HPT862, P.O. Box 8347, Canton, OH 44711. VISA, MasterCard, send card number and expiration date. Act now. Orders are fulfilled on a first come, first served basis.

© 2006 The Leader Co., Inc.

100   *Create a personal almanac page at* Almanac.com.   **2007**

How to Use This Almanac

The calendar pages (106–133) are the heart of *The Old Farmer's Almanac*. They present sky sightings and astronomical data for the entire year and are what make this book a true almanac, a "calendar of the heavens." In essence, these pages are unchanged since 1792, when Robert B. Thomas published his first edition. The long columns of numbers and symbols reveal all of nature's precision, rhythm, and glory—providing an astronomical look at the year 2007.

Why We Have Seasons

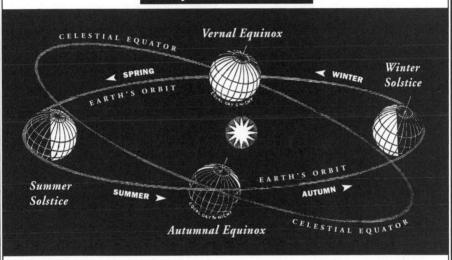

THE SEASONS OF 2007

Spring . . . . March 20, 8:07 P.M. EDT

Summer . . . . June 21, 2:06 P.M. EDT

Autumn . . . . . . September 23, 5:51 A.M. EDT

Winter . . . . December 22, 1:08 A.M. EST

■ The seasons occur because as Earth revolves around the Sun, its axis remains tilted at 23.5 degrees from the perpendicular. This tilt causes different latitudes on Earth to receive varying amounts of sunlight throughout the year.

In the Northern Hemisphere, the summer solstice (around June 21) marks the beginning of summer and occurs when the North Pole is tilted toward the Sun. The winter solstice (around December 21) marks the beginning of winter and occurs when the North Pole is tilted away from the Sun.

The equinoxes occur when the hemispheres equally face the Sun and receive equal amounts (12 hours each) of daylight and darkness. The vernal equinox (around March 21) marks the beginning of spring; the autumnal equinox (around September 23) marks the beginning of autumn. In the Southern Hemisphere, the seasons are the reverse of those in the Northern Hemisphere.

continued

The Left-Hand Calendar Pages • 106-132

A S A M P L E M O N T H

SKY WATCH ☆ *The box at the top of each Left-Hand Calendar Page describes the best times to view celestial highlights, including conjunctions, meteor showers, and planets. (The dates on which select astronomical events occur appear on the Right-Hand Calendar Pages.)*

1 **2** **3** **4** **5** **6** **7** **8**

All times are given in Eastern Standard Time. ☞ **Bold** = P.M. ☞ Light = A.M.

Day of Year	Day of Month	Day of Week	☀ Rises h. m.	Key	☀ Sets h. m.	Key	Length of Day h. m.	Sun Fast m.	Declina-tion of Sun ° '	High Tide Times Boston	☽ Rises h. m.	Key	☽ Sets h. m.	Key	☽ Place	☽ Age
1	1	M.	7:14	E	4:22	A	9 08	12	22 s.59	8¾ 9¼	2:14	A	5:40	E	TAU	12
2	2	Tu.	7:14	E	4:23	A	9 09	12	22 54	9¾ 10¼	3:12	A	6:46	E	AUR	13
3	3	W.	7:14	E	4:24	A	9 10	11	22 49	10½ 11¾	4:19	A	7:40	E	GEM	14

The Left-Hand Calendar Pages (detail above) contain daily Sun and Moon rise and set times, the length of day, high tide times, the Moon's place and age, and more for Boston. Examples of how to calculate astronomical times are shown below.

1 To calculate the sunrise/sunset times for your locale: Each sunrise/sunset time is assigned a Key Letter whose value is given in minutes in the **Time Corrections** table on **page 237**. Find your city in the table, or the city nearest you, and add or subtract those minutes to/from Boston's sunrise or sunset time given.

E X A M P L E :

■ To find the time of sunrise in Denver, Colorado, on the first day of the month:

Sunrise, Boston, with Key Letter E (above)	7:14 A.M. EST
Value of Key Letter E for Denver (p. 237)	+ 7 minutes
Sunrise, Denver	7:21 A.M. MST

2 To determine your city's length of day, find the sunrise/sunset Key Let-

ATTENTION, READERS: *All times given in this edition of the Almanac are for Boston, Massachusetts, and are in Eastern Standard Time (EST), except from 2:00 A.M., March 11, until 2:00 A.M., November 4, when Eastern Daylight Time (EDT) is given. Key Letters (A–E) are provided so that you can calculate times for other localities.*

ter values for your city on **page 237**. Add or subtract the sunset value to/from Boston's length of day. Then simply *reverse* the sunrise sign (from minus to plus, or plus to minus) and add or subtract this value to/from the result of the first step.

E X A M P L E :

■ To find the length of day in Richmond, Virginia:

Length of day, Boston (above)	9h. 08m.
Sunset Key Letter A for Richmond (p. 241)	+ 41m.
	9h. 49m.
Reverse sunrise Key Letter E for Richmond (p. 241, +11 to −11)	− 11m.
Length of day, Richmond	9h. 38m.

3 Use the Sun Fast column to change sundial time to clock time in Boston. A sundial reads natural time, or Sun time, which is neither Standard nor Daylight time except by coincidence. *Subtract* the minutes given in the Sun Fast column (except where the number is preceded by an asterisk [*], in which case *add* the minutes) to get Boston clock time, and use Key Letter C in the table on **page 237** to convert the time to your city.

Get local rise, set, and tide times at Almanac.com/astronomy. **2007**

E X A M P L E :

■ To change sundial time to clock time in Boston, or Salem, Oregon:

Sundial reading (Boston or Salem)	12:00 noon
Subtract Sun Fast (p. 102)	– 12 minutes
Clock time, Boston	11:48 A.M. EST
Use Key Letter C for Salem (p. 240)	+ 27 minutes
Clock time, Salem	12:15 P.M. PST

4 This column gives the degrees and minutes of the Sun from the celestial equator at noon EST or EDT.

5 This column gives the times of high tides in Boston. For example, the first high tide occurs at 8:45 A.M. and the second occurs at 9:30 P.M. the same day. (A dash indicates that high tide occurs on or after midnight and so is recorded on the next day.) Figures for calculating high tide times and heights for localities other than Boston are given in the Tide Corrections table on **page 234**.

-Beth Krommes

6 To calculate the moonrise/moonset times for localities other than Boston, follow the example in the next column, making a correction for longitude (see table, above right). For the longitude of your city, see **page 237**. (Note: A dash in the moonrise/moonset columns indicates that rise or set times occur on or after midnight and are recorded on the next day.)

Longitude of city	Correction minutes
58°–76°	0
77°–89°	+1
90°–102°	+2
103°–115°	+3
116°–127°	+4
128°–141°	+5
142°–155°	+6

E X A M P L E :

■ To determine the time of moonrise in Lansing, Michigan:

Moonrise, Boston, with Key Letter A (p. 102)	2:14 P.M. EST
Value of Key Letter A for Lansing (p. 239)	+ 52 minutes
Correction for Lansing longitude, 84°33'	+ 1 minute
Moonrise, Lansing	3:07 P.M. EST

Use the same procedure to determine the time of moonset.

7 The Moon's Place is its *astronomical* placement in the heavens. (This should not be confused with the Moon's *astrological* place in the zodiac, as explained on **page 226**.) All calculations in this Almanac are based on astronomy, not astrology, except for the information on **pages 226–230**.

In addition to the 12 constellations of the zodiac, this column may indicate others: Auriga **(AUR)**, a northern constellation between Perseus and Gemini; Cetus **(CET)**, which lies south of the zodiac, just south of Pisces and Aries; Ophiuchus **(OPH)**, a constellation primarily north of the zodiac but with a small corner between Scorpius and Sagittarius; Orion **(ORI)**, a constellation whose northern limit first reaches the zodiac between Taurus and Gemini; and Sextans **(SEX)**, which lies south of the zodiac except for a corner that just touches it near Leo.

8 The last column gives the Moon's Age, which is the number of days since the previous new Moon. (The average length of the lunar month is 29.53 days.)

continued

The Right-Hand Calendar Pages • 107–133

A SAMPLE MONTH

- Weather prediction rhyme.
- Civil holidays and astronomical events.
- Sundays and special holy days.
- The bold letter is the Dominical Letter (from A to G), a traditional ecclesiastical designation for Sunday determined by the date on which the first Sunday falls. For 2007, the Dominical Letter is **G**, because the first Sunday of the year falls on the seventh day of January.
- Symbols for notable celestial events. (See opposite page for explanations.)
- High tide heights, in feet, at Boston.
- Proverbs, poems, and adages.
- Noteworthy historical events, folklore, and legends.
- Religious feasts. A T indicates a major feast that the church has this year temporarily transferred to a date other than its usual one. This is to avoid conflict with Sundays, Holy Week, Easter Week, and other observances that take precedence.

Day of Month	Day of Week	Dates, Feasts, Fasts, Aspects, Tide Heights	Weather
1	Th.	St. David • ☌♄☾ • Congress authorized first U.S. Census, 1790 • Tides {9.9 8.9	*In*
2	Fr.	St. Chad • Ember Day • Puerto Rico became U.S. territory, 1917 • {10.0 9.2	*like*
3	Sa.	Ember Day • **Full Worm** ○ • **Eclipse** ☾ • *A good deed is never lost.*	*a*
4	**G**	**2nd S. in Lent** • ☾ ON EQ. • ☾ AT ☋ • {10.0 9.6	*lamb*
5	M.	St. Piran • ☌♅☉ • Piano maker William Steinway born, 1835	*a-bleating;*
6	Tu.	☾ AT APO. • Renaissance man Michelangelo born, 1475 • Tides {9.7 9.6	*sleeting,*
7	W.	St. Perpetua • ☿ STAT. • Brilliant nationwide aurora borealis, 1918 • {9.7 9.3	*but*
8	Th.	First train crossed Niagara Railway Suspension Bridge, Niagara River, 1855 • Tides {9.6 8.9	*it's*
9	Fr.	12" snow in parts of Ky., La., and N.C., 1960 • {9.4 8.5	*only*
10	Sa.	Abolitionist Harriet Tubman died, 1913 • First known U.S. fatality due to raccoon rabies, 2003	*fleeting.*
11	**G**	**3rd S. in Lent** • ☌♃☾ • **U.S. Daylight Saving time begins, 2:00 A.M.**	*Great*
12	M.	☾ RUNS LOW • *If you take a leap in the dark, you usually land in a pit.* • Tides {8.9 7.7	*days*
13	Tu.	Discovery of Pluto officially announced, 1930 • {9.0 7.8	*for*
14	W.	Cotton gin patented, 1794 • Musician Quincy Jones born, 1933 • Tides {9.3 8.1	*the*
15	Th.	Beware the ides of March. • ☌♂☾ • Tides {9.7 8.8	*Irish*
16	Fr.	☌☿☾ • ☌♆☾ • First Lady Pat Nixon born, 1912 • Tides {10.3 9.5	*and*
17	Sa.	St. Patrick • *If you would eat eggs, take care of the hen.* • Tides {10.8 10.3	*all*
18	**G**	**New** ● • **Eclipse** ☉ • ☾ ON EQ. • ☾ AT ☊ • {11.3 11.0	*of*
19	M.	St. Joseph • ☾ AT PERIG. • Chipmunks emerge from hibernation now. • {11.5 11.5	*their*
20	Tu.	**Vernal Equinox** • *Thunder in spring, Cold will bring.* • {11.5 —	*friends:*
21	W.	☌♀☾ • ☿ GR. ELONG. (28° WEST) • Singer Johnny Bristol died, 2004 • {11.8 11.2	*Look*
22	Th.	First women's basketball game, Smith College, Northampton, Mass., 1893 • Tides {11.8 10.7	*out,*
23	Fr.	World Meteorological Organization established, 1950	*below!*
24	Sa.	*Exxon Valdez* struck reef and spilled 240,000 barrels of oil, Prince William Sound, Alaska, 1989 • {11.0 9.3	*It's*
25	**G**	**5th S. in Lent** • ☾ RIDES HIGH • ☌♂♆ • {10.4 8.8	*snowing*
26	M.	Annunciation[T] • Oldest known black spider monkey died at age 53, 2005 • {9.9 8.4	*again!*

☞ *For explanations of Almanac terms, see the glossaries on pages 98, 134, and 236.*

Predicting Earthquakes

■ Note the dates in the **Right-Hand Calendar Pages** when the Moon rides high or runs low. The date of the high begins the most likely five-day period of earthquakes in the Northern Hemisphere; the date of the low indicates a similar five-day period in the Southern Hemisphere. Also noted are the two days each month when the Moon is on the celestial equator, indicating the most likely time for earthquakes in either hemisphere.

–Beth Krommes

Throughout the **Right-Hand Calendar Pages** are groups of symbols that represent notable celestial events. The symbols and names of the principal planets and aspects are:

⊙	Sun	Ψ	Neptune
○ ● ☾	Moon	♇	Pluto
☿	Mercury	♂	Conjunction (on the
♀	Venus		same celestial
⊕	Earth		longitude)
♂	Mars	☊	Ascending node
♃	Jupiter	☋	Descending node
♄	Saturn	☍	Opposition (180 degrees
♅	Uranus		from Sun)

E X A M P L E :

♂♃☾ on the eleventh day of the month (see opposite page) means that on that date a conjunction (♂) of Jupiter (♃) and the Moon (☾) occurs: They are aligned along the same celestial longitude and appear to be closest together in the sky.

Earth at Perihelion and Aphelion

■ Perihelion: January 3, 2007. Earth will be 91,399,728 miles from the Sun. Aphelion: July 6, 2007. Earth will be 94,508,728 miles from the Sun.

2007 Calendar Highlights

Movable Religious Observances

Septuagesima Sunday	February 4
Shrove Tuesday	February 20
Ash Wednesday	February 21
Palm Sunday	April 1
First day of Passover	April 3
Good Friday	April 6
Easter	April 8
Orthodox Easter	April 8
Rogation Sunday	May 13
Ascension Day	May 17
Whitsunday–Pentecost	May 27
Trinity Sunday	June 3
Corpus Christi	June 10
Rosh Hashanah	September 13
First day of Ramadan	September 13
Yom Kippur	September 22
First Sunday of Advent	December 2
First day of Chanukah	December 5

Chronological Cycles

Dominical Letter	G
Epact	11
Golden Number (Lunar Cycle)	13
Roman Indiction	15
Solar Cycle	28
Year of Julian Period	6720

–Beth Krommes

Eras

ERA	YEAR	BEGINS
Byzantine	7516	September 14
Jewish (A.M.)*	5768	September 13
Chinese (Lunar) [Year of the Pig/Boar]	4705	February 18
Roman (A.U.C.)	2760	January 14
Nabonassar	2756	April 22
Japanese	2667	January 1
Grecian (Seleucidae)	2319	September 14 (or October 14)
Indian (Saka)	1929	March 22
Diocletian	1724	September 12
Islamic (Hegira)*	1428	January 20

Year begins at sunset the evening before.

SKY WATCH ☆ *The evening sky is now nearly empty of planets, with Jupiter reaching conjunction with the Sun on the 21st. Venus is technically back, but it is actually too low to be easily observed. One bright spot this month is Saturn, which now rises by 11:00 P.M. at midmonth in Leo. However, the real highlight this month is the first transit of Mercury visible throughout North America in decades. Specially equipped solar telescopes or binoculars with strong appropriate filters (always use eye protection when viewing solar events) will show the innermost planet march across the Sun's face on the 8th. Orion and the brilliant winter stars return this month, rising well before midnight.*

○	**Full Moon**	5th day	7th hour	58th minute
☾	**Last Quarter**	12th day	12th hour	45th minute
●	**New Moon**	20th day	17th hour	18th minute
☽	**First Quarter**	28th day	1st hour	29th minute

To use this page, see p. 102; for Key Letters, see p. 237; for Tide Corrections, see p. 234.
All times are given in Eastern Standard Time. ☞ **Bold = P.M.** ☞ Light = A.M.

Day of Year	Day of Month	Day of Week	☀ Rises h. m.	Key	☀ Sets h. m.	Key	Length of Day h. m.	Sun Fast m.	Declination of Sun ° ′	High Tide Times Boston		☽ Rises h. m.	Key	☽ Sets h. m.	Key	☽ Place	☽ Age
305	1	W.	6:18	D	4:38	B	10 20	32	14 s. 32	6¾	7¼	2:37	D	1:15	C	AQU	10
306	2	Th.	6:19	D	4:37	B	10 18	32	14 51	7¾	8¼	3:00	C	2:32	D	PSC	11
307	3	Fr.	6:20	D	4:35	B	10 15	32	15 10	8¾	9¼	3:23	B	3:50	E	PSC	12
308	4	Sa.	6:21	D	4:34	B	10 13	32	15 29	9½	10	3:49	B	5:10	E	PSC	13
309	5	**A**	6:22	D	4:33	B	10 11	32	15 47	10¼	11	4:21	A	6:32	E	ARI	14
310	6	M.	6:24	D	4:32	B	10 08	32	16 05	11¼	11¾	4:59	A	7:54	E	ARI	15
311	7	Tu.	6:25	D	4:31	B	10 06	32	16 23	12	—	5:47	A	9:12	E	TAU	16
312	8	W.	6:26	D	4:29	A	10 03	32	16 40	12¾	12¾	6:45	A	10:20	E	AUR	17
313	9	Th.	6:27	D	4:28	A	10 01	32	16 57	1½	1¾	7:51	A	11:15	E	AUR	18
314	10	Fr.	6:29	D	4:27	A	9 58	32	17 14	2½	2½	8:59	A	11:58	E	GEM	19
315	11	Sa.	6:30	D	4:26	A	9 56	32	17 31	3¼	3½	10:07	B	12:32	E	CAN	20
316	12	**A**	6:31	D	4:25	A	9 54	32	17 47	4¼	4½	11:13	B	12:58	E	CAN	21
317	13	M.	6:32	D	4:24	A	9 52	31	18 03	5¼	5½	—	—	1:19	D	LEO	22
318	14	Tu.	6:34	D	4:23	A	9 49	31	18 19	6¼	6½	12:16	C	1:38	D	LEO	23
319	15	W.	6:35	D	4:23	A	9 48	31	18 34	7	7¼	1:17	D	1:56	C	LEO	24
320	16	Th.	6:36	D	4:22	A	9 46	31	18 50	7¾	8¼	2:18	D	2:13	C	VIR	25
321	17	Fr.	6:37	D	4:21	A	9 44	31	19 04	8½	9	3:19	E	2:31	B	VIR	26
322	18	Sa.	6:39	D	4:20	A	9 41	31	19 18	9¼	9¾	4:22	E	2:52	B	VIR	27
323	19	**A**	6:40	D	4:19	A	9 39	30	19 32	9¾	10½	5:27	E	3:16	A	VIR	28
324	20	M.	6:41	D	4:19	A	9 38	30	19 46	10½	11	6:34	E	3:46	A	LIB	0
325	21	Tu.	6:42	D	4:18	A	9 36	30	19 59	11	11¾	7:42	E	4:24	A	SCO	1
326	22	W.	6:44	D	4:17	A	9 33	30	20 12	11¾	—	8:48	E	5:11	A	OPH	2
327	23	Th.	6:45	D	4:17	A	9 32	29	20 24	12½	12½	9:47	E	6:10	A	SAG	3
328	24	Fr.	6:46	D	4:16	A	9 30	29	20 37	1	1¼	10:36	E	7:18	A	SAG	4
329	25	Sa.	6:47	D	4:15	A	9 28	29	20 49	2	2	11:17	E	8:31	B	SAG	5
330	26	**A**	6:48	D	4:15	A	9 27	28	21 00	2¾	2¾	11:49	E	9:46	B	CAP	6
331	27	M.	6:49	E	4:14	A	9 25	28	21 11	3½	3¾	12:16	E	11:01	C	CAP	7
332	28	Tu.	6:50	E	4:14	A	9 24	28	21 22	4½	4¾	12:40	D	—	—	AQU	8
333	29	W.	6:52	E	4:14	A	9 22	27	21 32	5½	5¾	1:02	C	12:16	D	PSC	9
334	30	Th.	6:53	E	4:13	A	9 20	27	21 s. 42	6½	7	1:24	C	1:31	D	PSC	10

C
A
L
E
N
D
A
R

NOVEMBER HATH 30 DAYS • 2006

In slack wind of November
The fog forms and shifts. –Christina Georgina Rossetti

Day of Month	Day of Week	Dates, Feasts, Fasts, Aspects, Tide Heights	Weather
1	W.	All Saints' • ☌♅☾ • Five-mile-long Mackinac Bridge, Mich., opened, 1957	*Dripping*
2	Th.	All Souls' • ☾ on Eq. • ☾ at ☊ • Tides { 10.3 10.4	*and*
3	Fr.	☾ at perig. • Canada's first bank opened, 1817 • { 11.0 10.7	*flaking,*
4	Sa.	*If you don't have what you like, you must like what you have.* • Gather milkweed pods for crafts now.	*then*
5	A	22nd S. af. P. • Full Beaver ○ • { 11.9 10.7	*sunny*
6	M.	Inventor of basketball, James Naismith, born, 1861 • *Genius, like water, will find its level.* • { 12.0 10.5	*for*
7	Tu.	Election Day • UN approved formation of United Nations Emergency Force, 1956 • { 11.9 —	*raking.*
8	W.	☿ in inf. ☌ • ☿ transits over ☉ • Tides { 10.2 11.5	*Showers*
9	Th.	☾ rides high • *A fox should not be of the jury at a goose's trial.* • Tides { 9.7 10.9	*ample;*
10	Fr.	Mammoth storm in Minnesota produced record-breaking low pressure, 1998 • Tides { 9.2 10.3	*now*
11	Sa.	St. Martin of Tours • Veterans Day • Sadie Hawkins Day • { 8.8 9.7	*a*
12	A	23rd S. af. P. • Indian Summer • ☌♄☾ • { 8.6 9.3	*sample*
13	M.	The Wall of Vietnam Veterans Memorial dedicated, 1982	*of*
14	Tu.	Journalist Nellie Bly left N.Y.C. for tour around the world in 72 days, 1889 • Tides { 8.5 8.8	*what's*
15	W.	☾ on Eq. • ☾ at ☋ • ☾ at apo. • Lobsters move to offshore waters. • { 8.7 8.8	*to*
16	Th.	Louis Riel, leader of Métis resistance vs. Canada, hanged, 1885 • *After black clouds, clear weather.*	*come!*
17	Fr.	St. Hugh of Lincoln • ☿ stat. • Crab apples are ripe now. • { 9.4 8.9	*Mild,*
18	Sa.	William Tell shot apple off son's head, 1307 • Tides { 9.7 8.9	*but*
19	A	24th S. af. P. • ☌☿☾ • Edsel car discontinued, 1959	*glum.*
20	M.	New ● • ♅ stat. • Photos required for U.S. passports, 1914 • Tides { 10.1 9.0	*Just*
21	Tu.	☌♃☉ • Truman became first U.S. president to ride underwater in a submarine, 1946	*enough*
22	W.	*Eat at pleasure, drink by measure.* • Humpback whales migrate to Hawaii now. • Tides { 10.3 —	*snow*
23	Th.	St. Clement • Thanksgiving • ☾ runs low • Tides { 8.9 10.3	*for*
24	Fr.	Suspected JFK assassin Lee Harvey Oswald murdered, 1963 • Tides { 8.8 10.3	*tracking—*
25	Sa.	☿ gr. elong. (20° west) • Robert S. Ledley granted patent for CAT scan, 1975 • { 8.8 10.2	*or*
26	A	25th S. af. P. • ☌♆☾ • First lion exhibited in America, 1716	*packing*
27	M.	The "Portland storm" brought 27 inches of snow to New London, Conn., 1898 • { 8.9 9.9	*it away*
28	Tu.	☌♅☾ • U.S. bill signed allowing states to set own speed limits, 1995 • { 9.2 9.8	*on*
29	W.	☾ on Eq. • ☾ at ☊ • *Pong* coin-operated video game debuted, 1972 • { 9.6 9.7	*Turkey*
30	Th.	St. Andrew • *A heavy November snow will last until April.*	*Day!*

Life is a combination of magic and pasta. –Federico Fellini

Farmer's Calendar

■ With the painful and protesting reluctance of a rusty hinge, the lazy householder turns again to his seasonal tasks. Procrastination ends at last. The leaves, the storm windows, the outdoor furniture, the tangled garden hose, the half-frozen garden itself—all these and many more must be attended to. Stiffly, slowly, not without creaks and groans, the work begins.

As it proceeds, however, the ordeal of the fall chores reveals a curious dynamic, a kind of automatic acceleration that lightens the whole job—maybe too much so. First, you do the things that must be done (the storm windows); then you do the things that might as well be done (the leaves); then those that it's nice to have done (the garden). You might call it a day at this point, but by now you're hooked. Your former inertia overcome—indeed, annihilated—you plunge on. You do jobs that never needed to be done and progress to others that, frankly, should have been omitted.

We have in action here a fundamental principle of behavior, hitherto little understood. Its algebraic expression might be $B = 1/t$, where B is the benefit of work and t is the time a worker has been at his tasks. The idea is that benefit is inversely proportional to time spent. It's a formula as rigorous, as inexorable, as Universal Gravitation, and in this humble space it has found its Newton. I call it the Iron Law of Puttering.

DECEMBER

THE TWELFTH MONTH • 2006

SKY WATCH ☆ *There's lots to see this month: A wonderfully tight Mercury/Mars/Jupiter conjunction stands low in the predawn twilight on the 9th. The next morning, Mercury and Jupiter are extremely close together, and Mercury remains visible during the whole first half of the month. Jupiter emerges from the solar glare as a morning star and crosses into Scorpius. Venus appears in the evening sky, although it is still low during twilight. Saturn rises by 9:30 P.M. at midmonth and is near the Moon on the 9th. The Geminid meteor showers should be visible before midnight on both the 13th and 14th. Winter officially arrives with the solstice on the 21st, at 7:22 P.M.*

○	**Full Moon**	4th day	19th hour	25th minute
☾	**Last Quarter**	12th day	9th hour	32nd minute
●	**New Moon**	20th day	9th hour	1st minute
☽	**First Quarter**	27th day	9th hour	48th minute

To use this page, see p. 102; for Key Letters, see p. 237; for Tide Corrections, see p. 234.
All times are given in Eastern Standard Time. ☞ **Bold = P.M.** ☞ Light = A.M.

Day of Year	Day of Month	Day of Week	☼ Rises h. m.	Key	☼ Sets h. m.	Key	Length of Day h.	m.	Sun Fast m.	Declination of Sun °	'	High Tide Times Boston		☽ Rises h. m.	Key	☽ Sets h. m.	Key	☽ Place	☽ Age
335	1	Fr.	6:54	E	**4:13**	A	9	19	27	21 s.	51	7¼	**8**	**1:48**	B	2:47	E	PSC	11
336	2	Sa.	6:55	E	**4:13**	A	9	18	26	22	00	8¼	**9**	**2:16**	B	4:05	E	ARI	12
337	3	**A**	6:56	E	**4:12**	A	9	16	26	22	09	9¼	**9¾**	**2:50**	A	5:26	E	ARI	13
338	4	M.	6:57	E	**4:12**	A	9	15	26	22	17	10	**10¾**	**3:34**	A	6:45	E	TAU	14
339	5	Tu.	6:58	E	**4:12**	A	9	14	25	22	25	10¾	**11½**	**4:27**	A	7:58	E	TAU	15
340	6	W.	6:59	E	**4:12**	A	9	13	25	22	32	11¾	—	**5:30**	A	9:00	E	AUR	16
341	7	Th.	7:00	E	**4:12**	A	9	12	24	22	39	12¼	**12½**	**6:39**	B	9:50	E	GEM	17
342	8	Fr.	7:01	E	**4:12**	A	9	11	24	22	45	1¼	**1¼**	**7:50**	B	10:28	E	CAN	18
343	9	Sa.	7:02	E	**4:12**	A	9	10	24	22	51	2	**2**	**8:58**	B	10:58	E	CAN	19
344	10	**A**	7:02	E	**4:12**	A	9	10	23	22	57	2¾	**3**	**10:03**	C	11:22	D	LEO	20
345	11	M.	7:03	E	**4:12**	A	9	09	23	23	02	3¾	**3¾**	**11:06**	C	11:42	D	LEO	21
346	12	Tu.	7:04	E	**4:12**	A	9	08	22	23	06	4½	**4¾**	—	–	**12:00**	D	LEO	22
347	13	W.	7:05	E	**4:12**	A	9	07	22	23	10	5¼	**5¾**	12:07	D	**12:17**	C	VIR	23
348	14	Th.	7:06	E	**4:12**	A	9	06	21	23	14	6¼	**6½**	1:07	D	**12:35**	B	VIR	24
349	15	Fr.	7:07	E	**4:13**	A	9	06	21	23	17	7	**7½**	2:09	E	**12:55**	B	VIR	25
350	16	Sa.	7:07	E	**4:13**	A	9	06	20	23	20	7¾	**8¼**	3:13	E	**1:17**	B	VIR	26
351	17	**A**	7:08	E	**4:13**	A	9	05	20	23	22	8½	**9¼**	4:19	E	**1:45**	A	LIB	27
352	18	M.	7:09	E	**4:14**	A	9	05	19	23	24	9¼	**10**	5:27	E	**2:19**	A	LIB	28
353	19	Tu.	7:09	E	**4:14**	A	9	05	19	23	25	10	**10½**	6:35	E	**3:04**	A	SCO	29
354	20	W.	7:10	E	**4:14**	A	9	04	18	23	26	10¾	**11¼**	7:37	E	**4:00**	A	SAG	0
355	21	Th.	7:11	E	**4:15**	A	9	04	18	23	26	11¼	—	8:31	E	**5:06**	A	SAG	1
356	22	Fr.	7:11	E	**4:15**	A	9	04	17	23	26	12	**12**	9:16	E	**6:20**	B	SAG	2
357	23	Sa.	7:11	E	**4:16**	A	9	05	17	23	26	12¾	**12¾**	9:51	E	**7:36**	B	CAP	3
358	24	**A**	7:12	E	**4:17**	A	9	05	16	23	25	1½	**1¾**	10:20	E	**8:52**	C	CAP	4
359	25	M.	7:12	E	**4:17**	A	9	05	16	23	23	2¼	**2½**	10:45	D	**10:07**	D	AQU	5
360	26	Tu.	7:12	E	**4:18**	A	9	06	15	23	22	3¼	**3½**	11:07	D	**11:21**	D	AQU	6
361	27	W.	7:13	E	**4:19**	A	9	06	15	23	19	4	**4½**	11:28	C	—	–	PSC	7
362	28	Th.	7:13	E	**4:19**	A	9	06	14	23	16	5	**5½**	11:51	B	12:35	E	PSC	8
363	29	Fr.	7:13	E	**4:20**	A	9	07	14	23	12	6	**6½**	**12:17**	B	1:51	E	PSC	9
364	30	Sa.	7:13	E	**4:21**	A	9	08	13	23	08	7	**7¾**	**12:47**	A	3:08	E	ARI	10
365	31	**A**	7:13	E	**4:22**	A	9	09	13	23 s.	04	8	**8¾**	**1:26**	A	4:25	E	TAU	11

DECEMBER HATH 31 DAYS • 2006

The icicles now fringe the trees
That swayed in summer's gentle breeze. –Dora Read Goodale

Day of Month	Day of Week	Dates, Feasts, Fasts, Aspects, Tide Heights	Weather
1	Fr.	☾ AT PERIG. • Rosa Parks arrested for not giving her bus seat to a white passenger, 1955 • { 10.6 / 9.8	*Snow*
2	Sa.	St. Viviana • Touro Synagogue, oldest in U.S., dedicated, Newport, R.I., 1763 • { 11.1 / 9.9	*lightly*
3	**A**	**1st S. of Advent** • Probe *Pioneer 10* reached Jupiter, 1973	*falls*
4	M.	**Full Cold** ○ • New Haven, Conn., received 20 inches of snow, 1786 • { 11.6 / 9.9	*outside*
5	Tu.	*A good example is the best sermon.* • Tides { 11.6 / 9.8	*the*
6	W.	St. Nicholas • ☾ RIDES HIGH • ♄ STAT. • Tides { 11.5 / —	*malls*
7	Th.	St. Ambrose • **National Pearl Harbor Remembrance Day** • Tides { 9.6 / 11.1	*on*
8	Fr.	Popeye creator, Elzie Crisler Segar, born, 1894	*shoppers*
9	Sa.	☌♂☿ • Quebec adopted a new coat of arms, 1939 • Tides { 9.1 / 10.2	*making*
10	**A**	**2nd S. of Advent** • ☌♃☿ • ☌♄☾	*cell phone*
11	M.	☌♂♃ • Cold air stopped Big Ben clock, 1981 • Winterberry fruits especially showy now.	*calls.*
12	Tu.	☾ AT ☋ • Pa. became second state in Union, 1787 • { 8.6 / 8.7	*It's*
13	W.	St. Lucia • ☾ ON EQ. • ☾ AT APO. • *A merry host makes merry guests.*	*cold*
14	Th.	Halcyon Days • Meteorite fell in Weston, Conn., 1807 • Tides { 8.7 / 8.3	*out;*
15	Fr.	Bill of Rights ratified, 1791 • "Great Blizzard" in Prairie provinces, 1964 • Tides { 8.9 / 8.2	*"The*
16	Sa.	First day of Chanukah • Novelist Jane Austen born, 1775	*Nut-*
17	**A**	**3rd S. of Advent** • 1st official NFL championship game, 1933	*cracker's*
18	M.	☌♂☾ • ☌♃☾ • ☌♇☉ • Pres. Wilson married Edith B. Galt, 1915	*sold*
19	Tu.	*He who would live in peace and at ease, Must not speak all he knows, nor judge all he sees.* • { 10.0 / 8.7	*out!"*
20	W.	Ember Day • **New** ● • ☾ RUNS LOW • Tides { 10.3 / 8.8	*Opening*
21	Th.	St. Thomas • **Winter Solstice** • 4-day snowstorm began, Portland, Oreg., 1892	*presents*
22	Fr.	Ember Day • Beware the Pogonip. • Tides { 9.0 / 10.7	*is*
23	Sa.	Ember Day • ☌♆☾ • G. Washington resigned army commission, 1783	*always*
24	**A**	**4th S. of Advent** • *Whistling parrots indicate rain.* • { 9.3 / 10.6	*a*
25	M.	**Christmas Day** • ☌♅☾ • Tides { 9.4 / 10.4	*thrill—*
26	Tu.	St. Stephen • **Boxing Day (Canada)** • **1st day of Kwanzaa** • ☾ ON EQ. • ☾ AT ☊	*'007's*
27	W.	St. John • ☾ AT PERIG. • Rubber rationing began in U.S., 1941 • { 9.8 / 9.7	*got*
28	Th.	Holy Innocents • First chewing gum patent granted, 1869	*a*
29	Fr.	Fred Newton completed 1,826-mile swim in Mississippi River, Minn. to La., 1930 • { 10.3 / 9.2	*license*
30	Sa.	Social reformer Amelia Bloomer died, 1894 • The Arroyo Seco Pkwy., California's first freeway, officially opened, 1940	*to*
31	**A**	**1st S. af. Ch.** • *Years know more than books.* • Tides { 10.7 / 9.1	*chill!*

Farmer's Calendar

■ In recent times, as the season for building and other outdoor projects draws to an end, a last flurry of construction has come to mark the dwindling year—an access of shelter-making that is dedicated, busy, and, at first, a little odd. I refer to the rearing of elaborate houses to protect the shrubs, hedges, and other plantings that adorn our dwellings.

We are not talking here about flimsy shelters thrown up just anyhow. The preferred form in these parts is a sturdy A-frame made of 2x4 stringers and ties of 1x4 stock at the lightest. Such a structure big enough to keep snow and ice from breaking down a good-size yew or rosebush has real weight and takes some building. It all seems a bit extreme. Sure, you build for your family, for your livestock, even for your dogs. Do you really have to build for your rhododendrons?

Formerly, these shrub castles were hardly seen. Twenty years ago, only the grandest places had them. There, perhaps, is a hint of the reason for the recent annual frenzy of plant-protection: Everybody's place is grand today—grand, at least, in expense. Nowadays, those hybrid honeysuckles come from a Garden Center, where you must leave serious money in exchange for serious botany. Come December, therefore, as you immure your fothergilla in lumber, don't be hard on yourself. You're not crazy; you're protecting your investment.

THE FIRST MONTH • 2007

SKY WATCH ☆ *Venus kicks off an exciting year as it begins its run as an evening star, low in the west after sunset. Throughout the month, inconspicuous Mars and bright Jupiter, both in the constellation Ophiuchus, appear as morning stars in the east before dawn. Saturn, in Leo, rises by 7:30 P.M. at midmonth and is easily seen after 9:00 P.M. The crescent Moon meets Venus low in the western twilight, half an hour after sunset, on the 20th. During the final days of the month, Mercury becomes brighter, is higher up, and can be viewed easily during the fading evening twilight. Earth reaches perihelion, its annual position closest to the Sun, on January 3.*

○	**Full Moon**	3rd day	8th hour	57th minute
☾	**Last Quarter**	11th day	7th hour	45th minute
●	**New Moon**	18th day	23rd hour	1st minute
☽	**First Quarter**	25th day	18th hour	1st minute

To use this page, see p. 102; for Key Letters, see p. 237; for Tide Tables, see p. 234.
All times are given in Eastern Standard Time. ☞ **Bold = P.M.** ☞ Light = A.M.

Day of Year	Day of Month	Day of Week	☼ Rises h. m.	Key	☼ Sets h. m.	Key	Length of Day h. m.	Sun Fast m.	Declination of Sun ° ′	High Tide Times Boston		☽ Rises h. m.	Key	☽ Sets h. m.	Key	☽ Place	☽ Age
1	1	M.	7:14	E	**4:22**	A	9 08	12	22 s.59	8¾	**9½**	**2:14**	A	5:40	E	TAU	12
2	2	Tu.	7:14	E	**4:23**	A	9 09	12	22 54	9¾	**10½**	**3:12**	A	6:46	E	AUR	13
3	3	W.	7:14	E	**4:24**	A	9 10	11	22 49	10½	**11¼**	**4:19**	A	7:40	E	GEM	14
4	4	Th.	7:14	E	**4:25**	A	9 11	11	22 43	11½	—	**5:30**	B	8:23	E	GEM	15
5	5	Fr.	7:14	E	**4:26**	A	9 12	11	22 36	12	**12¼**	**6:40**	B	8:56	E	CAN	16
6	6	Sa.	7:14	E	**4:27**	A	9 13	10	22 29	12¾	**1**	**7:47**	C	9:23	E	LEO	17
7	7	**G**	7:14	E	**4:28**	A	9 14	10	22 21	1½	**1¾**	**8:52**	C	9:44	D	LEO	18
8	8	M.	7:14	E	**4:29**	A	9 15	9	22 13	2¼	**2½**	**9:54**	D	10:03	D	LEO	19
9	9	Tu.	7:13	E	**4:30**	A	9 17	9	22 05	3	**3¼**	**10:55**	D	10:21	C	VIR	20
10	10	W.	7:13	E	**4:31**	A	9 18	8	21 57	3¾	**4**	**11:56**	D	10:39	C	VIR	21
11	11	Th.	7:13	E	**4:32**	A	9 19	8	21 47	4½	**4¾**	—	–	10:57	B	VIR	22
12	12	Fr.	7:12	E	**4:33**	A	9 21	8	21 38	5¼	**5¾**	12:59	E	11:18	B	VIR	23
13	13	Sa.	7:12	E	**4:35**	A	9 23	7	21 28	6	**6¾**	2:03	E	11:43	A	LIB	24
14	14	**G**	7:12	E	**4:36**	A	9 24	7	21 17	7	**7¾**	3:10	E	**12:14**	A	LIB	25
15	15	M.	7:11	E	**4:37**	A	9 26	6	21 06	7¾	**8½**	4:17	E	**12:53**	A	SCO	26
16	16	Tu.	7:11	E	**4:38**	A	9 27	6	20 55	8¾	**9½**	5:22	E	**1:44**	A	OPH	27
17	17	W.	7:10	E	**4:39**	A	9 29	6	20 44	9½	**10¼**	6:21	E	**2:47**	A	SAG	28
18	18	Th.	7:10	E	**4:40**	A	9 30	5	20 31	10¼	**11**	7:10	E	**4:00**	B	SAG	0
19	19	Fr.	7:09	E	**4:42**	A	9 33	5	20 19	11	**11¾**	7:49	E	**5:17**	B	CAP	1
20	20	Sa.	7:09	E	**4:43**	A	9 34	5	20 06	11¾	—	8:21	E	**6:36**	C	CAP	2
21	21	**G**	7:08	E	**4:44**	A	9 36	5	19 53	12½	**12½**	8:48	D	**7:54**	D	AQU	3
22	22	M.	7:07	E	**4:45**	A	9 38	4	19 39	1¼	**1½**	9:11	D	**9:10**	D	AQU	4
23	23	Tu.	7:07	D	**4:47**	A	9 40	4	19 25	2	**2¼**	9:33	C	**10:26**	E	PSC	5
24	24	W.	7:06	D	**4:48**	A	9 42	4	19 11	2¾	**3¼**	9:56	B	**11:41**	E	PSC	6
25	25	Th.	7:05	D	**4:49**	A	9 44	3	18 56	3½	**4**	10:20	B	—	–	PSC	7
26	26	Fr.	7:04	D	**4:50**	A	9 46	3	18 41	4½	**5¼**	10:49	A	12:58	E	ARI	8
27	27	Sa.	7:03	D	**4:52**	A	9 49	3	18 26	5½	**6¼**	11:24	A	2:15	E	TAU	9
28	28	**G**	7:02	D	**4:53**	A	9 51	3	18 10	6½	**7¼**	**12:08**	A	3:29	E	TAU	10
29	29	M.	7:01	D	**4:54**	A	9 53	3	17 54	7¾	**8½**	**1:01**	A	4:37	E	TAU	11
30	30	Tu.	7:00	D	**4:56**	A	9 56	2	17 38	8¾	**9½**	**2:05**	A	5:34	E	AUR	12
31	31	W.	7:00	D	**4:57**	A	9 57	2	17 s.21	9½	**10¼**	**3:13**	B	6:20	E	GEM	13

Janus am I; oldest of potentates!
Forward I look and backward. –Henry Wadsworth Longfellow

Farmer's Calendar

Day of Month	Day of Week	Dates, Feasts, Fasts, Aspects, Tide Heights	Weather
1	M.	New Year's Day • Holy Name • Patriot Paul Revere born, 1735 • { 10.8 / 9.1	*It's*
2	Tu.	☾ RIDES HIGH • Alice Sanger became first female staffer for the White House, 1890 • { 10.9 / 9.2	*teasing:*
3	W.	Full Wolf ○ • ⊕ AT PERIHELION • Tides { 10.9 / 9.3	*mild*
4	Th.	St. Elizabeth Ann Seton • Trains collided in Chase, Md., 1987 • { 10.9 / —	*and*
5	Fr.	Twelfth Night • Nixon announced NASA's space shuttle program, 1972 • { 9.3 / 10.6	*moist,*
6	Sa.	Epiphany • ☾♄☾ • In fair weather, prepare for foul. • { 9.2 / 10.3	*then*
7	G	1st ☘. af. Ep. • Distaff Day • ☿ IN SUP. ♂	*fine*
8	M.	☾ AT ☊ • Pres. Wilson's "Fourteen Points" speech, 1918 • Tides { 9.0 / 9.5	*but*
9	Tu.	Plough Monday • ☾ ON EQ. • 5.9 earthquake rattled eastern Canada and New England, 1982	*freezing!*
10	W.	☾ AT APO. • Showman "Buffalo Bill" Cody died, 1917	*Sunny*
11	Th.	*One joy scatters a hundred griefs.* • Tides { 8.8 / 8.1	*spells*
12	Fr.	America's first public museum, Charleston Museum in Charleston, S.C., organized, 1773 • { 8.7 / 7.8	*turn*
13	Sa.	St. Hilary • 13.5" snow, San Antonio, Tex., 1985 • { 8.8 / 7.7	*cold*
14	G	2nd ☘. af. Ep. • Physician Albert Schweitzer born, 1875 • { 9.0 / 7.8	*and*
15	M.	Martin Luther King Jr.'s Birthday (observed) • ☾♃☾ • Tides { 9.3 / 8.0	*sleety;*
16	Tu.	☾♂☾ • Avalanche in northern Idaho, 2005 • { 9.7 / 8.3	*Janus*
17	W.	Ben Franklin born, 1706 • ☾ RUNS LOW • Bridge game expert Norman Kay died, 2002 • { 10.1 / 8.7	*is*
18	Th.	New ● • ☾♀♀ • Dow Jones industrial average first passed 1,000 mark, 1966 • { 10.6 / 9.1	*a*
19	Fr.	Inventor James Watt born, 1736 • Law raised salary of U.S. president to $100,000, 1949 • { 11.0 / 9.5	*two-*
20	Sa.	Islamic New Year • ☾♃☾ • ☾♀☾ • Tides { 11.2 / —	*faced*
21	G	3rd ☘. af. Ep. • Kiwanis International founded, 1915 • { 9.9 / 11.3	*deity.*
22	M.	St. Vincent • ☾ AT ☊ • ☾ PERIG. • ☾⊙☾ • { 10.2 / 11.1	*Brrr!*
23	Tu.	☾ ON EQ. • China's giant pandas added to the endangered species list, 1984 • Tides { 10.4 / 10.7	*It's*
24	W.	Gymnast Mary Lou Retton born, 1968 • Tides { 10.5 / 10.2	*bitter,*
25	Th.	Conversion of Paul • G. D. Dows patented an improved soda fountain, 1870 • { 10.5 / 9.6	*with*
26	Fr.	Sts. Timothy & Titus • Tornado hit factory, Pottsville, Pa., 1843 • { 10.4 / 9.0	*snow*
27	Sa.	Three astronauts killed in fire during training for *Apollo 1* launch, 1967 • Tides { 10.2 / 8.6	*spitters.*
28	G	4th ☘. af. Ep. • Dancer Mikhail Baryshnikov born, 1948 • { 10.1 / 8.5	*Mush*
29	M.	*Fear to let fall a drop, and you will spill a lot.* • { 10.1 / 8.5	*and*
30	Tu.	☾ RIDES HIGH • Raccoons mate now. • Yerba Buena renamed San Francisco, 1847 • { 10.2 / 8.7	*slush,*
31	W.	First U.S. federal safety standards for vehicle safety issued, 1967 • Tides { 10.3 / 8.9	*by gush!*

■ Picture a black and brutal night of winter at its most merciless. It's ten below. A sharp wind is blowing right down from the Arctic, a gale so strong that you can hear in it the roaring of polar bears. The four feet of snow that have lain on the ground since New Year's have been whipped and whirled by the wind and fill the air, scouring and blinding. This is a night to freeze your tears and cause gridlock on the roads that go south.

On such a night, when no sane person is abroad, a light is seen moving between the house and the barn. A lantern struggles weakly along through the most miserable hours of this interminable night. It's lambing time.

Invariably, as any shepherd will tell you, ewes give birth in the most atrocious conditions available. Not at eleven on a bright and sunny winter's morning will they choose to embark upon motherhood, but in the middle of the biggest blizzard, the deepest freeze. A friend of mine, who has stood (or rather knelt) as midwife to many, many ewes, speculates that they begin labor when they do for reasons Darwinian. It's a matter of survival: Lambs are born in circumstances so horrible that even the foxes, wolves, and other predators are home in bed. Maybe it's true, but you can't help wondering: If Darwin justifies the sheep, who justifies the shepherd?

SKY WATCH ☆ *Mercury is conspicuous in the evening twilight during the first 12 days of February, when it floats between Venus and the western horizon. The month's headliner is Saturn, which reaches opposition on the 10th, when it is brightest and at its nearest point of the year. The ringed world rises at sunset and is out all night, shining at a bright— but not dazzling—magnitude zero. Small telescopes easily show the rings, more edgewise now than in several years, a circumstance that makes Saturn appear only half as brilliant as in recent oppositions. Venus climbs higher and grows brighter as it crosses from Aquarius into Pisces at midmonth and is striking when it meets the crescent Moon on the 19th.*

○	Full Moon	2nd day	0 hour	45th minute
☾	Last Quarter	10th day	4th hour	51st minute
●	New Moon	17th day	11th hour	14th minute
☽	First Quarter	24th day	2nd hour	56th minute

To use this page, see p. 102; for Key Letters, see p. 237; for Tide Tables, see p. 234.
All times are given in Eastern Standard Time. ☞ **Bold = P.M.** ☞ Light = A.M.

Day of Year	Day of Month	Day of Week	Rises h. m.	Key	Sets h. m.	Key	Length of Day h. m.	Sun Fast m.	Declination of Sun ° '	High Tide Times Boston		Rises h. m.	Key	Sets h. m.	Key	Place	Age
32	1	Th.	6:58	D	**4:58**	A	10 00	2	17 s.04	10½	11	**4:23**	B	6:56	E	CAN	14
33	2	Fr.	6:57	D	**5:00**	A	10 03	2	16 47	11¼	11¾	**5:32**	B	7:24	E	CAN	15
34	3	Sa.	6:56	D	**5:01**	A	10 05	2	16 29	12	—	6:37	C	7:47	D	LEO	16
35	4	**G**	6:55	D	**5:02**	A	10 07	2	16 11	12½	12½	**7:41**	D	8:07	D	LEO	17
36	5	M.	6:54	D	**5:03**	A	10 09	2	15 53	1	1¼	**8:43**	D	8:25	D	VIR	18
37	6	Tu.	6:53	D	**5:05**	A	10 12	2	15 35	1½	1¾	**9:44**	D	8:43	C	VIR	19
38	7	W.	6:52	D	**5:06**	A	10 14	2	15 17	2¼	2½	**10:46**	E	9:01	B	VIR	20
39	8	Th.	6:51	D	**5:07**	B	10 16	1	14 58	3	3¼	**11:49**	E	9:20	B	VIR	21
40	9	Fr.	6:49	D	**5:09**	B	10 20	1	14 39	3¾	4	—	–	9:43	B	LIB	22
41	10	Sa.	6:48	D	**5:10**	B	10 22	1	14 19	4½	5	12:54	E	10:10	A	SCO	23
42	11	**G**	6:47	D	**5:11**	B	10 24	1	13 59	5¼	6	2:00	E	10:45	A	OPH	24
43	12	M.	6:46	D	**5:13**	B	10 27	1	13 40	6¼	7	3:05	E	11:30	A	SAG	25
44	13	Tu.	6:44	D	**5:14**	B	10 30	1	13 19	7¼	8	4:06	E	**12:26**	A	SAG	26
45	14	W.	6:43	D	**5:15**	B	10 32	1	12 59	8	8¾	4:59	E	**1:34**	A	SAG	27
46	15	Th.	6:41	D	**5:16**	B	10 35	1	12 38	9	9¾	5:43	E	**2:49**	B	CAP	28
47	16	Fr.	6:40	D	**5:18**	B	10 38	1	12 18	9¾	10½	6:18	E	**4:09**	B	CAP	29
48	17	Sa.	6:39	D	**5:19**	B	10 40	2	11 57	10¾	11¼	6:47	E	**5:29**	C	AQU	0
49	18	**G**	6:37	D	**5:20**	B	10 43	2	11 35	11½	12	7:13	D	**6:49**	D	PSC	1
50	19	M.	6:36	D	**5:22**	B	10 46	2	11 14	12¼	—	7:36	C	**8:07**	D	PSC	2
51	20	Tu.	6:34	D	**5:23**	B	10 49	2	10 52	12¾	1	7:59	C	**9:26**	E	PSC	3
52	21	W.	6:33	D	**5:24**	B	10 51	2	10 31	1½	2	8:23	B	**10:45**	E	ARI	4
53	22	Th.	6:31	D	**5:25**	B	10 54	2	10 09	2¼	2¾	8:51	A	—	–	ARI	5
54	23	Fr.	6:30	D	**5:27**	B	10 57	2	9 47	3¼	3¾	9:24	A	**12:04**	E	TAU	6
55	24	Sa.	6:28	D	**5:28**	B	11 00	2	9 25	4¼	4¾	10:05	A	**1:20**	E	TAU	7
56	25	**G**	6:27	D	**5:29**	B	11 02	2	9 03	5¼	6	10:56	A	**2:31**	E	AUR	8
57	26	M.	6:25	D	**5:30**	B	11 05	3	8 40	6¼	7¼	11:56	A	**3:31**	E	GEM	9
58	27	Tu.	6:24	D	**5:32**	B	11 08	3	8 18	7½	8¼	**1:03**	A	**4:20**	E	GEM	10
59	28	W.	6:22	D	**5:33**	B	11 11	3	7 s.55	8½	9¼	**2:12**	B	4:58	E	CAN	11

Get local rise, set, and tide times at Almanac.com/astronomy.

CALENDAR

FEBRUARY HATH 28 DAYS • 2007

And in the winter, wild and cold,
'Tis merry, merry, too. –William Howitt

Day of Month	Day of Week	Dates, Feasts, Fasts, Aspects, Tide Heights	Weather
1	Th.	St. Brigid • Actor Clark Gable born, 1901 • Tides { 10.4 / 9.1	*Groundhog*
2	Fr.	Candlemas • Groundhog Day • **Full Snow** ○ • ☌♄☾	*peeks,*
3	Sa.	Air Force Lt. Col. Eileen Collins became first female shuttle pilot, for *Discovery,* 1995 • { 10.3 / —	*freaks!*
4	G	Septuagesima • ☾ AT ☋ • VP Dan Quayle born, 1947	*Six*
5	M.	St. Agatha • ☾ ON EQ. • Nat'l Zoo's first cheetah litter in 115 years went on display, 2005	*more*
6	Tu.	Massachusetts became the 6th U.S. state, 1788 • { 9.3 / 9.4	*weeks!*
7	W.	☾ AT APO. • ☌♅♀ • ☿ GR. ELONG. (18° EAST) • Tides { 9.3 / 9.0	*Where*
8	Th.	☌♆☉ • JFK administration banned travel of U.S. citizens to Cuba, 1963 • { 9.1 / 8.5	*are*
9	Fr.	*Good health is above wealth.* • 6.5 earthquake near Los Angeles, Calif., 1971 • Tides { 9.0 / 8.1	*the*
10	Sa.	♄ AT ☍ • Queen Victoria married Prince Albert, 1840 • Tides { 8.8 / 7.7	*snows*
11	G	Sexagesima • Mount Holyoke Seminary founded, 1836 • { 8.8 / 7.5	*of*
12	M.	☌♃☾ • Savannah, Ga., established, 1733 • Abe Lincoln born, 1809	*winters*
13	Tu.	☾ RUNS LOW • ☿ STAT. • Jesse James robbed his first bank, 1866 • Tides { 9.1 / 7.9	*past?*
14	W.	Sts. Cyril & Methodius • **Valentine's Day** • ☌♂☾	*We*
15	Th.	Susan B. Anthony born, 1820 • *Life is made up of tomorrows.* • Tides { 10.2 / 8.9	*forecast*
16	Fr.	Winter's back breaks. • Canadian Pacific Railway Company incorporated, 1881	*an*
17	Sa.	**New** ● • 27.5" snow, Logan airport, Boston, Mass., 2003 • { 11.2 / 10.2	*old-time*
18	G	Quinquagesima • **Chinese New Year** • ☾ AT ☊	*blast!*
19	M.	Pure Monday • ☾ ON EQ. • ☾ AT PERIG. • ☌♀☾ • { 11.5 / —	*Flurries;*
20	Tu.	Shrove Tuesday • John Glenn first American to orbit Earth, 1962 • { 11.1 / 11.3	*don't*
21	W.	Ash Wednesday • *A country can be judged by the quality of its proverbs.*	*forget*
22	Th.	George Washington born, 1732 • Tides { 11.2 / 10.2	*your*
23	Fr.	☿ IN INF. ☌ • Song "As Time Goes By," from movie *Casablanca,* copyrighted, 1943	*furries!*
24	Sa.	St. Matthias • Thermite explosive first used to break ice jam, Waddington, N.Y., 1925	*Hockey*
25	G	1st S. in Lent • Sunday of Orthodoxy • { 10.0 / 8.4	*players*
26	M.	☾ RIDES HIGH • Grand Canyon National Park established, 1919 • Tides { 9.8 / 8.2	*take*
27	Tu.	*The heart has its summer and its winter.* • Tides { 9.7 / 8.4	*off*
28	W.	Ember Day • Vincent Massey became first Canadian-born governor general of Canada, 1952	*layers.*

At least half the exercise I get every day comes from jumping to conclusions. –Bruce Dexter

Farmer's Calendar

■ Most of us are familiar, either by experience or information, with the winter doldrums, a pervasive state of midwinter depression, fatigue, and low energy. Today, of course, this condition has a fancy medical name: seasonal affective disorder (SAD—get it?); by whatever name, it's a fact of life for millions in the north, and its etiology is unclear.

Professor Bernd Heinrich, of the University of Vermont, lately proposed an ingenious theory to explain the winter blues. They are frustrated hibernation. Many northern mammals, when winter food runs low, can slow their bodily processes down and enter a torpid state that amounts to a more or less deep sleep. In the depths of winter, men and women, also mammals, wish to do the same. Their minds and bodies respond to winter with an impulse toward hibernation. But, being human, they can't sleep the winter away. Hence the winter doldrums, "a vestigial remnant of an adaptive hibernation response," as the professor writes.

It's a persuasive idea, but there are alternatives. The hypothesis seems to be that we're adapted to hibernate and go into the dumps at this time of year because we have to work instead. But couldn't it be that what we're adapted to, and denied, is not a long nap in a cold cave but a week at the beach in latitudes where hibernation isn't necessary?

MARCH

THE THIRD MONTH • 2007

SKY WATCH ☆ *The nearly full Moon floats alongside Saturn on the 1st, as both rise at nightfall. (The pair will meet again on the 28th.) On the 3rd, a total lunar eclipse is visible throughout the continental United States and Canada, except in the westernmost regions. As the Moon rises at sunset, the eclipse is already under way, offering a potentially photogenic event. (See page 90 for eclipse times.) Venus, crossing from Pisces into Aries at midmonth, is now much higher and continues to brighten in the west after sunset. Brilliant Jupiter is up by 1:00 A.M. at month's end. Mars is still dull and remains a predawn object. Spring begins with the vernal equinox on the 20th, at 8:07 P.M.*

○	**Full Moon**	3rd day	18th hour	17th minute
☾	**Last Quarter**	11th day	23rd hour	54th minute
●	**New Moon**	18th day	22nd hour	43rd minute
☽	**First Quarter**	25th day	14th hour	16th minute

To use this page, see p. 102; for Key Letters, see p. 237; for Tide Tables, see p. 234.

After 2:00 A.M. on March 11, Eastern Daylight Time is given. ☞ **Bold = P.M.** ☞ Light = A.M.

Day of Year	Day of Month	Day of Week	☼ Rises h. m.	Key	☼ Sets h. m.	Key	Length of Day h.	m.	Sun Fast m.	Declination of Sun °	'	High Tide Times Boston		☽ Rises h. m.	Key	☽ Sets h. m.	Key	☽ Place	☽ Age
60	1	Th.	6:20	D	**5:34**	B	11	14	3	7 s.	33	9½	**10**	**3:20**	B	5:28	E	CAN	12
61	2	Fr.	6:19	D	**5:35**	B	11	16	3	7	10	10¼	**10¾**	**4:26**	C	5:52	E	LEO	13
62	3	Sa.	6:17	D	**5:36**	B	11	19	3	6	47	11	**11¼**	**5:30**	C	6:13	D	LEO	14
63	4	**G**	6:16	D	**5:38**	B	11	22	4	6	24	11½	12	**6:32**	D	6:31	D	LEO	15
64	5	M.	6:14	D	**5:39**	B	11	25	4	6	01	**12¼**	—	**7:33**	D	6:48	C	VIR	16
65	6	Tu.	6:12	D	**5:40**	B	11	28	4	5	38	12½	**12¾**	**8:35**	E	7:06	B	VIR	17
66	7	W.	6:11	D	**5:41**	B	11	30	4	5	14	1	**1½**	**9:38**	E	7:25	B	VIR	18
67	8	Th.	6:09	D	**5:42**	B	11	33	5	4	51	1½	**2**	**10:42**	E	7:46	B	VIR	19
68	9	Fr.	6:07	D	**5:44**	B	11	37	5	4	27	2¼	**2¾**	**11:47**	E	8:11	A	LIB	20
69	10	Sa.	6:06	D	**5:45**	B	11	39	5	4	04	3	**3½**	—	–	8:43	A	LIB	21
70	11	**G**	7:04	D	**6:46**	B	11	42	5	3	40	4¾	**5½**	1:52	E	10:22	A	SCO	22
71	12	M.	7:02	C	**6:47**	B	11	45	6	3	17	5½	**6¼**	2:53	E	11:12	A	OPH	23
72	13	Tu.	7:00	C	**6:48**	B	11	48	6	2	53	6½	**7¼**	3:48	E	**12:13**	A	SAG	24
73	14	W.	6:59	C	**6:49**	B	11	50	6	2	29	7½	**8¼**	4:35	E	**1:23**	A	SAG	25
74	15	Th.	6:57	C	**6:51**	B	11	54	6	2	06	8½	**9¼**	5:13	E	**2:39**	B	CAP	26
75	16	Fr.	6:55	C	**6:52**	B	11	57	7	1	42	9½	**10¼**	5:44	E	**3:58**	C	CAP	27
76	17	Sa.	6:54	C	**6:53**	B	11	59	7	1	18	10½	**11**	6:11	D	**5:18**	D	AQU	28
77	18	**G**	6:52	C	**6:54**	B	12	02	7	0	55	11¼	**11¾**	6:35	D	**6:38**	D	AQU	0
78	19	M.	6:50	C	**6:55**	B	12	05	8	0	31	**12**	—	6:59	C	**7:58**	E	PSC	1
79	20	Tu.	6:48	C	**6:56**	C	12	08	8	0 s.	07	12½	**1**	7:23	B	**9:20**	E	PSC	2
80	21	W.	6:47	C	**6:58**	C	12	11	8	0 n.	17	1¼	**1¾**	7:50	B	**10:42**	E	ARI	3
81	22	Th.	6:45	C	**6:59**	C	12	14	8	0	40	2	**2¾**	8:22	A	—	–	ARI	4
82	23	Fr.	6:43	C	**7:00**	C	12	17	9	1	04	3	**3½**	9:01	A	12:03	E	TAU	5
83	24	Sa.	6:41	C	**7:01**	C	12	20	9	1	28	3¾	**4½**	9:50	A	1:19	E	TAU	6
84	25	**G**	6:40	C	**7:02**	C	12	22	9	1	51	4¾	**5½**	10:49	A	2:25	E	AUR	7
85	26	M.	6:38	C	**7:03**	C	12	25	10	2	15	5¾	**6¾**	11:54	A	3:18	E	GEM	8
86	27	Tu.	6:36	C	**7:04**	C	12	28	10	2	38	7	**8**	**1:03**	B	3:59	E	GEM	9
87	28	W.	6:35	C	**7:06**	C	12	31	10	3	02	8¼	**9**	**2:12**	B	4:32	E	CAN	10
88	29	Th.	6:33	C	**7:07**	C	12	34	11	3	25	9¼	**9¾**	**3:18**	C	4:57	E	LEO	11
89	30	Fr.	6:31	C	**7:08**	C	12	37	11	3	48	10	**10½**	**4:22**	C	5:19	D	LEO	12
90	31	Sa.	6:29	C	**7:09**	C	12	40	11	4 n.	12	10¾	**11¼**	**5:24**	D	5:38	D	LEO	13

MARCH HATH 31 DAYS • 2007

Now are the winds about us in their glee,
Tossing the slender tree. –William Gilmore Simms

Day of Month	Day of Week	Dates, Feasts, Fasts, Aspects, Tide Heights	Weather
1	Th.	St. David • ☌♄☾ • Congress authorized first U.S. Census, 1790 • Tides {9.9 / 8.9	*In*
2	Fr.	St. Chad • Ember Day • Puerto Rico became U.S. territory, 1917 • {10.0 / 9.2	*like*
3	Sa.	Ember Day • **Full Worm ○** • **Eclipse ☾** • *A good deed is never lost.*	*a*
4	G	**2nd S. in Lent** • ☾ on Eq. • ☾ at ☋ • {10.0 / 9.6	*lamb*
5	M.	St. Piran • ☌⛢☉ • Piano maker William Steinway born, 1835	*a-bleating;*
6	Tu.	☾ at apo. • Renaissance man Michelangelo born, 1475 • Tides {9.7 / 9.6	*sleeting,*
7	W.	St. Perpetua • ☿ stat. • Brilliant nationwide aurora borealis, 1918 • {9.7 / 9.3	*but*
8	Th.	First train crossed Niagara Railway Suspension Bridge, Niagara River, 1855 • Tides {9.6 / 8.9	*it's*
9	Fr.	12" snow in parts of Ky., La., and N.C., 1960 • {9.4 / 8.5	*only*
10	Sa.	Abolitionist Harriet Tubman died, 1913 • First known U.S. fatality due to raccoon rabies, 2003	*fleeting.*
11	G	**3rd S. in Lent** • ☌♃☾ • **U.S. Daylight Saving time begins, 2:00 A.M.**	*Great*
12	M.	☾ runs low • *If you take a leap in the dark, you usually land in a pit.* • Tides {8.9 / 7.7	*days*
13	Tu.	Discovery of Pluto officially announced, 1930 • {9.0 / 7.8	*for*
14	W.	Cotton gin patented, 1794 • Musician Quincy Jones born, 1933 • Tides {9.3 / 8.1	*the*
15	Th.	Beware the ides of March. • ☌♂☾ • Tides {9.7 / 8.8	*Irish*
16	Fr.	☌☿☾ • ☌♆☾ • First Lady Pat Nixon born, 1912 • Tides {10.3 / 9.5	*and*
17	Sa.	St. Patrick • *If you would eat eggs, take care of the hen.* • Tides {10.8 / 10.3	*all*
18	G	**New ●** • **Eclipse ☉** • ☾ on Eq. • ☾ at ☊ • {11.3 / 11.0	*of*
19	M.	St. Joseph • ☾ at perig. • Chipmunks emerge from hibernation now. • {11.5 / 11.5	*their*
20	Tu.	**Vernal Equinox** • *Thunder in spring, Cold will bring.* • {11.5 / —	*friends:*
21	W.	☌♀☾ • ☿ Gr. Elong. (28° West) • Singer Johnny Bristol died, 2004 • {11.8 / 11.2	*Look*
22	Th.	First women's basketball game, Smith College, Northampton, Mass., 1893 • Tides {11.8 / 10.7	*out,*
23	Fr.	World Meteorological Organization established, 1950	*below!*
24	Sa.	*Exxon Valdez* struck reef and spilled 240,000 barrels of oil, Prince William Sound, Alaska, 1989 • {11.0 / 9.3	*It's*
25	G	**5th S. in Lent** • ☾ rides high • ☌♂♆ • {10.4 / 8.8	*snowing*
26	M.	Annunciation[T] • Oldest known black spider monkey died at age 53, 2005 • {9.9 / 8.4	*again!*
27	Tu.	*Go to bed with the lamb and rise with the lark.* • {9.5 / 8.4	*Clouds*
28	W.	Mary Pickford married Douglas Fairbanks, 1920 • {9.4 / 8.5	*are*
29	Th.	☌♄☾ • Catherine Callbeck elected premier of P.E.I., Canada, 1993 • {9.4 / 8.8	*breaking,*
30	Fr.	Song "This Land Is Your Land" copyrighted, 1956	*bears*
31	Sa.	☾ at ☋ • ♇ stat. • Wabash, Ind., became first city to be lighted by electricity, 1880	*awaking.*

Farmer's Calendar

■ The past is where you find it. Recently, a friend with an interest in local history picked up at a flea market an old account book for a nearby village's store—at the time the old accounts were recorded, a typical general store for a tiny community well back in the foothills. The book gives a uniquely detailed view of that community and its economy in 1842–43.

The store accounts are kept in a fat, suede-covered ledger in a beautiful, ornate hand that looks more like the Declaration of Independence than a prosaic tally of nickels and dimes. The book has 452 pages, recording something like 6,000 transactions, remarkable chiefly in their diversity. This little store sold pretty much everything: nails, snuff, horseshoes, shot, calico, rum, shoe leather, baking soda, salt, scythe snathes, axe helves, butter, paint, pots and pans, baskets, panama hats, soap, oranges, tea, cloves, buttons, thread, molasses, oxbows, turpentine, whale oil, shingles.

The village store was not a place where the profits mounted quickly. A quart of rum cost a dime. The storekeeper was a hardworking man. He closed Sundays, Christmas, New Year's, and the Fourth of July. The rest of the year he was at his counter, cutting, measuring, weighing, selling—and recording. Would he be surprised at our interest?

C
A
L
E
N
D
A
R

SKY WATCH ☆ *Venus continues its ascent and is now 30 degrees above the horizon about one-half hour after sunset. It spends the first week in Aries and the rest of the month in Taurus, and is near the famous Pleiades star cluster from the 10th to the 12th. Saturn is prominent and at its highest point between 8:00 and 9:00 P.M. all month. The predawn scene starts to get lively, with Jupiter at its highest point each night before daybreak. The Moon meets Mars during the early morning hours on the 14th. The close conjunction of reddish Mars and faint-green Uranus on the 30th is a unique sight, best seen with binoculars. They will be six degrees above the horizon one hour before dawn.*

○ **Full Moon**	2nd day	13th hour	15th minute
☾ **Last Quarter**	10th day	14th hour	4th minute
● **New Moon**	17th day	7th hour	36th minute
☽ **First Quarter**	24th day	2nd hour	36th minute

To use this page, see p. 102; for Key Letters, see p. 237; for Tide Tables, see p. 234.
All times are given in Eastern Daylight Time. ☞ **Bold = P.M.** ☞ Light = A.M.

Day of Year	Day of Month	Day of Week	☼ Rises h. m.	Key	☼ Sets h. m.	Key	Length of Day h. m.	Sun Fast m.	Declination of Sun ° ′	High Tide Times Boston		☽ Rises h. m.	Key	☽ Sets h. m.	Key	Place	Age
91	1	**G**	6:28	B	**7:10**	C	12 42	11	4 N.35	11½	11¾	**6:25**	D	**5:55**	C	VIR	14
92	2	M.	6:26	B	**7:11**	C	12 45	12	4 58	12¼	—	**7:26**	E	**6:13**	C	VIR	15
93	3	Tu.	6:24	B	**7:12**	C	12 48	12	5 21	12¼	12¾	**8:29**	E	**6:31**	B	VIR	16
94	4	W.	6:22	B	**7:13**	C	12 51	12	5 44	1	1¼	**9:32**	E	**6:51**	B	VIR	17
95	5	Th.	6:21	B	**7:15**	D	12 54	13	6 07	1½	2	**10:37**	E	**7:15**	A	LIB	18
96	6	Fr.	6:19	B	**7:16**	D	12 57	13	6 29	2	2½	**11:42**	E	**7:44**	A	LIB	19
97	7	Sa.	6:17	B	**7:17**	D	13 00	13	6 52	2¾	3¼	—	–	**8:20**	A	SCO	20
98	8	**G**	6:16	B	**7:18**	D	13 02	14	7 15	3½	4	12:44	E	**9:06**	A	OPH	21
99	9	M.	6:14	B	**7:19**	D	13 05	14	7 37	4¼	5	1:40	E	**10:01**	A	SAG	22
100	10	Tu.	6:12	B	**7:20**	D	13 08	14	8 00	5	5¾	2:29	E	**11:06**	A	SAG	23
101	11	W.	6:11	B	**7:21**	D	13 10	14	8 22	6	6¾	3:09	E	**12:18**	B	CAP	24
102	12	Th.	6:09	B	**7:22**	D	13 13	15	8 44	7	7¾	3:42	E	**1:33**	B	CAP	25
103	13	Fr.	6:07	B	**7:24**	D	13 17	15	9 05	8	8¾	4:10	D	**2:50**	C	CAP	26
104	14	Sa.	6:06	B	**7:25**	D	13 19	15	9 27	9	9½	4:35	D	**4:08**	D	AQU	27
105	15	**G**	6:04	B	**7:26**	D	13 22	15	9 49	10	10½	4:58	C	**5:27**	D	PSC	28
106	16	M.	6:03	B	**7:27**	D	13 24	16	10 10	11	11¼	5:21	C	**6:48**	E	PSC	29
107	17	Tu.	6:01	B	**7:28**	D	13 27	16	10 31	11¾	—	5:47	B	**8:11**	E	PSC	0
108	18	W.	5:59	B	**7:29**	D	13 30	16	10 52	12	12½	6:17	B	**9:35**	E	ARI	1
109	19	Th.	5:58	B	**7:30**	D	13 32	16	11 13	12¾	1½	6:54	A	**10:56**	E	TAU	2
110	20	Fr.	5:56	B	**7:31**	D	13 35	17	11 33	1¾	2¼	7:40	A	—	–	TAU	3
111	21	Sa.	5:55	B	**7:33**	D	13 38	17	11 54	2½	3¼	8:36	A	12:09	E	TAU	4
112	22	**G**	5:53	B	**7:34**	D	13 41	17	12 14	3½	4¼	9:42	A	**1:10**	E	AUR	5
113	23	M.	5:52	B	**7:35**	D	13 43	17	12 34	4½	5¼	10:52	A	**1:57**	E	GEM	6
114	24	Tu.	5:50	B	**7:36**	D	13 46	17	12 54	5½	6¼	**12:02**	B	**2:33**	E	CAN	7
115	25	W.	5:49	B	**7:37**	D	13 48	17	13 13	6½	7½	**1:10**	B	**3:01**	E	CAN	8
116	26	Th.	5:47	B	**7:38**	D	13 51	18	13 33	7¾	8½	**2:14**	C	**3:24**	D	LEO	9
117	27	Fr.	5:46	B	**7:39**	D	13 53	18	13 52	8¾	9¼	**3:17**	C	**3:44**	D	LEO	10
118	28	Sa.	5:44	B	**7:40**	D	13 56	18	14 11	9½	10	**4:18**	D	**4:02**	C	VIR	11
119	29	**G**	5:43	B	**7:42**	D	13 59	18	14 30	10¼	10½	**5:19**	D	**4:19**	C	VIR	12
120	30	M.	5:42	B	**7:43**	D	14 01	18	14 N.48	11	11¼	**6:21**	E	**4:37**	B	VIR	13

APRIL HATH 30 DAYS • 2007

I have found violets. April hath come on,
And the cool winds feel softer. –Nathaniel Parker Willis

Day of Month	Day of Week	Dates, Feasts, Fasts, Aspects, Tide Heights	Weather
1	G	**Palm Sunday** • All Fools' • ☾ ON EQ. • ☌☿♅	*Spring's*
2	M.	Full Pink ○ • *The plough goes not well if the ploughman hold it not.* • { 9.7 / —	*dress*
3	Tu.	St. Richard of Chichester • First day of Passover • ☾ AT APO.	*rehearsal,*
4	W.	Augusta, Ga., hit by a tornado, 1804 • Statesman Jules Léger born, 1913 • Tides { 9.9 / 9.4	*then*
5	Th.	Maundy Thursday • ♃ STAT. • Pocahontas married John Rolfe, 1614	*reversal.*
6	Fr.	**Good Friday** • First modern Olympic games began, Athens, Greece, 1896 • { 9.8 / 8.9	*The*
7	Sa.	G. Washington devised Badge of Military Merit, later called Purple Heart, 1782 • Tides { 9.7 / 8.6	*snow*
8	G	**Easter** • ☌♃☾ • Figure skater Sonja Henie born, 1912 • { 9.5 / 8.3	*must*
9	M.	Easter Monday • ☾ RUNS LOW • Golfer Arnold Palmer won his third Masters Tournament, 1962	*go*
10	Tu.	3-D movie *House of Wax* premiered, N.Y.C., 1953 • { 9.3 / 8.1	*on!*
11	W.	*When April blows his horn, it's good for hay and corn.*	*Relief*
12	Th.	☌♆☾ • Nova Scotia's Moose River gold mine collapsed, trapping 3, 1936 • Tides { 9.5 / 8.8	*is*
13	Fr.	☌♂☾ • President Thomas Jefferson born, 1743	*coming,*
14	Sa.	☾ AT ☊ • ☌♅☾ • R.M.S. *Titanic* struck an iceberg, 1912 • { 10.3 / 10.2	*slowly*
15	G	**2nd S. of Easter** • ☾ ON EQ. • Tides { 10.7 / 11.0	*but*
16	M.	☌☿☾ • Severe freeze from Ga. to Tex. killed cotton crops, 1849 • { 11.0 / 11.6	*surely;*
17	Tu.	New ● • ☾ AT PERIG. • Song "Hail, Hail, the Gang's All Here" copyrighted, 1908	*get*
18	W.	33-inning baseball game began, Rochester Red Wings vs. Pawtucket Red Sox, 1981 • { 12.1 / 11.1	*your*
19	Th.	♄ STAT. • "Shot heard 'round the world," Lexington, Mass., 1775 • Tides { 12.2 / 10.8	*sugar*
20	Fr.	☌♀☾ • Hailstorm in San Antonio, Tex., 1878 • { 12.0 / 10.4	*snaps*
21	Sa.	☾ RIDES HIGH • John Adams sworn in as first U.S. vice president, 1789 • Tides { 11.6 / 9.9	*in*
22	G	**3rd S. of Easter** • Singer Glen Campbell born, 1936 • { 11.0 / 9.3	*early!*
23	M.	St. George • *When the fern is as high as a spoon, You may sleep an hour at noon.* • { 10.3 / 8.9	*Kids*
24	Tu.	Almanac maker Robert B. Thomas born, 1766 • { 9.8 / 8.7	*and*
25	W.	St. Mark • ☌♄☾ • 118°F, Volcano Springs, Calif., 1898 • { 9.4 / 8.6	*their*
26	Th.	Nine escaped buffalo caught on a tennis court in Md., 2005 • Tides { 9.2 / 8.8	*buddies*
27	Fr.	☾ AT ☋ • *He who speaks the truth should have one foot in the stirrup.* • { 9.1 / 9.1	*come*
28	Sa.	☾ ON EQ. • ☌♂♅ • Walter Sitch, at 98, became a great-great-great-grandfather, 1968	*home*
29	G	**4th S. of Easter** • Poplars leaf out about now.	*all*
30	M.	☾ AT APO. • U.S. Department of the Navy established, 1798 • Tides { 9.2 / 9.8	*muddy.*

A joke's a very serious thing. –Charles Churchill

Farmer's Calendar

■ The amateur lepidopterist, who chases butterflies with a net, inevitably comes to think of himself as a kind of hunter, and of the bright and agile insects he pursues as a kind of game. And so they are. Butterflies are fast, alert, and wary; catching them can be difficult. But (as with bigger game) if you leave your net at home, butterflies will sometimes come to you. They are gregarious and make good company.

Or at least some do. The showier species, like the swallowtails and the monarchs, are pretty standoffish. The smaller fritillaries and the white and red admirals are better natured. They seem curious, attentive, and eager to make your acquaintance. Often, walking down a country road, I have been joined by one or more of these species flying before, behind, beside me as I went along, for all the world like a friendly little spaniel.

My favorite of the companionable butterflies is the mourning cloak, a common species having velvety sable wings with golden borders. The mourning cloak is one of the butterflies that hibernate as winged adults. On a sunny day in March or April, when the snowbanks are by no means gone, one of these butterflies will tag along with you as you walk down the muddy road. After the long dark winter, it seems especially glad to see you, as you are to see it.

MAY

THE FIFTH MONTH • 2007

SKY WATCH ☆ *Mercury passes very near the thin crescent Moon on the 17th and is easy to see in fading western twilight during the last half of the month. Venus rises higher and becomes more dazzling in the western sky as it crosses from Taurus into Gemini. It has its own striking meeting with the Moon on the 19th, with Mercury a great distance below the pair. Saturn, sinking a bit lower, is still nicely visible in the southwest during the early evening hours. Jupiter, rising two hours earlier each month, pops up above the southeastern horizon by 11:00* P.M. *at midmonth. The Moon hovers below it on the 31st.*

○	**Full Moon**	2nd day	6th hour	9th minute
☾	**Last Quarter**	10th day	0 hour	27th minute
●	**New Moon**	16th day	15th hour	27th minute
☽	**First Quarter**	23rd day	17th hour	3rd minute
○	**Full Moon**	31st day	21st hour	4th minute

To use this page, see p. 102; for Key Letters, see p. 237; for Tide Tables, see p. 234.
All times are given in Eastern Daylight Time. ☞ **Bold = P.M.** ☞ Light = A.M.

Day of Year	Day of Month	Day of Week	☼ Rises h. m.	Key	☼ Sets h. m.	Key	Length of Day h.	m.	Sun Fast m.	Declination of Sun °	'	High Tide Times Boston		☽ Rises h. m.	Key	☽ Sets h. m.	Key	☽ Place	☽ Age
121	1	Tu.	5:40	B	**7:44**	D	14	04	18	15N.	07	11¾	**11¾**	**7:24**	E	4:57	B	VIR	14
122	2	W.	5:39	B	**7:45**	D	14	06	19	15	25	**12¼**	—	**8:28**	E	5:20	A	LIB	15
123	3	Th.	5:38	B	**7:46**	D	14	08	19	15	43	12¼	**1**	**9:34**	E	5:47	A	LIB	16
124	4	Fr.	5:36	A	**7:47**	D	14	11	19	16	00	1	**1½**	**10:37**	E	6:21	A	SCO	17
125	5	Sa.	5:35	A	**7:48**	D	14	13	19	16	17	1½	**2¼**	**11:35**	E	7:04	A	OPH	18
126	6	**G**	5:34	A	**7:49**	D	14	15	19	16	34	2¼	**3**	—	–	7:57	A	SAG	19
127	7	M.	5:32	A	**7:50**	D	14	18	19	16	51	3	**3¾**	12:26	E	8:58	A	SAG	20
128	8	Tu.	5:31	A	**7:52**	D	14	21	19	17	07	3¾	**4½**	1:08	E	10:07	A	SAG	21
129	9	W.	5:30	A	**7:53**	D	14	23	19	17	23	4¾	**5½**	1:42	E	11:19	B	CAP	22
130	10	Th.	5:29	A	**7:54**	D	14	25	19	17	39	5½	**6¼**	2:11	E	**12:33**	C	CAP	23
131	11	Fr.	5:28	A	**7:55**	D	14	27	19	17	55	6½	**7¼**	2:36	D	**1:47**	C	AQU	24
132	12	Sa.	5:27	A	**7:56**	D	14	29	19	18	10	7½	**8¼**	2:59	C	**3:02**	D	AQU	25
133	13	**G**	5:25	A	**7:57**	D	14	32	19	18	25	8½	**9**	3:21	C	**4:19**	E	PSC	26
134	14	M.	5:24	A	**7:58**	D	14	34	19	18	40	9½	**10**	3:45	B	**5:40**	E	PSC	27
135	15	Tu.	5:23	A	**7:59**	E	14	36	19	18	54	10½	**10¾**	4:12	B	**7:02**	E	ARI	28
136	16	W.	5:22	A	**8:00**	E	14	38	19	19	08	11½	**11¾**	4:45	A	**8:26**	E	ARI	0
137	17	Th.	5:21	A	**8:01**	E	14	40	19	19	21	**12¼**	—	5:27	A	**9:45**	E	TAU	1
138	18	Fr.	5:20	A	**8:02**	E	14	42	19	19	34	12½	**1¼**	6:19	A	**10:53**	E	TAU	2
139	19	Sa.	5:20	A	**8:03**	E	14	43	19	19	47	1¼	**2**	7:23	A	**11:48**	E	AUR	3
140	20	**G**	5:19	A	**8:04**	E	14	45	19	20	00	2¼	**3**	8:34	A	—	–	GEM	4
141	21	M.	5:18	A	**8:05**	E	14	47	19	20	13	3¼	**4**	9:46	B	12:30	E	CAN	5
142	22	Tu.	5:17	A	**8:06**	E	14	49	19	20	24	4	**5**	10:57	B	1:02	E	CAN	6
143	23	W.	5:16	A	**8:07**	E	14	51	19	20	36	5	**5¾**	**12:04**	C	1:27	E	LEO	7
144	24	Th.	5:15	A	**8:08**	E	14	53	19	20	47	6	**6¾**	**1:08**	C	1:48	D	LEO	8
145	25	Fr.	5:15	A	**8:09**	E	14	54	19	20	58	7	**7¾**	**2:10**	D	2:07	D	LEO	9
146	26	Sa.	5:14	A	**8:10**	E	14	56	19	21	09	8	**8½**	**3:11**	D	2:25	C	VIR	10
147	27	**G**	5:13	A	**8:11**	E	14	58	19	21	19	9	**9¼**	**4:12**	E	2:43	B	VIR	11
148	28	M.	5:13	A	**8:11**	E	14	58	18	21	29	9¾	**10**	**5:14**	E	3:02	B	VIR	12
149	29	Tu.	5:12	A	**8:12**	E	15	00	18	21	38	10½	**10½**	**6:19**	E	3:24	A	LIB	13
150	30	W.	5:11	A	**8:13**	E	15	02	18	21	47	11¼	**11¼**	**7:24**	E	3:50	A	LIB	14
151	31	Th.	5:11	A	**8:14**	E	15	03	18	21N.	56	**12**	12	**8:29**	E	4:22	A	SCO	15

MAY HATH 31 DAYS • 2007

Where shall we keep the holiday,
And duly greet the entering May? –Ralph Waldo Emerson

Day of Month	Day of Week	Dates, Feasts, Fasts, Aspects, Tide Heights	Weather
1	Tu.	Sts. Philip & James • May Day • Tides { 9.2 10.0	*Glum,*
2	W.	St. Athanasius • Vesak • Full Flower ○ • { 9.2 —	*chum,*
3	Th.	Invention of the Holy Cross • ☿ IN SUP. ☌ • Tides { 10.1 9.1	*but*
4	Fr.	6.5" snow, Missoula, Mont., 1961 • *You can not put an old head on young shoulders.* • { 10.1 8.9	*don't*
5	Sa.	Cinco de Mayo • ☌♃☾ • Comedian Michael Palin born, 1943 • { 10.0 8.8	*get*
6	G	5th S. of Easter • ☾ RUNS LOW • Tides { 9.9 8.6	*all*
7	M.	Canadian-bred horse Sunny's Halo won Kentucky Derby, 1983 • Tides { 9.8 8.5	*gloomy:*
8	Tu.	St. Julian of Norwich • The Beatles album "Let It Be" released, 1970 • { 9.7 8.5	*It's*
9	W.	St. Gregory of Nazianzus • FDA OK'd birth control pills, 1960	*warming,*
10	Th.	☌♆☾ • *Go to law for a sheep and lose your cow.* • Tides { 9.7 9.0	*storming,*
11	Fr.	☾ AT ☊ • Minn. became 32nd state, 1858 • Cranberries in bud now. • Three	*and*
12	Sa.	☾ ON EQ. • ☌♂☾ • ☌♅☾ • Chilly • { 9.9 10.2	*thunder-*
13	G	Rogation S. • 136 mph wind gust, Peru, Ind., 1995 • Saints	*boomy!*
14	M.	First permanent British settlement in North America, Jamestown, Va., 1607 • { 10.3 11.4	*Perfect*
15	Tu.	☾ AT PERIG. • *He who sows oats in May Gets little that way.* • Tides { 10.5 11.9	*days*
16	W.	New ● • Runner Joan Benoit Samuelson born, 1957	*for*
17	Th.	Ascension • ☌☿☾ • Joliet-Marquette Miss. R. expedition began, 1673	*biking*
18	Fr.	Selective Draft Act passed in U.S., 1917 • Actress Elizabeth Montgomery died, 1995 • { 12.1 10.3	*or*
19	Sa.	St. Dunstan • ☾ RIDES HIGH • ☌♀☾ • Tides { 11.8 10.0	*hiking;*
20	G	1st S. af. Asc. • First airplane catapulted from a dirigible, 1930 • { 11.4 9.7	*just*
21	M.	Victoria Day (Canada) • Patti Frustaci gave birth to first septuplets in U.S., 1985 • { 10.8 9.4	*watch*
22	Tu.	☌♄☾ • Wright brothers' "Flying Machine" patented, 1906 • Tides { 10.3 9.1	*out*
23	W.	Shavuot • Sledding in Farmington, Maine, 1858 • { 9.7 8.9	*for*
24	Th.	☾ AT ☋ • Jazz musician Duke Ellington died, 1974 • Tides { 9.2 8.9	*lightning*
25	Fr.	St. Bede • ☾ ON EQ. • ♆ STAT. • Brood XIII cicadas emerge about now.	*striking!*
26	Sa.	*The thought has good legs, and the quill a good tongue.*	*Lilacs*
27	G	Whit S. • Pentecost • ☾ AT APO. • Tides { 8.7 9.4	*in*
28	M.	Memorial Day (observed) • First author of *Nancy Drew* series, Mildred Benson, died, 2002	*bloom*
29	Tu.	Dime-size hail, Keene, N.H., 1987 • Tides { 8.7 9.8	*shed*
30	W.	Ember Day • First Indianapolis 500 auto race, Ind., 1911 • Tides { 8.8 10.0	*sweet*
31	Th.	Visit. of Mary • Full Milk ○ • Tides { 8.8 10.1	*perfume.*

Farmer's Calendar

■ A couple of years ago, as another lawn-mowing season began, I was persuaded to replace the gasoline-powered mower I had used for years with an electric model. The arguments for this change were three. The electric mower was far lighter than the old machine, and so easier to use. It ran on a battery, so you didn't need to buy fuel. Finally, the electric mower was quiet: no engine noise. After 30-plus years trailing a snarling gas-dragon around the place, I was sold.

I found that points one and two in favor of the new machine were fully in force. The difference between cutting grass with the light electric mower and its predecessor was the difference between walking the dog and pushing a load of bricks. And I liked not having to buy gas. I figure I buy enough gas, thanks.

On the final advantage of the new mower, however, I found myself ambivalent. Yes, it was quiet. Was it too quiet? The irritating roar of internal combustion was now a soft electric purr; using the new mower was like cutting the grass with a sewing machine. Could the task really be getting done? Missing the familiar racket of the gas engine, I found it hard to believe. Now, in fact, the grass looked fine. Improvement in our lives is possible, but sometimes it takes getting used to.

C
A
L
E
N
D
A
R

SKY WATCH ☆ *Jupiter is at opposition on the 5th; on the 7th, it is at its nearest point to Earth for the year. The largest planet is out all night and, at magnitude –2.1, outshone only during the first half of every night by Venus. Mercury, still easy to find during the first 12 days of the month, appears as the brightest star between Venus and the western horizon. The Moon hovers between Saturn and Venus on the 18th. Venus, which spends most of the month in Cancer, attains maximum brilliancy on the 29th and holds this extreme –4.4 magnitude for a month. Look for a close conjunction of Venus and Saturn on the 29th and 30th. Summer begins with the solstice on the 21st, at 2:06 P.M.*

☾	**Last Quarter**	8th day	7th hour	43rd minute
●	**New Moon**	14th day	23rd hour	13th minute
☽	**First Quarter**	22nd day	9th hour	15th minute
○	**Full Moon**	30th day	9th hour	49th minute

To use this page, see p. 102; for Key Letters, see p. 237; for Tide Tables, see p. 234.
All times are given in Eastern Daylight Time. ☞ **Bold** = P.M. ☞ Light = A.M.

Day of Year	Day of Month	Day of Week	Rises h. m.	Key	Sets h. m.	Key	Length of Day h. m.	Sun Fast m.	Declination of Sun ° '	High Tide Times Boston		Rises h. m.	Key	Sets h. m.	Key	Place	Age
152	1	Fr.	5:10	A	**8:15**	E	15 05	18	22N.04	12½	—	**9:29**	E	5:02	A	SCO	16
153	2	Sa.	5:09	A	**8:15**	E	15 06	18	22 12	12½	1¼	**10:23**	E	5:52	A	SAG	17
154	3	**G**	5:09	A	**8:16**	E	15 07	18	22 20	1¼	2	**11:07**	E	6:52	A	SAG	18
155	4	M.	5:09	A	**8:17**	E	15 08	17	22 27	2	2¾	**11:44**	E	7:59	A	SAG	19
156	5	Tu.	5:09	A	**8:18**	E	15 09	17	22 33	2¾	3¼	—	–	9:10	B	CAP	20
157	6	W.	5:08	A	**8:18**	E	15 10	17	22 40	3½	4¼	12:14	D	**10:23**	C	CAP	21
158	7	Th.	5:08	A	**8:19**	E	15 11	17	22 46	4¼	5	12:40	D	**11:36**	C	AQU	22
159	8	Fr.	5:08	A	**8:19**	E	15 11	17	22 51	5¼	5¾	1:02	D	**12:49**	D	AQU	23
160	9	Sa.	5:08	A	**8:20**	E	15 12	17	22 57	6¼	6¾	1:24	C	**2:02**	D	PSC	24
161	10	**G**	5:08	A	**8:21**	E	15 13	16	23 02	7¼	7¾	1:46	B	**3:19**	E	PSC	25
162	11	M.	5:07	A	**8:21**	E	15 14	16	23 06	8¼	8½	2:11	B	**4:38**	E	PSC	26
163	12	Tu.	5:07	A	**8:22**	E	15 15	16	23 10	9¼	9½	2:41	A	**5:59**	E	ARI	27
164	13	W.	5:07	A	**8:22**	E	15 15	16	23 13	10¼	10½	3:17	A	**7:19**	E	TAU	28
165	14	Th.	5:07	A	**8:23**	E	15 16	16	23 16	11¼	11¼	4:04	A	**8:33**	E	TAU	0
166	15	Fr.	5:07	A	**8:23**	E	15 16	15	23 19	**12**	—	5:03	A	**9:34**	E	TAU	1
167	16	Sa.	5:07	A	**8:23**	E	15 16	15	23 21	12¼	1	6:11	A	**10:22**	E	GEM	2
168	17	**G**	5:07	A	**8:24**	E	15 17	15	23 23	1	1¾	7:25	B	**10:59**	E	GEM	3
169	18	M.	5:07	A	**8:24**	E	15 17	15	23 25	2	2¾	8:38	B	**11:27**	E	CAN	4
170	19	Tu.	5:07	A	**8:24**	E	15 17	14	23 26	2¾	3½	9:48	C	**11:51**	D	LEO	5
171	20	W.	5:07	A	**8:25**	E	15 18	14	23 26	3¾	4¼	10:55	C	—	–	LEO	6
172	21	Th.	5:07	A	**8:25**	E	15 18	14	23 26	4½	5¼	11:58	D	12:11	D	LEO	7
173	22	Fr.	5:08	A	**8:25**	E	15 17	14	23 26	5½	6	**1:00**	D	12:29	C	VIR	8
174	23	Sa.	5:08	A	**8:25**	E	15 17	14	23 25	6¼	6¾	**2:01**	E	12:47	C	VIR	9
175	24	**G**	5:08	A	**8:25**	E	15 17	13	23 24	7¼	7½	**3:03**	E	1:05	B	VIR	10
176	25	M.	5:08	A	**8:25**	E	15 17	13	23 23	8¼	8½	**4:07**	E	1:26	B	VIR	11
177	26	Tu.	5:09	A	**8:26**	E	15 17	13	23 22	9	9¼	**5:12**	E	1:51	A	LIB	12
178	27	W.	5:09	A	**8:26**	E	15 17	13	23 19	9¾	10	**6:17**	E	2:20	A	LIB	13
179	28	Th.	5:10	A	**8:26**	E	15 16	13	23 17	10¾	10¾	**7:20**	E	2:58	A	SCO	14
180	29	Fr.	5:10	A	**8:25**	E	15 15	12	23 13	11½	11½	**8:17**	E	3:45	A	OPH	15
181	30	Sa.	5:11	A	**8:25**	E	15 14	12	23N.10	12¼	—	**9:05**	E	4:42	A	SAG	16

JUNE HATH 30 DAYS • 2007

And since all this loveliness can not be Heaven,
I know in my heart it is June. –Abba Goold Woolson

Day of Month	Day of Week	Dates, Feasts, Fasts, Aspects, Tide Heights	Weather
1	Fr.	Ember Day • ☌♃☾ • Kentucky became 15th state, 1792 • {8.8 / —	*Blushing*
2	Sa.	Ember Day • ☾ RUNS LOW • ☿ GR. ELONG. (23° EAST) • Tides {10.2 / 8.8	*brides*
3	G	**Trinity** • **Orthodox All Saints'** • Tides {10.2 / 8.8	*may*
4	M.	Sierra Club organized, San Francisco, 1892 • *If you pay peanuts, you get monkeys.* • {10.3 / 8.9	*wed*
5	Tu.	**St. Boniface** • ♃ AT ☍ • Teton Dam failed, SE Idaho, 1976	*outside,*
6	W.	D-Day, 1944 • ☌♆☾ • Psychologist Carl Jung died, 1961	*accepting*
7	Th.	☾ AT ☊ • Delegate Richard Henry Lee proposed independence of American colonies, 1776	*friends'*
8	Fr.	☾ ON EQ. • ☌♅☾ • ☿ GR. ELONG. (45° EAST)	*congratulations.*
9	Sa.	Donald Duck debuted in cartoon "The Wise Little Hen," 1934 • Tides {9.8 / 10.2	*Dads,*
10	G	**Corpus Christi** • ☌♂☾ • *Storms burst as the tide turns.* • {9.7 / 10.7	*provide*
11	M.	**St. Barnabas** • 112°F, Los Angeles, 1877 • Tides {9.7 / 11.1	*a*
12	Tu.	☾ AT PERIG. • Portsmouth Navy Yard, N.H., est., 1800	*place*
13	W.	Spacecraft *Pioneer 10* became the first manmade object to leave solar system, 1983 • Tides {9.8 / 11.7	*to*
14	Th.	**St. Basil** • **New** ● • Singer Burl Ives born, 1909 • {9.9 / 11.8	*hide*
15	Fr.	☾ RIDES HIGH • ☿ STAT. • Oregon Treaty set 49th parallel as U.S.-British border, 1846 • {9.9 / —	*in*
16	Sa.	☌☿☾ • Eye protectors for chickens patented, 1903 • {11.7 / 9.9	*case*
17	G	**3rd S. af. P.** • Methodism founder John Wesley born, 1703 • {11.5 / 9.7	*of*
18	M.	☌♀☾ • Sally K. Ride became first U.S. woman in space, 1983 • Tides {11.1 / 9.6	*sudden*
19	Tu.	♇ AT ☍ • ☌♄☾ • FCC established, 1934	*precipitation!*
20	W.	☾ AT ☋ • Columbia Records introduced the LP record, N.Y.C., 1948	*Commencement*
21	Th.	**Summer Solstice** • ☾ ON EQ. • Jim Bunning pitched a perfect baseball game, 1964	*speakers,*
22	Fr.	**St. Alban** • Henry Hudson, son, and 7 crew set adrift by mutineers, 1611 • Tides {9.1 / 9.1	*keep*
23	Sa.	♅ STAT. • *He that pries into every cloud may be stricken with a thunderbolt.* • Tides {8.7 / 9.1	*it*
24	G	**4th S. af. P.** • Midsummer Day • ☾ AT APO.	*brief:*
25	M.	**Nativ. John the Baptist**[T] • Architect Stanford White killed, 1906 • {8.3 / 9.3	*Those*
26	Tu.	Actor Peter Lorre born, 1904 • JFK gave "Ich bin ein Berliner" speech, 1963 • {8.2 / 9.5	*sun-*
27	W.	Muhammad Ali announced his retirement from boxing, 1979 • Tides {8.3 / 9.7	*baked*
28	Th.	**St. Irenaeus** • ☌♃☾ • ☿ IN INF. ☌ • {8.4 / 9.9	*graduates*
29	Fr.	**Sts. Peter & Paul** • ☾ RUNS LOW • Poet Elizabeth Barrett Browning died, 1861	*need*
30	Sa.	**Full Strawberry** ○ • *Flattery sits in the parlor, when plain-dealing is kicked out of doors.*	*relief!*

A good heart is better than all the heads in the world. –E. Bulwer-Lytton

Farmer's Calendar

■ The dark, inert mass in the upper branches of a hemlock proves to be not a crow's nest but a large porcupine, an unusual sighting hereabouts in recent years. Porcupines, today fairly scarce, used to abound in this region—to the point, indeed, that they figured in the local economy.

Porcupines eat the living inner bark of trees, eventually killing them. Early in the last century, comparatively unchecked by predators because of their quills, porcupines reached numbers in Vermont that threatened whole forests. The state responded by putting a bounty on porcupines. Those famous quills might have kept off a fox or a bobcat, but they were little protection against a farmboy with a .22 rifle.

In this town, according to older residents, the porcupine bounty was a nickel, payable by the Town Clerk on presentation of a pair of the animal's ears. That was good money in, say, 1920. Good enough that enterprising hunters found a way to increase the supply side of the market. They discovered that the unquilled belly skin of a porcupine resembles the skin of the ears, so one porcupine carcass could be hand cut to yield five or six pairs. By the time the state caught on, the bounty had done its work, and the porcupines were largely gone.

SKY WATCH ☆ *Venus, in Leo, maintains its extreme brilliance during the first 24 days of the month, but it sinks rapidly toward the western horizon. By midmonth, it is close to Earth and looks like a crescent Moon through steadily braced binoculars. Saturn is slipping lower in the southwest at nightfall. During midmonth, Jupiter is at its highest at 10:00 P.M., outshining the famous red star, Antares, just below it. Mars, brightening in Aries, rises in the east by 2:00 A.M. Mercury is technically a morning star before dawn for the whole month, but it makes a low, mediocre appearance. Earth reaches aphelion, its position farthest from the Sun in 2007, on the 6th.*

☾ Last Quarter	7th day	12th hour	54th minute
● New Moon	14th day	8th hour	4th minute
☽ First Quarter	22nd day	2nd hour	29th minute
○ Full Moon	29th day	20th hour	48th minute

To use this page, see p. 102; for Key Letters, see p. 237; for Tide Tables, see p. 234.
All times are given in Eastern Daylight Time. ☞ **Bold = P.M.** ☞ Light = A.M.

Day of Year	Day of Month	Day of Week	☼ Rises h. m.	Key	☼ Sets h. m.	Key	Length of Day h. m.	Sun Fast m.	Declination of Sun ° '	High Tide Times Boston		☽ Rises h. m.	Key	☽ Sets h. m.	Key	☽ Place	☽ Age
182	1	G	5:11	A	8:25	E	15 14	12	23 N.06	12¼	12¾	9:45	E	5:48	A	SAG	17
183	2	M.	5:12	A	8:25	E	15 13	12	23 01	12¾	1½	10:17	E	7:00	B	CAP	18
184	3	Tu.	5:12	A	8:25	E	15 13	12	22 57	1½	2¼	10:44	D	8:13	B	CAP	19
185	4	W.	5:13	A	8:25	E	15 12	11	22 52	2¼	3	11:07	D	9:27	C	AQU	20
186	5	Th.	5:13	A	8:24	E	15 11	11	22 46	3¼	3¾	11:29	C	10:40	D	AQU	21
187	6	Fr.	5:14	A	8:24	E	15 10	11	22 41	4	4½	11:51	B	11:53	D	PSC	22
188	7	Sa.	5:15	A	8:24	E	15 09	11	22 34	5	5½	—	—	1:07	E	PSC	23
189	8	G	5:15	A	8:23	E	15 08	11	22 28	5¾	6¼	12:14	A	2:23	E	PSC	24
190	9	M.	5:16	A	8:23	E	15 07	11	22 21	7	7¼	12:41	A	3:42	E	ARI	25
191	10	Tu.	5:17	A	8:23	E	15 06	10	22 13	8	8¼	1:14	A	5:00	E	ARI	26
192	11	W.	5:18	A	8:22	E	15 04	10	22 05	9	9¼	1:55	A	6:15	E	TAU	27
193	12	Th.	5:19	A	8:22	E	15 03	10	21 57	10	10¼	2:47	A	7:20	E	TAU	28
194	13	Fr.	5:19	A	8:21	E	15 02	10	21 49	11	11	3:51	A	8:13	E	AUR	29
195	14	Sa.	5:20	A	8:20	E	15 00	10	21 40	11¾	—	5:03	A	8:55	E	GEM	0
196	15	G	5:21	A	8:20	E	14 59	10	21 31	12	12¾	6:17	B	9:26	E	CAN	1
197	16	M.	5:22	A	8:19	E	14 57	10	21 21	12¾	1½	7:29	B	9:52	D	CAN	2
198	17	Tu.	5:22	A	8:18	E	14 56	10	21 11	1¾	2¼	8:38	C	10:13	D	LEO	3
199	18	W.	5:23	A	8:18	E	14 55	9	21 00	2½	3	9:44	D	10:32	D	LEO	4
200	19	Th.	5:24	A	8:17	E	14 53	9	20 49	3¼	3¾	10:47	D	10:51	C	VIR	5
201	20	Fr.	5:25	A	8:16	E	14 51	9	20 38	4	4½	11:49	D	11:09	B	VIR	6
202	21	Sa.	5:26	A	8:15	E	14 49	9	20 27	4¾	5¼	12:51	E	11:29	B	VIR	7
203	22	G	5:27	A	8:14	E	14 47	9	20 15	5½	6	1:54	E	11:51	B	VIR	8
204	23	M.	5:28	A	8:14	E	14 46	9	20 03	6½	6¾	2:58	E	—	—	LIB	9
205	24	Tu.	5:29	A	8:13	E	14 44	9	19 51	7½	7¾	4:03	E	12:19	A	LIB	10
206	25	W.	5:30	A	8:12	E	14 42	9	19 38	8¼	8½	5:07	E	12:53	A	SCO	11
207	26	Th.	5:31	A	8:11	D	14 40	9	19 25	9¼	9¼	6:06	E	1:35	A	OPH	12
208	27	Fr.	5:32	A	8:10	D	14 38	9	19 11	10	10¼	6:58	E	2:28	A	SAG	13
209	28	Sa.	5:33	A	8:09	D	14 36	9	18 57	11	11	7:42	E	3:32	A	SAG	14
210	29	G	5:34	A	8:08	D	14 34	9	18 43	11¾	11¾	8:17	E	4:43	A	SAG	15
211	30	M.	5:35	A	8:07	D	14 32	9	18 29	12¼	—	8:46	E	5:57	B	CAP	16
212	31	Tu.	5:36	A	8:06	D	14 30	9	18 N.14	12½	1	9:11	D	7:13	C	CAP	17

JULY HATH 31 DAYS • 2007

Old wortermelon time is a-comin' round ag'in,
And they ain't no man a-livin any tickleder'n me. –James Whitcomb Riley

Day of Month	Day of Week	Dates, Feasts, Fasts, Aspects, Tide Heights	Weather
1	G	**5th S. af. P.** • **Canada Day** • ☌♀♄	*Storm clouds*
2	M.	Charles Guiteau shot Pres. Garfield, 1881 • { 10.5 9.1	*mutter,*
3	Tu.	Dog Days begin. • ☌♆☾ • 105°F in Allentown, Pa., 1966 • { 10.6 9.4	*then*
4	W.	**Independence Day** • ☾ AT ☊ • 15-lb., 3-oz., American lobster caught, N.J., 2003	*fill*
5	Th.	☌⛢☾ • Graham cracker inventor, Sylvester Graham, born, 1794 • Tides { 10.5 9.9	*the*
6	Fr.	☾ ON EQ. • ⊕ AT APHELION • Musician Louis Armstrong died, 1971	*gutter.*
7	Sa.	Composer Gustav Mahler born, 1860 • Jim Thorpe won Olympic pentathlon, 1912 • { 10.0 10.4	*Great*
8	G	**6th S. af. P.** • *Wall Street Journal* debuted, 1889 • Tides { 9.7 10.6	*for*
9	M.	☾ AT PERIG. • ☌♂☾ • ☿ STAT. • Tides { 9.4 10.8	*clambakes*
10	Tu.	*If you have no courage, you must have fast legs.* • { 9.2 10.9	*(bring*
11	W.	Wilfrid Laurier became prime minister of Canada, 1896 • Actor Sir Laurence Olivier died, 1989	*lots*
12	Th.	☾ RIDES HIGH • ☌☿☾ • ♀ GR. ILLUM. EXTENT • Tides { 9.2 11.2	*of*
13	Fr.	Cornscateous air is everywhere. • Gold discovered near Cochrane, Ontario, 1909 • { 9.4 11.2	*butter!).*
14	Sa.	**Bastille Day** • **New** ● • Armadillos mate now. • Tides { 9.5 —	*Millions*
15	G	**7th S. af. P.** • *Molasses catches more flies than vinegar.* • { 11.2 9.6	*of*
16	M.	OCCN. ♄☾ • 22.22" rain in 24 hrs. ends, Altapass, N.C., 1916 • { 11.0 9.6	*drops*
17	Tu.	☾ AT ☋ • ☌♀☾ • Maiden flight of B-2 stealth bomber, 1989 • Tides { 10.8 9.6	*save*
18	W.	Marie and Pierre Curie announced discovery of polonium, 1898 • Tides { 10.4 9.5	*the*
19	Th.	☾ ON EQ. • Fla. hit with third hurricane within a month, 1886 • Tides { 9.9 9.4	*crops,*
20	Fr.	☿ GR. ELONG. (20° WEST) • E. Lamson first woman astronomer at U.S. Naval Observatory, 1900	*smelling*
21	Sa.	*When pigs carry sticks, the clouds will play tricks.* • { 8.9 9.2	*lovely*
22	G	**8th S. af. P.** • ☾ AT APO. • Game show host Alex Trebek born, 1940	*when*
23	M.	**St. Mary Magdalene**[T] • Adult gypsy moths emerge. • Tides { 8.2 9.1	*it*
24	Tu.	Cyclist Lance Armstrong became first seven-time winner in Tour de France history, 2005 • { 7.9 9.1	*stops.*
25	W.	**Sts. James & Christopher** • ☌♃☾ • ♀ STAT.	*Lightning*
26	Th.	**St. Anne** • New York became the 11th U.S. state, 1788 • Tides { 8.0 9.6	*flashes*
27	Fr.	☾ RUNS LOW • 5.2 earthquake in Sharpsburg, Ky., 1980 • Tides { 8.2 9.9	*send*
28	Sa.	*Nature, time, and patience are the three great physicians.* • Egg fried on steps of U.S. Capitol, 1944	*cosmic*
29	G	**9th S. af. P.** • **Full Buck** ○ • Tides { 8.9 10.6	*dots*
30	M.	☌♆☾ • *Apollo 15* landed on Moon, 1971 • Tides { 9.3 —	*and*
31	Tu.	**St. Ignatius of Loyola** • Samuel Hopkins granted first patent for potash, 1790	*dashes.*

Farmer's Calendar

■ Every six to eight weeks in the warm months, the garter snake prepares for the ceremony of renewal peculiar to its kind: It sheds its skin. The process is a curious one. The snake seeks a dark, sheltered, confined spot—inside a stone wall, say, or in a brush pile or a stack of cordwood. There it rubs its head and jaws against some rough surface until the outermost layer of epidermis, which over the past few days will have become soft and dull in color, has torn. The snake then hooks or catches the loosened covering on some projection and slowly crawls out of its own skin, turning the skin inside out behind it as it goes, much as a woman removes a nylon stocking.

The cast-off skin is a remarkable thing, a kind of airy, gossamer replica of the snake itself. Every tiny scale and plate, even the empty lenses that covered the eyes, is present. Weirdly, the snake seems to have departed, leaving behind its hologram, the ghost of a garter snake.

Folklore, always tough on snakes, says that their shed skins are bad luck, not to be touched. But I have always liked and enjoyed snakes, and when I find these uncanny remnants of their lives in the woodpile or hidden under the squash vines in the garden, I'm charmed and somehow reassured, as though I'd received a postcard from a long-absent friend.

AUGUST

THE EIGHTH MONTH • 2007

SKY WATCH ☆ *Mars, in Taurus, keeps brightening as it now rises by 1:00 A.M. and hovers near the Moon during the early hours of the 7th. The month's highlight is the famous Perseid meteor shower, occurring this year under ideal new Moon conditions. It will peak on the night of the 11th–12th, with the intensity increasing after midnight to about one meteor per minute. Two nights later, Neptune comes into opposition in Capricornus, where it remains a dim, 8th-magnitude object requiring a telescope to see. Venus finally vanishes into the setting Sun's glare and is at inferior conjunction on the 18th. It reappears during the final days of the month in its new role as a morning star in the east.*

☾	**Last Quarter**	5th day	17th hour	20th minute
●	**New Moon**	12th day	19th hour	3rd minute
☽	**First Quarter**	20th day	19th hour	54th minute
○	**Full Moon**	28th day	6th hour	35th minute

To use this page, see p. 102; for Key Letters, see p. 237; for Tide Tables, see p. 234.
All times are given in Eastern Daylight Time. ☞ **Bold = P.M.** ☞ Light = A.M.

Day of Year	Day of Month	Day of Week	☼ Rises h. m.	Key	☼ Sets h. m.	Key	Length of Day h. m.	Sun Fast m.	Declination of Sun ° ′	High Tide Times Boston		☽ Rises h. m.	Key	☽ Sets h. m.	Key	☽ Place	☽ Age
213	1	W.	5:37	A	**8:04**	D	14 27	9	17 N.59	1¼	**1¾**	**9:34**	C	8:28	C	AQU	18
214	2	Th.	5:38	A	**8:03**	D	14 25	9	17 44	2	**2½**	**9:56**	C	9:42	D	PSC	19
215	3	Fr.	5:39	A	**8:02**	D	14 23	9	17 28	2¾	**3¼**	**10:19**	B	10:57	E	PSC	20
216	4	Sa.	5:40	A	**8:01**	D	14 21	9	17 13	3¾	**4¼**	**10:44**	B	**12:13**	E	PSC	21
217	5	**G**	5:41	A	**8:00**	D	14 19	10	16 57	4½	**5**	**11:15**	A	**1:31**	E	ARI	22
218	6	M.	5:42	A	**7:58**	D	14 16	10	16 40	5½	**6**	**11:52**	A	**2:49**	E	ARI	23
219	7	Tu.	5:43	A	**7:57**	D	14 14	10	16 23	6¾	**7**	—	–	**4:04**	E	TAU	24
220	8	W.	5:44	A	**7:56**	D	14 12	10	16 06	7¾	**8**	12:40	A	**5:11**	E	TAU	25
221	9	Th.	5:45	A	**7:54**	D	14 09	10	15 49	8¾	**9**	1:39	A	**6:08**	E	AUR	26
222	10	Fr.	5:46	A	**7:53**	D	14 07	10	15 32	9¾	**10**	2:46	A	**6:52**	E	GEM	27
223	11	Sa.	5:47	A	**7:52**	D	14 05	10	15 14	10¾	**11**	3:59	B	**7:26**	E	CAN	28
224	12	**G**	5:48	A	**7:50**	D	14 02	10	14 56	11¾	**11¾**	5:11	B	**7:54**	E	CAN	0
225	13	M.	5:49	A	**7:49**	D	14 00	11	14 38	**12½**	—	6:21	C	**8:16**	D	LEO	1
226	14	Tu.	5:50	A	**7:48**	D	13 58	11	14 20	12½	**1**	7:28	D	**8:36**	D	LEO	2
227	15	W.	5:51	B	**7:46**	D	13 55	11	14 01	1¼	**1¾**	8:33	D	**8:55**	C	LEO	3
228	16	Th.	5:52	B	**7:45**	D	13 53	11	13 42	2	**2¼**	9:36	D	**9:13**	B	VIR	4
229	17	Fr.	5:53	B	**7:43**	D	13 50	11	13 23	2¾	**3**	10:38	E	**9:32**	B	VIR	5
230	18	Sa.	5:55	B	**7:42**	D	13 47	12	13 04	3¼	**3¾**	11:41	E	**9:53**	B	VIR	6
231	19	**G**	5:56	B	**7:40**	D	13 44	12	12 44	4	**4½**	**12:45**	E	**10:18**	A	VIR	7
232	20	M.	5:57	B	**7:39**	D	13 42	12	12 25	5	**5¼**	**1:49**	E	**10:49**	A	LIB	8
233	21	Tu.	5:58	B	**7:37**	D	13 39	12	12 05	5¾	**6**	**2:53**	E	**11:27**	A	SCO	9
234	22	W.	5:59	B	**7:35**	D	13 36	12	11 45	6¾	**7**	**3:54**	E	—	–	SCO	10
235	23	Th.	6:00	B	**7:34**	D	13 34	13	11 24	7¾	**8**	**4:48**	E	12:15	A	SAG	11
236	24	Fr.	6:01	B	**7:32**	D	13 31	13	11 04	8¾	**8¾**	**5:35**	E	1:13	A	SAG	12
237	25	Sa.	6:02	B	**7:31**	D	13 29	13	10 43	9½	**9¾**	**6:14**	E	2:21	A	SAG	13
238	26	**G**	6:03	B	**7:29**	D	13 26	14	10 22	10¼	**10½**	**6:46**	E	3:34	B	CAP	14
239	27	M.	6:04	B	**7:27**	D	13 23	14	10 01	11	**11¼**	**7:13**	D	4:50	B	CAP	15
240	28	Tu.	6:05	B	**7:26**	D	13 21	14	9 40	11¾	—	**7:36**	D	6:07	C	AQU	16
241	29	W.	6:06	B	**7:24**	D	13 18	14	9 19	12	**12½**	**7:59**	C	7:24	D	AQU	17
242	30	Th.	6:07	B	**7:22**	D	13 15	15	8 57	12¾	**1¼**	**8:22**	B	8:41	D	PSC	18
243	31	Fr.	6:08	B	**7:21**	D	13 13	15	8 N.36	1¾	**2**	**8:47**	B	9:59	E	PSC	19

AUGUST

AUGUST HATH 31 DAYS • 2007

Upon her throne Queen August lies
With languor in her dreamful eyes. –Samuel Minturn Peck

Day of Month	Day of Week	Dates, Feasts, Fasts, Aspects, Tide Heights	Weather
1	W.	Lammas Day • ☾ AT ☊ • ☌ ♅ ☾ • Tides { 11.0 / 10.1	*Too*
2	Th.	☾ ON EQ. • Einstein wrote to Pres. FDR about the possibility of an atomic bomb, 1939 • { 11.0 / 10.5	*cool*
3	Fr.	☾ AT PERIG. • 6.25" rain, Warsaw, Ind., 1929 • Gray squirrels have second litters now.	*for*
4	Sa.	Canada entered WWI, 1914 • *Let not thy tongue run away with thy brains.* • Tides { 10.4 / 10.8	*the*
5	G	**10th S. af. P.** • Poet Conrad Aiken born, 1889 • { 9.9 / 10.8	*pool.*
6	M.	**Transfiguration** • Microsoft and Apple agreed to share technology, 1997 • { 9.5 / 10.7	*Rain-*
7	Tu.	☌ ♂ ☾ • ♃ STAT. • First picture of Earth transmitted from space, 1959 • { 9.1 / 10.6	*outs*
8	W.	**St. Dominic** • First red-footed falcon spotted in Western Hemisphere, Edgartown, Mass., 2004	*come*
9	Th.	☾ RIDES HIGH • Tornado tore through northern Wallingford, Conn., 1878 • { 8.8 / 10.6	*rarely,*
10	Fr.	**St. Lawrence** • President Herbert Hoover born, 1874	*then*
11	Sa.	**St. Clare** • Dog days end. • Jackson Pollock, artist, died, 1956 • { 9.2 / 10.7	*beaches*
12	G	**11th S. af. P.** • **New ●** • Tides { 9.4 / 10.7	*are*
13	M.	♆ AT ☍ • First National Hurricane Research Project flight, 1956 • { 9.6 / —	*covered*
14	Tu.	☾ AT ☋ • *Footprints on the sands of time are not made by sitting down.* • { 10.6 / 9.7	*with*
15	W.	**Assumption** • ☾ ON EQ. • ☿ IN SUP. ☌ • Tides { 10.4 / 9.7	*bathers*
16	Th.	Battle of Bennington, Vt., 1777 • Baseball player Babe Ruth died, 1948 • { 10.1 / 9.7	*(some*
17	Fr.	Cat Nights commence. • Frontiersman Davy Crockett born, 1786 • { 9.7 / 9.6	*barely!).*
18	Sa.	☾ AT APO. • ♀ IN INF. ☌ • First child born in America from English parents, 1587	*Golfers*
19	G	**12th S. af. P.** • Ragweed in bloom. • { 8.8 / 9.3	*scatter*
20	M.	Talk show host Regis Philbin set world record for most hours on camera, 2004 • Tides { 8.3 / 9.1	*when*
21	Tu.	☌ ♄ ☉ • ☌ ♃ ☾ • American Bar Association formed, 1878	*dark*
22	W.	*August sunshine and bright nights ripen the grapes.*	*clouds*
23	Th.	☾ RUNS LOW • Fannie Farmer opened a cooking school, Boston, Mass., 1902 • { 7.8 / 9.2	*gather,*
24	Fr.	**St. Bartholomew** • Jockey Julie Krone won Pacific Classic, 2003 • { 8.0 / 9.5	*seeking*
25	Sa.	Hoax about life on Moon printed in *The New York Sun,* 1835 • Tides { 8.3 / 10.0	*shelter*
26	G	**13th S. af. P.** • Krakatau erupted, Neth. East Indies, 1883 • { 8.9 / 10.4	*while*
27	M.	☌ ♆ ☾ • Missionary Mother Teresa born, 1910 • Tides { 9.4 / 10.9	*they*
28	Tu.	**Full Sturgeon ○** • **Eclipse ☾** • ☾ AT ☊ • { 10.0 / —	*swelter.*
29	W.	**St. John the Baptist** • ☾ ON EQ. • ☌ ♅ ☾ • { 11.2 / 10.6	*Damper*
30	Th.	☾ AT PERIG. • Streetcar service ended in Montreal, Quebec, 1959 • Tides { 11.3 / 11.0	*for*
31	Fr.	Princess Diana died, 1997 • *Go abroad and you'll hear news of home.* • { 11.2 / 11.3	*campers.*

Farmer's Calendar

■ Planted in the icy mud of April, each in its own finger-poked hole, then watched over, weeded, supported in weakness, this year's peas have at last gone by. Their vines have died, dried, turned the color of hay. They lean upon the head-high wire fences erected to prop them up, where they make a hopeless, tangled brake of obsolete vegetation. The job now is to tear them down, lay them on the compost pile, and call it another year for the garden's first and most reliable bumper crop.

Was there ever a more feeble and contemptible plant than a pea? This is the vegetable version of a consumptive poet: pale, languid, exhausted. When you pull the vines up to discard them, you find they have hardly any roots at all. Their stalks flop and sag against the fence, which they soon overtop, whereupon they collapse in a lazy, disorderly mass.

And yet, from this weakling, what bounty! Beginning in late June, the peas pour out of the garden like a river. They never fail. Even when they have run their course and the time has come to dispose of their remains, a few pods hide among the wilderness of dying vines. You find them as you strip the plants from their fences. There's always one more pod lurking in the thicket, its peas yellow, dry, beginning to shrivel. They look like something you'd find at the bottom of your aunt's handbag.

SEPTEMBER

THE NINTH MONTH • 2007

SKY WATCH ☆ *Venus returns as a morning star, rising higher each day before dawn; it hits its greatest brilliancy (magnitude –4.5) on the 12th and maintains it for more than a month. Dim Uranus reaches opposition on the 9th. In Aquarius at magnitude 5.8, the aqua-green planet can barely be glimpsed by the unaided eye. (See "Seventh Heaven" on page 76.) Saturn, now a predawn star, is close to Leo's bright star Regulus during the first half of September, the duo hovering between Venus and the point of sunrise. Jupiter remains bright in the west after sunset, above the red star Antares. Mars, in Taurus, rises at midnight. Autumn officially begins with the equinox on the 23rd, at 5:51* A.M.

☾	**Last Quarter**	3rd day	22nd hour	32nd minute
●	**New Moon**	11th day	8th hour	44th minute
☽	**First Quarter**	19th day	12th hour	48th minute
○	**Full Moon**	26th day	15th hour	45th minute

To use this page, see p. 102; for Key Letters, see p. 237; for Tide Tables, see p. 234.
All times are given in Eastern Daylight Time. ☞ **Bold = P.M.** ☞ Light = A.M.

Day of Year	Day of Month	Day of Week	☼ Rises h. m.	Key	☼ Sets h. m.	Key	Length of Day h.	Length of Day m.	Sun Fast m.	Declination of Sun °	Declination of Sun '	High Tide Times Boston		☽ Rises h. m.	Key	☽ Sets h. m.	Key	☽ Place	☽ Age
244	1	Sa.	6:09	B	**7:19**	D	13	10	15	8 N.	14	2½	**2¾**	**9:16**	B	11:18	E	ARI	20
245	2	**G**	6:10	B	**7:17**	D	13	07	16	7	52	3½	**3¾**	**9:52**	A	**12:38**	E	ARI	21
246	3	M.	6:11	B	**7:16**	D	13	05	16	7	30	4¼	**4¾**	**10:37**	A	**1:55**	E	TAU	22
247	4	Tu.	6:12	B	**7:14**	D	13	02	16	7	08	5¼	**5¾**	**11:32**	A	**3:05**	E	TAU	23
248	5	W.	6:14	B	**7:12**	D	12	58	17	6	46	6½	**6¾**	—	–	**4:04**	E	AUR	24
249	6	Th.	6:15	B	**7:11**	D	12	56	17	6	24	7½	**7¾**	12:37	A	**4:52**	E	GEM	25
250	7	Fr.	6:16	B	**7:09**	D	12	53	17	6	01	8¾	**9**	1:47	B	**5:28**	E	GEM	26
251	8	Sa.	6:17	B	**7:07**	D	12	50	18	5	39	9¾	**10**	2:59	B	**5:57**	E	CAN	27
252	9	**G**	6:18	B	**7:05**	C	12	47	18	5	16	10½	**10¾**	4:09	B	**6:21**	D	LEO	28
253	10	M.	6:19	B	**7:04**	C	12	45	18	4	54	11¼	**11½**	5:16	C	**6:41**	D	LEO	29
254	11	Tu.	6:20	B	**7:02**	C	12	42	19	4	31	**12**	—	6:21	D	**7:00**	C	LEO	0
255	12	W.	6:21	B	**7:00**	C	12	39	19	4	08	12¼	**12½**	7:24	D	**7:18**	C	VIR	1
256	13	Th.	6:22	B	**6:58**	C	12	36	19	3	45	12¾	**1¼**	8:26	D	**7:37**	B	VIR	2
257	14	Fr.	6:23	B	**6:57**	C	12	34	20	3	22	1½	**1¾**	9:29	E	**7:57**	B	VIR	3
258	15	Sa.	6:24	B	**6:55**	C	12	31	20	2	59	2¼	**2¼**	10:32	E	**8:21**	A	VIR	4
259	16	**G**	6:25	B	**6:53**	C	12	28	20	2	36	2¾	**3**	11:36	E	**8:49**	A	LIB	5
260	17	M.	6:26	B	**6:51**	C	12	25	21	2	13	3½	**3¾**	**12:40**	E	**9:23**	A	LIB	6
261	18	Tu.	6:27	B	**6:49**	C	12	22	21	1	50	4¼	**4½**	**1:41**	E	**10:07**	A	SCO	7
262	19	W.	6:28	B	**6:48**	C	12	20	22	1	27	5¼	**5¼**	**2:38**	E	**10:59**	A	OPH	8
263	20	Th.	6:29	C	**6:46**	C	12	17	22	1	03	6	**6¼**	**3:27**	E	—	–	SAG	9
264	21	Fr.	6:30	C	**6:44**	C	12	14	22	0	40	7	**7¼**	**4:08**	E	12:02	A	SAG	10
265	22	Sa.	6:32	C	**6:42**	C	12	10	23	0 N.	17	8	**8¼**	**4:42**	E	1:11	B	CAP	11
266	23	**G**	6:33	C	**6:41**	C	12	08	23	0 S.	07	9	**9¼**	**5:11**	E	2:25	B	CAP	12
267	24	M.	6:34	C	**6:39**	C	12	05	23	0	30	9¾	**10**	**5:36**	D	3:40	C	CAP	13
268	25	Tu.	6:35	C	**6:37**	C	12	02	24	0	53	10½	**10¾**	**6:00**	D	4:57	C	AQU	14
269	26	W.	6:36	C	**6:35**	C	11	59	24	1	17	11¼	**11¾**	**6:23**	C	6:14	D	PSC	15
270	27	Th.	6:37	C	**6:34**	C	11	57	24	1	40	**12**	—	**6:48**	B	7:34	E	PSC	16
271	28	Fr.	6:38	C	**6:32**	B	11	54	25	2	04	12½	**12¾**	**7:16**	B	8:55	E	PSC	17
272	29	Sa.	6:39	C	**6:30**	B	11	51	25	2	27	1¼	**1½**	**7:50**	A	10:18	E	ARI	18
273	30	**G**	6:40	C	**6:28**	B	11	48	25	2 S.	50	2¼	**2½**	**8:33**	A	11:39	E	TAU	19

SEPTEMBER HATH 30 DAYS • 2007

Here and yonder, high and low,
Goldenrod and sunflowers glow. –Robert Kelley Weeks

Day of Month	Day of Week	Dates, Feasts, Fasts, Aspects, Tide Heights	Weather
1	Sa.	Bobby Fischer became first American to win the world chess championship, 1972 • Tides {10.8 11.3	A
2	**G**	**14th S. af. P.** • Author J.R.R. Tolkien died, 1973	hint
3	M.	**Labor Day** • Hailstone 17.5" in circumference, Coffeyville, Kans., 1970 • {9.8 10.9	of
4	Tu.	☌♂☾ • Cranberry bog harvest begins, Cape Cod, Mass. • Tides {9.2 10.6	fall,
5	W.	☾ RIDES HIGH • Treaty signed, Portsmouth, N.H., ending Russo-Japanese War, 1905 • {8.8 10.3	then
6	Th.	*An apple pie without some cheese Is like a kiss without a squeeze.* • Tides {8.7 10.1	heat
7	Fr.	♇ STAT. • ♀ STAT. • Google Inc. founded, 1998 • {8.8 10.2	that's
8	Sa.	☌♀☾ • Cruise ship S.S. *Morro Castle* burned near Asbury Park, N.J., 1934 • {9.0 10.2	brutal;
9	**G**	**15th S. af. P.** • ♅ AT ☍ • Tides {9.3 10.3	in
10	M.	☾ AT ☋ • ☌♄☾ • Air terminal building of Halifax Int'l Airport, Nova Scotia, opened, 1960	all
11	Tu.	**New** ● • **Eclipse** ☉ • ☾ ON EQ. • Terrorist attacks on United States, 2001	the
12	W.	Astronauts Jan Davis and Mark Lee became first married couple to be in space, 1992 • {10.2 9.9	orchards,
13	Th.	**Rosh Hashanah • First day of Ramadan** • ☌☿☾	ripening
14	Fr.	**Holy Cross** • *There's many a slip 'Twixt the cup and the lip.* • Tides {9.7 9.9	fruit'll
15	Sa.	☾ AT APO. • Author Agatha Christie born, 1890 • Prince Harry of Wales born, 1984	soon
16	**G**	**16th S. af. P.** • American Legion incorporated, 1919 • Tides {9.0 9.6	be
17	M.	Musician Hank Williams born, 1923 • 20.5" snow in Lander, Wyo., 1965 • {8.6 9.3	picked,
18	Tu.	☌♃☾ • Shirley Temple made film debut at age 3, in *War Babies,* 1932 • Tides {8.2 9.1	or
19	W.	Ember Day • ☾ RUNS LOW • Pres. James Garfield died, 1881 • {7.9 9.0	pressed
20	Th.	**St. Eustace** • *A curdly sky will not leave the earth long dry.* • Tides {7.8 9.0	for
21	Fr.	**St. Matthew** • Ember Day • NFL's longest punt, 98 yards, by Steve O'Neal, 1969	cider.
22	Sa.	Ember Day • **Yom Kippur** • Patriot Nathan Hale died, 1776 • {8.2 9.6	Skies
23	**G**	**Autumnal Equinox** • Harvest Home • ☌♆☾ • ♀ GR. ILLUM. EXTENT	seem
24	M.	☾ AT ☊ • Aircraft carrier U.S.S. *Enterprise* launched, Newport News, Va., 1960	clearer,
25	Tu.	☌♅☾ • First glimpse of Pacific Ocean by explorer Vasco Núñez de Balboa, 1513	bluer,
26	W.	**Full Harvest** ○ • ☾ ON EQ. • 104°F, Death Valley, Calif., 1979 • {10.9 11.2	wider,
27	Th.	**St. Vincent de Paul • Sukkoth** • ☾ AT PERIG. • {11.4 —	dreading
28	Fr.	*A statement once let loose can not be caught by four horses.* • Tides {11.3 11.8	winter's
29	Sa.	**St. Michael** • ☿ GR. ELONG. (26° EAST) • Canadian satellite *Alouette 1* launched, 1962	first
30	**G**	**18th S. af. P.** • Woodchucks hibernate now. • {10.7 11.8	outrider.

You can't catch the wind in a net. –Charles Haddon Spurgeon

Farmer's Calendar

■ Science is perpetual revision. Its findings often seem to be unstable, provisional—and never more than in the field of paleontology, where, you'd think, discoveries about prehistoric life would have the permanence of the ancient rock that preserves the fossil record.

Not at all. Take, for example, the scientific view of the earliest mammals. Evolving more or less along with the dinosaurs, mammals were formerly thought to have had a timid, inconspicuous existence in the shadow of the great reptiles. They were, we were told, plucky little shrew-like mites, scurrying around trying to dodge the heavy tread of boxcar-size lizards.

Recent discoveries in China have altered this standard account. Fossils dated to 130 million years ago have been found to be the remains of mammals resembling badgers or wolverines. These creatures, of the genus *Repenomamus,* were carnivores. They ate small or immature dinosaurs, as evidenced by fossil dinosaur bones found inside one of the fossil mammals. Clearly, the larger members of *Repenomamus* were no pip-squeaks.

Here the science of paleontology, doing its appointed work, has revised science's whole picture of the history of life on Earth. As in so much of our experience, the more we learn, the less we know.

OCTOBER

THE TENTH MONTH • 2007

CALENDAR

SKY WATCH ☆ *The best action happens on the 7th, from 4:30 to 6:30* A.M.*, when Venus is high and absolutely dazzling at its greatest brilliancy. Look for a beautiful tight bunching of Venus, Saturn, the blue star Regulus, and the crescent Moon. Venus and Saturn are closest together from the 11th to the 15th, and they are especially striking before daybreak when viewed with a small telescope. Mercury starts to appear in that vicinity, too, during the last days of the month, but it is much lower than the others. The Moon makes its closest approach to Earth for the year on the 26th, the night it is full; its surface will then be approximately 221,688 miles from ours.*

☾	**Last Quarter**	3rd day	6th hour	6th minute
●	**New Moon**	11th day	1st hour	1st minute
☽	**First Quarter**	19th day	4th hour	33rd minute
○	**Full Moon**	26th day	0 hour	52nd minute

To use this page, see p. 102; for Key Letters, see p. 237; for Tide Tables, see p. 234.
All times are given in Eastern Daylight Time. ☞ **Bold = P.M.** ☞ Light = A.M.

Day of Year	Day of Month	Day of Week	☼ Rises h. m.	Key	☼ Sets h. m.	Key	Length of Day h. m.	Sun Fast m.	Declination of Sun ° '	High Tide Times Boston		☽ Rises h. m.	Key	☽ Sets h. m.	Key	☽ Place	☽ Age
274	1	M.	6:41	C	**6:27**	B	11 46	26	3s.13	3	**3¼**	**9:26**	A	**12:55**	E	TAU	20
275	2	Tu.	6:42	C	**6:25**	B	11 43	26	3 37	4	**4¼**	**10:29**	A	**1:59**	E	TAU	21
276	3	W.	6:43	C	**6:23**	B	11 40	26	4 00	5	**5¼**	**11:39**	A	**2:51**	E	AUR	22
277	4	Th.	6:45	C	**6:21**	B	11 36	27	4 23	6¼	**6½**	—	–	**3:30**	E	GEM	23
278	5	Fr.	6:46	C	**6:20**	B	11 34	27	4 46	7¼	**7¾**	12:50	A	**4:01**	E	CAN	24
279	6	Sa.	6:47	C	**6:18**	B	11 31	27	5 09	8½	**8¾**	2:00	B	**4:26**	D	LEO	25
280	7	**G**	6:48	C	**6:16**	B	11 28	28	5 32	9¼	**9¾**	3:07	C	**4:47**	D	LEO	26
281	8	M.	6:49	C	**6:15**	B	11 26	28	5 55	10¼	**10½**	4:12	C	**5:06**	D	LEO	27
282	9	Tu.	6:50	C	**6:13**	B	11 23	28	6 18	10¾	**11¼**	5:15	D	**5:25**	C	VIR	28
283	10	W.	6:51	C	**6:11**	B	11 20	28	6 41	11½	**11¾**	6:17	D	**5:43**	B	VIR	29
284	11	Th.	6:52	C	**6:10**	B	11 18	29	7 04	**12**	—	7:19	E	**6:03**	B	VIR	0
285	12	Fr.	6:54	C	**6:08**	B	11 14	29	7 26	12½	**12½**	8:22	E	**6:25**	B	VIR	1
286	13	Sa.	6:55	C	**6:06**	B	11 11	29	7 49	1	**1¼**	9:26	E	**6:51**	A	LIB	2
287	14	**G**	6:56	D	**6:05**	B	11 09	29	8 11	1¾	**1¾**	10:30	E	**7:24**	A	LIB	3
288	15	M.	6:57	D	**6:03**	B	11 06	30	8 34	2¼	**2½**	11:32	E	**8:03**	A	SCO	4
289	16	Tu.	6:58	D	**6:01**	B	11 03	30	8 56	3	**3¼**	**12:30**	E	**8:52**	A	OPH	5
290	17	W.	6:59	D	**6:00**	B	11 01	30	9 18	3¾	**4**	**1:21**	E	**9:50**	A	SAG	6
291	18	Th.	7:01	D	**5:58**	B	10 57	30	9 40	4¾	**4¾**	**2:04**	E	**10:54**	B	SAG	7
292	19	Fr.	7:02	D	**5:57**	B	10 55	30	10 01	5½	**5¾**	**2:40**	E	—	–	SAG	8
293	20	Sa.	7:03	D	**5:55**	B	10 52	31	10 23	6½	**6¾**	**3:10**	E	12:04	B	CAP	9
294	21	**G**	7:04	D	**5:54**	B	10 50	31	10 44	7½	**7¾**	**3:36**	D	1:16	C	CAP	10
295	22	M.	7:05	D	**5:52**	B	10 47	31	11 05	8¼	**8¾**	**3:59**	D	2:30	C	AQU	11
296	23	Tu.	7:06	D	**5:51**	B	10 45	31	11 26	9¼	**9½**	**4:22**	C	3:45	D	PSC	12
297	24	W.	7:08	D	**5:49**	B	10 41	31	11 47	10	**10½**	**4:46**	C	5:03	D	PSC	13
298	25	Th.	7:09	D	**5:48**	B	10 39	31	12 08	10¾	**11¼**	**5:12**	B	6:23	E	PSC	14
299	26	Fr.	7:10	D	**5:46**	B	10 36	32	12 29	11½	—	**5:44**	A	7:46	E	ARI	15
300	27	Sa.	7:11	D	**5:45**	B	10 34	32	12 49	12¼	**12¼**	**6:24**	A	9:11	E	ARI	16
301	28	**G**	7:13	D	**5:44**	B	10 31	32	13 09	2	**1¼**	**7:14**	A	10:33	E	TAU	17
302	29	M.	7:14	D	**5:42**	B	10 28	32	13 29	2	**2**	**8:16**	A	11:45	E	TAU	18
303	30	Tu.	7:15	D	**5:41**	B	10 26	32	13 49	2¾	**3**	**9:26**	A	12:44	E	AUR	19
304	31	W.	7:16	D	**5:40**	B	10 24	32	14s.08	3¾	**4**	**10:39**	B	1:29	E	GEM	20

OCTOBER HATH 31 DAYS • 2007

His store of nuts and acorns now
The squirrel hastes to gain. –Alice Cary

Day of Month	Day of Week	Dates, Feasts, Fasts, Aspects, Tide Heights	Weather
1	M.	St. Gregory • Racer's Storm approached Galveston, Tex., 1837 • Tides 10.2 / 11.4	*Red*
2	Tu.	☾ RIDES HIGH • ☌♂☾ • Redwood National Park established, 1968 • 9.6 / 10.9	*and*
3	W.	*Little Women* first published, 1868 • Actor Roddy McDowall died, 1998 • 9.1 / 10.4	*gold*
4	Th.	St. Francis of Assisi • First U.S. Open golf championship, Newport, R.I., 1895	*leaf-fire*
5	Fr.	*Mere wishes are silly fishes.* • Inventor Louis Lumière born, 1864 • Tides 8.8 / 9.8	*roars*
6	Sa.	☌♀☾ • Submarine U.S.S. *Seawolf* surfaced after record-breaking 60 days underwater, 1958	*from*
7	G	**19th S. af. P.** • ☾ AT ☋ • ☌♄☾ • 9.2 / 9.8	*Canada*
8	M.	**Columbus Day** • **Thanksgiving Day (Canada)** • Great Chicago Fire began, 1871	*to*
9	Tu.	☾ ON EQ. • Peach, blue, and green U.S. $20 bill debuted, 2003 • 9.7 / 9.8	*Connecticut*
10	W.	Quebec Labor Minister Pierre Laporte kidnapped, 1970 • Tides 9.9 / 9.7	*shores,*
11	Th.	**New ●** • YMCA founder, Sir George Williams, born, 1821 • Tides 10.0 / —	*harried*
12	Fr.	☌☿☾ • ☿ STAT. • *Opportunities, like eggs, come one at a time.* • 9.5 / 10.0	*by*
13	Sa.	☾ AT APO. • Cornerstone of the White House laid, 1792 • Tides 9.3 / 10.0	*the*
14	G	**20th S. af. P.** • First piloted supersonic flight, 1947 • 9.1 / 9.9	*snow's*
15	M.	☌♄♀ • China became third country to send a person into orbit, 2003 • 8.8 / 9.7	*pale*
16	Tu.	☌♃☾ • John Brown's raid at Harper's Ferry in what is now W.Va., 1859	*horsemen,*
17	W.	St. Ignatius of Antioch • ☾ RUNS LOW • Tides 8.2 / 9.3	*like*
18	Th.	St. Luke • St. Luke's little summer. • Football's Mike Ditka born, 1939 • Tides 8.0 / 9.1	*a*
19	Fr.	*Rainbow to windward, foul fall the day; Rainbow to leeward, damp runs away.* • Tides 8.0 / 9.1	*horde*
20	Sa.	☌♆☾ • John Bardeen won his second Nobel Prize in Physics, 1972 • Tides 8.2 / 9.3	*of*
21	G	**21st S. af. P.** • Timber rattlesnakes move to winter dens. • 8.7 / 9.6	*howling*
22	M.	☾ AT ☊ • ☌♅☾ • College of N.J. (later Princeton) chartered, 1746	*Norsemen.*
23	Tu.	☾ ON EQ. • ☿ IN INF. ☌ • Massive wildfire burned parts of Bar Harbor, Maine, 1947	*Sunshine*
24	W.	Cartoonist Bob Kane born, 1915 • Tides 10.8 / 10.7	*stems*
25	Th.	S.S. *Princess Sophia* sank near Juneau, Alaska, 1918	*the*
26	Fr.	**Full Hunter's ○** • ☾ AT PERIG. • Tides 12.0 / —	*tide,*
27	Sa.	Little brown bats hibernate now. • U.S. and Spain signed Treaty of San Lorenzo, 1795 • 11.0 / 12.2	*but*
28	G	**22nd S. af. P.** • ♀ GR. ELONG. (46° WEST) • Tides 10.8 / 12.2	*time*
29	M.	Sts. Simon & Jude† • *Monday is the key of the week.* • Tides 10.4 / 11.9	*is on*
30	Tu.	☾ RIDES HIGH • ☌♂☾ • 24-second shot clock debuted in NBA, 1954 • 10.0 / 11.4	*winter's*
31	W.	All Hallows' Eve • St. Wolfgang • ♆ STAT. • Tides 9.5 / 10.8	*side.*

Farmer's Calendar

■ Nobody knows for sure what accounts for the cycle in the lives of oak trees in which they make a huge crop of acorns every four or five years after several years of far lower production. Some botanists say the superabundant years are due to ideal weather conditions when the trees are in flower. Some think the wide swings in acorn production are adapted to foil insect parasites.

In a big year (a "mast" year, so-called), the woods seem to be flooded with acorns. They're treacherous underfoot; going down a woods road in an acorn super-year is like walking on marbles. An acre of oak woods in a normal year may produce a quarter-million acorns. In a mast year that crop might be doubled or trebled.

Whatever causes it, the extraordinary production of acorns is good news in the forest. Acorns are the bread of the woods. Deer, bear, squirrels, wild turkeys, partridge thrive in mast years. If you take to the woods in the spring following a bountiful acorn year, you'll be hard pressed to find a handful. That tidal wave of acorns has been consumed on the spot, or it has been cached by squirrels in safe places—some of them so safe that the provident squirrels themselves have overlooked them. Those acorns are the ones that will grow the oaks that will make the acorns that will turn the ankles of our grandchildren.

SKY WATCH ☆ *Mercury has its year's-best morning showing during the first 24 days of the month. It's bright in the predawn east, but it can't approach the dazzle of higher-up Venus. The crescent Moon has a close encounter with Venus on the 5th, then floats below Mercury on the 8th, 40 minutes before sunrise. With its orbit temporarily more oval than usual, the Moon is at its farthest distance of the year—about 252,705 miles—on the 9th. A week later, Saturn makes a comeback and rises by 1:00 A.M. The big story is Mars, now brightening rapidly in Gemini and rising by 8:30 P.M at midmonth. The evening sky finds Jupiter sinking; it's conspicuous early in the month but very low by Thanksgiving.*

☾	**Last Quarter**	1st day	17th hour	18th minute
●	**New Moon**	9th day	18th hour	3rd minute
☽	**First Quarter**	17th day	17th hour	33rd minute
○	**Full Moon**	24th day	9th hour	30th minute

To use this page, see p. 102; for Key Letters, see p. 237; for Tide Tables, see p. 234.
After 2:00 A.M. on November 4, Eastern Standard Time is given. ☞ **Bold = P.M.** ☞ Light = A.M.

Day of Year	Day of Month	Day of Week	☼ Rises h. m.	Key	☼ Sets h. m.	Key	Length of Day h. m.	Sun Fast m.	Declination of Sun ° '	High Tide Times Boston	☽ Rises h. m.	Key	☽ Sets h. m.	Key	☽ Place	Age
305	1	Th.	7:17	D	5:38	B	10 21	32	14s.27	4¾ 5	11:51	B	2:03	E	CAN	21
306	2	Fr.	7:19	D	5:37	B	10 18	32	14 46	6 6¼	—	–	2:30	E	CAN	22
307	3	Sa.	7:20	D	5:36	B	10 16	32	15 05	7 7¼	1:00	B	2:53	D	LEO	23
308	4	**G**	6:21	D	4:34	B	10 13	32	15 24	7 7¼	1:05	C	2:13	D	LEO	24
309	5	M.	6:22	D	4:33	B	10 11	32	15 43	7¾ 8¼	2:08	D	2:31	C	LEO	25
310	6	Tu.	6:24	D	4:32	B	10 08	32	16 01	8½ 9	3:10	D	2:49	C	VIR	26
311	7	W.	6:25	D	4:31	B	10 06	32	16 19	9¼ 9¾	4:12	E	3:08	B	VIR	27
312	8	Th.	6:26	D	4:30	A	10 04	32	16 36	10 10½	5:14	E	3:30	B	VIR	28
313	9	Fr.	6:27	D	4:29	A	10 02	32	16 53	10½ 11	6:18	E	3:55	A	LIB	0
314	10	Sa.	6:29	D	4:28	A	9 59	32	17 10	11 11¾	7:21	E	4:26	A	LIB	1
315	11	**G**	6:30	D	4:27	A	9 57	32	17 27	11¾ —	8:24	E	5:03	A	SCO	2
316	12	M.	6:31	D	4:26	A	9 55	32	17 43	12¼ 12¼	9:23	E	5:49	A	OPH	3
317	13	Tu.	6:33	D	4:25	A	9 52	31	17 59	1 1	10:16	E	6:44	A	SAG	4
318	14	W.	6:34	D	4:24	A	9 50	31	18 15	1¾ 1¾	11:01	E	7:46	A	SAG	5
319	15	Th.	6:35	D	4:23	A	9 48	31	18 31	2½ 2½	11:39	E	8:52	B	SAG	6
320	16	Fr.	6:36	D	4:22	A	9 46	31	18 46	3¼ 3¼	12:10	E	10:02	B	CAP	7
321	17	Sa.	6:37	D	4:21	A	9 44	31	19 01	4 4¼	12:36	D	11:12	B	CAP	8
322	18	**G**	6:39	D	4:20	A	9 41	31	19 15	5 5¼	1:00	D	—	–	AQU	9
323	19	M.	6:40	D	4:19	A	9 39	30	19 29	5¾ 6¼	1:22	D	12:24	C	AQU	10
324	20	Tu.	6:41	D	4:19	A	9 38	30	19 43	6¾ 7¼	1:45	C	1:37	D	PSC	11
325	21	W.	6:42	D	4:18	A	9 36	30	19 56	7½ 8	2:09	B	2:53	E	PSC	12
326	22	Th.	6:44	D	4:17	A	9 33	30	20 09	8½ 9	2:37	B	4:13	E	PSC	13
327	23	Fr.	6:45	D	4:17	A	9 32	29	20 22	9¼ 10	3:13	A	5:36	E	ARI	14
328	24	Sa.	6:46	D	4:16	A	9 30	29	20 34	10¼ 10¾	3:58	A	7:00	E	TAU	15
329	25	**G**	6:47	D	4:16	A	9 29	29	20 46	11 11¾	4:55	A	8:19	E	TAU	16
330	26	M.	6:48	D	4:15	A	9 27	29	20 58	12 —	6:04	A	9:27	E	AUR	17
331	27	Tu.	6:49	E	4:14	A	9 25	28	21 09	12¾ 12¾	7:19	B	10:20	E	GEM	18
332	28	W.	6:50	E	4:14	A	9 24	28	21 19	1½ 1¾	8:35	B	11:00	E	CAN	19
333	29	Th.	6:52	E	4:14	A	9 22	28	21 30	2½ 2¾	9:47	C	11:31	E	CAN	20
334	30	Fr.	6:53	E	4:13	A	9 20	27	21s.39	3½ 3¾	10:55	C	11:56	D	LEO	21

NOVEMBER HATH 30 DAYS • 2007

The woodland foliage now
Is gathered by the wild November blast. –J. Howard Bryant

Day of Month	Day of Week	Dates, Feasts, Fasts, Aspects, Tide Heights	Weather
1	Th.	All Saints' • ☿ STAT. • Architect James Renwick Jr. born, 1818 • {9.2 / 10.2}	*Bright*
2	Fr.	All Souls' • Storm blocked Ben Franklin's view of a lunar eclipse, 1743 • Tides {8.9 / 9.7}	*and*
3	Sa.	Sadie Hawkins Day • ☾ AT ☋ • ☌♄☾ • Tides {8.9 / 9.4}	*still:*
4	G	**23rd S. af. P.** • **U.S. Daylight Saving time ends, 2:00 A.M.**	*Raindrops*
5	M.	☾ ON EQ. • ☌♀☾ • Pres. FDR won third term in office, 1940 • Tides {9.3 / 9.2}	*fill*
6	Tu.	**Election Day** • Canada's second national Thanksgiving Day after confederation, 1879	*the*
7	W.	*In the decay of the Moon, a cloudy morning bodes a fair afternoon.* • Tides {9.7 / 9.2}	*lakes,*
8	Th.	☌☿☾ • ☿ GR. ELONG. (19° WEST) • William Frost's electric insect destroyer patented, 1910	*then*
9	Fr.	**New ●** • ☾ AT APO. • Great fire in Boston raged for two days, 1872 • {10.0 / 9.1}	*turn*
10	Sa.	*Sesame Street* debuted on television, 1969 • Tides {10.0 / 8.9}	*to*
11	G	**24th S. af. P.** • **Veteran's Day** • Tides {10.0 / —}	*flakes.*
12	M.	Indian Summer • ☌♃☾ • Lobsters move to offshore waters. • {8.8 / 9.9}	*Streams*
13	T.	☾ RUNS LOW • Newfoundland co-proprietorship granted to David Kirke, 1637 • {8.6 / 9.8}	*are*
14	W.	Melville's *Moby Dick* first published in U.S., 1851 • Actress Veronica Lake born, 1919 • {8.5 / 9.7}	*hardly*
15	Th.	♂ STAT. • *When the Sun is highest, it casts the least shadow.* • Tides {8.3 / 9.5}	*flowing,*
16	Fr.	6" snow, Tucson, Ariz., 1958 • Crab apples are ripe now. • {8.3 / 9.4}	*their*
17	Sa.	St. Hugh of Lincoln • ☌♆☾ • Athlete Bob Mathias born, 1930	*pulses*
18	G	**25th S. af. P.** • ☾ AT ☊ • Tides {8.7 / 9.4}	*slowing;*
19	M.	☾ ON EQ. • ☌⛢☾ • Lincoln's Gettysburg Address, 1863 • {9.2 / 9.5}	*Again,*
20	Tu.	City of Moose Jaw, Sask., incorporated, 1903 • {9.9 / 9.7}	*it's*
21	W.	Mayflower Compact signed by Pilgrim settlers, 1620 • Skunks hibernate now.	*snowing.*
22	Th.	**Thanksgiving** • *The company makes the feast.* • {11.2 / 10.2}	*But*
23	Fr.	St. Clement • ☾ AT PERIG. • Comedian Harpo Marx born, 1888 • {11.7 / 10.4}	*just*
24	Sa.	**Full Beaver ○** • ⛢ STAT. • Tides {12.1 / 10.4}	*before*
25	G	**26th S. af. P.** • 160 mph winds, Mt. Washington, N.H., 1950 • {12.2 / 10.3}	*all*
26	M.	☾ RIDES HIGH • Stan Berenstain, "Berenstain Bears" co-creator, died, 2005 • {12.1 / —}	*freezes*
27	Tu.	☌♂☾ • Basketball's Wilt Chamberlain hit 18 field goals in a row, 1963 • Tides {10.1 / 11.7}	*up,*
28	W.	First recorded U.S. auto race, Ill., 1895 • Storm on Lake Superior caused 20- to 40-foot-high waves, 1960	*it*
29	Th.	*Forsaken by the wind, you must use your oars.* • {9.5 / 10.6}	*eases*
30	Fr.	St. Andrew • ☾ AT ☋ • Lucille Ball married Desi Arnaz, 1940 • {9.3 / 10.0}	*up.*

Celebration is a communal experience of joy. –Jean Vanier

Farmer's Calendar

■ It was only a few years ago that up-to-date Enhanced 911 wireless telephone service for emergency response arrived in this neighborhood. Formerly, emergency calls went to a local dispatch center that summoned responders who, you hoped, knew where you were and how to get there. The new service is more efficient. It relies not only on responders knowing their beat, but also on precise, minutely detailed maps locating every dwelling in town.

Those maps revealed the unappreciated magnitude and complexity of the local road system—unappreciated by me, anyhow. I was surprised to learn what a wealth of ways we have for such a small place. We have high roads, low roads, back roads, way-back roads, highways, byways, lanes. Until the advent of E911 service, many of our roads had been nameless and unknown to all but those who lived on them.

Giving names is a mysterious and powerful act. Almost, to name a thing is to call it into being. Certainly in this town there seem to be an awful lot more roads than there used to be. Upper Eager Road, Sears Road—who knew of them before E911? Like Adam in the Garden of Eden, we set out to assign names to our surroundings. And like Adam we got a little more than we bargained for.

DECEMBER

THE TWELFTH MONTH • 2007

SKY WATCH ☆ *The Geminid meteors will be best after the Moon sets on the evening of December 13. Venus loses some of its height and dazzle in the predawn sky but remains prominent. The headliner is Mars, retrograding in Gemini, arriving at its closest and brightest of the year on the 18th and at opposition on the 24th. Mars is exceptionally high up at midnight, not far from the zenith. The year's 13th full Moon rises on the 23rd at sunset, right next to Mars, making a striking sight. Winter begins with the solstice on the 22nd, at 1:08 A.M., although the year's earliest sunset occurs two weeks earlier.*

☾	**Last Quarter**	1st day	7th hour	44th minute
●	**New Moon**	9th day	12th hour	40th minute
☽	**First Quarter**	17th day	5th hour	18th minute
○	**Full Moon**	23rd day	20th hour	16th minute
☾	**Last Quarter**	31st day	2nd hour	51st minute

To use this page, see p. 102; for Key Letters, see p. 237; for Tide Tables, see p. 234.
All times are given in Eastern Standard Time. ☞ **Bold = P.M.** ☞ Light = A.M.

Day of Year	Day of Month	Day of Week	☼ Rises h. m.	Key	☼ Sets h. m.	Key	Length of Day h.	Length of Day m.	Sun Fast m.	Declination of Sun °	Declination of Sun ′	High Tide Times Boston	High Tide Times Boston	☽ Rises h. m.	Key	☽ Sets h. m.	Key	☽ Place	☽ Age
335	1	Sa.	6:54	E	**4:13**	A	9	19	27	21s.	49	4½	**4¾**	12:00	C	**12:17**	D	LEO	22
336	2	**G**	6:55	E	**4:13**	A	9	18	27	21	58	5¼	**5¾**	—	–	**12:36**	C	LEO	23
337	3	M.	6:56	E	**4:12**	A	9	16	26	22	07	6¼	**6¾**	1:03	D	**12:54**	C	VIR	24
338	4	Tu.	6:57	E	**4:12**	A	9	15	26	22	15	7¼	**7½**	2:04	E	**1:13**	B	VIR	25
339	5	W.	6:58	E	**4:12**	A	9	14	25	22	23	8	**8½**	3:06	E	**1:34**	B	VIR	26
340	6	Th.	6:59	E	**4:12**	A	9	13	25	22	30	8¾	**9¼**	4:09	E	**1:58**	B	VIR	27
341	7	Fr.	7:00	E	**4:12**	A	9	12	25	22	37	9¼	**10**	5:13	E	**2:27**	A	LIB	28
342	8	Sa.	7:01	E	**4:12**	A	9	11	24	22	43	10	**10¾**	6:16	E	**3:02**	A	SCO	29
343	9	**G**	7:02	E	**4:12**	A	9	10	24	22	49	10¾	**11¼**	7:17	E	**3:46**	A	SCO	0
344	10	M.	7:03	E	**4:12**	A	9	09	23	22	55	11¼	12	8:12	E	**4:39**	A	OPH	1
345	11	Tu.	7:03	E	**4:12**	A	9	09	23	23	01	**12**	—	9:00	E	**5:39**	A	SAG	2
346	12	W.	7:04	E	**4:12**	A	9	08	22	23	05	12¾	**12¾**	9:40	E	**6:45**	B	SAG	3
347	13	Th.	7:05	E	**4:12**	A	9	07	22	23	09	1¼	**1¼**	10:12	E	**7:54**	B	CAP	4
348	14	Fr.	7:06	E	**4:12**	A	9	06	21	23	13	2	**2**	10:40	D	**9:03**	C	CAP	5
349	15	Sa.	7:07	E	**4:13**	A	9	06	21	23	16	2¾	**2¾**	11:04	D	**10:13**	C	AQU	6
350	16	**G**	7:07	E	**4:13**	A	9	06	20	23	19	3½	**3¾**	11:25	D	**11:23**	C	AQU	7
351	17	M.	7:08	E	**4:13**	A	9	05	20	23	21	4½	**4¾**	11:47	C	—	–	PSC	8
352	18	Tu.	7:09	E	**4:13**	A	9	04	19	23	23	5¼	**5¾**	**12:09**	C	12:35	D	PSC	9
353	19	W.	7:10	E	**4:14**	A	9	04	19	23	25	6¼	**6¾**	**12:35**	B	1:50	E	PSC	10
354	20	Th.	7:10	E	**4:14**	A	9	04	18	23	26	7	**7¾**	**1:05**	B	3:08	E	ARI	11
355	21	Fr.	7:11	E	**4:15**	A	9	04	18	23	26	8	**8¾**	**1:44**	A	4:30	E	ARI	12
356	22	Sa.	7:11	E	**4:15**	A	9	04	17	23	26	9	**9¾**	**2:35**	A	5:50	E	TAU	13
357	23	**G**	7:11	E	**4:16**	A	9	05	17	23	26	10	**10½**	**3:38**	A	7:04	E	TAU	14
358	24	M.	7:11	E	**4:16**	A	9	05	16	23	25	10¾	**11½**	**4:51**	A	8:04	E	AUR	15
359	25	Tu.	7:12	E	**4:17**	A	9	05	16	23	24	11¾	—	**6:09**	B	8:52	E	GEM	16
360	26	W.	7:12	E	**4:18**	A	9	06	15	23	22	12½	**12½**	**7:25**	B	9:28	E	CAN	17
361	27	Th.	7:12	E	**4:18**	A	9	06	15	23	20	1¼	**1½**	**8:37**	C	9:56	D	LEO	18
362	28	Fr.	7:13	E	**4:19**	A	9	06	14	23	17	2	**2¼**	**9:46**	D	10:19	D	LEO	19
363	29	Sa.	7:13	E	**4:20**	A	9	07	14	23	13	3	**3**	**10:50**	D	10:39	D	LEO	20
364	30	**G**	7:14	E	**4:21**	A	9	07	13	23	09	3¾	**4**	**11:54**	D	10:58	C	VIR	21
365	31	M.	7:14	E	**4:21**	A	9	07	13	23s.	05	4½	**5**	—	–	11:17	B	VIR	22

 Get local rise, set, and tide times at Almanac.com/astronomy.

DECEMBER HATH 31 DAYS • 2007

Good-by, kind year, we walk no more together,
But here in quiet happiness we part. –Sarah Doudney

Day of Month	Day of Week	Dates, Feasts, Fasts, Aspects, Tide Heights	Weather
1	Sa.	☌♄☾ • Temperature rose 80 degrees in one day, Kipp, Mont., 1896 • Tides { 9.1 9.4	*Mercy,*
2	G	**1st S. of Advent** • ☾ ON EQ. • Tides { 9.0 9.0	*it's*
3	M.	First public performance of G. Gershwin's "Concerto in F," Carnegie Hall, N.Y.C., 1925 • { 9.1 8.7	*mild,*
4	Tu.	*One eyewitness is better than two hear-so's.* • { 9.2 8.5	*but*
5	W.	**First day of Chanukah** • ☌♀☾ • Tides { 9.3 8.5	*turning*
6	Th.	**St. Nicholas** • ☾ AT APO. • 362 killed in coal mine explosion, Monongah, W. Va., 1907	*wild!*
7	Fr.	**St. Ambrose** • **National Pearl Harbor Remembrance Day** • Tides { 9.7 8.6	*On*
8	Sa.	American Bird Banding Association formed, first such society in U.S., 1909 • Tides { 9.8 8.6	*every*
9	G	**2nd S. of Advent** • **New ●** • Tides { 9.9 8.6	*rooftop*
10	M.	**St. Eulalia** • ☾ RUNS LOW • Winterberry fruits especially showy now. • { 10.0 8.6	*snow*
11	Tu.	Canada granted legislative independence from Britain, 1931	*is*
12	W.	Orange soil discovered on Moon by *Apollo 17* astronauts, 1972 • Beware the Pogonip. • { 8.6 10.0	*piled*
13	Th.	**St. Lucia** • *Lucy light, Lucy light Shortest day and longest night.* • { 8.6 10.0	*like*
14	Fr.	Halcyon Days • ☌♆☾ • Tilt-a-Whirl trademark registered, 1926	*wedding*
15	Sa.	☾ AT ☊ • Sioux chief Sitting Bull killed, 1890 • { 8.8 9.7	*cake!*
16	G	**3rd S. of Advent** • ☌♅☾ • Tides { 9.1 9.5	*Sunny*
17	M.	☾ ON EQ. • ☿ IN SUP. ☌ • Airport renamed for Bob Hope, Burbank, Calif., 2003	*break*
18	Tu.	♂ CLOSEST APPROACH • 13th Amendment, prohibiting slavery, went into effect, 1865 • { 9.8 9.3	*to*
19	W.	Ember Day • Fictional Robinson Crusoe left island after 28 years, 1686 • { 10.2 9.3	*hit*
20	Th.	☌♇☉ • ♄ STAT. • *Tomorrow never comes.* • { 10.7 9.4	*the*
21	Fr.	**St. Thomas** • Ember Day • Actress Jane Fonda born, 1937 • { 11.1 9.5	*malls,*
22	Sa.	Ember Day • **Winter Solstice** • ☾ AT PERIG. • Tides { 11.5 9.7	*roast*
23	G	**Full Cold ○** • ☾ RIDES HIGH • ☌♂☾ • ☌♃☉ • { 11.8 9.9	*the*
24	M.	♂ AT ☍ • Fire at Library of Congress destroyed 35,000 volumes, 1851	*chestnuts,*
25	Tu.	**Christmas Day** • –57°F, Fort Smith, N.W.T., 1917	*deck*
26	W.	**St. Stephen** • **Boxing Day (Canada)** • **First day of Kwanzaa** • Tides { 9.9 11.5	*the*
27	Th.	**St. John** • ☾ AT ☋ • Carry Nation smashed Hotel Carey bar, Wichita, Kans., 1900	*halls!*
28	Fr.	**Holy Innocents** • ☌♄☾ • Tides { 9.6 10.4	*Cryogenic*
29	Sa.	☾ ON EQ. • *A cake eaten in peace is worth two in trouble.* • Tides { 9.4 9.8	*cold*
30	G	**1st S. af. Ch.** • Golfer Tiger Woods born, 1975	*abates*
31	M.	**St. Sylvester** • C. B. Darrow received patent for *Monopoly* game, 1935 • { 9.0 8.6	*in '08!*

Farmer's Calendar

■ For as long as there have been weather prognosticators, apparently, there have been those who loved to mock them. Benjamin Franklin was known to poke fun at weather prediction—a business he himself was very much in. Writing in 1737 in *Poor Richard's Almanack,* Franklin gave an ironic defense of his forecasts. The promised weather would turn up, he assured readers; it was merely a matter of *when.* "We modestly desire only the favorable allowance of a day or two before and a day or two after the precise day" whose weather Poor Richard was predicting, wrote Ben. And "if it does not come to pass accordingly, let the fault be laid upon the printer."

Our attitude toward weather prediction and those who practice it is complex. On the one hand, we follow the forecasters closely and rely on them implicitly. On the other hand, we feel a perverse little satisfaction on the rare occasions when they're wrong. We almost seem to want the forecaster to fail. Why?

Perhaps we're ambivalent about the forecasts just because they're so good. We want there to be a realm of our experience that has a power, a mystery beyond our control and understanding. To the extent that scientific forecasting makes that mystery less in the case of the weather, we may accept it, but we won't entirely like it.

Glossary of Almanac Oddities

■ Many readers have expressed puzzlement over the rather obscure notations that appear on our **Right-Hand Calendar Pages, 107–133.** These "oddities" have long been fixtures in the Almanac, and we are pleased to provide some definitions. (Once explained, they may not seem so odd after all!)

–Beth Krommes

Ember Days: The Almanac traditionally marks the four periods formerly observed by the Roman Catholic and Anglican churches for prayer, fasting, and the ordination of clergy. These Ember Days are the Wednesdays, Fridays, and Saturdays that follow in succession after (1) the First Sunday in Lent; (2) Whitsunday–Pentecost; (3) the Feast of the Holy Cross, September 14; and (4) the Feast of St. Lucia, December 13. The word *ember* is perhaps a corruption of the Latin *quatuor tempora,* "four times."

Folklore has it that the weather on each of the three days foretells the weather for the next three months; that is, for September's Ember Days, Wednesday forecasts the weather for October, Friday for November, and Saturday for December.

Distaff Day (January 7): This was the first day after Epiphany, when women were expected to return to their spinning following the Christmas holiday. (Plough Monday was the day the men returned to work; every few years, Distaff Day and Plough Monday fall on the same day.) A distaff is the staff for holding the flax or wool in spinning, and it symbolized the domestic sphere. "The distaff side" indicated the women. One proverb notes that "Yule is come and Yule is gone, and we have feasted well; so Jack must to his flail again and Jenny to her wheel."

Plough Monday (January): Traditionally, the first Monday after Epiphany was called Plough Monday because it was the day that men returned to their plough, or daily work, following the Christmas holiday. It was customary for farm laborers to draw a plough through the village, soliciting money for a "plough-light," which was kept burning in the parish church all year. In some areas, the custom of blessing the plough is still observed today.

Three Chilly Saints (May): Mamertus, Pancras, and Gervais were three early Christian saints. Because their feast days, on May 11, 12, and 13, respectively, are traditionally cold, they have come to be known as the Three Chilly Saints. An old French saying translates to: "St. Mamertus, St. Pancras, and St. Gervais do not pass without a frost."

Midsummer Day (June 24): Although it occurs near the summer solstice, to the farmer this day is the midpoint of the growing season, halfway between planting and harvest and an occasion for festivity. The English church considered it a "Quarter Day," one of the four major divisions of the liturgical year. It also marks the feast day of St. John the Baptist.

Cornscateous Air (July): First used by early almanac makers, this term signifies

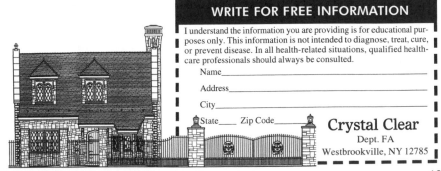

warm, damp air. Though it signals ideal climatic conditions for growing corn, it also poses a danger to those affected by asthma, pneumonia, and other respiratory problems.

Dog Days (July 3–August 11): These are the hottest and most unhealthy days of the year. Also known as Canicular Days, their name derives from the Dog Star, Sirius. The traditional period of Dog Days is the 40 days beginning July 3 and ending August 11, coinciding with the heliacal (at sunrise) rising of Sirius.

Lammas Day (August 1): Derived from the Old English *hlaf maesse,* meaning "loaf mass," Lammas Day marked the beginning of the harvest. Traditionally, loaves of bread were baked from the first-ripened grain and brought to the churches to be consecrated. Eventually, "loaf mass" became "Lammas." In Scotland, Lammastide fairs became famous as the time when trial marriages could be made. These marriages could end after a year with no strings attached.

Cat Nights Begin (August 17): This term harks back to the days when people believed in witches. An old Irish legend says that a witch could turn into a cat and regain herself eight times, but on the ninth time, August 17, she couldn't change back, hence the saying: "A cat has nine lives." Because August is a "yowly" time for cats, this may have prompted the speculation about witches on the prowl in the first place.

Harvest Home (September): In Europe and Britain, the conclusion of the harvest each autumn was once marked by festivals of fun, feasting, and thanksgiving known as "Harvest Home." It was also a time to hold elections, pay workers, and collect rents. These festivals usually took place around the time of the autumnal equinox. Certain groups in this country, particularly the Pennsylvania Dutch, have kept the tradition alive.

St. Luke's Little Summer (October): A spell of warm weather that occurs about the time of the saint's feast day, October 18, this period is sometimes referred to as Indian summer.

Indian Summer (November): A period of warm weather following a cold spell or a hard frost, Indian summer can occur between St. Martin's Day (November 11) and November 20. Although there are differing dates for its occurrence, for more than 200 years the Almanac has adhered to the saying "If All Saints' brings out winter, St. Martin's brings out Indian summer." As for the origin of the term, some say that it comes from the early Native Americans, who believed that the condition was caused by a warm wind sent from the court of their southwestern god, Cautantowwit.

Halcyon Days (December): About 14 days of calm weather follow the blustery winds of autumn's end. The ancient Greeks and Romans believed them to occur around the time of the winter solstice, when the halcyon, or kingfisher, was brooding. In a nest floating on the sea, the bird was said to have charmed the wind and waves so that the waters were especially calm during this period.

Beware the Pogonip (December): The word *pogonip* is a meteorological term used to describe an uncommon occurrence—frozen fog. The word was coined by Native Americans to describe the frozen fogs of fine ice needles that occur in the mountain valleys of the western United States and Canada. According to their tradition, breathing the fog is injurious to the lungs. □□

Holidays and Observances

For Movable Religious Observances, see page 105.

Jan. 17	Benjamin Franklin's Birthday
Jan. 19	Robert E. Lee Day *(Ark., Fla., Ky., La., S.C.)*
Feb. 2	Groundhog Day
Feb. 12	Abraham Lincoln's Birthday
Feb. 14	Valentine's Day
Feb. 15	Susan B. Anthony's Birthday *(Fla., Wis.)*
Feb. 20	Mardi Gras *(Baldwin & Mobile counties, Ala.; La.)*
Mar. 2	Texas Independence Day
Mar. 6	Town Meeting Day *(Vt.)*
Mar. 15	Andrew Jackson Day *(Tenn.)*
Mar. 17	St. Patrick's Day Evacuation Day *(Suffolk Co., Mass.)*
Mar. 26	Seward's Day *(Alaska)*
Apr. 2	Pascua Florida Day
Apr. 16	Patriots Day *(Maine, Mass.)*
Apr. 21	San Jacinto Day *(Tex.)*
Apr. 22	Earth Day
Apr. 27	National Arbor Day
May 1	May Day
May 5	Cinco de Mayo
May 8	Truman Day *(Mo.)*
May 13	Mother's Day
May 19	Armed Forces Day
May 21	Victoria Day *(Canada)*
May 22	National Maritime Day
June 5	World Environment Day
June 11	King Kamehameha I Day *(Hawaii)*
June 14	Flag Day
June 17	Father's Day Bunker Hill Day *(Suffolk Co., Mass.)*

June 19	Emancipation Day *(Tex.)*
June 20	West Virginia Day
July 1	Canada Day
July 24	Pioneer Day *(Utah)*
Aug. 6	Colorado Day Civic Holiday *(Canada)*
Aug. 16	Bennington Battle Day *(Vt.)*
Aug. 19	National Aviation Day
Aug. 26	Women's Equality Day
Sept. 9	Grandparents Day Admission Day *(Calif.)*
Sept. 17	Citizenship Day
Oct. 1	Child Health Day
Oct. 8	Native Americans Day *(S.Dak.)* Thanksgiving Day *(Canada)*
Oct. 9	Leif Eriksson Day
Oct. 18	Alaska Day
Oct. 24	United Nations Day
Oct. 26	Nevada Day
Oct. 31	Halloween
Nov. 4	Will Rogers Day *(Okla.)*
Nov. 6	Election Day
Nov. 11	Remembrance Day *(Canada)*
Nov. 19	Discovery Day *(Puerto Rico)*
Nov. 23	Acadian Day *(La.)*
Nov. 25	John F. Kennedy Day *(Mass.)*
Dec. 7	National Pearl Harbor Remembrance Day
Dec. 15	Bill of Rights Day
Dec. 17	Wright Brothers Day
Dec. 26	Boxing Day *(Canada)* First day of Kwanzaa

Federal Holidays

Jan. 1	New Year's Day
Jan. 15	Martin Luther King Jr.'s Birthday *(observed)*
Feb. 19	George Washington's Birthday *(observed)*
May 28	Memorial Day *(observed)*

July 4	Independence Day
Sept. 3	Labor Day
Oct. 8	Columbus Day *(observed)*
Nov. 12	Veterans Day *(observed)*
Nov. 22	Thanksgiving Day
Dec. 25	Christmas Day

2006

January 2006

S	M	T	W	T	F	S
						1
2?						

S	M	T	W	T	F	S
1	2	3	4	5	6	7
8	9	10	11	12	13	14
15	16	17	18	19	20	21
22	23	24	25	26	27	28
29	30	31				

February 2006

S	M	T	W	T	F	S
			1	2	3	4
5	6	7	8	9	10	11
12	13	14	15	16	17	18
19	20	21	22	23		
26	27	28				

March 2006

S	M	T	W	T	F	S
			1	2	3	4
5	6	7	8	9	10	11
12	13	14	15	16	17	18
19	20	21	22	23	24	25
26	27	28	29	30	31	

April 2006

S	M	T	W	T	F	S
						1
2	3	4	5	6	7	8
9	10	11	12	13	14	15
16	17	18	19	20	21	22
23	24	25	26	27	28	29
30						

May 2006

S	M	T	W	T	F	S
	1	2	3	4	5	6
7	8	9	10	11	12	13
14	15	16	17	18	19	20
21	22	23	24	25	26	27
28	29	30	31			

June 2006

S	M	T	W	T	F	S
				1	2	3
4	5	6	7	8	9	10
11	12	13	14	15	16	17
18	19	20	21	22	23	24
25	26	27	28	29	30	

July 2006

S	M	T	W	T	F	S
						1
2	3	4	5	6	7	8
9	10	11	12	13	14	15
16	17	18	19	20	21	22
23	24	25	26	27	28	29
30	31					

August 2006

S	M	T	W	T	F	S
		1	2	3	4	5
6	7	8	9	10	11	12
13	14	15	16	17	18	19
20	21	22	23	24	25	26
27	28	29	30	31		

September 2006

S	M	T	W	T	F	S
					1	2
3	4	5	6	7	8	9
10	11	12	13	14	15	16
17	18	19	20	21	22	23
24	25	26	27	28	29	30

October 2006

S	M	T	W	T	F	S
1	2	3	4	5	6	7
8	9	10	11	12	13	14
15	16	17	18	19	20	21
22	23	24	25	26	27	28
29	30	31				

November 2006

S	M	T	W	T	F	S
			1	2	3	4
5	6	7	8	9	10	11
12	13	14	15	16	17	18
19	20	21	22	23	24	25
26	27	28	29	30		

December 2006

S	M	T	W	T	F	S
					1	2
3	4	5	6	7	8	9
10	11	12	13	14	15	16
17	18	19	20	21	22	23
24	25	26	27	28	29	30
31						

2007

January 2007

S	M	T	W	T	F	S
	1	2	3	4	5	6
7	8	9	10	11	12	13
14	15	16	17	18	19	20
21	22	23	24	25	26	27
28	29	30	31			

February 2007

S	M	T	W	T	F	S
				1	2	3
4	5	6	7	8	9	10
11	12	13	14	15	16	17
18	19	20	21	22	23	24
25	26	27	28			

March 2007

S	M	T	W	T	F	S
				1	2	3
4	5	6	7	8	9	10
11	12	13	14	15	16	17
18	19	20	21	22	23	24
25	26	27	28	29	30	31

April 2007

S	M	T	W	T	F	S
1	2	3	4	5	6	7
8	9	10	11	12	13	14
15	16	17	18	19	20	21
22	23	24	25	26	27	28
29	30					

May 2007

S	M	T	W	T	F	S
		1	2	3	4	5
6	7	8	9	10	11	12
13	14	15	16	17	18	19
20	21	22	23	24	25	26
27	28	29	30	31		

June 2007

S	M	T	W	T	F	S
					1	2
3	4	5	6	7	8	9
10	11	12	13	14	15	16
17	18	19	20	21	22	23
24	25	26	27	28	29	30

July 2007

S	M	T	W	T	F	S
1	2	3	4	5	6	7
8	9	10	11	12	13	14
15	16	17	18	19	20	21
22	23	24	25	26	27	28
29	30	31				

August 2007

S	M	T	W	T	F	S
			1	2	3	4
5	6	7	8	9	10	11
12	13	14	15	16	17	18
19	20	21	22	23	24	25
26	27	28	29	30	31	

September 2007

S	M	T	W	T	F	S
						1
2	3	4	5	6	7	8
9	10	11	12	13	14	15
16	17	18	19	20	21	22
23	24	25	26	27	28	29
30						

October 2007

S	M	T	W	T	F	S
	1	2	3	4	5	6
7	8	9	10	11	12	13
14	15	16	17	18	19	20
21	22	23	24	25	26	27
28	29	30	31			

November 2007

S	M	T	W	T	F	S
				1	2	3
4	5	6	7	8	9	10
11	12	13	14	15	16	17
18	19	20	21	22	23	24
25	26	27	28	29	30	

December 2007

S	M	T	W	T	F	S
						1
2	3	4	5	6	7	8
9	10	11	12	13	14	15
16	17	18	19	20	21	22
23	24	25	26	27	28	29
30	31					

2008

January 2008

S	M	T	W	T	F	S
		1	2	3	4	5
6	7	8	9	10	11	12
13	14	15	16	17	18	19
20	21	22	23	24	25	26
27	28	29	30	31		

February 2008

S	M	T	W	T	F	S
					1	2
3	4	5	6	7	8	9
10	11	12	13	14	15	16
17	18	19	20	21	22	23
24	25	26	27	28	29	

March 2008

S	M	T	W	T	F	S
						1
2	3	4	5	6	7	8
9	10	11	12	13	14	15
16	17	18	19	20	21	22
23	24	25	26	27	28	29
30	31					

April 2008

S	M	T	W	T	F	S
		1	2	3	4	5
6	7	8	9	10	11	12
13	14	15	16	17	18	19
20	21	22	23	24	25	26
27	28	29	30			

May 2008

S	M	T	W	T	F	S
				1	2	3
4	5	6	7	8	9	10
11	12	13	14	15	16	17
18	19	20	21	22	23	24
25	26	27	28	29	30	31

June 2008

S	M	T	W	T	F	S
1	2	3	4	5	6	7
8	9	10	11	12	13	14
15	16	17	18	19	20	21
22	23	24	25	26	27	28
29	30					

July 2008

S	M	T	W	T	F	S
		1	2	3	4	5
6	7	8	9	10	11	12
13	14	15	16	17	18	19
20	21	22	23	24	25	26
27	28	29	30	31		

August 2008

S	M	T	W	T	F	S
					1	2
3	4	5	6	7	8	9
10	11	12	13	14	15	16
17	18	19	20	21	22	23
24	25	26	27	28	29	30
31						

September 2008

S	M	T	W	T	F	S
	1	2	3	4	5	6
7	8	9	10	11	12	13
14	15	16	17	18	19	20
21	22	23	24	25	26	27
28	29	30				

October 2008

S	M	T	W	T	F	S
			1	2	3	4
5	6	7	8	9	10	11
12	13	14	15	16	17	18
19	20	21	22	23	24	25
26	27	28	29	30	31	

November 2008

S	M	T	W	T	F	S
						1
2	3	4	5	6	7	8
9	10	11	12	13	14	15
16	17	18	19	20	21	22
23	24	25	26	27	28	29
30						

December 2008

S	M	T	W	T	F	S
	1	2	3	4	5	6
7	8	9	10	11	12	13
14	15	16	17	18	19	20
21	22	23	24	25	26	27
28	29	30	31			

Love calendar lore? Find more at Almanac.com.

For centuries, jokers around the world have reveled in April Fools' Day as a prank-playing free-for-all. Exactly how this started isn't crystal clear, but many agree that the tradition seems to have arisen in 1582, when France switched to the Gregorian calendar and moved New Year's Day from March 25 back to January 1. Prior to this change, the new year's celebration had begun on March 25 and ended on April 1. Those who were unaware of the change were called April fools.

The jesting spread and is still going strong. In France, for instance, children secretly stick paper fishes on the backs of victims and then shout "Poisson d'Avril!" ("April Fish!"). Scots call the holiday "Huntigowk Day" and send

This is the day upon which we are reminded of what we are on the other three hundred and sixty-four.

–from Pudd'nhead Wilson's calendar in *The Tragedy of Pudd'nhead Wilson* by Mark Twain, American writer (1835–1910)

APRIL FOOLS' DAY
(Honest!)

people to "hunt the gowk another mile"—a wild goose chase. In other places far and wide, young and old dream up mischief April after April.

Why is this day of harmless fun so universally popular? Alex Boese, an author whose Web site (www.museumofhoaxes.com) chronicles such shenanigans, cites "the guilty pleasure of chuckling at other people's gullibility."

While most are content with putting salt in the sugar bowl or gluing a penny to the sidewalk, some jokers cook up elaborate schemes. Here are some famous examples.

BY ALICE CARY

–illustrated by Paul Meisel

A Swift End

- John Partridge, an English cobbler-turned-astrologer, began publishing predictions in almanacs in the late 1600s. By 1708, satirist Jonathan Swift (later famous for *Gulliver's Travels*) had grown so disgusted with Partridge's rantings that under a pseudonym he published a parody: *Predictions for the Ensuing Year,* by Isaac Bickerstaff. There, Swift predicted Partridge's death on March 29. A day or so after the supposed death, Swift wrote an elegy—signed by Bickerstaff—reporting that on his deathbed, Partridge had admitted to being a fraud. On April Fools' Day and for days afterward, Partridge had to explain to many that he was not dead.

CAVE OF TREASURES

■ In the mid-1800s, an April Fools' Day article in the *Boston Post* reported that workmen removing trees from the Boston Common had uncovered a hidden trapdoor leading to a cave filled with treasure. Treasure seekers flocked to the Common, but, alas, no door was found.

See the Spaghetti Grow

■ In 1957, the BBC aired a newsreel explaining how the mild winter had produced a higher-than-normal harvest for Swiss spaghetti farmers. Swiss women were shown plucking strands of pasta from trees, while a well-known broadcaster noted that the disappearance of the "spaghetti weevil" had also boosted growth. The broadcaster noted that years of careful cultivation had allowed the spaghetti to grow to a uniform length. Viewers were so intrigued that they called the BBC and asked where they might buy their own spaghetti bushes.

Gravity Gone Berserk

■ Well-known British astronomer Patrick Moore announced on BBC Radio 2 that at 9:47 A.M. on April 1, 1976, a special alignment of Pluto and Jupiter would counteract Earth's gravity for an instant and make people weigh less. He said that listeners who jumped in the air at that moment would experience a floating sensation. Callers immediately jammed phone lines to report that, indeed, they had felt the gravity change. One woman reported that she and her friends had actually floated above their chairs.

(continued)

Superstar Pitcher Discovered

■ On April 1, 1985, *Sports Illustrated* featured a story about a whiz pitcher named Sidd Finch capable of hurling a 168-mph fastball. Writer George Plimpton described how this Harvard University dropout had perfected his style by throwing rocks and meditating in Tibet. A *Sports Illustrated* photographer convinced his friend, Illinois middle school teacher Joe Berton, to pose as Sidd Finch for a photo shoot during the New York Mets' spring training. Berton donned a uniform and wound up on the mound. Finch had his own trademark style, so the lanky Berton fell into character and pitched with one bare foot and the other in a work boot. More than 20 years later, fans still occasionally recognize Berton and ask him to show his stuff. (One of the definitions of "finch," by the way, is "small lie.")

BIG APPLE BUST

In need of more April 1 fun? If you happen to be in New York City, don't miss the **APRIL FOOLS' DAY PARADE** down Fifth Avenue, a Big Apple tradition since 1986. Media hoaxer Joey Skaggs sends out press releases detailing each year's theme, and a bevy of camera crews and spectators arrive on the scene to secure a spot. Of course, there's no parade.

Blue Sky: Going, Going, . . .

▨ The sky is becoming less blue, warned a 2001 article in *The Mail on Sunday,* a British newspaper. According-ing to researchers from a university in Amsterdam, the "coefficient of blueness" had decreased from 9.3 percent in 1996 to 6.9 percent in 2001. Readers were asked to help investigate this phenomenon by mailing in their own observations using a special "Skyometer" printed in the newspaper.

Internet Spring Cleaning

■ A flurry of e-mails warned that the Internet would be out of service for cleaning for 24 hours between March 31 and April 2, 1997. Users were advised to disconnect all devices. This was an updated version of an old phone joke, in which customers were instructed to place bags over phone receivers to catch dust blown out during phone line cleaning. □□

THE JOKE'S ON . . . WHOM?

Have you played a great April Fools' prank? Tell us about it at **Almanac.com/extras**.

CLICK ON!

Visit **The Old Farmer's Almanac** online if you enjoy:

- watching the weather
- gardening
- fishing
- astronomy
- cooking
- historical facts
- chatting with other Almanac users

Come explore **Almanac.com** if you are planning a:

- wedding
- special vacation
- bike ride
- company outing
- family reunion
- camping trip

You'll find weather forecasts, the Sun and Moon rise and set times, tide information, and much, much more to make your event or trip successful!

JEEPERS, CREEPERS,

-Tom Brakefield/Superstock

Getting a Peek at a Peeper

Peepers can be found in southeastern parts of Canada and in areas east of the Mississippi River from New England to as far south as northern Florida. The northern peeper sings from March to June; the southern peeper, from November to March. Their brown to gray to olive-green colorings are similar, but the southern peeper has a prominent dark marking on its belly.

Peepers can modify their color to match their surroundings, making them difficult to see during the day. The best time to go looking for them is at night. Bring a flashlight; a peeper will sit still if it's captured in a beam of light. The

'S THE

PEEPERS

BY MARY MARVIN

And spring has arrived!

Some folks in the Northeast have learned to mark the end of winter when they hear the "doorbells of spring." These are nature's seasonal trumpeters—tiny male tree frogs whose swamp song warms the hearts of humans but is actually a suitor's serenade to the females of the species.

The tree frog known as the peeper was once classified in scientific circles as *Hyla crucifer; Hyla* designated its genus, and the species name *crucifer* came from the Latin word *crucis,* for the X, or cross, on its back. But herpetologists heard the collective cry and, recognizing that this is no common tree frog, renamed it *Pseudacris crucifer, pseudacris* being from the Greek words *pseudes* ("false") and *akris* ("locust").

Theirs is a constantly changing choir; a peeper's life span is about three years. As the weather warms, often after the first warm rain, tree frogs abandon the forest habitat where they have been hibernating under logs or stones and head for marshes and shallow pools. Before the male begins his solo, he stakes out

male, with its distended sac, is the easiest to spot. Look for him on twigs or branches, but don't try to sneak up on him. He will stop peeping if he senses footsteps approaching.

PEEP PREDICTIONS

If you hear peepers during the day, expect rain.

Expect a frost three times after you hear the peepers sing.

147

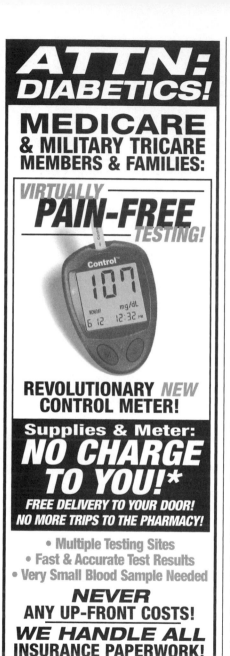
a territory separating him by about three feet from any others. To increase the projection of his peep, he perches on a blade of grass or a twig. (The peeper doesn't climb as high as other varieties of tree frog—it seldom ventures more than about three feet up into vegetation.)

He makes his shrill mating call by pushing air in and out of a balloonlike sac, or pouch, that stretches from his throat to his mouth; when the sac is fully inflated, it's as big as he is—only an inch to an inch and a half long when fully grown. He calls at dusk and after dark, about once every second. When a female hears a peep she likes, she joins the male that is making the sound and they head off to the water.

> **TADPOLE TRIVIA**
>
> To learn how a newborn tree frog develops, go to **Almanac.com/extras.**

As the female lays her eggs (700 to 1,000 of them), the male simultaneously fertilizes them. The female then attaches them to underwater vegetation, such as stems. The tadpoles emerge four to 14 days later.

When mating season is over, the adult frogs return to the woods; they have no parental responsibility for the tadpoles. The young ones are on their own against their natural predators—aquatic insects, turtles, fish, wading birds, and bullfrogs, which like to eat the tadpoles. Conditions such as water mold and drought are also threats. For each tadpole that survives to maturity, hundreds die—but those males that do survive are ready to join the chorus the following spring. ☐☐

Mary Marvin, a nature writer who lives in southwestern New York, has peepers in her backyard. One year, she heard the first peepers on March 14; contrary to lore, five frosts followed—three in March, one in April, and one in May.

How to IMPRESS *the* OPI

There is no surefire way to impress all men or all women all the time. However, we can suggest some ways to improve your chances.

RULE

1

Stop trying so hard.

The art of impressing someone is a hit-or-miss proposition at best. It's tough and wearisome work getting out of bed each day obsessed with thoughts of how you're going to look, smell, talk, or even walk. To complicate matters more, socially acceptable behaviors, fashion and style trends, and role models keep changing.

Experts say that you might as well throw caution and self-critical thinking to the wind. The odds are in favor of there being someone out there for you, so why bother with a painful and expensive masquerade?

Women may be inclined to spend time improving their appearance.

by Jeff Brein

–illustrated by Eldon Doty

OSITE SEX

Guys will do some
outlandish things:
bungee jump, prize
fight, sky dive.

RULE 2

Ignore Rule 1.

You can't help trying to impress people. You are genetically disposed to show off.

"Our efforts to impress others began with a basic biological urge to reproduce," says Todd Shackelford, associate professor of psychology at Florida Atlantic University.

"As we try to impress, we're actually manipulating by sending hidden signals to other people. We do our best to appear intelligent, kind, interested in what others are saying, and even funny. We just can't help it."

RULE 3

Do well what you do best.

Men and women both want to impress others—not just the opposite sex—with their unique talents, but there are some very basic differences in how they do it. Guys will do some outlandish things: bungee jump, prize fight, sky dive, mountain climb, or even get a full-body tattoo. Women, on the other hand, may be just as inclined to spend time improving their appearance, making a nice home, or nurturing others. (This isn't to say that a woman wouldn't jump off a bridge with a cord around her ankle or summit Mt. Everest, but the distaff side is less likely to take extreme physical risks.)

RULE 4

Make sure that you smell good.

Men have been using animal scents, or pheromones, to impress women for thousands of years. Primitive tribesmen in New Guinea covered themselves in cow dung, early settlers used musk oil, and Europeans doused themselves with peppermint oil, which had the added benefit of lowering fatigue and was presumably most helpful on blind dates.

(continued)

Not much has changed—in principle. Today, many men use cologne, aftershave, and even deodorants to impress themselves and others. People who think that they smell good—including women, who purchase 75 percent of all fragrances—have more confidence.

Sometimes, however, less is more. Napoleon reportedly told Josephine not to bathe for a week because he liked her natural scent.

Learn how to "talk" and translate body language. Maintain eye contact. Be poised.

RULE 5

Dress the part.

"Since the beginning of fashion history, we've tried to impress others by wearing either too much or too little," says Kevin Jones, curator of the Fashion Institute of Design and Merchandising Museum in Los Angeles. "The object is to stand out in a crowd, and if you're successful, you'll always make an impression."

Color is very important and can send different messages, depending on where you are.

"In Asia, red is a romantic or wedding color, while in the United States it's white," says Jones. "Black works for a formal date, just as well as for a funeral. The brighter the colors, the more confidence the wearer is likely to have, and this translates into someone who is more outgoing."

RULE 6

Stop blowing smoke and start sending signals.

Save your romantic French and Italian idioms for a dinner date and then use them on the menu. Learn how to "talk"—and translate—the anatomical lingua franca, body language.

Gloria Starr, a Charlotte, North Carolina, image consultant, suggests: "Establish and maintain eye contact."

And be poised. "Don't fidget. Keep your hands and feet still. When you wiggle, you send signals of agitation or disinterest. Rubbing your ear, for example, tells the other person that you don't trust them."

"Smile when appropriate and nod approvingly every so often. Whisper or speak softly. Shouts or loud conversations are threatening. And don't stand directly in front of someone, but instead position yourself slightly to the side.

"If you feel compelled to touch the person, do it lightly in the neutral zone—between the wrist and elbow. Anywhere else just may send the wrong message."

(continued)

RULE

Spend time, not (lots of) money.

People have always tried to impress each other with wealth and what it can buy. But often it's the little things that make the biggest impressions:

Men buy most of the millions of boxes of candy and bouquets of flowers that are sold each year, but women should not be afraid to reciprocate. In a poll conducted by the Society of American Florists, 60 percent of the men said that they liked to receive flowers, usually in vivid or loud colors such as yellow, orange, and red—but at their homes, not in their places of work, within sight of the other guys.

Ladies, your mother probably told you that the way to a man's heart is through his stomach. Still true. Men, take a hint: Women enjoy home-cooked meals, too.

Finally, keep in mind that simple good deeds are sometimes the most impressive, so write a poem, turn off the cell phone when you're together, or hand over the TV remote.

RULE

Be yourself.

When all is said and done, we are all unique people, with strengths, weaknesses, fantasies, faults, and foibles. So just be yourself. Enjoy life. People will notice—and be impressed.

Jeff Brein lives on a small island near Seattle, Washington, and feels compelled to impress only his wife, who is known to forgive him for how he smells, dresses, and eats. He does, however, bribe her with flowers and candy.

Quick Tips to Impress Someone Fast

Most experts say that "first impressions" are made within 30 seconds of meeting, so when time is of the essence, consider this advice:

IN PREPARATION . . .

- Ladies, avoid clothing with shoulder pads.
- Men, don't shave your legs.
- Both: Perfume only your body, not your clothes, and ignore all scientific studies that suggest human sweat is desirable.

UPON MEETING . . .

- Smile.
- Look the other person in the eye, but from a distance of at least 18 inches so as not to intrude into their personal space.
- Use the most effective pick-up line ever invented: "Hi."

TO BREAK THE ICE . . .

- Ladies, send a man a drink or ask him to dance.
- Men, compliment a woman on her hair or jewelry.

TO CREATE A BIT OF MYSTERY . . .

- Ladies, keep your age to yourself. (Some say that a woman who will tell her age will tell anything.)
- Men, it's OK to inflate your age.

TO LEAVE A LASTING IMPRESSION . . .

- Put your best foot forward: Walk in a straight line and avoid the "duck walk," in which your feet point outward.
- Speaking of feet, don't put them in your mouth: Never monopolize the conversation, talk too much about yourself, or exaggerate your accomplishments. Be impressed with your true self, and others will be, too.

□ □

Just Put Your Lips Together ...

Whistling in public has often been considered rude and uncouth. Finally, this traditional American pastime is getting the respect it deserves.

by Martie Majoros

People have been whistling ever since someone realized what would happen if air were blown through puckered lips. Many scientists believe that primitive man's early language was based on nonverbal sounds, including clicking, clucking, and ... whistling. In ancient times, shepherds whistled when they needed to communicate with each other across long distances. (Even today, young residents of La Gomera, one of Spain's Canary Islands, are required to learn Silbo, the nearly extinct whistled language of the island.) Seamen, too, whistled messages to each other, and in Henry Wadsworth Longfellow's "Christus: A Mystery," characters whistle "for a capful of wind to fill our sail," invoking a long-held superstition that whistling at sea will bring a good sailing wind.

In the late 19th century, whistling took center stage in vaudeville shows and musical reviews as performers incorporated birdcalls into their songs. So popular were these concerts that, in 1923, Agnes Woodward, director of the California School of Artistic Whistling, published an instructional book on the subject. In it, she offers general tips, such as how to produce short, quick staccato notes: "... keep the lips firm and tense and whistle very rapidly a plain, sharp sound on each note." She also describes bird-mimicking techniques, such as the Hewie chirp. "The Hewie chirp is one of the familiar figures used continuously by the [northern mockingbird]. It is ...

whistled exactly as it sounds ("*hew*-ie"), with a
very definite accent on the first note. Keep the
jaw and under lip still." Woodward
includes instructions for performing other bird-specific sounds,
including the reverse chirp,
the quiver, the trill, and
the whip.

Woodward claimed
that with the mastery
of such techniques,
"the intelligent and
capable instructor,"
as well as the "com-
petent and finished"
solo performer,
could make lucra-
tive livelihoods—
and many did. One,
then-well-known whistler Alice
Shaw, earned the equivalent of
$8,000 per week in today's dol-
lars for her whistling performances. Amateur enthusiasts
could benefit physically, if not fi-
nancially. According to Wood-

-courtesy Cal Fenwick

Cal Fenwick performs at the 2005 International Whistlers Convention.

The Whistler

One of the most successful radio programs of the 1940s and '50s was "The Whistler," an anthology of mystery tales. The narrator was a character called The Whistler, who opened each broadcast with the words, "I am the Whistler and I know many things." Dorothy Roberts provided the 13-note whistle, which became the show's trademark. In the 1940s, the concept evolved into a series of "unusually intelligent and affecting" movies based on the stories of Cornell Woolrich.

ward, whistling "strengthens, by the constant practice of deep breathing, the lungs, the throat, and the diaphragm."

Spurred on by the development of talking movies and radio, whistling—and whistlers—gained greater respect. In the 1927 film *The Jazz Singer,* Al Jolson whistles "Toot-Toot-Tootsie." In the 1930s, whistlers often appeared with big bands and, like the horn players and drummers, they took turns performing solo riffs.

Nevertheless, the skill has long had its detractors. The ancient Roman philosopher Cicero reportedly preferred listening to a nightingale to hearing a whistler imitate one. In the 1930s, New York University philosophy professor Dr. Charles Shaw (no relation to Alice Shaw) proclaimed that "no great or successful man ever whistles." He suggested that those who whistled were "inferior and maladjusted individuals." (Shaw's comments hit a collective nerve in the American public, and he received an onslaught of letters, including several from writers who refuted Shaw's assertion by claiming to have heard Thomas Edison and Albert Einstein whistle.) As recently as the mid–20th century, the pastime was regarded as unseemly, and many mothers discouraged their sons and daughters from whistling.

Fortunately, many whistlers would not be silenced. In the 1930s, a new generation was introduced to the art through Walt Disney's seven dwarfs, who became famous for whistling merrily while they worked. A decade later, whistler Fred Lowery earned a reputation for his melancholy rendition of "Indian Love Call." By the 1960s, the entertainment industry had relegated whistling to the category of background music. Ironically, some of those tunes became pop culture classics. For example, "The Fishin' Hole," written and performed by Earle Hagen for *The Andy Griffith Show,* is instantly recognizable—although perhaps not by name—by fans of that television program.

Phyllis Heil, of Hickory, North Carolina, recalls that as a child she was advised by her mother, "A

whistling woman and a cackling hen will never come to any good end." However, this did not stop Heil from enlisting her four older brothers to teach her how to whistle. They showed her how to position her lips by placing her little finger in her mouth and using it as a guide to form the letter "O." By the time she was a preteen, young Heil was whistling tunes that she heard on the radio and television and in church, and she continued to whistle throughout her early years.

Cal Fenwick, on the other hand, had the support of his parents but suffered the rebuke of his siblings. As a three-year-old growing up in rural Uphill, Ontario, Fenwick started "tooth whistling," which means using the tongue, roof of the mouth, and teeth, but not the lips. A few years later, he whistled in imitation of

Fred Lowery and Bing Crosby appear together during a *Kraft Music Hall* broadcast, 1945.

How Do You Get to Carnegie Hall?

Practice, practice, practice—every day, to keep your lip, tongue, and mouth muscles in shape and to become familiar with the music that you plan to perform. And . . .

- Use lip balm to keep your lips from drying out. Avoid waxy lip products; they tend to distort the tone.

- Stay hydrated. Water wards off "dry mouth" that may result from nervousness.

- Avoid eating or drinking dairy products right before whistling. Milk, cheese, and yogurt can upset the saliva-mucus balance in your mouth and throat and make whistling very difficult.

- Abstain from kissing (that is, for several hours prior to a performance). Some professional whistlers claim that it makes their lips "mushy," which makes them unable to maintain the proper amount of tension needed to reach the high notes.

"Taxi!"

Learn to hail a cab with this traffic-stopping whistle, and you'll never have to walk a city block again.

■ Open your mouth slightly. Keep your bottom lip taut as you pull it over the top edge of your lower teeth.

■ Keep your tongue flat, and lightly press it against the inside edge of your lower lip. Lift the sides of your tongue up a bit so that it forms a slight "V." Pull your tongue back from your lower teeth a bit so that there is a small hole between the tip of your tongue and inside edge of your lower lip. You will need to lift your tongue from the floor of your mouth about $\frac{1}{8}$ to $\frac{1}{16}$ of an inch. In this position, your tongue creates the "bottle," or cavity, that you will be blowing across.

■ Close your mouth slightly, keeping your lower lip tensed. Keep your upper lip out of the way.

■ Gently blow and direct air over the hole. Increase the tension of both lips and, if necessary, adjust the V shape of your tongue. Avoid blowing too hard at first, and listen for the slightest beginnings of a whistle. Once you hear that, continue to practice and adjust.

–adapted from *Mouth Sounds* by Fred Newman (Workman Publishing, 2004)

–courtesy Franklin County Arts Council

Before competitions, Emily Edwards practices her chosen performance pieces about four times a day.

the birds that he heard in his backyard—and they whistled back. Encouraged by that success, he began making up melodies for his own amusement. Fenwick's father says that although his son was whistling with notable skill and ability, his musical pastime often drove his brothers and sister crazy.

World-champion whistler Steve Herbst puckers up for a 2005 performance at New York City's Gramercy Theater.

If the International Whistlers Convention is any measure, the art and its practitioners may be more esteemed today than ever. The 2005 gathering, which was held in Louisburg, North Carolina, attracted 150 competitors and an audience of more than 1,000.

Those in attendance heard some remarkable performances. Emily Edwards, from Zebulon, North Carolina, who began whistling at the age of four with more of a chirp than a true whistle, took first place in the Children's category with renditions of the "Battle Hymn of the Republic" and "Edelweiss" at the tender age of 12. Phyllis Heil, now 57, proved her mother's adage wrong when she competed with 14 other women from places such as Canada, China, Germany, Holland, and Japan. Ultimately, her performances of Puccini's "O Mio Babbino Caro" and "When the Saints Go Marchin' In" earned her a trophy and some medals. She went on to be named the convention's 2005 Female Entertainer of the Year.

Cal Fenwick, who found a more appreciative audience in high school (the principal asked him to record a whistling version of the national anthem, which was played once a week during the morning announcements), walked away with second prize in the Teenage category. Today, he performs in churches, theaters, and opera halls in and around Ontario. Like most of those who whistle, he continues to win high praise from his peers. "My friends love it," says Fenwick. "They think it's amazing. If nothing else, it's a fun thing to do at a party."

Martie Majoros is the research editor at *The Old Farmer's Almanac*. She has written about prizewinning pets, unique career choices, and the marvelous zucchini.

WHISTLE STOPS
To link to Steve Herbst's Web site, plus learn more about ways to whistle, where to whistle, and whistling a happy tune, go to **Almanac.com/extras.**

Use It or Lose It

Practice these simple exercises to keep your lips and tongue in good whistling form:

■ Place your bottom lip up over your top lip. Hold that position for a few seconds. Now, reverse lip positions, putting your top lip over your bottom lip.

■ Point your tongue so that the tip protrudes slightly from your mouth. Return your tongue to its normal position, then relax your tongue so that the front of it rests gently against your inside lower lip. Alternate between pointing and spreading your tongue.

■ Open your mouth about halfway. Move the tip of your tongue back and forth, touching the left corner of your mouth and then the right. Repeat several times.

■ Stick your tongue out as far as it can go and try to touch the tip of your nose. Relax. Then try to touch the tip of your chin with your tongue. Relax, and repeat.

□ □

THE

There's a wonderful family called
    Stein—
There's Gert, and there's Epp, and
    there's Ein;
Gert's poems are bunk;
Epp's statues are junk;
And no one can understand Ein.

–Unknown

At a time when we seem to be surrounded by sameness, some parents want their children to stand out. This quest for individuality is fueling a radical evolution in baby names.

Whether 21st-century parents look to their favorite places (Brooklyn), hobbies (Gardener), or ideals (Justice) for inspiration, they are, ironically, like a school of fish swimming in sync. As they move subconsciously in the same direction, many of the "new" and different names they choose are gaining in popularity, cracking Top 1,000

–ThinkStock LLC/Index Stock

by Genevieve Rajewski

BROOKLYN · ZACHARY · JANIE · JUAN

GAME

lists faster than ever before and becoming—gasp!—common.

Like weather and fashion, naming trends tend to be cyclical. Here is a survey of the novelties in nomenclature today, with a few peeks into past traditions. Perhaps you'll find a clue about how you arrived at what you're called—or maybe you'll start thinking about changing the name you have.

WHEN  IS NEW

Strong towers decay, but a great name shall never pass away.

–Park Benjamin, American journalist (1809–64)

In search of fresh, new names, some of today's parents are searching through history for monikers, leading to a surge of interest in "antique" varieties.

"An 'antique' name goes back to at least your great-grandparents' generation," says Laura Wattenberg, author of *The Baby Name Wizard: A Magical Method for Finding the Perfect Name for Your Baby.* "It doesn't even feel 'old.' . . . It just feels unusual." Sophia, Sebastian, and Oliver are currently popular antique names.

(continued)

ISABELLA • JACOB • TYRESE • BRADEN

Similarly, ancestral surnames—especially those of maternal forebears—are making a comeback. "Parents are reviving a grandmother's maiden name that otherwise would be lost to time or are using the mother's maiden name," says Pamela Redmond Satran, who has written with coauthor Linda Rosenkrantz numerous name guides, including *The Baby Name Bible: The Know-All, Tell-All Guide to Choosing the Perfect Name.* Recycling the names of prior generations is not new. Euro-American folk traditions suggest that attaching a family name conveys magical strength and power. The hope is that the child will develop the admirable qualities of the name he bears. Laplanders set even higher expectations: They believe that the deceased ancestor will provide earthly assistance to the one who bears his name.

There is old, and then there is ancient. In the first Book of Samuel, penned in about 500 B.C., it is written: "As his name is, so is he." That philosophy has inspired some people to change their name and so confuse evil spirits.

The Old Testament has long been a wellspring of name ideas for parents of sons, with Joshua being one of the most often chosen for years—bested only by Jacob and Michael. More recently, Noah, Caleb, and Zachary have found favor. Biblical girls' names currently in vogue include Hannah and Abigail.

TO NICKNAMES

Nicknames stick to people, and the most ridiculous are the most adhesive.

–Thomas C. Haliburton, Canadian writer (1796–1865)

A few decades ago, almost everyone had two names: a formal, given name and an abbreviated version of that—a nickname. For example, Andrew was altered to Andy, Thomas turned into Tom or Tommy, and Margaret reemerged as Marge, Margo, or Peg. Even plain Jane blossomed into the more lyrical Janie.

Today, nicknames are for naught. "I don't know if parents want more control over the child's name than ever before or if it is just a move toward formality," says Wattenberg, "but many parents are looking for names that can not be shortened."

"Even parents who choose a name that has a traditional nickname aren't using it anymore," she continues. "Maybe it is because over the last several generations, names like Jim and Bill have grown to sound extremely ordinary, whereas James and William, because they were so seldom heard in their full form, have a more elegant cast to them."

Today, nicknames are for naught. Many parents are looking for names that can not be shortened.

A RETURN TO
ROOTS

Fate tried to conceal him by naming him Smith.

–Oliver Wendell Holmes Sr., American writer (1809–94)

The melting pot of multicultural influences has long dictated naming patterns in North America. "In the 1950s and '60s, immigrant families were looking to give their children names that were more assimilated, more American," says Satran. "If the Italian grandmother's name was Elisabeta, the parents might have named their child Betsy."

"It's going in the opposite direction now. If parents like the name Elizabeth, they might look for a more ethnic version, such as Elisabeta," she notes. For the same reason, Irish-American parents might celebrate their heritage by naming a son O'brien.

Wattenberg believes that Irish names, which have been in vogue for years, will shortly give way to a wave of Welsh names. "They have that feeling of familiarity and also a romanticism that comes from Celtic mythology," she says. For example, the name of the Welsh goddess Rhiannon is familiar to many because it's also the title of a Fleetwood Mac song.

LUCKY 7
Seven-letter names bring very good luck. Having 13 letters in a given or surname name is bad luck. Add or subtract one letter for good luck.

ALMOST
FAMOUS

What a heavy burden is a name that has become too famous.

–Voltaire, French writer (1694–1778)

Although the entertainment media are often credited with making a name trendy, the name itself must both be "new" and fit in with the fashionable sounds of the times, says Cleveland Kent Evans, Ph.D., president of the American Name Society. "Most people do not conceive of themselves as naming a child 'after' the celebrity or fictional character, but rather use the popular media as a place to find 'cool-sounding' new names," he says.

In some immigrant circles, the naming conventions mimic the American celebrity culture, but with native names. For example, some Indian parents are naming sons Arjun and daughters Shreya, after Bollywood film personalitics. ("Bollywood" refers to India's Bombay-based film industry.) In areas of North America with large Spanish-speaking populations, classic Spanish boys' names such as Jose, Juan, and Angel rank near the top. However, among Spanish-speaking parents of baby girls, names from the entertainment world trump tradition. Yesenia, a character on two popular telenovelas, and Shakira, a Colombian singer, are among the preferred.

(c o n t i n u e d)

ARJUN • SHAKIRA • KAYTLAN • LEO

SOUNDALIKES

I don't care what the papers say about me, as long as they spell my name right.

—attributed to "Big Tim" Sullivan, American politician (1862–1913)

Every once in a while, you hear of a family in which all of the children's names begin with the same letter. Call it cute, clever, or even corny, but it's also fairly common. Naming trends tend to follow the letter fashions of their day.

"'J' names, such as Jennifer and Jason, were wildly popular in the 1980s, and 'k' names, such as Kyle and Kayla, were really big in the '90s," says Satran. Notably, Cy Young Award–winning pitcher Roger "Rocket" Clemens gave his four children names that start with "k": Koby, Kory, Kacy, and Kody. Baseball enthusiasts will recognize K as the scoring notation for a strikeout.

Olympic gold medalist and two-time heavyweight boxing champion George Foreman may have taken the soundalike concept to an extreme. He famously named all five of his sons George. Foreman says that he "kept it simple" so he wouldn't forget the kids' names.

Today, the aural emphasis is on names that begin or end with vowels. This means more Emmas, Isabellas, Ethans, and Owens—for starters. Endings with a long "o" sound are coming to the fore. "There is a lot of interest right now in Italian names like Leo and Enzo in the general population," says Evans. "If that trend continues, Hispanic names such as Mateo and Julio have a chance of crossing over to other ethnic groups."

WHAT'S IN A NAME?
To learn more about naming traditions, what your name says about you, and what your name means, go to **Almanac.com/extras**.

THE INVENTION CONVENTION

What a deal of talking there would be in the world if we desired at all costs to change the names of things into definitions.

—Georg Christoph Lichtenberg, German physicist and writer (1742–99)

In African-American communities and, to a lesser extent, Mormon communities, there has been a long-standing tradition of inventing names and creating new spellings for familiar names.

"African-Americans are the only group in which a very large percentage of children are given completely invented names," says Evans. "Before the 1960s, the names that black parents and white parents gave their children were actually quite similar. But in the early 20th century, prejudiced whites stereotyped blacks as having 'weird' names."

(continued)

166

Flatten your stomach without gut-wrenching exercises.

Clogged arteries could virtually disappear when you add this to your life once a day.

"HONEY Can Heal WHAT?"

(By Frank K. Wood)

If you want to learn how to use gentle folk remedies to unleash your body's healing power instead of resorting to dangerous prescription drugs or risky surgery, you need *The Folk Remedy Encyclopedia*.

You'll be amazed by how many inexpensive, easy, natural cures you can find all around you — in your pantry, garden, garage, and grocery store.

► One super vitamin protects your vision, fights infections, keeps skin, bones, and cells healthy, plus fights heart disease, cancer, memory loss, arthritis, liver disease, Parkinson's, and complications of diabetes. Are you getting 100%?

► Flatten your stomach without gut-wrenching exercises. These tips turn ugly flab into rock-hard abs!

► A natural way to rejuvenate your veins and arteries that will have you feeling brand new.

► Miracle healing seed lowers blood pressure, reduces risk of stroke, plus fights arthritis, heart disease, type 2 diabetes, stomach disorders, and even mental problems!

► Prevent high blood pressure, colon cancer, senility, and fragile bones. All with one — yes, one — inexpensive daily supplement that keeps you healthy and strong.

► That "spare tire" around your waist is doing more than just slowing you down. It also increases your risk of many life-threatening illnesses. Burn it off without gut-wrenching sit-ups and grueling fitness regimens.

► Nature's wonder food for your body — once praised by Gandhi. Fights heart disease, high blood pressure, stroke, arthritis, type 2 diabetes, and even protects against breast, colon, and prostate cancer!

► Clogged arteries virtually disappear when you add this to your life every day.

► Here's the secret to naturally block out calories from foods. Just add this when you eat — and watch the weight melt away.

► It protects your heart, lowers your cholesterol, fights cancer, and much more! Researchers take a good look at this "miracle" mineral.

► Kills cancer cells dead in their tracks! Duke University study proves this tiny seed packs a powerful punch!

► Just 2 glasses a day of (you won't believe this — but it's true!) lowers your cholesterol — and prevents heart attacks too!

► Trick your body into losing weight! Melts off fat safely, naturally and best yet, easily.

► Give your brain the nutrients it needs for a better memory. Don't let your brain deteriorate when you can so easily power it up.

Learn about all these natural healing folk remedies and more. To order a copy, just return this notice with your name and address and a check for $9.99 plus $3.00 shipping and handling to: **FC&A, Dept. POF07**, 103 Clover Green, Peachtree City, GA 30269. We will send you a copy of *The Folk Remedy Encyclopedia: Olive Oil, Vinegar, Honey and 1,001 Other Home Remedies*.

You get a no-time-limit guarantee of satisfaction or your money back.

You must cut out and return this notice with your order. Copies will not be accepted!

IMPORTANT — FREE GIFT
OFFER EXPIRES IN 30 DAYS

All orders mailed within 30 days will receive a free gift, *Simple Solutions to Common Health Problems*, guaranteed. Order right away! ©FC&A 2006

This shift toward originality in naming is still in its nascent stage but seems to be growing.

"In the 1960s, African-Americans took this negative stereotype and turned it into a positive, essentially saying, 'We are the people who give creative, beautiful new names to our children.'" Popular invented African-American names include DeJuan, DeVonte, DeMario, Tyrese, and Jamarion for boys, and Lakeisha, LaToya, Shanika, and Tanish for girls.

Some Mormon parents have adapted the blended-family concept to names. According to Cari Bilyeu Clark, the cocreator (with her husband, Wes) of the Utah Baby Namer Web site (http://wesclark.com/ubn), it's a common Mormon practice to combine two or more names into one, such as using Truman and Ann to make Truann; to insert a French-sounding prefix or suffix, such as LaDawn or Dorette; or to add the ending "en" to a familiar name to make Braden, for example. Creative spellings for conventional names, such as Kaytlan for Caitlin, are also common.

This shift toward originality in naming is still in its nascent stage but seems to be growing. "Most white Americans still have to 'find' a name somewhere to think that it's legitimate, but this may be changing," says Evans. "Since Aidan and [like-sounding names such as] Caden, Hayden, and Jayden are all popular for boys,

I am now seeing a few each year with [invented] names like Bladen, Daden, Graden, Shayden, Taeden, and Zaden."

"It would not surprise me if, 50 years from now, about half of all children receive names that their parents invent. It's the ultimate in finding a unique 'different' name," says Evans.

NAME THE CURE

TO QUIET A COUGH . . .

Eat a piece of bread given to you by a woman who has successively married two men of the same name and from different families.

TO REMEDY SICKNESS . . .

Change your name. Some Native American tribes believed that sickness was a sign that a name did not agree with the bearer. "Washing off" the original name and giving a new one was expected to restore health.

□□

Genevieve Rajewski was named after her maternal grandmother, following the long-standing tradition of her Irish ancestors. The name "Genevieve" hit its peak in American popularity in the early 1900s—meaning that a comeback for it should be in order.

Indiana Firm Discovers:

Special ^New cream for arthritis

(SPECIAL)–A small company in central Indiana has developed a special cream that relieves arthritis pain in minutes, even chronic arthritis pain—deep in the joints. The product which is called **PAIN-BUST-R-II,** is one of the fastest acting therapeutic formulas ever developed in the fight against arthritis. Immediately upon application it goes to work by penetrating deep to the areas most affected—the joints themselves, bringing fast relief where relief is needed most. Men and women who have suffered arthritis pain for years are reporting incredible results with this product. Even a single application seems to work remarkably well in relieving pain and bringing comfort to cramped, knotted joints. *PAIN-BUST-R-II was researched and formulated to be absorbed directly into the joints and muscles—where the pain originates. Long-time arthritis sufferers will be glad to know that this formula will help put an end to agonizing days and sleepless nights. It is highly recommended by users who have resumed daily activities and are enjoying life again.

Read what our users have to say:

"I use **PAIN BUST** because I suffer from tension in my back and shoulders. I can't praise your product enough, I've used other ointments, but they don't seem to work as fast nor last as long. Thank you. Thank you...Thank you!" *C.K.F.*

"Last night when I went to sleep I rubbed some **PAIN BUST** on my sore aching knee. 15 minutes later I fell sound asleep and woke 8 hours later with absolutely no pain. I wish I knew about **PAIN BUST** long ago." *B.M.S.*

NO-RISK FREE TRIAL
We Trust You — Send No Money!

TO ORDER: Just write **"PAIN BUST-R-II"** on a sheet of paper and send it along with your name, address and the number of tubes you wish to order. We will promptly ship you 1 large tube for **$9.90**, 2 large tubes for **$16.80** *(Saves $3)* or 3 large tubes for only **$21.90** *(SAVES $7.80).* Prices include all shipping and handling. We will enclose an invoice and if for any reason you don't agree that **PAIN BUST-R-II** relieves pain more effectively than anything you've tried, simply mark "cancel" on the invoice and there will be no charge to you. You don't even have to bother returning the merchandise. Act quickly—this offer may not be repeated. **CALL NOW! 1-800-451-5773 and ask for offer# OFA-07** or write today to: Continental Quest/Research Corp., 1015 - 3rd Ave SW, Dept. OFA-07, Carmel, IN 46032 ©2006 Continental Quest/Research Corp.

Winners in the 2006 Essay Contest

My Marriage Proposal

First Prize

On February 13, 2005, a cold, snowy day in Holland, Michigan, Brad decided that we should go ice fishing. We headed to a river, found the perfect spot, and pitched the tent. Then we drilled the first hole. The fish weren't biting, so Brad drilled a second hole and set me up to fish at it while he worked at the first hole. After a few minutes he called me over, saying he had a bite! Since I had never been ice fishing before, he asked if I wanted to reel it in. I took the fishing pole and started winding. It didn't feel that heavy to me, but Brad insisted that I keep going. I was very surprised when, instead of a fish, I pulled up a diamond ring! I looked at Brad slightly confused and he professed his love and asked me to become his wife. We were married in August 2005.

–Jenny Vander Zwaag, Zeeland, Michigan

Second Prize

Joe and I had known each other for several years. One evening, we were playing Scrabble while watching television. Between turns, Joe would hold my hand and play with my birthstone ring, which I always wore on my left ring finger. He would twist my ring around, take it off, and put it back on again. After the last game, he was playing around with the letters on the board, spelling out different phrases. He then took all the tiles off the board, except for the last phrase, which read WILL YOU MARRY ME. When I answered yes, Joe handed me my birthstone ring. He had exchanged it for the engagement ring, which was now shining brightly on my finger.

–Elaine Kyrylchuk, Regina, Saskatchewan

Third Prize

We were in our 20s and didn't have the income for extravagances, so I was shocked when Jim took me to a fine restaurant overlooking the Hudson River. As the meal ended, he swept the wine cork and beverage napkins into his pockets. Bemused, I said, "Don't forget the forks!" and excused myself to go to the rest room. When I returned, I found him already outside, standing on the dock.

When I joined him, he said, "Do you remember what I said to you the night we met?" I did. We were at a pub and, through mutual friends, had introduced ourselves over a game of pool. "You said you needed a partner," I said. Just then, Jim got down on one knee, displayed a beautiful solitaire, and said, "Yes, I need a partner." After I accepted his proposal, he pulled the cork from his right pocket. On it, he had written the date and the word, "Yes."

"What if I had said, 'No'?" I asked. From his left pocket, he pulled out the napkins and said, "That is what these were for."

–Deb Morris, Saratoga Springs, New York

Honorable Mention

In 24 hours, my boyfriend Esteban had stood me up three times. Finally, he picked me up on Saturday evening.

He took me to a new restaurant in a baroque-style building in Querétaro, Mexico. Soon after we arrived, a video was projected on the wall of Esteban playing the guitar and singing a song that he had written for me.

The waiter led us up a spiral staircase into a candlelit room with balconies and a cupola. Amid violets and roses was one large table, elegantly set. Heart balloons floated overhead and on one wall was written in silver glitter: "Will you marry me?" All the customers and waiters were at the door clapping and shouting. Suddenly they all said good-bye—and only later did I understand why. It was an uninhabited house, not a restaurant, that Esteban had rented and prepared for two days. After everyone left, we dined, talked, and danced for hours. Now when I tell this story, everyone asks me where this restaurant is, but I have to say it existed for only one wonderful night.

–Yolanda Alegria Moreno, Thomaston, Maine

Thanks to all who participated in the essay contest. We received many stories. Here are a few more, in brief:

■ We went to a hat party as a medieval prince and princess. Later, he appeared as a knight in full armor on a white horse and proposed to me on one knee (not easy in armor).

■ I was doing housework while my Romeo watched TV. During a commercial break, he asked me to "fetch him another cold one." When I returned with his beer, he looked into my eyes and said, "How would ya like to do this full-time?"

■ On a large "Item of the Week" sign that hung from the ceiling in the retail store where I worked, my boyfriend wrote, "Sarah, will you marry me?"

■ Using washable markers, I wrote "will you" on her left foot and "marry me" on her right foot. The next day, the markings bled through her socks, leaving a perfect imprint of my proposal. I cut out the soles and framed the words.

■ "I never asked your mother to marry me. I

merely wanted to know if she could marry a man like me. I didn't have the heart to tell her that she had misinterpreted my question, so I thought it best to go along with her."

■ He looked at me very seriously and asked if I wanted to get married. If I did, I could get an engagement ring; if not, he was going to get a new gun.

■ We met on a blind date. We talked for hours, through a cruise on Boston Harbor and dinner. That evening he said, "Someone is going to marry you and it might as well be me."

Announcing the 2007 Essay Contest Topic

The Best Thing I Ever Bought at a Yard Sale

In 200 words or less, please tell us an amusing or instructive tale about one item that you purchased at a yard or garage sale. See page 173 for contest rules.

Winners in the 2006 Recipe Contest

Rice

First Prize

SHRIMP AND CREAMY SPINACH FETA RICE

2 tablespoons olive oil
1/2 cup julienned red pepper
6 ounces baby spinach, washed and dried
1/2 teaspoon salt
1/2 teaspoon pepper
1 pound shrimp, cooked, peeled, and
  deveined
1 1/2 cups cooked brown rice
1 cup feta cheese
1/3 to 1/2 cup pine nuts, toasted

Heat the oil in a large skillet over medium heat, add the red pepper, and sauté for 1 minute. Add the spinach, salt, and pepper and sauté just until the spinach begins to wilt. Drain the excess liquid. Add the shrimp and sauté for 30 seconds, or until warm. Add the rice and feta, and toss until heated through and the cheese is creamy. Top with pine nuts. **Serves 2 to 4.**

–Cathleen Billig, Canton, Ohio

Second Prize

CHICKEN AND WILD RICE CASSEROLE

1 box wild rice mix
4 chicken breasts, boned and skinned
1 medium tomato, seeded and chopped
1 small red onion, diced
2 ribs celery, diced
1/3 cup pecans, chopped
1 cup light mayonnaise
1 teaspoon salt, or to taste
1/2 teaspoon black pepper
1/4 teaspoon nutmeg
8 ounces shredded Monterey Jack cheese

Preheat the oven to 350°F. Prepare the rice according to the package directions. Place the chicken breasts in the bottom of a greased 13x9-inch casserole dish. In a large bowl, combine the rice with all of the remaining ingredients *except* the cheese. Spoon the rice mixture around the chicken breasts. Sprinkle the cheese on the chicken and rice. Cover and bake for 30 minutes. Remove the cover and cook 15 minutes more, or until the cheese is brown and bubbly and the chicken is cooked through. **Serves 4 to 6.**

–Glenna Anderson Muse, Springfield, Missouri

Third Prize

CONFETTI RICE SALAD

1 box long grain or wild rice mix with herbs
1 cup walnut pieces
1 cup sweetened dried cranberries
3/4 cup chopped yellow bell pepper
3/4 cup chopped red bell pepper

1/2 cup finely chopped red onion (or Vidalia onion)
3/4 cup raspberry walnut vinaigrette
1 cup mandarin orange slices, drained

Prepare the rice according to the package directions. While the rice is cooking, heat the oven to 325°F, place the walnuts on a cookie sheet, and toast them in the oven for 6 to 8 minutes, stirring once or twice to toast evenly. When the rice is cooked, place it into a large bowl and toss it to fluff. Add the cranberries, peppers, onions, and vinaigrette and toss well. Set aside for 1 hour at room temperature to let the flavors blend and the rice absorb the juices. Just before serving, adjust the flavor, adding more vinaigrette if necessary. Add the oranges and walnuts, saving a few to garnish the top, and toss to mix. **Serves 6 to 8.**

–Fran Drummond, Gray, Georgia

| Honorable Mention |

MOCK WILD RICE STUFFING

2/3 cup plus 2 tablespoons butter
1 tablespoon salt, or to taste
4 cups quick-cooking rice
3/4 cup diced onion
1 1/2 pounds sliced fresh mushrooms
3 cups diced celery
3/4 cup chopped celery leaves

1 teaspoon marjoram
1 tablespoon dried sage
3/4 teaspoon dried thyme
dash of pepper
4 1/2 cups chicken broth
1 cup chopped pecans

Melt the butter in a large skillet or pot. Add all of the ingredients, except the broth and pecans. Sauté on medium-high heat for 10 to 15 minutes, stirring constantly. Add the broth. Turn the heat to high and bring to a boil, then reduce the heat and simmer for 5 to 10 minutes, uncovered. The rice will absorb the liquid; remove it from the heat as directed or when it reaches the desired consistency. Add the pecans and mix to combine. **Makes 8 cups.**

–Diann Miller, Urbanville, Iowa

☐ ☐

STILL HUNGRY?

We received many different and appealing recipes using rice. To try them, go to **Almanac.com/extras.**

| Announcing the 2007 Recipe Contest: Peanut Butter |

Send us your best recipe using peanut butter (smooth or crunchy). Amateur cooks only, please. See contest rules below.

RECIPE AND ESSAY CONTEST RULES

Cash prizes (first prize, $100; second prize, $75; third prize, $50) will be awarded for the best recipe using peanut butter and for the best original essay on the subject "The Best Thing I Ever Bought at a Yard Sale." All entries become the property of Yankee Publishing, which reserves all rights to the material. The deadline for entries is Friday, January 26, 2007. Label "Recipe Contest" or "Essay Contest" and mail to The Old Farmer's Almanac, P.O. Box 520, Dublin, NH 03444; or e-mail recipecontest@yankeepub.com or essaycontest@yankeepub.com. Include your name, mailing address, and e-mail address. Winners will be announced in *The 2008 Old Farmer's Almanac* and on Almanac.com.

A Blue Ribbon Banquet

Endive Salad With Walnuts, Cherries, and Roquefort

1 small head endive, rinsed and drained
1 small head butter lettuce, rinsed and drained
3/4 cup walnut oil
3 tablespoons sherry wine vinegar
1 tablespoon lemon juice
salt and pepper, to taste
1/2 cup walnuts, toasted
1/2 cup fresh sweet cherries, rinsed and pitted
4 ounces Roquefort cheese, crumbled
2 tablespoons minced fresh chives

Tear the endive and lettuce into bite-size pieces and place in a salad bowl. In a small bowl, combine the walnut oil, vinegar, and lemon juice. Beat with a wire whisk until well blended. Season with salt and pepper to taste. Drizzle over the greens and mix well. Arrange the greens on individual salad plates and top each serving with a portion of toasted walnuts, cherries, Roquefort cheese, and chives. *Makes 4 to 6 servings.*

–Joy Cassens, National Cherry Festival, Traverse City, Michigan

Stuffed Chicken With Apple Glaze

CHICKEN:
1 broiler-fryer chicken
1/2 teaspoon salt
1/4 teaspoon freshly ground black pepper
2 tablespoons oil
1 package (6 ounces) stuffing mix
1 cup grated apple
1/2 teaspoon grated lemon rind
1/4 cup chopped walnuts
1/4 cup raisins
1/4 cup finely chopped celery

GLAZE:
1/2 cup apple jelly
1 tablespoon lemon juice
1/2 teaspoon ground cinnamon

For chicken: Preheat the oven to 350°F. Sprinkle the chicken cavity with the salt and pepper. Rub the outside of the chicken with the oil.

In a large bowl, prepare the stuffing according to the package directions. Add the apple, lemon rind, walnuts, raisins, and celery, mixing well. Stuff the chicken and place on a rack in a baking pan. Cover loosely with foil and roast for 25 minutes per pound (a little under 2 hours for a stuffed 4-pound bird). Place any extra stuffing in a covered casserole and bake for 1 hour.

For glaze: While the chicken

is cooking, combine the apple jelly, lemon juice, and cinnamon in a small saucepan. Bring to a boil, then lower the heat and simmer for 3 minutes, stirring to prevent scorching. After 1 hour of roasting the chicken, remove the foil and brush the chicken with the glaze. Continue roasting, brushing frequently with glaze, for about 30 minutes more. The chicken is done when the leg moves freely when lifted and the internal temperature registers 180°F on a meat thermometer. *Makes 4 to 6 servings.*

–Ruth Dykes, Delmarva Chicken Festival, Georgetown, Delaware

Death Row Bourbon Sauce
Use as a barbecue or table sauce on pork, beef, and chicken, or in baked beans.

2 tablespoons vegetable oil
1/2 cup finely chopped onion
1 clove garlic, minced
2 cups ketchup
1/2 cup bourbon
*   whiskey, divided*
1/4 cup raspberry vinegar
1/4 cup Worcestershire sauce
3 tablespoons molasses
2 tablespoons prepared mustard
2 tablespoons soy sauce
2 tablespoons hot sauce or 1 tablespoon
*   Tabasco*
1/2 teaspoon coarsely ground black pepper
1/4 teaspoon cayenne pepper
1/4 teaspoon liquid smoke (optional)

In a medium saucepan, heat the oil over medium heat. Add the onion and garlic and sauté until tender, about 5

minutes. Add the ketchup, ¼ cup of the whiskey, vinegar, Worcestershire sauce, molasses, mustard, soy sauce, hot sauce, black pepper, and cayenne. Mix thoroughly. Add the liquid smoke and simmer for 20 minutes over low heat on the stovetop. (Or, omit the liquid smoke and cook for 2 hours in a smoker.) Stir in the remaining ¼ cup of whiskey. This sauce will keep for several weeks in the refrigerator. *Makes 3½ cups.*

–Barbara Correll, Jack Daniel's Cook-off, Lynchburg, Tennessee

Decadent Brownies

BROWNIES:
15 ounces fine European semisweet
*   chocolate*
3/4 cup (1 1/2 sticks) unsalted butter
3/4 cup confectioners' sugar
2 tablespoons flour

(c o n t i n u e d)

Festival Food Facts

■ **Michigan produces 70 percent of the tart cherries grown in the United States.**

■ **Some cooks at the Delmarva Chicken Festival tend a 10-foot-long frying pan with garden rakes, cooking up to 800 chicken quarters at a time.**

■ **Hamburgers are the most popular choice for at-home barbecues. Next in line on the menu are steak, hot dogs, and chicken breasts.**

■ **According to food lore, the Brownie was discovered by accident in the early 1900s when someone baked a chocolate cake and forgot to add baking powder.**

Food

4 eggs, separated
1 teaspoon vanilla extract
3/4 cup sour cream
GLAZE:
1/4 cup (1/2 stick) unsalted butter
4 ounces fine European semisweet chocolate
1 1/2 cups confectioners' sugar
3 tablespoons boiling water or strong coffee
2 teaspoons vanilla extract

For brownies: Preheat the oven to 375°F. Lightly grease a 9-inch square glass baking dish. Melt the chocolate and butter in a large saucepan or a double boiler. Whisk in the confectioners' sugar and flour and remove from the heat. Add the egg yolks one at a time, beating well after each addition. Stir in the vanilla. Beat the egg whites in a separate bowl until stiff, then fold into the chocolate mixture. Remove 1 cup of this mixture and blend with the sour cream; set aside. Pour the chocolate-egg mixture into the prepared pan. Top with the chocolate–sour cream mixture and swirl with a knife. Bake for 30 minutes. Cool completely.

For glaze: In a medium saucepan or a double boiler, melt the butter and chocolate together over low heat. Remove from the heat and beat in the confectioners' sugar, water or coffee, and vanilla. Spread over the cooled brownies. *Makes 1 dozen brownies.*

–Jill Anderson, Georgia National Fair, Perry, Georgia

□ □

HUNGRY FOR MORE?

These truly award-winning recipes are excerpted from The Old Farmer's Almanac *Blue Ribbon Recipes* and *Best Home Baking* cookbooks. For more recipes, go to **Almanac.com/food.**

Table of Measures

APOTHECARIES'
1 scruple = 20 grains
1 dram = 3 scruples
1 ounce = 8 drams
1 pound = 12 ounces

AVOIRDUPOIS
1 ounce = 16 drams
1 pound = 16 ounces
1 hundredweight = 100 pounds
1 ton = 2,000 pounds
1 long ton = 2,240 pounds

LIQUID
4 gills = 1 pint
63 gallons = 1 hogshead
2 hogsheads = 1 pipe or butt
2 pipes = 1 tun

DRY
2 pints = 1 quart
4 quarts = 1 gallon
2 gallons = 1 peck
4 pecks = 1 bushel

LINEAR
1 hand = 4 inches
1 link = 7.92 inches

1 span = 9 inches
1 foot = 12 inches
1 yard = 3 feet
1 rod = 5½ yards
1 mile = 320 rods = 1,760 yards = 5,280 feet
1 Int. nautical mile = 6,076.1155 feet
1 knot = 1 nautical mile per hour
1 fathom = 2 yards = 6 feet
1 furlong = ⅛ mile = 660 feet = 220 yards
1 league = 3 miles = 24 furlongs
1 chain = 100 links = 22 yards

SQUARE
1 square foot = 144 square inches
1 square yard = 9 square feet
1 square rod = 30¼ square yards = 272¼ square feet
1 acre = 160 square rods = 43,560 square feet
1 square mile = 640 acres = 102,400 square rods
1 square rod = 625 square links

1 square chain = 16 square rods
1 acre = 10 square chains

CUBIC
1 cubic foot = 1,728 cubic inches
1 cubic yard = 27 cubic feet
1 cord = 128 cubic feet
1 U.S. liquid gallon = 4 quarts = 231 cubic inches
1 Imperial gallon = 1.20 U.S. gallons = 0.16 cubic foot
1 board foot = 144 cubic inches

KITCHEN
3 teaspoons = 1 tablespoon
16 tablespoons = 1 cup
1 cup = 8 ounces
2 cups = 1 pint
2 pints = 1 quart
4 quarts = 1 gallon

To convert Fahrenheit and Celsius:
°C = (°F − 32) × ⁵⁄₉
°F = (°C × ⁹⁄₅) + 32

Metric Conversions

LINEAR
1 inch = 2.54 centimeters
1 centimeter = 0.39 inch
1 meter = 39.37 inches
1 yard = 0.914 meter
1 mile = 1.61 kilometers
1 kilometer = 0.62 mile

SQUARE
1 square inch = 6.45 square centimeters
1 square yard = 0.84 square meter
1 square mile = 2.59 square kilometers
1 square kilometer = 0.386 square mile

1 acre = 0.40 hectare
1 hectare = 2.47 acres

CUBIC
1 cubic yard = 0.76 cubic meter
1 cubic meter = 1.31 cubic yards

HOUSEHOLD
½ teaspoon = 2 mL
1 teaspoon = 5 mL
1 tablespoon = 15 mL
¼ cup = 60 mL
⅓ cup = 75 mL
½ cup = 125 mL
⅔ cup = 150 mL
¾ cup = 175 mL
1 cup = 250 mL

1 liter = 1.057 U.S. liquid quarts
1 U.S. liquid quart = 0.946 liter
1 U.S. liquid gallon = 3.78 liters
1 gram = 0.035 ounce
1 ounce = 28.349 grams
1 kilogram = 2.2 pounds
1 pound = 0.45 kilogram

"What's That, La
Speak

Communicating with our pets comes naturally.

"Woof! Woof! Woof!"

Lassie runs up to us on the TV screen, her silken tail waving with excitement. It's trouble, we can tell, but what kind? And where?

Luckily, Lassie always gets the message across. She leaps for a rope. Tugs on a sleeve. Fingers the bad guy. Or, in one oh-c'mon-now episode, runs to fetch a C-clamp from the workbench. So Lassie's communication skills are a notch above those of that furry lump at your feet.

Or are they?

A few years ago, Joe Woods of Wagontown, Pennsylvania, was socializing at a large gathering. As usual, his friendly dog Bosun, a shepherd/collie mix, was at his side. Bent on causing trouble, some strangers arrived and soon started a brief scuffle inside the house. Woods, who was outside, wasn't involved at all.

But later, one of the strangers approached him, staring in a menacing way or, as Woods describes it, "giving me 'stink eye.'"

"My dog, who's normally very friendly, sees this and starts giving him 'stink eye' back," says Woods. "He was glaring at the guy and snarling."

"The guy says to me, 'Hey, your dog is scaring

BOSUN
scared off a stranger with his snarl.

by Sally Roth

178

ssie?

Jp, Girl!"

me!' and he left," says Woods. "Man, I loved that dog."

Bubba the cat used a more vocal version of the stink-eye technique when a thief came to call.

"It was spring break," says Samantha Hall, who shared a house with college roommates and Bubba, a gray-striped shorthair with white paws, in Stroudsburg, Pennsylvania. "So we were all in and out of the place. The door was rarely locked."

"A guy decided to come in and help himself. When I confronted him, he made up some story and ran out."

Money was missing, and so was some electronics gear. "I called 911," says Hall, "and while I was on the phone, Bubba started freaking out at my bedroom window. I told him to stop, but he kept howling and clawing at the window. When I finally came over to him, I realized that the robber was outside looking in my window! He took off again, thank God, and Bubba ran to the back door to try to get out."

"Bubba didn't save our lives, exactly," says Hall, "but we listen to what he has to say now."

SEBASTIAN
shows affection with his bite.

Even if our pets don't scare away bad guys or burglars, we trust their instincts. Take Sebastian, a huge orange tabby owned by Laura Webb of Stillwater, New Jersey. When he approves of someone, Webb knows it right away. "He bites people he likes," she says. "It's a sign of affection for him. That's how I knew that Michael was okay when we first started dating—Sebastian bit him!"

Laura and Michael married a year later. They now share their home with the heartily approving Sebastian.

No matter how wacky their habits, our pets seem to have no problem in getting their points across. "My 'tuxedo cat' Sigi will squeak out a little 'Eek!' noise when he wants affection," says Larry Miller, of Evansville, Indiana. "But instead of jumping up on my lap, he turns and walks slowly away, expecting that I will go pick him up. His legs go limp when I grab him off the floor,

Figuring out what our pets are trying to tell us seems to come naturally.

and by the time I have him up to my face to give him a little kiss, he's purring away. He likes to be cradled like a little baby on his back in my arms, looking up at me."

Ah, that purr. That relaxed body. Or that wagging tail and adoring canine gaze. They all spell "happy pet," and we get the message loud and clear. Unconsciously, we pay attention to the signals that reveal our pet's mood: the squirming that indicates discomfort or the purring that says pleasure. So figuring out what our pets are trying to tell us seems to come naturally.

And when it comes to understanding the message of a barking dog, we're so good at instant translation—danger/no danger—that researchers suggest the skill may be hardwired into our brains. Is a friend coming for a visit? A danger sneaking up in the dark? A saber-toothed tiger on the prowl? Or is it just the pizza delivery person? A deep bark means aggression; it's a warning we heed. But we can dismiss continual, high-pitched yelping, which usually means, "Hey, I'm tired of being home alone, and I'm bored."

When researchers at Eötvös Loránd University in Budapest, Hungary, tested their subjects' ability to distinguish between different kinds of dog barks, they found that most could instantly tell the difference between an aggressive bark and a happy bark. The subjects matched 21 recordings of barks to seven possible situations—confronting an intruder; being provoked by someone; anticipating a treat, a toy, or a walk; playing with other dogs; or being tied up and left alone. They got it right nearly half the time, even if they didn't own a dog.

Okay, so most of us can understand dog language. But can our pets understand our language?

Corinne Bowers of Minneapolis, Minnesota, says that her sheltie, Rapha, does a great job of deciphering English. "He becomes very attentive when I talk to him," she says. "If I say, 'We're going in the car,' he goes all the way down to the garage, instead of going to the side door where we go to walk outside."

RAPHA
understands his owner's language.

A pet with a big vocabulary is fun. But our pets don't need to understand words to figure out what we mean. Feeling blue? Chances are that your pet will sense it before you say a word and come over to comfort you.

Cory, a small Tonkinese cat, had a sixth sense when it came to consolation. "If anyone was sad, she could sense it," says Patrice Jacob, who lived in Lake Oswego, Oregon, with Cory. "Normally, she was shy around strangers, but if someone was upset, she'd come cuddle up. People often remarked about how

CORY

can sense when a person is blue.

sensitive she was. For years, whenever I had a burning question, I'd go talk to her about it. She was a wise, wise cat."

And a homebody—except for once, when Patrice was away on a two-week business trip and her mother was minding her house. "On one of my calls home," Patrice says, "my three-year-old, Michael, let slip an awful secret: Cory was missing."

"I felt heartsick. Every time I called my mother, I'd get the same report: No cat."

"When I got home and opened the door, my mother and son were ecstatic— Cory had come home!" Great news, with an incredible twist: Cory had returned less than an hour before Patrice herself arrived. "She had been gone for a week and a half in the Northwest winter. We never found out where she had been. It was a miracle to me."

A lot of our communication with our pets comes down to interpreting the signals. But sometimes, as with Cory the cat, it seems like something larger is at work. Intuition? Mind reading?

"I would love to have a visit with a pet psychic," says Rapha's owner. "Once, I was in the living room, thinking to myself that I needed to go in the bedroom and get my nail file. I was too lazy to go get it, but I kept thinking about it. After a short time, Rapha came running out of the bedroom with my nail file in his mouth. I can think of no other explanation but that he read my mind."

Mind reading is exactly what a booming crop of animal communicators suggest they can do. If you and your pet don't seem to be getting through to one another, you can hire a communication specialist to translate what it's thinking.

Joane Ventresca called on her pet communicator for advice when litter box problems cropped up in her Los Angeles home. The communicator tuned in on the cat— by phone—and told Ventresca that a recent earthquake had rattled its nerves. Noisy construction crews working to repair the damage only made matters worse.

"So my cat was going in the corner of my bedroom, which was as far away as she could possibly get from these loud, noisy workers," says Ventresca. It all added up.

Communicating with our pets is an everyday miracle that never gets old. Well . . . maybe sometimes: "What's that, Lassie? You want to go out again?" □ □

Sally Roth, author of nature and gardening books, lives in Washington State with her two shaggy dogs, Duke and Willy.

MEET ALEX THE PARROT

Learn about bird behavior and share your tales of talking to animals at **Almanac.com/extras.**

How We Predict the Weather

■ **We derive our weather forecasts from** a secret formula that was devised by the founder of this Almanac, Robert B. Thomas, in 1792. Thomas believed that weather on Earth was influenced by sunspots, which are magnetic storms on the surface of the Sun.

—Beth Krommes

Over the years, we have refined and enhanced that formula with state-of-the-art technology and modern scientific calculations. We employ three scientific disciplines to make our long-range predictions: solar science, the study of sunspots and other solar activity; climatology, the study of prevailing weather patterns; and meteorology, the study of the atmosphere. We predict weather trends and events by comparing solar patterns and historical weather conditions with current solar activity.

Our forecasts emphasize temperature and precipitation deviations from averages, or normals. These are based on 30-year statistical averages prepared by government meteorological agencies and updated every ten years. The most-recent tabulations span the period 1971 through 2000.

We believe that nothing in the universe happens haphazardly, that there is a cause-and-effect pattern to all phenomena. However, although neither we nor any other forecasters have as yet gained sufficient insight into the mysteries of the universe to predict the weather with *total* accuracy, our results are almost always *very* close to our traditional claim of 80 percent.

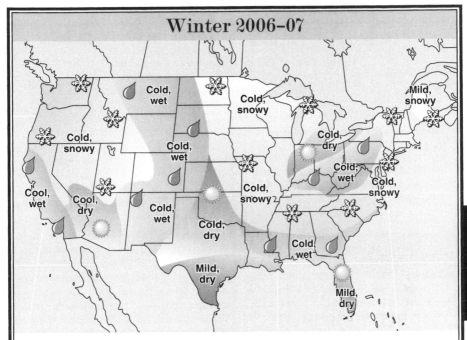

Winter 2006–07

Cold, wet
Cold, snowy
Mild, snowy
Cold, snowy
Cold, dry
Cold, wet
Cold, wet
Cold, snowy
Cool, wet
Cool, dry
Cold, wet
Cold, snowy
Cold, dry
Cold, wet
Mild, dry
Mild, dry

These seasonal weather maps correspond to the winter (November through March) and summer (June through August) forecasts on page 184. To see these maps in color, go to Almanac.com/extras.

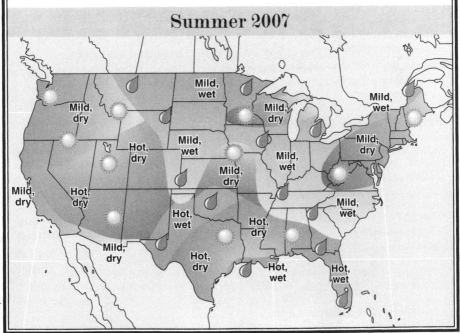

Summer 2007

Mild, wet
Mild, dry
Mild, wet
Mild, dry
Mild, wet
Mild, dry
Hot, dry
Mild, wet
Mild, dry
Mild, dry
Mild, wet
Mild, dry
Hot, dry
Mild, dry
Hot, wet
Hot, dry
Mild, wet
Mild, dry
Hot, dry
Hot, wet
Hot, wet

–maps: AccuWeather, Inc.

WEATHER

General Weather Forecast and Report

To see maps of the forecast, turn to page 183.

Our study of solar activity suggests that a weak El Niño will develop this winter, resulting in below-normal temperatures, on average, in much of the country. Snowfall will be above normal in most areas, especially in the Upper Midwest and Heartland. But, with the Atlantic warmer than normal (and getting warmer still) and the Pacific also relatively warm, most regions will have at least one mild month. (If the El Niño fails to develop as expected, the very cold periods will be brief and most of the country will experience a mild winter overall—perhaps even a *very* mild winter.)

Spring will come relatively early in most regions. Summer will be mild in most areas, but continuing drought will lead to wildfires and water management challenges in western regions. A major hurricane will threaten the Northeast in late September.

W E A T H E R

November through March will be colder than normal, on average, in all areas except northern New England, Florida, and southern Texas. Snowfall will be below normal in the High Plains, much of the eastern Great Lakes, and the Southwest; near normal in the Ohio Valley; and above normal in other areas that normally receive snow.

April and May will be warmer than normal, on average, in all areas except eastern New England, southern Florida, southern Texas, the Intermountain region, and the Pacific Northwest. Rainfall will be above normal in the northwestern quarter of the country, Texas, and portions of the Ohio Valley and below normal in most other places.

June through August will be hotter than normal, on average, across most of the southern states and the Intermountain region, and cooler than normal in most other areas. Rainfall will be below normal from the Intermountain region and Desert Southwest westward to the Pacific, northward from Virginia through most of New England, parts of the Upper Midwest, and in much of the area from the Gulf states northward through Iowa. Rainfall elsewhere will generally be above normal.

September and October will be warmer than normal, on average, in most of the western half of the country and cooler than normal in most of the eastern half. Precipitation will be above normal in most of the Pacific regions and western portions of the Intermountain region, and the northern Atlantic region. Elsewhere, precipitation will be near or below normal.

How accurate was our forecast last winter?

Our snowfall forecast for winter 2005–06 was accurate in more than 99% of the country: The area from just south of Boston southward to Baltimore and in much of the area in the lee of the Great Lakes had above-normal snowfall, and most other areas that receive snow had below-normal snowfall, as predicted. We also accurately forecast a milder-than-normal winter in the southwestern half of the country.

We accurately predicted wild swings in the winter weather. Much of the country experienced colder-than-normal temperatures from November through most of December, followed by one of the warmest Januarys on record. Winter returned in February, as New York City had its heaviest snowfall in history (beating even the Blizzard of 1888), and the eastern half of the nation had some of its coldest late-month temperatures ever.

Our prediction for winter temperatures in the northeastern half of the country was not on target—but it was on trend. We expected the colder-than-normal November and December temperatures to continue into January, with a very mild February to follow. But a weak La Niña developed in the Pacific earlier than we expected, bringing instead (as noted above) one of the mildest Januarys ever.

For more on "How We Predict the Weather," turn to page 182.

U.S. Weather Regions

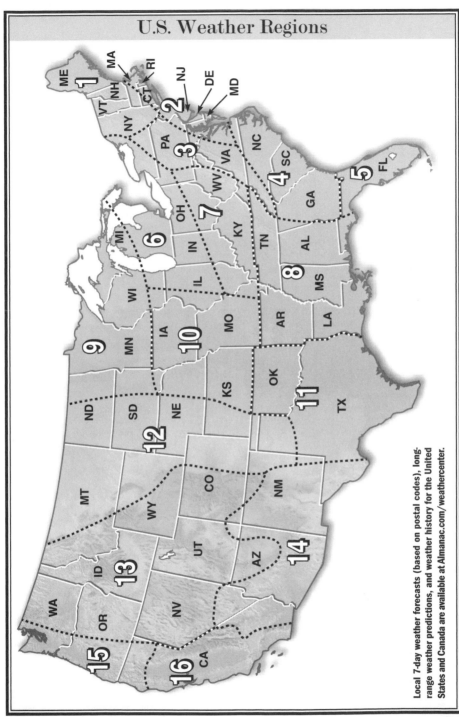

ME 1

MA · NH · RI · VT · CT · NJ · DE · MD

NY

2

PA 3 WV VA NC SC FL 5

MI 6 OH 7 KY TN GA 4

IN

IL

WI MO AR LA 8 AL MS

MN IA 10

9 OK TX 11

ND SD NE 12 KS

MT WY CO NM 14

ID 13 UT AZ

WA OR NV CA 16

15

WEATHER

Local 7-day weather forecasts (based on postal codes), long-range weather predictions, and weather history for the United States and Canada are available at Almanac.com/weathercenter.

Northeast

SUMMARY: Winter temperatures will be near normal, on average: a bit above in the north and a bit below in the south. Precipitation and snowfall will be near or slightly below normal. The snowiest periods will be in mid-November, in mid-December and just before Christmas, in mid-February, and in early and late March. The coldest temperatures will be in mid- to late January, with other cold periods in late December, early January, and much of February.

April and May will be drier than normal, despite an early April snowstorm. Temperatures, on average, will be a bit cooler than normal in the east and a bit warmer in the west.

Summer will be cooler than normal, on average, with rainfall near normal in the north and below normal in the south. The hottest periods will be mid-May, mid-June, early July, and mid- to late August, with no prolonged heat waves.

September and October will be cooler than normal, on average, with above-normal precipitation.

NOV. 2006: Temp. 39° (3° above avg. north; 1° below south); precip. 3" (0.5" below avg.). 1–6 Rain and snow, then sunny, cold. 7–12 Mild, showers. 13–16 Snow, cold. 17–19 Mild, rain. 20–25 Cold, snow showers. 26–30 Mild; rain, then sunny.

DEC. 2006: Temp. 27.5° (3° above avg. north; avg. south); precip. 3" (0.5" below avg. north; 1" above south). 1–7 Mild, snow showers. 8–11 Cold, snow showers. 12–16 Mild, rain and snow. 17–18 Sunny. 19–23 Heavy snow. 24–27 Sunny, cold. 28–31 Rain and snow.

JAN. 2007: Temp. 19° (1° below avg.); precip. 2" (1" below avg.). 1–3 Mild, rain. 4–8 Sunny, cold. 9–13 Rain, then sunny, cold. 14–21 Mild, rain and snow showers. 22–27 Very cold; snow showers. 28–31 Mild, rain and snow.

FEB. 2007: Temp. 16° (5° below avg.); precip. 2.5" (avg.). 1–3 Sunny, then snow; cold. 4–7 Sunny, very cold. 8–15 Snowy periods, cold. 16–19 Snowstorm, very cold. 20–22 Rain and snow. 23–25 Sunny, very cold. 26–28 Snow, then sunny.

MAR. 2007: Temp. 36° (3° above avg.); precip. 2.5" (0.5" below avg.). 1–5 Sunny. 6–11 Rain and snow, then sunny, mild. 12–19 Sunny; cool, then mild. 20–24 Warm; sunny, then showers. 25–28 Heavy rain and snow, then sunny, cold. 29–31 Sunny, mild.

APR. 2007: Temp. 45° (1° below avg. east; 1° above west); precip. 3" (0.5" above avg. north; 1" below south). 1–5 Mild; showers,

then sunny. 6–13 Snow, then sunny, cold. 14–19 Sunny. 20–23 Showers north; sunny, warm south. 24–30 Showers.

MAY 2007: Temp. 56.5° (1° below avg. east; 2° above west); precip. 2" (1.5" below avg.). 1–7 Cool; showers, then sunny. 8–15 Very warm; t-storms. 16–23 Sunny. 24–25 T-storms. 26–31 Sunny, then showers.

JUNE 2007: Temp. 64° (1° below avg.); precip. 1.5" (2" below avg.). 1–4 Sunny, very warm. 5–12 T-storms, then sunny, warm. 13–18 Warm, t-storms. 19–24 Sunny, seasonable. 25–30 T-storms, then sunny, cool.

JULY 2007: Temp. 68° (2° below avg.); precip. 4" (2" above avg. north; 2" below south). 1–2 Sunny, hot. 3–6 Warm, t-storms. 7–13 Showers north, sunny south. 14–23 Showers. 24–31 T-storms, then sunny, warm.

AUG. 2007: Temp. 65° (2° below avg.); precip. 4" (avg.). 1–5 Showers, cool. 6–13 Comfortable; scattered showers. 14–21 T-storms, then sunny, warm. 22–26 Hot, t-storms. 27–31 Cool; sunny, then rain.

SEPT. 2007: Temp. 57° (2° below avg.); precip. 3.5" (avg.; 2" above south). 1–3 Sunny, cool. 4–8 Warm, t-storms. 9–16 Cool, showers. 17–23 Showers. 24–30 Sunny, then rain.

OCT. 2007: Temp. 45° (3° below avg.); precip. 4" (0.5" above avg.). 1–6 Showers, warm. 7–9 Sunny, cool. 10–16 Showers, warm. 17–20 Rain and snow showers, then sunny. 21–25 Cool; showers, snow north. 26–31 Cold, snow showers.

Caribou ⊙

Augusta ⊙

Burlington ⊙

Concord ⊙

Albany ⊙

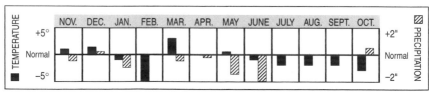

Get your local forecast at Almanac.com/weathercenter. **2007**

Atlantic Corridor

SUMMARY: Winter temperatures will be slightly below normal, on average, with near-normal precipitation and above-normal snowfall, especially in the southeast. February will be the coldest, snowiest month. The snowiest periods will be in mid-December and mid- and late February. The coldest periods will be around Christmas and in early and late January and early and late February.

Spring will come early, with temperatures slightly above normal, on average, from mid-March through May. Rainfall will be below normal, on average, with many sunny days.

Summer temperatures will be slightly below normal, on average, with the hottest periods in mid-June and mid-August. Below-normal rainfall will continue, stressing crops and lawns.

A major hurricane will threaten in late September. Otherwise, September and October will be cooler than normal, with near-normal rainfall.

NOV. 2006: Temp. 48.5° (0.5° above avg.); precip. 3" (0.5" below avg.). 1–5 Rain, then sunny, cold. 6–11 Mild, rainy periods. 12–16 Rain and snow, then sunny. 17–21 Rain, then sunny, mild. 22–30 Sunny; cold, then mild.

DEC. 2006: Temp. 36° (2° below avg.); precip. 5.5" (1" above avg. north; 4" above south). 1–2 Sunny, cold. 3–6 Snow, then rain. 7–9 Sunny, cold. 10–13 Rain, mild. 14–18 Sunny, then rain and snow. 19–22 Sunny, then rain. 23–25 Sunny, cold. 26–29 Snow east, then warm. 30–31 Heavy rain.

JAN. 2007: Temp. 32° (1° below avg.); precip. 1.5" (2" below avg.). 1–8 Snow south, then very cold. 9–12 Rain, then sunny, cold. 13–15 Cold, snow showers. 16–21 Mild, showers. 22–25 Snow, then sunny, very cold. 26–31 Snow, then warm.

FEB. 2007: Temp. 29° (4° below avg.); precip. 4" (1" above avg.). 1–7 Snow, then sunny, very cold. 8–11 Snow north, rain south; seasonable. 12–18 Rainy periods south, rain and snow north. 19–22 Mild, rain. 23–26 Sunny, very cold. 27–28 Northeaster.

MAR. 2007: Temp. 45° (3° above avg. north; 1° above avg. south); precip. 3.5" (0.5" below avg.). 1–4 Flurries, cold. 5–12 Heavy rain, then sunny, seasonable. 13–21 Rain, then sunny, seasonable. 22–26 Warm; sunny, then rain. 27–31 Sunny, cool.

APR. 2007: Temp. 53° (1° above avg.); precip. 3" (0.5" below avg.). 1–7 T-storms; warm, then cool. 8–14 Cool, showers. 15–22 Sunny, very warm. 23–25 T-storms; cool north, warm south. 26–30 Sunny, warm.

MAY 2007: Temp. 64° (2° above avg.); precip. 2.5" (1.5" below avg.). 1–7 Cool, showers. 8–15 Sunny, hot. 16–27 Very warm; scattered t-storms. 28–31 Showers.

JUNE 2007: Temp. 70.5° (0.5° below avg.); precip. 4" (0.5" above avg.). 1–5 Sunny, warm. 6–14 Warm, t-storms. 15–21 Seasonable; t-storms north. 22–26 Sunny, cool. 27–30 Sunny, comfortable north; rain south.

JULY 2007: Temp. 74° (2° below avg.); precip. 2" (2" below avg.). 1–7 Sunny, warm. 8–18 Seasonable; scattered t-storms. 19–23 T-storms, then sunny, cool. 24-31 Sunny, warm.

AUG. 2007: Temp. 72° (2° below avg.); precip. 3.5" (1" above avg. north; 2" below south). 1–7 T-storms, then sunny, cool. 8–15 Hot; scattered t-storms. 16–21 Sunny, warm. 22–31 Showers; hot, then cool.

SEPT. 2007: Temp. 65° (2° below avg.); precip. 3.5" (avg.). 1–3 Sunny, cool. 4–9 Sunny, warm. 10–19 Rain, then sunny, cool. 20–26 Rain, then sunny, cool. 27–30 Hurricane.

OCT. 2007: Temp. 54.5° (2.5° below avg. north; 0.5° below south); precip. 3.5" (1" above avg. north; 1" below south). 1–6 Warm; showers north, sunny south. 7–11 Sunny, warm. 12–17 Seasonable, showers. 18–21 Cold; rain south, snow north. 22–24 Sunny. 25–31 Heavy rain, then sunny, cold.

Boston
Hartford
New York
Philadelphia
Baltimore
Atlantic City
Washington
Richmond

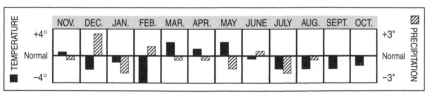

	NOV.	DEC.	JAN.	FEB.	MAR.	APR.	MAY	JUNE	JULY	AUG.	SEPT.	OCT.	

TEMPERATURE +4° Normal ■ –4°

PRECIPITATION +3" Normal –3"

W
E
A
T
H
E
R

Appalachians

SUMMARY: Winter will be colder than normal, with above-normal precipitation but near-normal snowfall. The coldest periods will be in mid- and late December, mid-January, and early February. The snowiest periods will occur in mid-December, early and late February, and early March.

Spring will come early, with some of the hottest temperatures of the year in mid- to late April and mid-May. Temperatures in April and May will be well above normal, on average, with well-below-normal precipitation.

Summer will be a bit cooler than normal, on average, with below-normal rainfall in most of the region. While this will provide many great days for outdoor activities, it will stress farms, gardens, and lawns.

September and October will be cooler than normal, on average, with near-normal precipitation and an early snow in mid- to late October.

NOV. 2006: Temp. 43° (avg.); precip. 3.5" (avg.). 1–5 Chilly, rain and snow showers. 6–11 Mild; rainy periods. 12–14 Snow, cold. 15–21 Sunny, then rain, mild. 22–24 Sunny, chilly. 25–30 Mild, sunny, then rain.

DEC. 2006: Temp. 32° (2° below avg.); precip. 5" (2" above avg.). 1–3 Chilly, flurries. 4–6 Rain, mild. 7–9 Sunny, cold. 10–14 Mild; rainy periods. 15–21 Cold; snow, then flurries. 22–27 Snow, then sunny, very cold. 28–31 Mild; sunny, then rain.

JAN. 2007: Temp. 26.5° (1.5° below avg.); precip. 2" (1" below avg.). 1–8 Sunny, very cold. 9–13 Rain, then sunny, cold. 14–19 Snow, then sunny, mild. 20–25 Rain to snow, then sunny, very cold. 26–31 Snow showers, then mild.

FEB. 2007: Temp. 24° (4° below avg.); precip. 3.5" (1" above avg.). 1–7 Snow, then sunny, very cold. 8–19 Seasonable; occasional rain and snow. 20–22 Rain, mild. 23–28 Cold; sunny, then snow.

MAR. 2007: Temp. 39.5° (2° above avg. north; 1° below south); precip. 3.5" (0.5" above avg.). 1–4 Cold, snow. 5–12 Rain, then sunny, seasonable. 13–15 Rain, seasonable. 16–24 Sunny, pleasant. 25–31 Heavy rain, then sunny, cool.

APR. 2007: Temp. 51° (2° above avg. north; avg. south); precip. 2.5" (1" below avg.). 1–4 T-storms, then sunny. 5–11 Chilly; rain, then snow. 12–15 Sunny, cool. 16–22 Sunny, very warm. 23–30 T-storms, then sunny.

MAY 2007: Temp. 63° (3° above avg.); precip. 2.5" (1.5" below avg.). 1–7 Cool; sunny north, rainy periods south. 8–13 Sunny, hot. 14–20 Warm, t-storms. 21–24 Sunny north, rain south. 25–31 Seasonable, t-storms.

JUNE 2007: Temp. 67.5° (0.5° below avg.); precip. 3" (1" below avg.). 1–4 Sunny, warm. 5–8 Cool, rain. 9–13 Sunny, hot. 14–20 Seasonable, t-storms. 21–26 Sunny, comfortable. 27–30 Sunny north, showers south.

JULY 2007: Temp. 72° (1° below avg.); precip. 3" (3" below avg. north; 2" above south). 1–3 Sunny, hot. 4–9 Seasonable, t-storms. 10–15 Sunny, warm. 16–19 Seasonable, t-storms. 20–25 Sunny, then t-storms; cool. 26–31 Humid, t-storms.

AUG. 2007: Temp. 70° (1° below avg.); precip. 3.5" (avg.). 1–2 Sunny, warm. 3–5 Cool; rain north, sunny south. 6–11 Seasonable, t-storms. 12–14 Sunny, hot. 15–20 T-storms, then sunny. 21–26 T-storms, then sunny, very warm. 27–31 Showers, seasonable.

SEPT. 2007: Temp. 61° (3° below avg.); precip. 4.5" (1" above avg.). 1–3 Sunny, cool. 4–9 Rain, then sunny, warm. 10–18 Cool; showers, then sunny. 19–25 Cool; rain, then sunny. 26–30 Seasonable; rain, then sunny.

OCT. 2007: Temp. 52° (1° below avg.); precip. 2" (1" below avg.). 1–6 Warm; showers north, sunny south. 7–14 Sunny; warm, then seasonable. 15–19 Rain, then sunny, cold. 20–23 Snow. 24–27 Chilly; rain, then sunny. 28–31 Cold; snow north, rain south.

Elmira ⊙
Scranton ⊙
Harrisburg ⊙
Frederick ⊙
Roanoke ⊙
Asheville ⊙

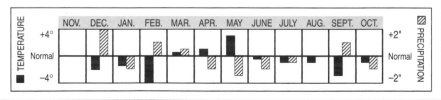

	NOV.	DEC.	JAN.	FEB.	MAR.	APR.	MAY	JUNE	JULY	AUG.	SEPT.	OCT.	

TEMPERATURE +4° Normal −4° PRECIPITATION +2" Normal −2"

Southeast

SUMMARY: Winter will be colder and wetter than normal, on average, with above-normal snowfall, especially in eastern North Carolina. The coldest periods will be in mid- to late December, early January, and early and late February. The heaviest and most widespread snowfalls will occur around Christmas and in early and mid-January and late February.

April and May will be warmer and drier than normal, on average, with an early heat wave in mid-May.

Summer temperatures will be about a degree below normal, on average, with above-normal rainfall. The hottest temperatures will occur in mid- to late July and late August.

September and October will be cooler and drier than normal, on average, with especially chilly temperatures in the second half of October.

NOV. 2006: Temp. 56° (1° above avg.); precip. 2.5" (0.5" below avg.). 1–5 Sunny, cool. 6–10 Showers, warm. 11–16 Sunny, cool. 17–21 Rain, then sunny, warm. 22–25 Sunny, cool. 26–30 Mild; sunny, then rain.

DEC. 2006: Temp. 45° (2° below avg.); precip. 7.5" (4" above avg.). 1–3 Sunny, cool. 4–11 Rain; mild, then chilly. 12–16 T-storms, then sunny, cool. 17–20 Rain, then sunny, cold. 21–24 Rain, then sunny, very cold. 25–29 Rain and snow, then sunny, mild. 30–31 Heavy rain.

JAN. 2007: Temp. 43° (2° below avg.); precip. 4" (0.5" below avg.). 1–4 Chilly; sunny, then rain and snow. 5–8 Sunny, very cold. 9–15 Cold; sunny, then rain south and snow north. 16–20 Warm; showers north, sunny south. 21–23 Turning colder; rain south, snow north. 24–31 Sunny; cool, then warm.

FEB. 2007: Temp. 45.5° (3° below avg. north; 2° above south); precip. 4.5" (0.5" above avg.). 1–2 Sunny, cold. 3–5 Rain, then sunny. 6–9 Snow north, then sunny, warm. 10–13 Mild, rain. 14–18 T-storms, warm. 19–22 Rain, then sunny; warm. 23–28 Cold; rain and snow north, rain south.

MAR. 2007: Temp. 53° (2° below avg.); precip. 5" (0.5" above avg.). 1–3 Cold; snow north, rain south. 4–9 Cool; sunny north, rain south. 10–14 Sunny, cool. 15–18 T-storms, then sunny. 19–22 Rain, then sunny. 23–25 T-storms, warm. 26–31 Cool; sunny, then rain.

APR. 2007: Temp. 63° (1° above avg. north; 1° below south); precip. 2.5" (0.5" below avg.). 1–5 Warm, rain. 6–15 Sunny, cool. 16–22 Sunny, then t-storms. 23–30 Sunny, warm.

MAY 2007: Temp. 75° (4° above avg.); precip. 2.5" (1" below avg.). 1–3 Sunny, warm. 4–11 T-storms, then sunny, very warm. 12–15 Sunny, hot. 16–22 T-storms north, then sunny, hot. 23–31 Seasonable; sunny, then t-storms.

JUNE 2007: Temp. 75° (2° below avg.); precip. 7" (2.5" above avg.). 1–8 T-storms, some heavy; seasonable. 9–12 Sunny, comfortable. 13–16 T-storms, seasonable. 17–19 Sunny, warm. 20–23 T-storms, cool. 24–30 Sunny, then heavy t-storms; seasonable.

JULY 2007: Temp. 81° (avg.); precip. 6" (1" above avg.). 1–6 T-storms, seasonable. 7–11 Sunny, warm. 12–19 T-storms, seasonable. 20–25 Sunny, hot east; t-storms west. 26–31 T-storms; warm north, hot south.

AUG. 2007: Temp. 78° (1° below avg.); precip. 3" (2" below avg.). 1–3 T-storms, seasonable. 4–8 Sunny, comfortable. 9–14 T-storms, then sunny; warm. 15–21 Seasonable, t-storms. 22–31 Warm, sunny, then t-storms.

SEPT. 2007: Temp. 72° (2° below avg.); precip. 4.5" (avg.). 1–3 Sunny, cool. 4–11 Warm, t-storms. 12–19 Sunny, cool. 20–25 T-storms, then sunny, cool. 26–30 Warm, showers.

OCT. 2007: Temp. 63° (1° below avg.); precip. 1" (2" below avg.). 1–11 Sunny, warm. 12–16 Showers. 17–25 Sunny; cold, then seasonable. 26–31 Cold; rain, then sunny.

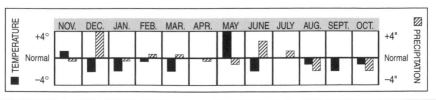

Florida

SUMMARY: Winter will be warmer and drier than normal. Expect temperatures to be slightly above normal, on average, and rainfall to be well below normal. The coldest temperatures will occur in mid- to late December, early January, and late February, but a damaging freeze is unlikely.

April and May will be much drier than normal, with much-below-normal rainfall, stressing crops and lawns and increasing the threat of fires. Temperatures will be near or a bit above normal.

Summer rainfall will be above normal, lowering the fire threat but not making up for the accumulated rainfall deficit, especially with temperatures slightly above normal, on average. The hottest periods will occur in mid-June, most of July, and early and late August.

September and October will be cooler and drier than normal, with temperatures cooler than normal, on average, and well-below-normal rainfall.

NOV. 2006: Temp. 71° (2° above avg.); precip. 1.5" (1" below avg.). 1–9 Sunny; cool, then warm. 10–17 Warm; scattered t-storms. 18–24 Sunny, seasonable. 25–30 Warm; scattered showers south.

DEC. 2006: Temp. 62° (1° below avg.); precip. 1.5" (1" below avg.). 1–6 Sunny, warm. 7–13 Warm; scattered t-storms. 14–20 Sunny, chilly. 21–25 T-storms, then sunny, cold. 26–29 Showers, then sunny, chilly. 30–31 T-storms.

JAN. 2007: Temp. 61.5° (1° below avg. north; 2° above south); precip. 1.5" (1" below avg.). 1–3 Sunny, cool. 4–7 Rain, then sunny, cold. 8–12 Partly sunny, mild. 13–15 Sunny. 16–22 Warm; scattered showers. 23–28 Sunny, cool. 29–31 Mild, showers.

FEB. 2007: Temp. 65° (4° above avg.); precip. 2" (0.5" below avg.). 1–3 T-storms. 4–6 Showers, then sunny, chilly. 7–15 Warm; scattered showers. 16–22 Sunny, very warm. 23–28 T-storms, then sunny, cold.

MAR. 2007: Temp. 65.5° (2° below avg. north; 1° below south); precip. 2.5" (0.5" below avg.). 1–6 Sunny; cold, then warm. 7–10 T-storms, cool. 11–15 Sunny; cool, then warm. 16–20 T-storms, seasonable. 21–23 Sunny, cool. 24–29 T-storms, then sunny, cool. 30–31 Showers.

APR. 2007: Temp. 71° (avg.); precip. 0.5" (2" below avg.). 1–5 Showers, then sunny; warm. 6–16 T-storms, then sunny, cool. 17–20 Sunny, seasonable. 21–26 Warm; t-storms, then sunny. 27–30 Seasonable; scattered t-storms.

MAY 2007: Temp. 78.5° (3° above avg. north; avg. south); precip. 1.5" (2.5" below avg.). 1–3 Sunny, warm. 4–12 Seasonable; scattered t-storms. 13–21 Hot, humid; t-storms. 22–31 Seasonable, t-storms.

JUNE 2007: Temp. 81° (avg.); precip. 7" (0.5" above avg.). 1–7 Seasonable, t-storms. 8–18 Seasonable; scattered t-storms. 19–21 Sunny, hot. 22–30 Seasonable; scattered t-storms.

JULY 2007: Temp. 84° (2° above avg.); precip. 8.5" (2" above avg.). 1–7 Hot; scattered t-storms. 8–12 Sunny, hot. 13–21 Hot, humid; scattered t-storms. 22–31 Seasonable; scattered t-storms.

AUG. 2007: Temp. 82° (1° above avg.); precip. 7.5" (avg.). 1–5 Hot, t-storms mainly south. 6–11 Seasonable; scattered t-storms. 12–21 Seasonable, t-storms. 22–24 Sunny, hot. 25–31 Hot, t-storms.

SEPT. 2007: Temp. 78.5° (1.5° below avg.); precip. 6" (1" below avg.). 1–7 Seasonable, then hot; scattered t-storms. 8–13 Seasonable, t-storms. 14–18 Cool, t-storms. 19–24 T-storms; cool north, warm south. 25–30 Hot, t-storms.

OCT. 2007: Temp. 73.5° (1.5° below avg.); precip. 1" (3" below avg.). 1–7 T-storms, then sunny; warm. 8–15 T-storms, then sunny, seasonable. 16–23 T-storms, then sunny, cool. 24–31 T-storms, then sunny, chilly.

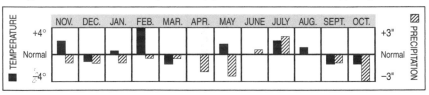

Lower Lakes

SUMMARY: Winter will be colder than normal, on average, especially in the west. Precipitation will be below normal, with below-normal snowfall except in the west and in areas that receive lake snows in a southwesterly flow. The coldest temperatures will be around Christmas and in early and mid- to late January and early and late February. The heaviest lake snows will be in early and mid-December and mid-January. The heaviest general snowfalls will be in mid-December, early and late January, and mid-February.

April and May will be warmer and drier than normal. The period from mid-April through mid-May will be much warmer than normal, with summerlike temperatures in mid- to late April and mid-May.

Summer will be a bit cooler and wetter than normal, on average. The hottest period will be in late July.

September and October will be a bit cooler and drier than normal, on average.

NOV. 2006: Temp. 41.5° (0.5° below avg. east; 3° above west); precip. 3.5" (0.5" above avg.). 1–4 Cold, snow showers. 5–10 Mild, rain. 11–15 Cold, snow showers. 16–20 Mild, rain, then sunny. 21–23 Cold, snow showers. 24–30 Warm; sunny, then showers.

DEC. 2006: Temp. 27° (1° below avg. east; 3° below west); precip. 2.5" (0.5" below avg.). 1–3 Snow, cold. 4–6 Showers, mild. 7–10 Cold; lake snows. 11–13 Showers, mild. 14–17 Snow, cold. 18–21 Snow showers. 22–26 Very cold; snow showers, lake snows. 27–31 Mild, rain and snow showers.

JAN. 2007: Temp. 20.5° (1° below avg. east; 6° below west); precip. 2" (0.5" below avg.). 1–6 Snowstorm, then bitter cold. 7–14 Rain, then snow showers, very cold. 15–20 Mild; rainy periods. 21–27 Snow showers, bitter cold. 28–31 Mild, then cold; rain to snow.

FEB. 2007: Temp. 20° (4° below avg.); precip. 1.5" (0.5" below avg.). 1–6 Snow showers, very cold. 7–11 Seasonable, snow showers. 12–18 Cold; snowy periods. 19–21 Mild, showers. 22–28 Very cold, snow showers.

MAR. 2007: Temp. 37° (3° above avg. east; 1° below west); precip. 2" (1" below avg.). 1–7 Seasonable, periods of rain and snow. 8–16 Seasonable, rain and snow showers. 17–23 Sunny, turning warm. 24–28 Cold, rain to snow, then sunny. 29–31 Mild, showers.

APR. 2007: Temp. 50° (3° above avg.); precip. 2.5" (1" below avg.). 1–5 Showers, cool.

6–11 Cool; snow, then sunny. 12–16 Warm, showers. 17–22 Sunny, warm. 23–30 Heavy t-storms, then showers, warm.

MAY 2007: Temp. 63° (5° above avg.); precip. 2.5" (avg. south; 2" below north). 1–5 Showers, then sunny; cool. 6–14 Showers, then warm. 19–22 Showers. 23–25 Warm, t-storms. 26–31 Cool; sunny, then showers.

JUNE 2007: Temp. 67° (avg.); precip. 3" (0.5" below avg.). 1–2 Sunny. 3–7 Showers; warm, then cool. 8–12 Sunny, very warm. 13–19 Showers; cool, then warm. 20–23 Sunny, hot. 24–30 T-storms, then sunny; seasonable.

JULY 2007: Temp. 70° (2° below avg.); precip. 4.5" (1" above avg.). 1–4 Showers east, sunny west. 5–11 Cool; sunny east, t-storms west. 12–16 Scattered t-storms. 17–22 Cool; rainy periods. 23–31 Hot; scattered t-storms.

AUG. 2007: Temp. 69° (1° below avg.); precip. 4" (avg.). 1–12 Cool; t-storms east, sunny west. 13–20 Warm; scattered t-storms. 21–24 Sunny, hot. 25–31 T-storms, then sunny, cool.

SEPT. 2007: Temp. 62° (1° below avg.); precip. 3" (0.5" below avg.). 1–4 T-storms, turning warmer. 5–7 Sunny, very warm. 8–17 Cool; t-storms, then sunny. 18–23 Cool, showers. 24–30 Turning warmer; sunny, then showers.

OCT. 2007: Temp. 52° (avg.); precip. 2" (0.5" below avg.). 1–4 Showers, mild. 5–9 Sunny, warm. 10–14 Showers, mild. 15–20 Turning cold; rain to snow. 21–26 Cool; rainy periods. 27–31 Chilly, rain and snow.

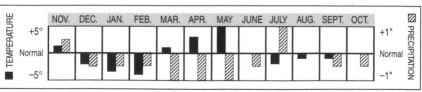

Ohio Valley

SUMMARY: Winter temperatures will be slightly below normal, on average, with near-normal snowfall. Rainfall will be above normal, especially in the southwest. The coldest temperatures will be around Christmas and in early, mid-, and late January and early February. The most widespread snowfalls will be in early December, mid- and late January, and late February.

The first half of April will be rather cold, but mid-April through May will be much warmer than normal, with some of the year's hottest temperatures in mid-May. Precipitation in April and May will be near or slightly below normal.

Summer temperatures will be near normal, on average. Rainfall will be a bit below normal in the east, a bit above in the west. The hottest periods will be in late July and mid-August.

September and October will be cool, with near- or slightly below-normal precipitation. Expect the first widespread snowfall in mid- to late October.

NOV. 2006: Temp. 46° (avg. east; 2° above west); precip. 4" (0.5" above avg.). 1–4 Cold, flurries. 5–10 Rain, warm. 11–15 Cold, snow showers. 16–20 Rain, then sunny, mild. 21–24 Sunny, cold. 25–30 Mild, showers.

DEC. 2006: Temp. 34° (1° below avg.); precip. 3.5" (1" below avg. northeast; 2" above southwest). 1–3 Cold; sunny, then snow. 4–6 Rain, mild. 7–9 Sunny, cold. 10–13 Mild, showers. 14–19 Seasonable, rain and snow showers. 20–27 Very cold, snow showers. 28–31 Mild; sunny, then rain.

JAN. 2007: Temp. 27° (4° below avg.); precip. 2.5" (0.5" below avg.). 1–7 Very cold; snow showers, then sunny. 8–9 Mild, rain. 10–14 Cold; sunny, then snow. 15–20 Mild, showers. 21–27 Cold, snow showers. 28–31 Sunny, warm, then snow showers.

FEB. 2007: Temp. 31.5° (2° below avg. north; 1° above south); precip. 5" (2" above avg.). 1–6 Cold, snow showers. 7–14 Seasonable; sunny, then rain and snow showers. 15–21 Snow, then mild, t-storms. 22–28 Cold; sunny, then snowstorm.

MAR. 2007: Temp. 43.5° (0.5° below avg.); precip. 4.5" (0.5" above avg.). 1–5 Seasonable, rain and snow showers. 6–12 Chilly, flurries. 13–16 T-storms, mild. 17–23 Sunny, turning warm. 24–29 Rain to snow, then sunny; cold. 30–31 Mild, showers.

APR. 2007: Temp. 54.5° (2° above avg. north; 1° below south); precip. 3" (0.5" below avg.). 1–3 Showers. 4–6 Rain, cold. 7–11

Snow, then sunny. 12–17 Cool, showers. 18–23 Sunny, warm. 24–30 T-storms, then sunny.

MAY 2007: Temp. 69° (6° above avg.); precip. 4" (0.5" below avg.). 1–4 T-storms, then sunny; cool. 5–12 Showers, then sunny, hot. 13–22 Warm; t-storms. 23–31 Warm; sunny, then t-storms.

JUNE 2007: Temp. 72° (avg.); precip. 4" (0.5" above avg.). 1–6 Warm; sunny, then t-storms. 7–11 Sunny, cool. 12–18 Seasonable; scattered t-storms. 19–24 Sunny, warm. 25–30 Rain, then sunny; seasonable.

JULY 2007: Temp. 75° (1° below avg.); precip. 4" (2" below avg. east; 2" above west). 1–5 T-storms, then sunny, comfortable. 6–12 Warm, humid; t-storms. 13–19 Scattered t-storms. 20–22 Sunny, cool. 23–28 T-storms, then sunny. 29–31 Hot; sunny, then t-storms.

AUG. 2007: Temp. 74° (avg.); precip. 4" (0.5" above avg.). 1–5 Cool; t-storms east. 6–12 Comfortable, t-storms then sunny. 13–21 Hot; sunny, then t-storms. 22–25 Sunny, warm. 26–31 T-storms, warm, then cool.

SEPT. 2007: Temp. 63° (4° below avg.); precip. 3" (avg.). 1–4 Cool; sunny, then t-storms. 5–7 Sunny, warm. 8–12 T-storms, then sunny, cool. 13–18 Chilly; showers, then sunny. 19–25 Cool; rain, then sunny. 26–30 Showers.

OCT. 2007: Temp. 54° (2° below avg.); precip. 2" (0.5" below avg.). 1–9 Showers, then sunny, warm. 10–14 Showers, then sunny, seasonable. 15–18 Showers, then sunny, cold. 19–21 Snow, cold. 22–27 Rain, then sunny, cold. 28–31 Cold, rain and snow showers.

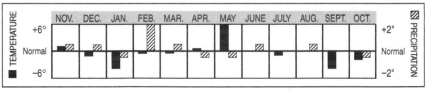

Deep South

SUMMARY: Winter will be a bit cooler than normal, on average, with record cold bringing a freeze all the way to the Gulf Coast in early January. Other cold periods will be in mid- to late December and in early and late February. The snowiest periods will be in early January and in early and late February. Rainfall will be well above normal in the north and near or slightly above normal in the south.

April will have near- or slightly below-normal temperatures, followed by an exceptionally warm May. Rainfall will be near normal in the north and below normal in the south.

Summer temperatures and rainfall will be near normal, on average. The hottest periods will be in mid- and late July and early and mid-August.

September and October will be a bit cooler and wetter than normal in the north and a bit warmer and drier in the south.

NOV. 2006: Temp. 56.5° (1.5° above avg.); precip. 6" (0.5" below avg. east; 2" above west). 1–4 Sunny, cool. 5–9 Mild, t-storms. 10–15 Showers, then sunny, cool. 16–24 T-storms, then sunny, cool. 25–30 Warm; sunny, then showers.

DEC. 2006: Temp. 45° (2° below avg.); precip. 10" (5" above avg.). 1–6 Warm; heavy t-storms. 7–11 T-storms, cool, then warm. 12–16 Sunny, cool. 17–27 Cold; rain showers south, snow showers north. 28–31 Mild; sunny, then rain.

JAN. 2007: Temp. 42° (2° below avg.); precip. 4.5" (0.5" below avg.). 1–7 Snow north, rain south, then sunny, record cold. 8–14 Cool, showers. 15–20 Rain, then sunny, warm. 21–25 T-storms, then sunny, seasonable. 26–31 Warm, sunny, then rain.

FEB. 2007: Temp. 49° (3° above avg.); precip. 6" (3" above avg. north; 1" below south). 1–4 Cold; flurries, then sunny. 5–8 Sunny, warm. 9–14 Cool; scattered t-storms. 15–21 Warm, t-storms. 22–28 Flurries, then sunny.

MAR. 2007: Temp. 54° (2° above avg.); precip. 6" (2" above avg. north; 2" below south). 1–5 Showers, mild. 6–12 Sunny, cool. 13–20 Scattered t-storms. 21–24 Sunny, then t-storms. 25–31 Cool; sunny, then showers.

APR. 2007: Temp. 62.5° (0.5° below avg.); precip. 4" (1" above avg. north; 2" below south). 1–6 Seasonable, t-storms. 7–14 Sunny, cool. 15–21 Sunny north, t-storms

south. 22–30 T-storms, then sunny, seasonable.

MAY 2007: Temp. 76° (5° above avg.); precip. 4" (1" below avg.). 1–8 Sunny, warm. 9–22 Hot, mostly dry. 23–31 Seasonable, t-storms.

JUNE 2007: Temp. 77° (1° below avg.); precip. 6" (1" above avg.). 1–5 Seasonable, t-storms. 6–11 Sunny, comfortable. 12–23 Scattered t-storms. 24–30 Sunny, then t-storms.

JULY 2007: Temp. 83° (1° below avg. north; 3° above south); precip. 4" (1" below avg.). 1–8 Warm; t-storms, then sunny. 9–15 T-storms, then sunny, seasonable. 16–19 Warm, t-storms. 20–23 Cool north, t-storms south. 24–31 Hot, humid; scattered t-storms.

AUG. 2007: Temp. 82° (1° above avg.); precip. 4.5" (1" above avg. north; 1.5" below south). 1–6 T-storms, then sunny, hot. 7–11 Warm; sunny north, t-storms south. 12–18 Hot; scattered t-storms. 19–24 Seasonable, t-storms. 25–31 Hot; scattered t-storms.

SEPT. 2007: Temp. 75.5° (2° below avg. north; 1° above south); precip. 2.5" (2" below avg.; 3" above north). 1–6 Cool, rain, then sunny. 7–11 T-storms, then sunny. 12–17 Showers, then sunny, cool. 18–24 Rain, then sunny, chilly. 25–30 Showers, then sunny.

OCT. 2007: Temp. 65.5° (0.5° above avg.); precip. 2" (1" below avg.). 1–6 T-storms, then sunny, warm. 7–10 Warm; scattered t-storms. 11–16 Seasonable, mainly dry. 17–21 Showers, then sunny, very cool. 22–31 Showers, then sunny, very cool.

Map labels: Nashville, Little Rock, Tupelo, Montgomery, Shreveport, Jackson, Mobile, New Orleans

W E A T H E R

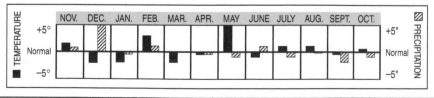

Upper Midwest

SUMMARY: Winter will be much colder and snowier than normal, with temperatures a couple of degrees below normal. The coldest periods will be occurring in early and late December, early and mid-January, and mid-February. The snowiest periods will be in early December; early, mid-, and late February; and early March.

April will have a cold, snowy start, but temperatures from midmonth through May will be milder than normal, on average. Precipitation will be a bit below normal in the east and a bit above in the west.

Summer will be a bit cooler than normal, with near-normal rainfall. The hottest periods will be in late June, late July, and mid-August.

September will be slightly cooler and wetter than normal. October will be slightly milder and drier than normal.

NOV. 2006: Temp. 32° (4° above avg.); precip. 1" (1" below avg.). 1–7 Sunny; cold, then mild. 8–16 Snow showers, seasonable. 17–22 Sunny, mild. 23–30 Mild; showers, then flurries.

DEC. 2006: Temp. 10° (4° below avg.); precip. 1.5" (0.5" above avg.). 1–3 Snowstorm. 4–9 Very cold, snow showers. 10–14 Snow showers, seasonable, then cold. 15–19 Mild, flurries. 20–25 Flurries, very cold, then seasonable. 26–28 Sunny, mild. 29–31 Cold, snow showers.

JAN. 2007: Temp. 6° (3° below avg.); precip. 1" (avg.). 1–4 Very cold, snow showers. 5–13 Snow showers, then sunny, record cold. 14–20 Snow showers, then sunny, mild. 21–26 Cold, snow showers. 27–31 Mild, then cold, snow showers.

FEB. 2007: Temp. 4° (7° below avg.); precip. 1.5" (0.5" above avg.). 1–6 Flurries, turning mild. 7–11 Snow, then sunny, cold. 12–18 Cold, periods of snow. 19–23 Sunny, record cold. 24–28 Snowstorm, then sunny, cold.

MAR. 2007: Temp. 26.5° (0.5° below avg.); precip. 1" (0.5" below avg.). 1–6 Heavy snow east, mild west. 7–12 Cold, snow showers. 13–16 Sunny, seasonable. 17–24 Snow, then sunny, cold. 25–31 Snow showers, then sunny, cold.

APR. 2007: Temp. 41.5° (0.5° above avg.); precip. 1.5" (0.5" below avg.). 1–5 Cold, snow showers. 6–9 Snow, then sunny, cold. 10–14 Sunny, seasonable. 15–20 Showers, then sunny, very warm. 21–24 Seasonable, showers. 25–28 Sunny, warm. 29–30 T-storms, then cool.

MAY 2007: Temp. 55.5° (0.5° above avg.); precip. 4" (0.5" below avg. east; 2" above west). 1–4 Cool, showers. 5–12 T-storms, warm. 13–17 Seasonable; scattered t-storms. 18–21 Sunny, cool. 22–27 T-storms, then sunny, cool. 28–31 T-storms, then sunny.

JUNE 2007: Temp. 64° (avg.); precip. 4.5" (2" above north; 1" below south). 1–4 T-storms. 5–8 Sunny, seasonable. 9–14 Cool; t-storms, then sunny. 15–20 Sunny, seasonable. 21–30 T-storms; hot, then seasonable.

JULY 2007: Temp. 67° (2° below avg.); precip. 4" (0.5" above avg.). 1–7 T-storms, then sunny, cool. 8–12 Cool, showers. 13–21 T-storms, then sunny, cool. 22–26 Showers, then sunny, cool. 27–31 Scattered t-storms, warm.

AUG. 2007: Temp. 66° (1° below avg.); precip. 3" (0.5" below avg.). 1–6 Cool; scattered t-storms. 7–12 Sunny, seasonable. 13–17 Warm; sunny, then t-storms. 18–21 Sunny, warm. 22–25 Cool, t-storms east. 26–31 T-storms, then chilly.

SEPT. 2007: Temp. 57° (1° below avg.); precip. 3.5" (0.5" above avg.). 1–4 Rain, chilly. 5–10 Showers, seasonable. 11–15 Sunny, cool. 16–22 Showers, then sunny, cool. 23–30 Showers, then sunny; seasonable.

OCT. 2007: Temp. 48° (2° above avg.); precip. 2" (0.5" below avg.). 1–8 T-storms, then sunny, warm. 9–14 Showers, then sunny, seasonable. 15–20 Rain and snow showers, then sunny, cold. 21–25 Sunny, mild. 26–31 Cool, rain and snow showers.

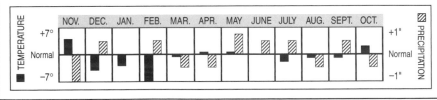

Heartland

SUMMARY: Winter will be much colder and snowier than normal, with temperatures a couple of degrees below normal, on average. The coldest periods will be occurring in early and mid-to-late December, early and mid-January, and early February. Significant snowfalls will be in mid-November; early, mid-, and late December; mid-January; and mid-February.

Early April will be cool, but mid-April through May will be very warm, with temperatures about eight degrees above normal, on average. Rainfall will be above normal in the north and below normal in the south.

Summer will be cooler than normal, on average, especially in the southeast. The hottest temperatures will be in late June and mid-August. Rainfall will be near normal in the north and below normal in the south.

September will be cooler and wetter than normal. October will be warmer and drier than normal, on average.

NOV. 2006: Temp. 44° (2° above avg.); precip. 2.5" (avg.). 1–3 Sunny, cool. 4–6 Mild, showers. 7–13 Turning colder; rain, then snow. 14–20 Rain, then sunny; mild. 21–24 Sunny, cool. 25–30 Sunny, warm, then rain.

DEC. 2006: Temp. 26° (4° below avg.); precip. 2" (0.5" above avg.). 1–9 Snowstorm, then sunny, very cold. 10–12 Milder, rain and snow showers. 13–18 Snowstorm, then sunny, cold. 19–25 Very cold, flurries. 26–31 Sunny, mild, then snowstorm.

JAN. 2007: Temp. 20° (6° below avg.); precip. 1" (avg.). 1–5 Sunny, bitter cold. 6–8 Sunny, mild. 9–11 Snow, then very cold. 12–17 Snowstorm, then sunny, very cold. 18–23 Rain, then sunny; mild. 24–29 Sunny, very mild. 30–31 Cold, flurries.

FEB. 2007: Temp. 26° (3° below avg.); precip. 2" (0.5" above avg.). 1–7 Rain and snow, then sunny, mild. 8–12 Seasonable; snow north, rain south. 13–19 Snow, cold north; rain south. 20–24 Sunny, record cold. 25–28 Cold, snow showers.

MAR. 2007: Temp. 42° (1° below avg.); precip. 2" (0.5" below avg.). 1–5 Seasonable; showers south, snow north. 6–10 Flurries, cold. 11–19 Seasonable; scattered t-storms. 20–22 Sunny, warm. 23–28 Cold, rain and snow showers. 29–31 Showers, seasonable.

APR. 2007: Temp. 55° (1° above avg.); precip. 2.5" (1" below avg.). 1–5 Chilly, rain. 6–12 Sunny; cold, then seasonable. 13–16 Warm, t-storms. 17–20 Sunny; cool, then

warm. 21–24 Warm, t-storms. 25–30 Sunny, warm.

MAY 2007: Temp. 71° (7° above avg.); precip. 4.5" (2" above avg. north; 2" below south). 1–12 Rain, then sunny; very warm. 13–16 Very warm, t-storms. 17–25 Warm; scattered t-storms. 26–31 Warm, t-storms.

JUNE 2007: Temp. 72.5° (1° above avg. northwest; 2° below southeast); precip. 4.5" (avg.). 1–11 T-storms, then sunny; comfortable. 12–18 Seasonable; scattered t-storms. 19–22 Sunny, warm. 23–30 T-storms, then sunny, hot.

JULY 2007: Temp. 75° (3° below avg.); precip. 3.5" (1" above avg. north; 2" below south). 1–6 Seasonable; scattered t-storms. 7–13 Cool; t-storms north, sunny south. 14–18 Seasonable, t-storms. 19–26 Cool; t-storms, then sunny. 27–31 Seasonable, t-storms.

AUG. 2007: Temp. 75° (1° below avg.); precip. 3" (0.5" below avg.). 1–11 T-storms, then sunny; cool. 12–18 Hot; scattered t-storms. 19–22 Sunny, warm. 23–29 Seasonable, t-storms. 30–31 Sunny, cool.

SEPT. 2007: Temp. 65° (2° below avg.); precip. 4.5" (1" above avg.). 1–7 T-storms, then sunny, hot. 8–12 T-storms, then sunny; warm. 13–22 Showers, then sunny; cool. 23–30 Showers, seasonable.

OCT. 2007: Temp. 57° (1° above avg.); precip. 2" (1" below avg.). 1–9 Warm; sunny, then t-storms. 10–16 Seasonable; scattered showers. 17–20 Sunny, chilly. 21–23 Showers, mild. 24–31 Cold; sunny, then rain.

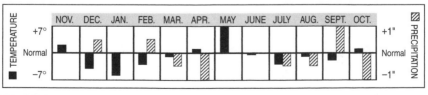

Texas–Oklahoma

SUMMARY: Winter will be cooler than normal in the north and a bit milder than normal in the south. Rainfall will be slightly below normal, with near-normal snowfall. The coldest temperatures will be in early January, with other cold periods in early to mid- and late December and mid-January. The snowiest periods in the north will be in late December and early January.

April and May will be much warmer and wetter than normal in the north, but temperatures and precipitation will be near normal in the south.

Summer temperatures will be near or a bit hotter than normal. Rainfall will be above normal in Oklahoma, but most of Texas will have much-below-normal rainfall, with a severe drought continuing in The Valley and Hill Country. The hottest temperatures will be in mid- and late June, early and late July, and early August.

September and October will be warmer and drier than normal, on average.

NOV. 2006: Temp. 57° (1° above avg.); precip. 4" (1" above avg.). 1–4 Sunny, cool. 5–9 Rain, seasonable. 10–16 T-storms; cool north, warm south. 17–21 Sunny, warm. 22–24 Cloudy, cool. 25–30 Warm showers north.

DEC. 2006: Temp. 47° (3° below avg. north; 1° above south); precip. 2.5" (0.5" above avg. north; 1" below south). 1–3 Showers, mild. 4–8 Cold; snow north, rain south. 9–11 Seasonable, t-storms. 12–20 Sunny, mild. 21–26 Sunny, cool. 27–31 Mild, then cold; snow north, rain south.

JAN. 2007: Temp. 43° (3° below avg.); precip. 1" (1" below avg.). 1–6 Rain to snow, then sunny, record cold. 7–11 Rain, then sunny, cool. 12–18 Cold; snow showers north, light rain south. 19–29 Sunny, turning mild. 30–31 Sunny, cold.

FEB. 2007: Temp. 50.5° (1° above avg. north; 4° above south); precip. 1" (1" below avg.). 1–7 Sunny, warm. 8–13 T-storms, then sunny; mild. 14–17 Showers, mild. 18–28 Rain, then sunny, cold.

MAR. 2007: Temp. 57° (1° below avg.); precip. 2.5" (avg.). 1–5 Showers, mild. 6–11 Rain south, snow north, then sunny, cold. 12–23 Warm, mainly dry. 24–31 Cool, t-storms.

APR. 2007: Temp. 67° (2° above avg. north; 0.5° below south); precip. 4" (1" above avg.). 1–5 Showers, mild. 6–11 Sunny, seasonable. 12–16 Showers, then sunny, warm. 17–24 Warm; t-storms. 25–30 Sunny, comfortable.

MAY 2007: Temp. 77° (8° above avg. north;

Oklahoma City ◎

Dallas ◎

Houston ◎

◎ San Antonio

avg. south); precip. 5.5" (2" above avg. north; 1" below south). 1–13 Sunny, warm. 14–21 Warm; scattered t-storms. 22–31 Seasonable, t-storms.

JUNE 2007: Temp. 80° (avg.); precip. 3" (1" below avg.). 1–6 T-storms north, sunny south; seasonable. 7–11 Sunny, hot. 12–19 Warm; scattered t-storms. 20–24 Humid, t-storms. 25–30 Sunny, very warm.

JULY 2007: Temp. 84° (1° above avg.); precip. 2.5" (2" above avg. north; 3" below south). 1–8 Sunny, hot. 9–19 Sunny, widely separated t-storms. 20–27 T-storms north; sunny, hot south. 28–31 Sunny, hot.

AUG. 2007: Temp. 83° (avg. north; 2° above south); precip. 2" (1" above avg. north; 2" below south). 1–7 Sunny, record heat. 8–16 T-storms, then sunny, hot. 17–22 T-storms, then not as hot north; scattered t-storms, hot south. 23–31 T-storms; turning cool north, hot south.

SEPT. 2007: Temp. 76.5° (1° below avg. east; 2° above west); precip. 2.5" (1" below avg.). 1–5 T-storms, then sunny; cool north, warm south. 6–12 Warm; sunny, then t-storms. 13–18 Sunny, warm. 19–25 T-storms, then sunny, cool. 26–30 Warm; scattered t-storms.

OCT. 2007: Temp. 69° (2° above avg.); precip. 3.5" (0.5" below avg.). 1–10 Very warm; scattered t-storms. 11–20 T-storms, then sunny, seasonable. 21–31 T-storms, then sunny, chilly.

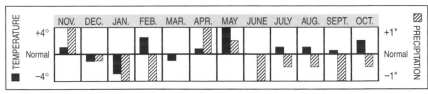

High Plains

SUMMARY: Winter will be much colder than normal in the northwest but near normal in the southeast. Precipitation will be near or a bit above normal, with near- or below-normal snowfall. The snowiest periods will be in early November, early January, mid-February, and early and late March. The coldest temperatures will be in early December, early and mid-January, and mid- and late February.

Although April will be warmer and drier than normal, on average, Denver will receive a heavy, wet snow in the latter half of the month. May will be cool and wet in the north and warm and dry in the south.

Summer will be cooler than normal, with near- to above-normal rainfall. The hottest temperatures will be in mid-June, late July, and early and mid-August.

September and October will be warmer and drier than normal, on average, despite an early September snowstorm in the northwest.

NOV. 2006: Temp. 36.5° (3° above avg. northeast; 2° below southwest); precip. 1" (avg.). 1–4 Sunny, mild. 5–10 Snow, seasonable. 11–19 Sunny; cold, then mild. 20–23 Rain and snow showers, seasonable. 24–27 Sunny, mild. 28–30 Snow showers.

DEC. 2006: Temp. 25° (2° below avg.); precip. 0.5" (avg.). 1–7 Snow showers, then sunny, very cold. 8–11 Seasonable, flurries. 12–16 Snow showers; cold north, mild south. 17–22 Sunny, seasonable. 23–29 Snow showers, then sunny, mild. 30–31 Snow showers.

JAN. 2007: Temp. 21° (4° below avg.); precip. 1" (0.5" above avg.). 1–5 Snowstorm, then sunny, very cold. 6–16 Snow showers, very cold. 17–28 Sunny, turning very mild. 29–31 Snow showers, cold.

FEB. 2007: Temp. 25.5° (7° below avg. north; 4° above south); precip. 1" (0.5" above avg.). 1–3 Sunny, mild. 4–8 Mild; showers, then sunny. 9–14 Snow, turning colder. 15–22 Record cold, snow showers. 23–28 Very cold, snow showers north; sunny, seasonable south.

MAR. 2007: Temp. 38.5° (0.5° above avg.); precip. 1" (avg.). 1–8 Snowstorm, then sunny, cold. 9–16 Sunny, mild. 17–21 Showers, then sunny, warm. 22–27 Snow, then sunny, cold. 28–31 Seasonable; rain south.

APR. 2007: Temp. 52° (4° above avg.); precip. 0.5" (1" below avg.). 1–8 Rain and snow, then sunny, seasonable. 9–14 Sunny, warm.

15–19 Showers, then sunny, warm. 20–28 Rain and snow, then sunny, mild. 29–30 Showers.

MAY 2007: Temp. 59° (2° below avg. north; 4° above south); precip. 3.5" (3" above avg. north; 1" below south). 1–7 Scattered t-storms; seasonable north, hot south. 8–14 Seasonable, t-storms. 15–21 Showers, cool north; sunny, very warm south. 22–31 T-storms, then sunny; seasonable.

JUNE 2007: Temp. 67.5° (2° above avg. north; 1° below south); precip. 2.5" (avg.). 1–8 Warm; scattered t-storms. 9–16 Seasonable; scattered t-storms. 17–22 Sunny, very warm. 23–30 Seasonable, t-storms.

JULY 2007: Temp. 69° (3° below avg.); precip. 3" (1" above avg.). 1–11 Scattered t-storms; cool north, hot south. 12–18 Sunny, comfortable. 19–25 Cool, t-storms. 26–31 Sunny, warm.

AUG. 2007: Temp. 70° (1° below avg.); precip. 1.5" (0.5" below avg.). 1–4 Sunny, hot. 5–14 T-storms, then sunny, seasonable. 15–21 T-storms, then sunny, hot. 22–31 T-storms, then sunny, cool.

SEPT. 2007: Temp. 61° (avg.); precip. 1.5" (avg.). 1–4 Rain southeast, snow northwest; then sunny, cool. 5–8 Sunny, warm. 9–14 Showers, then sunny, seasonable. 15–22 Showers, mild. 23–30 Seasonable; sunny, then rain.

OCT. 2007: Temp. 52° (3° above avg.); precip. 0.5" (0.5" below avg.). 1–8 Sunny, warm. 9–15 Mild; scattered showers. 16–25 Sunny; chilly, then mild. 26–31 Scattered showers.

WEATHER

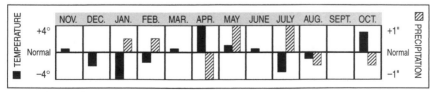

Intermountain

SUMMARY: Winter will be colder and snowier than normal, with near-normal precipitation. The coldest temperatures will occur in mid-January, with other cold periods in early December, early January, and mid-February. The snowiest periods will occur in mid-November, mid-January, mid- and late February, and early and mid-March.

Temperatures in April and May will be near normal, on average, with above-normal precipitation.

Summer will be drier than normal, with below-normal temperatures in the north and slightly above-normal temperatures in the south, on average. The hottest temperatures will be in mid-June, mid-July, and early and mid-August.

September and October will be warmer than normal, on average, with precipitation near normal in the east and above normal in the west.

NOV. 2006: Temp. 38.5° (2° below avg. northwest; 1° above southeast); precip. 1" (0.5" below avg.). 1–8 Sunny, cool. 9–13 Cold, snow showers. 14–19 Snow, then sunny, mild. 20–26 Showers, then sunny, mild. 27–30 Seasonable; scattered showers.

DEC. 2006: Temp. 29° (2° below avg.); precip. 1" (0.5" below avg.; 1" above northwest). 1–7 Snow showers, then sunny; cold. 8–13 Snow, seasonable. 14–20 Sunny, seasonable. 21–28 Rain and snow showers, then sunny, mild. 29–31 Rain and snow showers.

JAN. 2007: Temp. 28° (3° below avg.); precip. 1" (0.5" below avg.). 1–6 Sunny, cold. 7–11 Cold; snow northeast, sunny elsewhere. 12–18 Snowstorm, then sunny, very cold. 19–25 Sunny, mild northwest; flurries, cold elsewhere. 26–31 Flurries, seasonable.

FEB. 2007: Temp. 32° (1° below avg.); precip. 2" (0.5" above avg.). 1–9 Mild; rainy periods. 10–16 Seasonable, snow showers. 17–22 Snow, then sunny, cold. 23–28 Snow, cold.

MAR. 2007: Temp. 41° (1° below avg.); precip. 1.5" (avg.). 1–8 Snow, then sunny, cold. 9–13 Sunny, seasonable. 14–21 Snow, then sunny, seasonable. 22–28 Showers, then sunny seasonable. 29–31 Showers.

APR. 2007: Temp. 51° (2° above avg.); precip. 1.5" (0.5" above avg.). 1–3 Seasonable; showers east. 4–13 Sunny, warm days. 14–18 Showers, then sunny; mild. 19–23 Turning colder; snow east, rain west. 24–30 Sunny, turning warm.

MAY 2007: Temp. 55° (2° below avg.); precip. 2" (1" above avg.). 1–5 Showers northeast; sunny, warm elsewhere. 6–10 Sunny, cool. 11–14 Cool, rain and snow. 15–21 Cool; rainy periods. 22–28 Sunny, seasonable. 29–31 Showers, cool.

JUNE 2007: Temp. 67° (1° below avg. north; 3° above south); precip. 0.2" (0.3" below avg.). 1–8 Seasonable; scattered showers. 9–19 Sunny; cool, then hot. 20–30 Showers, then sunny, cool.

JULY 2007: Temp. 72° (1° below avg.); precip. 0.5" (avg.). 1–5 Sunny, warm. 6–11 T-storms, then sunny, cool. 12–17 Sunny, warm. 18–25 T-storms, then sunny; warm. 26–31 Showers, then cool.

AUG. 2007: Temp. 71° (1° below avg.); precip. 0.5" (0.5" below avg.). 1–5 Showers, then sunny, cool. 6–11 Hot; scattered t-storms. 12–19 Sunny, warm. 20–25 T-storms, then sunny, cool. 26–31 Sunny, warm.

SEPT. 2007: Temp. 62.5° (0.5° above avg.); precip. 1.5" (0.5" above avg.). 1–12 Showers, then sunny; warm. 13–20 T-storms, then sunny; warm. 21–30 T-storms, then sunny, cool.

OCT. 2007: Temp. 52.5° (avg. north; 3° above south); precip. 1" (0.5" below avg. east, 1" above west). 1–7 Mild; scattered showers. 8–16 Sunny, seasonable. 17–28 Sunny, warm days. 29–31 Scattered showers.

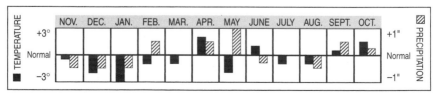

Get your local forecast at Almanac.com/weathercenter. **2007**

Desert Southwest

SUMMARY: Winter will be colder than normal with near-normal snowfall. Precipitation will be above normal in the east and slightly below normal in the west. The coldest temperatures will occur in early January, with other cold periods in early December, mid-February, and early March. The snowiest periods will be in mid-November, early December, and early and mid-January.

April will be warmer than normal and May will be cooler than normal, on average. Both months will have below-normal rainfall.

Summer temperatures will be near normal, on average. The hottest temperatures will be in mid-June, early and mid-July, and early and mid-August. Rainfall will be above average in the east but below normal in the west, continuing drought conditions.

September and October will be drier than normal, with temperatures near normal in the east and above normal in the west, on average.

NOV. 2006: Temp. 54° (1° below avg.); precip. 0.5" (avg.; 1" above east). 1–3 Showers, cool east; sunny west. 4–6 Sunny, seasonable. 7–13 Cold; snow, then sunny east; sunny west. 14–19 Cool, then warm; scattered showers. 20–30 Sunny, mild.

DEC. 2006: Temp. 46° (1° below avg.); precip. 0.5" (0.1" above avg. east; 0.1" below west). 1–5 Cold, showers west; mild, sunny east; sunny, then snow north. 6–10 Cool; scattered showers. 11–19 Sunny, cool. 20–31 Sunny, mild.

JAN. 2007: Temp. 47° (1° below avg. east; 1° above west); precip. 0.9" (0.4" above avg.). 1–3 Sunny, mild. 4–9 Record cold; snow showers north and east, rain showers south and west. 10–16 Showers; cool, then mild. 17–31 Snow north, rain south, then sunny, mild.

FEB. 2007: Temp. 50.5° (2° above avg. east; 1° below west); precip. 0.4" (0.1" below avg.). 1–7 Mild, showers. 8–13 Sunny, seasonable. 14–23 Showers, then sunny, cold. 24–28 Seasonable; sunny, then showers.

MAR. 2007: Temp. 55° (2° below avg.); precip. 0.3" (0.2" below avg.). 1–9 Showers, then sunny, cold. 10–19 Showers, then sunny, seasonable. 20–31 Sunny, mild.

APR. 2007: Temp. 68° (4° above avg.); precip. 0.2" (0.3" below avg.). 1–14 Sunny, warm. 15–19 Sunny, seasonable. 20–25 Showers, then sunny, cool. 26–30 Sunny, very warm.

MAY 2007: Temp. 71° (2° below avg.); precip. 0.2" (0.3" below avg.). 1–6 Sunny, very warm. 7–22 Sunny, cool. 23–31 Seasonable; widely separated t-storms.

JUNE 2007: Temp. 82° (1° below avg.); precip. 0.4" (0.1" below avg.). 1–7 Sunny, seasonable. 8–11 T-storms, then sunny, cool. 12–20 Sunny, hot. 21–30 Seasonable; scattered t-storms.

JULY 2007: Temp. 86° (1° below avg.); precip. 1.2" (0.3" below avg.). 1–6 Hot; scattered t-storms east, sunny west. 7–11 Sunny, comfortable. 12–20 Hot; scattered t-storms east, sunny west. 21–31 Seasonable; widely separated t-storms.

AUG. 2007: Temp. 87° (2° above avg.); precip. 0.5" (1" below avg.; 1" above east). 1–15 Sunny, hot. 16–24 T-storms, then sunny, hot. 25–31 Cool, t-storms east; sunny, seasonable west.

SEPT. 2007: Temp. 78° (avg.); precip. 0.7" (0.3" below avg.). 1–9 Seasonable; scattered t-storms east, sunny west. 10–15 Sunny, hot. 16–21 T-storms, cool. 22–27 Sunny, seasonable. 28–30 Showers, then cool.

OCT. 2007: Temp. 68.5° (avg. east; 3° above west); precip. 0.7" (0.3" below avg.). 1–9 Sunny; cool, then warm. 10–16 Cool, showers, then sunny. 17–31 Showers, then sunny east; sunny, warm west.

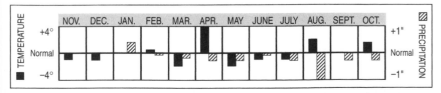

Pacific Northwest

SUMMARY: Winter will be a bit colder than normal, on average, with above-normal snowfall. Precipitation will be below normal in Washington and above normal in Oregon and California. The heaviest snow will fall in mid- to late February, with other snowfalls in mid-November, early to mid-December, and early to mid-January. The stormiest periods will be in early and mid-November, mid-December, and mid-March. The coldest temperatures will be in early December, mid-January, and mid-February.

April and May will be cooler and wetter than normal, on average, with the stormiest period in mid- to late April. The first half of April will be warmer than normal, with below-normal temperatures most of the time from the latter half of April through May.

Summer will be slightly cooler and drier than normal, on average, with the hottest temperatures in mid-July. Other warm periods will be in mid-June and mid- and late August.

September and October will be wetter and warmer than normal, on average.

NOV. 2006: Temp: 45.5° (1.5° below avg.); precip. 8" (avg. north; 3" above south). 1–2 Sunny. 3–5 Stormy, with heavy rain. 6–10 Sunny, cool. 11–14 Cool; light rain. 15–18 Cold; heavy rain, then snow. 19–24 Rain, mild. 25–30 Misty, cool.

DEC. 2006: Temp: 43° (1° above avg.); precip. 7.5" (1" above avg.). 1–4 Showers, then sunny, cold. 5–14 Snow, then heavy rain, mild. 15–23 Mild; rainy periods. 24–26 Sunny, mild. 27–31 Rain, mild.

JAN. 2007: Temp. 42° (avg.); precip. 2" (4" below avg.). 1–4 Sunny, mild. 5–13 Chilly, rain and wet snow. 14–17 Sunny, very cold. 18–21 Misty, mild. 22–28 Sunny, mild. 29–31 Rain, mild.

FEB. 2007: Temp. 43.5° (0.5° below avg.); precip. 5.5" (1" below avg. north; 2" above south). 1–11 Mild; rainy periods. 12–15 Sunny, seasonable. 16–21 Rain and snow, then sunny, very cold. 22–28 Heavy snow, then rain, mild.

MAR. 2007: Temp. 47° (avg.); precip. 4.5" (avg.). 1–8 Rain south, snow north, then sunny, cool. 9–14 Misty, seasonable. 15–21 Heavy rain, seasonable. 22–27 Sunny, mild. 28–31 Rain, mild.

APR. 2007: Temp. 49.5° (0.5° below avg.); precip. 4" (1" above avg.). 1–7 Rain, then sunny, warm. 8–12 Warm, showers. 13–17 Misty, mild. 18–24 Stormy, with heavy rain, cool. 25–30 Cool; rainy periods.

MAY. 2007: Temp. 51° (4° below avg.); precip. 2" (avg.). 1–3 Seasonable, mild. 4–15 Cool; occasional showers. 16–20 Rainy periods, cool. 21–31 Cool; occasional showers.

JUNE 2007: Temp. 60° (avg.); precip. 0.5" (1" below avg.). 1–7 Cool; showers north, sunny south. 8–18 Sunny; seasonable, then warm. 19–24 Showers, then sunny; seasonable. 25–30 Cool; showers north, sunny south.

JULY 2007: Temp. 63° (1° below avg.); precip. 1" (0.5" above avg.). 1–5 Sunny, cool. 6–13 Cool; showers, then sunny. 14–24 Sunny, hot. 25–31 Showers, cool.

AUG. 2007: Temp. 65.5° (0.5° above avg.); precip. 1" (avg.). 1–5 Showers, then sunny; seasonable. 6–12 Seasonable; showers north, sunny south. 13–19 Sunny, very warm. 20–22 Showers, cool. 23–31 Sunny, warm.

SEPT. 2007: Temp. 61.5° (0.5° above avg.); precip. 2.5" (1" above avg.). 1–8 Showers, seasonable. 9–19 Sunny, seasonable. 20–25 Rain, then sunny, mild. 26–30 Cool, showers.

OCT. 2007: Temp. 55° (1° above avg.); precip. 4" (avg. north; 2" above south). 1–7 Heavy rain, cool. 8–11 Sunny, cool. 12–27 Sunny, mild. 28–31 Rain, mild.

Seattle
Portland
Eugene
Eureka

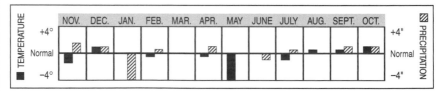

| | NOV. | DEC. | JAN. | FEB. | MAR. | APR. | MAY | JUNE | JULY | AUG. | SEPT. | OCT. | |

Pacific Southwest

SUMMARY: Winter will be slightly cooler than normal near the coast and much cooler inland, on average. Rainfall will be well above normal, with above-normal snowfall in the mountains. The most widespread snow will be in mid-January. The stormiest periods will be in mid- and late November and early and mid-February. The coldest periods will be in early December, mid-January, and mid- to late February.

April and May will be drier than normal, with temperatures above normal in April and below normal in May, on average. Summer will be cooler than normal in coastal sections, but hotter than normal inland, on average. The hottest temperatures will be in mid-June and mid-August.

Expect stormy weather in early October, with total rainfall in September and October above normal in the north and below normal in the south. Despite very warm temperatures in mid-September and mid- to late October, temperatures will be near normal, on average.

NOV. 2006: Temp. 57.5° (0.5° below avg.); precip. 4" (4" above avg. north; 1" above south). 1–9 Sunny, seasonable. 10–14 Cool, t-storms. 15–20 Seasonable; rainy periods. 21–27 Sunny, then heavy rain. 28–30 Sunny, cool.

DEC. 2006: Temp. 52° (1° below avg.); precip. 0.5" (1.5" above avg.). 1–8 Cool; sunny north, rainy periods south. 9–15 Cool, showers. 16–31 Valley and coastal fog, otherwise sunny; cool.

JAN. 2007: Temp. 53° (3° below avg. east; 3° above west); precip. 2.5" (2" below avg. north; 1" above south). 1–5 Sunny, mild. 6–12 Showers, then sunny, cool. 13–16 Cold; rain, ending as snow north. 17–27 Sunny; cold, then mild. 28–31 Seasonable; showers north, sunny south.

FEB. 2007: Temp. 54° (1° below avg.); precip. 8" (5" above avg.). 1–14 Rainy periods with heavy t-storms; mild, then cool. 15–19 Cool; sunny, then showers. 20–24 Sunny, cold. 25–28 Showers, seasonable.

MAR. 2007: Temp. 56° (1° below avg.); precip. 1.5" (1" below avg.). 1–4 Cool, showers. 5–9 Cool; showers north, sunny south. 10–13 Seasonable; sunny north, showers south. 14–19 Rain, then sunny; cool. 20–31 Sunny; seasonable, then warm.

APR. 2007: Temp. 63° (3° above avg.); precip. 0.1" (0.9" below avg.). 1–8 Sunny, warm. 9–13 Seasonable; sunny, then cloudy with showers north. 14–17 Sunny, warm.

18–22 Seasonable; scattered showers. 23–30 Sunny; seasonable, then warm.

MAY. 2007: Temp. 62° (2° below avg.); precip. 0.5" (0.5" below avg. north; 0.5" above south). 1–5 Sunny, seasonable. 6–9 Cool, showers. 10–18 Sunny, cool. 19–21 Cool, sprinkles. 22–31 Sunny, seasonable.

JUNE 2007: Temp. 68.5° (2° above avg. east; 1° below west); precip. 0" (0.1" below avg.). 1–5 Seasonable; sunny inland, coastal clouds. 6–10 Cool, sprinkles. 11–14 Sunny; hot north, seasonable south. 15–30 Sunny, seasonable.

JULY 2007: Temp. 70° (1° below avg.); precip. 0" (avg.). 1–4 Sunny, seasonable. 5–10 Scattered t-storms, then sunny, cool. 11–31 Sunny, seasonable.

AUG. 2007: Temp. 72.5° (0.5° above avg.); precip. 0.1" (avg.). 1–4 Cool north, coastal clouds south; sunny, warm south. 5–18 Sunny, warm. 19–22 Sunny; hot north, seasonable south. 23–31 Seasonable; coastal clouds north, sunny south.

SEPT. 2007: Temp. 69.5° (0.5° below avg.); precip. 0.1" (0.1" below avg.). 1–9 Sunny, seasonable. 10–19 Sunny, warm. 20–30 Showers north, then sunny, cool.

OCT. 2007: Temp. 65.5° (0.5° above avg.); precip. 2.7" (4" above avg. north; 0.5" below south). 1–3 Sunny, seasonable. 4–8 Gusty, heavy t-storms north; showers south. 9–22 Sunny, seasonable. 23–26 Sunny, very warm. 27–31 Showers, then sunny; cool.

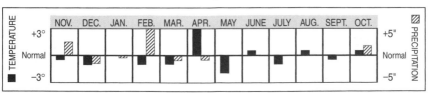

THE GOOD NEWS

BY EVELYN BROWNING-GARRISS

HUH? Perhaps, like many people, you haven't heard that there **is** any.

Melting glaciers, rising oceans, increasing storms: The future, with global warming, looks bleak. There certainly are severe problems associated with the present warming trend, but there are also some significant benefits. Here are a few.

Warmer Weather Is Healthier

Where do many seniors go when they retire? Not north. They generally go south—or in whatever direction leads them to warmer climes. Statistics show that warmer weather is healthier for people. Some of Britain's leading medical experts have calculated that a rise in the average temperature by 3.6°F (2°C) over the next 50 years would increase yearly heat-related deaths in Britain by about 2,000—but would reduce cold-related deaths by about 20,000. A similar study by American doc-

ABOUT CLIMATE CHANGE

tors estimated that a warming of 4.5°F (2.5°C) would lower the annual death rate in the United States by 40,000, while reducing medical costs by almost $20 billion per year. Both studies found that the decrease in the number of cold-related deaths would be much greater than the rise of heat-related deaths.

Of course, this doesn't mean that heat is good for everyone. Sudden heat waves can be catastrophic, as they were in Chicago in 1995 and France in 2003. However, since then, both of those places have taken the precautions of making available cooled local shelters and checking on the elderly during hot

Statistics show that populations are moving into climates that enjoy less extreme cold weather.

spells—steps that have been effective in maintaining good health and saving lives. Other regions have adapted to heat waves with long lunch breaks and siestas, concentrating work in the cooler hours of the morning and late afternoon.

Thanks to improved medical care, increased access to air-conditioning, and social adaptations over the past 40 years, the populations in North America, Europe, and most of Asia have become much less susceptible to heat stress. Studies from these areas now show that their highest death rates occur in winter, with the leading causes being respiratory problems (flu and pneumonia) and heart disease.

One of the primary medical concerns about global warming in North America has been the possible spread of diseases such as malaria, cholera, and yellow fever. In fact, these diseases were widespread in the United States in the colder 19th century. Their absence today is due to modern sanitation, which prevents the microbes from getting a foothold, and increased mosquito control efforts. As another example, the Gulf Coast is free of dengue fever, even though its average temperatures are warmer than those on many of the Caribbean islands where the disease is commonplace.

As air-conditioning has mitigated the rigors of hot summers, the population of the United States has been moving south and west, into climates that enjoy less extreme cold weather. A similar but smaller pattern is being seen in Europe. People seem to prefer warmer winters, and statistics are showing that this move is much better for their health. The good news is that you don't have to move now. Warmer winters are heading your way.

Warmer Temperatures Save Energy

The Intergovernmental Panel on Climate Change (the United Nations body that has been studying global warming for more than a decade) has forecast that, by the end of the 21st century, the world's climate will be about 3.6°F (2°C) warmer than it is today. Records show that for the past 100 years, most of the warming has been in the form of warmer nighttime and winter temperatures. A study of 45 U.S. cities by Dr. Thomas Gale Moore of Stanford University in 1996 showed that for each increase of 1.8°F (1°C) yearly, July's average temperatures went up by only 0.9°F (0.5°C),

For the past 100 years, the main impact of global warming has been milder winters.

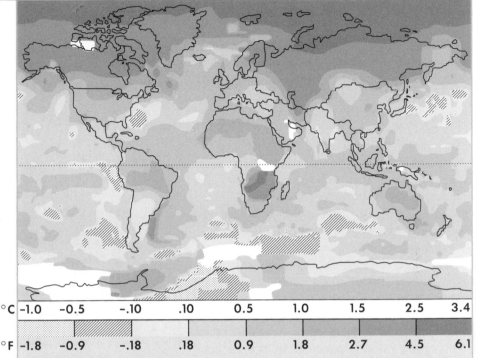

°C	-1.0	-0.5	-.10	.10	0.5	1.0	1.5	2.5	3.4
°F	-1.8	-0.9	-.18	.18	0.9	1.8	2.7	4.5	6.1

Deviation of global temperatures, based on 1951–80 averages. White indicates insufficient data. To see this map in color, go to Almanac.com/extras.

–adapted from NASA/GISS

while January's average temperatures climbed by 2.7°F (1.5°C). The main impact of global warming has been milder winters.

Note, too, that global warming is not evenly distributed in the oceans. Temperatures have increased more around the poles, but only slight increases have occurred near the equator. (See map above.) Thus northern cities have enjoyed more warming than southern ones.

U.S. Department of Energy studies show that a warmer climate would reduce heating bills more than it would boost outlays for air-conditioning. If energy prices remained constant and we currently enjoyed the weather predicted for the 21st century, expenditures for heating and cooling would be cut by at least $12.2 billion annually. If energy prices go up, the savings will be greater.

IN JANUARY 2006, NASA REPORTED THE TOP FIVE WARMEST YEARS SINCE THE 1890S. IN ORDER STARTING WITH THE WARMEST, THEY WERE 2005, 1998, 2002, 2003, AND 2004.

(CONTINUED)

Water Is More Abundant

Since 2000, the North American West has suffered from a drought that is raising the price of both water and hydro-electricity. This has led some states—California and Arizona, for example—to battle each other for water rights. Drought is irritating and expensive in the wealthy United States, but it is disastrous in other parts of the world. According to the World Bank, 80 nations now have water shortages that threaten their health and economies, while 40 percent of the world—more than 2 billion people—have no access to clean water or sanitation.

While the scientific community is divided over many aspects of the global warming theory, they agree on the impact of global warming on precipitation. Warmer air holds more moisture. Global warming will mean more condensation and more evaporation, producing more and/or heavier rains. With warmer world temperatures, we will see more moisture, which will be carried farther inland before it cools enough to precipitate out as rain or snow. Not all areas will receive more precipitation, but globally there will be more rain and snow. To the parched millions in Asia and Africa, this will be life-saving.

With warmer world temperatures, we will see more moisture, which will be carried farther inland.

Plants Thrive in Heat and CO_2

The June 6, 2003, issue of *Science* magazine reported that Earth is greener now than it has ever been during the past 100 years. Specifically, *Science* found that the climate changes that occurred between 1980 and 2000, a time of dramatic warming, had resulted in 6 percent more plant growth globally. The Amazon jungle, an area that had been dwindling, accounted for 42 percent of the increased plant growth.

The findings defied computer models, which had forecast little change. What happened was that tropical monsoon rainfall became heavier and more reliable in areas such as India. The skies have become less hazy over

IT IS ESTIMATED THAT 386,100
SQUARE MILES OF SEA ICE HAVE
DISAPPEARED SINCE 1974.

**The skies have become
less hazy over Brazil,
allowing sunlight to
pour onto the jungles.**

Brazil, allowing sunlight
to pour onto the South
American jungles. Plants
have flourished, and—
more important to
poverty-stricken nations
in Africa, Asia, and South
America—crops have
thrived, too.

The climate is helping
plant growth in three
ways. The warming tem-
peratures are lengthening
growing seasons. The
warmer air usually holds
more moisture. And, the
increased man-made and
natural CO_2 in the
warmer air is increasing
photosynthesis. The gas
indirectly acts as a fertilizer and increases plant
growth, especially in
crops such as wheat, rice,
and soybeans. If you en-
joy eating, the increased
warmth is good news.

Arctic Shipping Routes Will Save Time and Energy

T he rate of global warming is greatest in the
oceans around the poles. As the ice has
melted, new opportunities have opened up.

Access to new oil and gas fields has caught international attention. According to the U.S. Geological
Survey, one-fourth of the world's undiscovered oil
and gas resources are in the Arctic. These new fields
lie within the borders of stable nations—Norway,
Russia, Denmark, Canada, and the United States—
and major corporations are investing in exploration
and development.

(CONTINUED)

**As the ice
melts, new
waterways
are being
freed up,
saving time,
energy,
and freight
costs.**

The real story is that for many reasons, the world is changing. We must learn to change with it.

In addition to being a possible new source of energy, the Arctic is also a potential new location for maritime commerce. As the ice melts, new waterways are being freed up, whose use will save time, energy, and international freight costs. Shipping across the top of Russia—along what is known as the Northern Sea Route—was a monopoly while under the control of the Soviet Union. With the demise of that regime, the route fell into almost complete disuse. As Arctic waters warm, attempts are being made to rejuvenate this shipping lane. Doing so has the potential to reduce the transport distance from Asia to Europe by 40 percent—more than 4,500 miles. Also, this lane has become attractive to shipping concerns because they could avoid the increased piracy now occurring in some more southerly latitudes.

Two other shipping lanes are being studied; unlike the Northern Sea Route, they are not yet in use. The melting ice is opening up the Northwest Passage, across Canada, and the Transpolar Route, the deep-sea version of a course already taken by airplanes to reduce mileage. Access by ships could cut some ocean travel in half. In a growing global economy, these three new shipping routes would result in dramatic savings.

The View From Here

This is, of course, a distorted picture that identifies only the benefits of the changing climate. It is as distorted as the bleak scenarios that show only the problems of global warming. The real story is that for many reasons—both natural and man-made—the world is changing. This change is going to cause enormous hardships and create enormous opportunities. We must learn to change with it. Just as we should not ignore the suffering that results, we should not overlook the fact that for many throughout the world, the changing climate will be beneficial. □□

Evelyn Browning-Garriss, editor of the *Browning Newsletter,* has been writing, speaking, and consulting about the social and economic impact of climate change for more than 30 years. She tracks weather trends and cycles from her office in New Mexico.

WATCH THE WARMING EFFECTS
To see animated maps of the effects of global warming on plant productivity, temperature, and moisture, go to **Almanac.com/extras.**

208

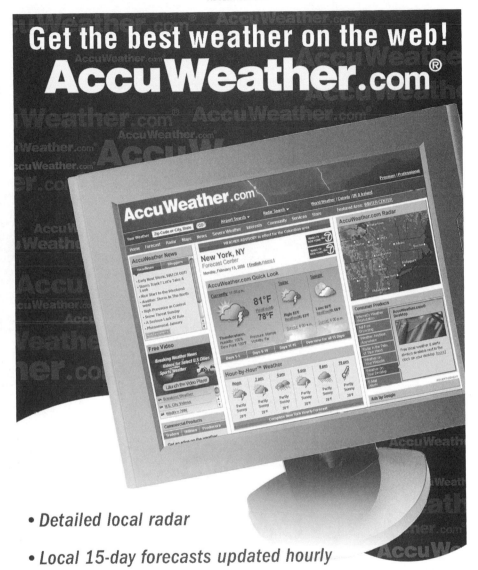

Powered by oats, don't step in exhaust.

–a sign in the barn at the Russells' farm in Poplarville, Mississippi

Kenny Russell (left) gives student Steve Dimick a demonstration of how to plow with a team of draft horses.

The New Old-Fashio

When Kenny Russell started his "Farming with Draft Horses" school in Poplarville, Mississippi, in 1993, people wondered who would come. Kenny's dad, granddad, and uncles had all worked draft animals when he was growing up. He loved it, and he figured

that maybe others would, too. Sure enough, from across the United States and Canada, the calls came in—and they've not let up. "We thought at first that it was just a fad," says Russell. "I meet people every day who are wanting to farm with horses. We're about three generations away from when farmers had to use them. We might be

Story and
photos
by Christine
Schultz

*The wise farmer
likes the assurance—
and insurance—
of a reliable team of
horses to fall back
on in case something
happens to the tractor.*

–The Old Farmer's Almanac, 1949

ned Way to Farm

headed back to it. People say that we're reaching into the past, but really we're reaching into the future."

People from all walks of life have come to the 86-acre farm near the Gulf Coast that Russell owns with his wife, Renée. Monks from Alabama arrived to learn how to set up a self-sustaining monastery. Snowboard instructors from

Boulder, Colorado, came to learn how to homestead with horses in the off-season. A few people came out of fear that Y2K was going to change the world. Farmers and want-to-be-farmers have come, some of whom have learned that they simply aren't suited to the lifestyle.

"The only reason they couldn't do it

is because they don't," says Kenny Russell. "It's all practice. That's all it takes, but you've got to know what to practice. I can teach them to use a tractor in 20 minutes, but I can't possibly teach them to farm with horses in three days."

One session in Autumn 2005 was attended by more than a dozen folks, including farmers and other horse people, from ten different states and Canada. Gina Miller, who hitches some of the 30 horses on her Oklahoma farm to carriages for weddings and proms, came with her husband, a large-animal veterinarian. It was their seventh visit. Another couple, Nancy Denson and Nick Stemm, who run a sustainable

Good Horse Sense

"[Horses] help plant and harvest their own 'fuel,'" writes Gail Damerow, editor of *Rural Heritage* magazine, in her article "Horse Power vs. Horsepower." Kenny Russell says that with diesel over three dollars per gallon, he can run a team of horses cheaper than gas-powered equipment. "What's more, draft horses work an average of 16 to 18 years and birth their own replacements," he adds.

Lynn Miller, who works his own 2,000-acre farm with draft animals in Sisters, Oregon, and also edits and publishes *Small Farmer's Journal*, notes that a small farmer dedicated to making the most of his horses can actually earn three times more per acre than an agribusiness can.

organic farm in Washington State, drove three days to learn about working draft horses into their operation to reduce their dependence on gas-powered machines. "People are going back to the old ways because they work," says Renée Russell.

The Russells' nine horses are especially well-mannered Belgians, a breed

It takes only three things to train a horse: time, time, and time. If you don't have all three, don't even try.

Clockwise from left: The author learns how to keep a straight line with a mower; farrier Jimmy Klein of Trenton, Tennessee, plies his trade; Kenny Russell pitches hay into a cattle feeder.

often called "the gentle giants." (Four of them appeared in the movie *O Brother, Where Art Thou?*) Each horse, however, has its own personality; they don't show up in your stable automatically suited to your needs. "I often tell people that it takes only three things to train a horse: time, time, and time," says Jimmy Klein, an expert horseman (as well as farrier) who teaches the workshop with Kenny Russell. "If you don't have all three, don't even try."

In addition to training the horses, you must train yourself not only to know the ins and outs of harnesses and farm equipment, but also to have the finesse to lead a team of living creatures from behind. "It's a skill you have to develop, not a knowledge that you can acquire," says Klein. "There's pitifully little that we can teach you about driving horses, but we can teach you your own limitations."

Barry Coco and Steve Dimick are especially thankful for that. Coco, a Louisiana draft horse owner who has been to the Russells' clinic three times, says, "I would've been dead by now if I hadn't met up with these folks. I was fixing to buy a harness without knowing the first thing about it. There's no

213

Students, instructors, and horses pause for a photo at the Russells' farm after clearing trees knocked down by Hurricane Katrina.

telling where I would've ended up—probably dragged all the way to Canada." Dimick had come to the clinic from Ohio after already having farmed with his own team of Percherons. As he listened to Klein and Russell run through the basics of harnessing a horse, he made a list of all the things he'd done wrong.

While most of the people at the workshop had been around quarter horses, not everyone had been up close to the towering flanks of Belgians. All were warned not to startle or irritate them. You don't need to

TAKE THE REINS
To learn more about Russell's Workhorse Farm or either of the publications mentioned, go to **Almanac.com/extras.**

look a tractor in the eye to know if you've got a good one, Klein told them, but horses require an introduction. A kind and gentle eye is the first sign of a cooperative animal, he says, explaining what to look for in the conformation of a horse. Beyond that, there are many parts to consider—anvil-size hooves, the knees and nose, hips and hocks, fetlocks and buttocks, cannons, crests, croups, pasterns, polls, elbows. Those parts become more familiar as the participants learn how to harness, ground drive, and work those horses during the three-day program.

By afternoon of the first day, the students had harnessed a team of Belgians to the number-9 horse-drawn hay

Leaning powerfully against the weight, the horses dragged the logs, billowing dust behind and stepping over brush ahead that would have encumbered a tractor.

Draft Numbers

Draft horses, by definition, are any that pull a load, but when people in North America speak of draft horses, they generally mean the heavy breeds that stand between 17 and 18 hands tall (about 5½ feet from the ground to the shoulders) and weigh 1,600 pounds or more. Clydesdales have stolen the limelight as beer-sponsored parade hitches, but Belgians and Percherons are the breeds that actually make up 95 percent of the registered draft horses in the United States and Canada.

Lynn Miller of *Small Farmer's Journal* estimates that some 400,000 North Americans use some form of animal power these days (a large percentage are Amish). Interest is spreading in people from ages 18 to 80 in every state and from every background imaginable. He estimates that roughly seven out of ten people who try farming with horses stick with it.

If you are thinking of keeping a horse, plan on one to two acres per draft horse for grazing, with a tie-stall space of 6 by 12 feet in your barn. Assume roughly 2 percent of the horse's body weight for hay per day. Plan to supplement that with oats and corn, depending on the time of year, the quality of the hay and grass, and how much you work the horse.

mower that dates from the 1930s. Russell oiled its iron gears and then lowered the cutter bar. Eric Elam took his place in the cupped iron seat. He raised the leather lines and made a kissing noise to the Belgians. Elam grew up on a Kentucky tobacco farm but now spends his days at the head of a construction crew. He and his wife, Jamie Smith, were there to learn more about training their Percherons and the mule they had at home in Alabama. Jamie's Canadian mother, Madho Smith, had flown down to join them. Smith hopes someday to find the couple a patch of land in Canada for a horse-powered farm.

On Elam's cue, the horses leaned into the harness and stepped thick-muscled legs across the field, moving at a slow but steady pace. The musky scent of hay and horses simmered in the warm Mississippi sun as the cutter laid down a line through the field. Later, after handing over the lines to another student, Elam grinned from under his cowboy hat and said, "Driving that team makes me want to trade in every car I ever owned."

Later, the group gathered the hay with a horse-drawn hay rake, loaded it onto a horse-drawn sled, and drove the hay to the cattle feeder. After they'd tried their hand at driving a wagon, hauling a manure spreader, and tilling a field with a horse-drawn plow, someone wanted to know how to tell when a horse is overheated. "No bells ring or lights flash on the dashboard to tell you," said Kenny Russell. "You have to check for sweat under the forelock, look for flaring nostrils or heaving sides."

Other lessons they would learn included how to shoe a draft horse; how to control an ornery draft horse that needs treatment from a veterinarian; the pros and cons of working oxen and mule teams vs. horses; and how to put your horse into a stall. "At the end of the day, you can't just drive into the barn and turn your key off," says Russell. "You have to tend to your animals. But that allows *you* time to cool down and unwind, as well."

A common criticism of the horse-powered farm is that it's nothing more than an expensive hobby with no real use—an ironic echo of early observations about the motorcar. However, when a calamity hits, the old ways seem suddenly efficient and civilized. Following Hurricane Katrina, with the phones and power out and the roads strewn with trees and abandoned cars and trucks, the Russells set to work cleaning up their farm with their horses. When they had finished, they helped a neighbor whose truck had gotten stuck. "When it got dark, we went to bed tired—but a 'good' tired from working the horses," Kenny Russell says.

Before using the third day to focus on the specific needs of each participant, the group spent the second session gaining more practical experience. They harnessed three teams of Belgians to a wagon, a forecart, and a sled, and took off to clear the fallen trees on the far side of the property. One by one, they lashed a log to a team of horses and then took turns driving the team up the hill. Leaning powerfully against the weight, the horses dragged the logs, billowing dust behind and stepping over brush ahead that would have encumbered a tractor. As the sunlight sent shadows down the valley, the group posed with the horses for a portrait. They looked like pioneers in the wilderness. Some said that they felt like it, too.

□ □

Writer and photographer **Christine Schultz** has been a contributor to this Almanac since 1988. She and her husband would like to work draft horses on their acre in Taylor, Mississippi, but for now they raise chickens.

Gestation and Mating Table

	Proper Age for First Mating	Period of Fertility (years)	Number of Females for One Male	Period of Gestation (days) AVERAGE	RANGE
Ewe	90 lbs. or 1 yr.	6		147 / 151[1]	142–154
Ram	12–14 mos., well matured	7	50–75[2] / 35–40[3]		
Mare	3 yrs.	10–12		336	310–370
Stallion	3 yrs.	12–15	40–45[4] / Record 252[5]		
Cow	15–18 mos.[6]	10–14		283	279–290[7] 262–300[8]
Bull	1 yr., well matured	10–12	50[4] / Thousands[5]		
Sow	5–6 mos. or 250 lbs.	6		115	110–120
Boar	250–300 lbs.	6	50[2] / 35–40[3]		
Doe goat	10 mos. or 85–90 lbs.	6		150	145–155
Buck goat	Well matured	5	30		
Bitch	16–18 mos.	8		63	58–67
Male dog	12–16 mos.	8	8–10		
Queen cat	12 mos.	6		63	60–68
Tom cat	12 mos.	6	6–8		
Doe rabbit	6 mos.	5–6		31	30–32
Buck rabbit	6 mos.	5–6	30		

[1]For fine wool breeds. [2]Hand-mated. [3]Pasture. [4]Natural. [5]Artificial. [6]Holstein and beef: 750 lbs.; Jersey: 500 lbs. [7]Beef; 8–10 days shorter for Angus. [8]Dairy.

Incubation Period of Poultry (days)	Maximum Life Span of Animals in Captivity (years)	
Chicken. 21	Cat (domestic). 34	Duck (domestic) 23
Duck 26–32	Chicken (domestic). 25	Goat (domestic). 20
Goose 30–34	Dog (domestic) 29	Goose (domestic) 20
Guinea 26–28		Horse 62
		Rabbit . . . . 18+

	Estral/Estrous Cycle (including heat period) AVERAGE	RANGE	Length of Estrus (heat) AVERAGE	RANGE	Usual Time of Ovulation	When Cycle Recurs if Not Bred
Mare	21 days	10–37 days	5–6 days	2–11 days	24–48 hours before end of estrus	21 days
Sow	21 days	18–24 days	2–3 days	1–5 days	30–36 hours after start of estrus	21 days
Ewe	16½ days	14–19 days	30 hours	24–32 hours	12–24 hours before end of estrus	16½ days
Goat	21 days	18–24 days	2–3 days	1–4 days	Near end of estrus	21 days
Cow	21 days	18–24 days	18 hours	10–24 hours	10–12 hours after end of estrus	21 days
Bitch	24 days		7 days	5–9 days	1–3 days after first acceptance	Pseudo-pregnancy
Cat		15–21 days	3–4 days, if mated	9–10 days, in absence of male	24–56 hours after coitus	Pseudo-pregnancy

Really BIG Fish

Anyone who goes fishing holds a secret dream that maybe a once-in-a-lifetime fish awaits. Sometimes, it really does.

"It wore me smooth out."

THE FISH: Alligator gar *(Lepisosteus spatula),* one of the largest freshwater fish in North America

THE ANGLER: Deryl Landers of Bokchito, Oklahoma

THE WATER: Red River, Oklahoma

THE DAY: July 17, 2002

THE BAIT: Cut buffalofish

THE RECORD: 30-pound line class; 180 pounds; recognized by the National Freshwater Fishing Hall of Fame

THE FACTS: The gar's scales are so hard that Native Americans once used them as arrowheads. Because gar can breathe both air and water, they can often be found in the shallow, muddy waters of the South.

—courtesy Deryl Landers

THE TALE:

We were fishing for catfish, and when this one hit, I thought that it was a catfish. When it splashed, it was like someone threw a Volkswagen into the river. The fish was taking out line so fast that I had to put my thumb on the reel to slow it down. I played it for an hour and 45 minutes. I've caught a lot of fish in my life, and I don't think that I've ever caught anything

Tales

by Mel R. Allen

that fought like that gar. It just about killed me. It wore me smooth out.

The fish was finally tired. I had to climb down a steep bank to get it. When I did, it flipped, knocked me right off my feet, and flipped me right over. That fish was nearly eight feet long. I tied a rope through its mouth, backed my pickup up to the bank, and pulled it up. We put it in a small swimming pool to keep it wet, and the next day we took it to the fish hatchery. The biologist there looked at the scales and estimated that the fish was 125 years old. I had no idea they lived that long.

As I began to reel in my lure, my rod shook violently and suddenly bent almost into a U shape.

"We all gasped ..."

THE FISH: Chinook salmon (king, sea-run) *(Oncorhynchus tshawytscha)*

THE ANGLER: Eugene Marre of Oakbrook, Illinois, current holder of 17 different National Freshwater Fishing Hall of Fame line-class records for various North Atlantic salmon species

THE WATER: Kenai River, Alaska

THE DAY: July 31, 1991

THE BAIT: King salmon eggs

THE RECORD: 10-pound line class; 63 pounds, 3 ounces; recognized by the National Freshwater Fishing Hall of Fame

THE FACTS: Chinook may spend from one to eight years in the ocean before returning to their birth rivers to spawn.

THE TALE:

It was the last day of the season for king salmon fishing on the Kenai River. We fished

—courtesy Eugene Marre

the entire morning without getting a strike. At about 11:15, the guide said that the next drift would be our last.

At the conclusion of the next drift, we reeled in our lures for the trip home. I was last to reel in because I was seated in the bow of the boat. As I began to reel in my lure, my rod shook violently and suddenly bent almost into a U shape. Then pandemonium broke out. People scurried about the boat, everyone yelling instructions at the same time. All the while, the fish was swimming upriver so fast that suddenly I realized that all my line was practically gone.

During the next 30 minutes, the fish went upriver, downriver, and from one side of the river to the other. Only my wife was quiet. She sat in the boat with her rosary beads. Suddenly, the fish turned toward the boat and then swam under it, fouling the line under the motor shaft. The guide shut the motor down. After leaning over the back of the boat and carefully unwinding the line from the shaft, he restarted the motor. He asked if I could still feel the fish. I could not. I reeled in some line and suddenly felt resistance. Yes, the fish was still hooked.

I brought the huge fish to the boat, and we all gasped as we got our first glimpse of it. The guide made one pass with the net and landed it. As he netted the fish, the hook broke free—but the fish was ours.

I have caught many large kings, but never have I experienced the feeling of exhilaration that I had at that final moment.

"My arms were killing me!"

THE FISH: Wahoo *(Acanthocybium solandri)*

THE ANGLER: Sara Hayward of Nacogdoches, Texas, who broke the existing all-tackle record by over 25 pounds when she was 15 years old

THE WATER: Sea of Cortez, Cabo San Lucas, Mexico

THE DAY: July 29, 2005

THE BAIT: "Mean Joe Green" artificial lure

THE RECORDS: Three classes (all-tackle, women's 80-pound line, junior female); 184 pounds; recognized by the International Game Fish Association (IGFA)

THE FACTS: Wahoo can swim up to 50 miles per hour. When first hooked, they can take several hundred yards of line off a reel in a few seconds.

THE TALE:

All of a sudden, the rod closest to me hit. It was vibrating. Whatever it was had taken the hook and run with it. The reel was spinning and I just reacted—I reached for it. I was struggling, but I hooked into the fighting chair. My dad was next to me, coaching me.

Every time I reeled the fish in, it would take the line back out. There was no way

Sara Hayward (center) with her brother and sister.

–courtesy Sara Hayward

Every time I reeled the fish in, it would take the line back out.

---

to stop it. My dad was shouting, "Pull it back! Pull the reel back!"

After 45 minutes, I had the most intense feeling of tiredness I had ever felt. My arms were killing me! My dad kept saying, "You can do it!"

Then it felt like I had lost the fish. I was so upset. Suddenly I saw its shape next to me, and I reeled even faster. We finally got it close enough to gaff. It took all four of us—my dad, the captain, the deckhand, and me—to land the fish. When we got it into the boat, all I could say was, "Oh, my gosh."

My dad wanted to release it, but the captain said no. "That's the biggest wahoo I have ever seen. You can't put it back." He raced to the dock to weigh it. The fish was so heavy that we needed ten people to carry it to the scale. Nobody could believe that I had caught it.

Canada's Most Famous Catch

THE FISH: Bluefin tuna *(Thunnus thynnus)*

THE ANGLER: Captain Ken Fraser of North Lake, Prince Edward Island

—IGFA

THE WATER: Aulds Cove, Nova Scotia

THE DAY: October 26, 1979

THE RECORD: All-tackle. Fraser's 1,496-pound bluefin tuna is the largest ever landed; recognized by the IGFA

THE FACTS: The trophy tail resides in Fraser's basement. The runner-up is a 1,170-pound bluefin landed by Dr. Colette Peras of Montreal in P.E.I. waters in 1978, for a women's 130-pound line class world record, also recognized by the IGFA.

continued

"Save us from this beast."

THE FISH: Shortfin mako shark *(Isurus oxyrinchus)*

THE ANGLER: Luke Sweeney of Lakeville, Massachusetts

THE WATER: Atlantic Ocean, off Chatham, Massachusetts

THE DAY: July 21, 2001

THE BAIT: Fresh bonito and bluefish on hooks, plus bluefish and bonito ground up in a wood chipper for chum

THE RECORD: All-tackle; 1,221 pounds; recognized by the IGFA

THE FACTS: The mako shark preys on broadbill swordfish. Startled fishermen once discovered a 120-pound swordfish inside a 730-pound mako. The IGFA calls the mako "the undisputed leader in attacks on boats."

—courtesy Luke Sweeney

THE TALE:

There were 170 boats in the Oak Bluffs [Martha's Vineyard] Monster Shark Tourney, and we were on the smallest one, a 24-foot catboat. We had the best chum, hands down. We flipped a coin to see which one of us would be on the rod if we got a strike. I won. I strapped into the harness and belt. The captain put a bluefish on a hook and threw the bait overboard. In a few minutes we saw it—a huge mako.

We let it swim for 15 seconds before I set the hook. The fish started peeling off line. We followed, and suddenly the line grew slack. It was coming toward us! We tried to get away, to keep the line tight, but we couldn't get away as fast as the fish could swim. The line went slack. I thought that the fish was gone.

Suddenly, this fish rockets 12 feet out

We got it close to the boat, saw its mouth opened wide and that jaw and those teeth—and we knew that it could bite us in half.

of the water right beside us! When it hit the water, the boat rocked. We were scared.

For over an hour, I fought to keep the line tight. I was absolutely spent, played out. My lower back was killing me. Finally, we got it close to the boat, saw its mouth opened wide and that jaw and those teeth—and we knew that it could bite us in half. I said to myself, "Jesus, Mary, and Joseph, save us from this beast."

We got a gaff into its back near the dorsal fin. It thrashed around, slamming the boat so hard that the fiberglass cracked. Then it took off again, towing the boat on the gaff rope. The shark bent that gaff straight and shook it free, and it came flying back and slammed into the boat.

Finally, we were able to get a rope around its tail and, once the tail was out of the water, we had it—a 13-foot-long giant. We had four guys. There was no way that we could haul the thing over the gunwale, so we tied it to the boat and headed for the dock. Running the motors at full speed, we were getting only about 7 knots.

Halfway back to port, we realized that we were going to run out of gas. We radioed Oak Bluffs: "We have the biggest fish you've ever seen. Get guys out here with gas!"

Word got around, and there were maybe 2,000 people waiting at the dock. We donated the meat to the Boston Food Bank. It made 4,800 individual servings! We won $24,000 in the fishermen's pool, and we knew that we had caught one of Martha's Vineyard's most famous fish ever. □□

Mel R. Allen once went fly-fishing for Atlantic salmon on the Miramachi River in New Brunswick, Canada, with famed angler and baseball immortal Ted Williams. The legend's advice for Allen? "Stay out of my way, kid."

The Hardest Record to Beat

Because they are so abundant in rivers, ponds, and lakes, yellow perch (*Perca flavescens*) are one of the species most often caught in North America—especially by young anglers. It is somewhat ironic, then, that yellow perch is also the category for the longest-standing world record. In May 1865, Dr. C. Abbott landed a 4-pound, 3-ounce, yellow perch in Bordentown, New Jersey. It has never been topped.

The Youngest Record Holder

David White landed the all-tackle record for sea-run rainbow trout (*Oncorhynchus mykiss*) on June 22, 1970, on Bell Island, Alaska. His fish weighed 42 pounds, 2 ounces. He was 8 years old.

The Lightest Record

In December 2005, Dr. Mark Everard of Great Somerford, England, set the British record for catching the largest minnow. His $4\frac{1}{2}$-inch-long, $\frac{1}{2}$-ounce monster bested the previous record holder by about $\frac{1}{10}$ of an ounce.

GET HOOKED!

These and other records are made to be broken. Why shouldn't it be you who does it? For information on landing million-dollar fish (and tips on where you can find one), as well as advice on what to do if you think you've caught a record setter, go to **Almanac.com/extras.**

Best Fishing Days and Times

■ **The best times to fish are when the fish are naturally most active. The Sun,** Moon, tides, and weather all influence fish activity. For example, fish tend to feed more at sunrise and sunset. During a full Moon, tides are higher than average and fish tend to feed more. However, most of us go fishing when we can get the time off, not because it is the best time. But there *are* best times, according to fishing lore:

The Best Days for 2007, when the Moon is between new and full:

January 1–3

January 18–February 2

February 17–March 3

March 18–April 2

April 17–May 2

May 16–31

June 14–30

July 14–29

August 12–28

September 11–26

October 11–26

November 9–24

December 9–23

■ One hour before and one hour after high tides, and one hour before and one hour after low tides. (The times of high tides for Boston are given on pages 106–132; also see pages 234–235. Inland, the times for high tides correspond with the times when the Moon is due south. Low tides are halfway between high tides.)

■ During the "morning rise" (after sunup for a spell) and the "evening rise" (just before sundown and the hour or so after).

■ When the barometer is steady or on the rise. (But even during stormy periods, the fish aren't going to give up feeding. The smart fisherman will find just the right bait.)

■ When there is a hatch of flies—caddis flies or may-flies, commonly. (The fisherman will have to match *his* fly with the hatching flies or go fishless.)

■ When the breeze is from a westerly quarter rather than from the north or east.

■ When the water is still or rippled, rather than during a wind.

Tackle-Box Checklist

❏ Fishing line

❏ Bobbers

❏ Swivels, to keep fishing line from twisting

❏ Leaders

❏ Sinkers

❏ Different sizes of hooks

❏ Pliers, to help remove hooks

❏ Stringer, to hold all the fish you catch

❏ Sharp knife

❏ Ruler/scale

❏ Flashlight

❏ First-aid kit

❏ Insect repellent

❏ Sunscreen

trout

catfish

salmon

New lure's catch rate may be too high for some tournaments.

Out-fishes other bait 19 to 4 in one contest.

Uses aerospace technology to mimic a real fish.

Swims with its tail.

New lure swims like a real fish--nearly triples catch in Florida contest.

ORLANDO, FL— A small company in Connecticut has developed a new lure that mimics the motion of a real fish so realistically eight professionals couldn't tell the difference between it and a live shad when it "swam" toward them on retrieval. The design eliminates wobbling, angled swimming and other unnatural motions that problem other hard bait lures. It swims upright and appears to propel itself with its tail.

Curiously, the company may have designed it too well. Tournament fishermen who have used it said it's possible officials will not allow it in contests where live bait is prohibited. They claim it swims more realistically than anything they have ever seen. If so, that would hurt the company's promotional efforts. Winning tournaments is an important part of marketing a new lure.

Fish would probably prefer to see it restricted. I watched eight veteran fishermen test the new lure (called The KickTail®) on a lake outside Orlando FL for about four hours. Four used the KickTail and four used a combination of their favorite lures and shiners (live bait). The four using the KickTail caught 41 fish versus 14 for the other four. In one boat the KickTail won 19 to 4. The KickTail also caught bigger fish, which suggests it triggers larger, less aggressive fish to strike.

The KickTail's magic comes from a patented technology that breaks the tail into five segments. As water rushes by on retrieval, a little-known principle called aeronautical flutter causes the tail to wag left and right, as if the lure were propelling itself with its tail. Unlike other hard baits, the head remains stationary—only the tail wags. A company spokesman told me this.

"Marine biologists will tell you that the more a lure swims like a real fish, the more fish it will catch. Well, the only live thing the KickTail doesn't do is breathe. It's always swimming wild and free. Fish can't stand it. We've seen fish that have just eaten go for the KickTail. It's like having another potato chip."

Whether you fish for fun or profit, if you want a nearly 3 to 1 advantage, I would order now before the KickTail becomes known. The company even guarantees a refund, if you don't catch more fish and return the lures within 30 days. There are three versions: a floater, a diver and a "dying shad" with a weed guard. Each lure costs $9.95 and you must order at least two. There is also a "Super 10-Pack" with additional colors for only $79.95, a savings of almost $20.00. S/h is only $6.00 no matter how many you order.

To order call **1-800-873-4415** or click **www.ngcsports.com** anytime of any day or send a check or M.O. (or cc number and exp. date) to NGC Sports **(Dept. KT-1025)**, 60 Church Street, Yalesville, CT 06492. CT orders add sales tax. The KickTail is four inches long and works in salt and fresh water.

KTS-5   © NGC Worldwide, Inc. 2007 **Dept. KT-1025**

Secrets of the Zodiac

The Man of the Signs

Ancient astrologers believed that each astrological sign influenced a specific part of the body. The first sign of the zodiac—Aries—was attributed to the head, with the rest of the signs moving down the body, ending with Pisces at the feet.

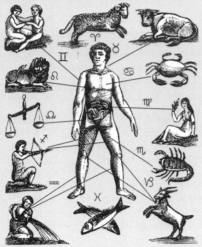

♈ Aries, head . . . . **ARI** *Mar. 21–Apr. 20*
♉ Taurus, neck . . . . . . **TAU** *Apr. 21–May 20*
♊ Gemini, arms . . . . . **GEM** *May 21–June 20*
♋ Cancer, breast . . . . **CAN** *June 21–July 22*
♌ Leo, heart . . . . **LEO** *July 23–Aug. 22*
♍ Virgo, belly . . . . **VIR** *Aug. 23–Sept. 22*
♎ Libra, reins . . . . **LIB** *Sept. 23–Oct. 22*
♏ Scorpio, secrets . . . **SCO** *Oct. 23–Nov. 22*
♐ Sagittarius, thighs . . **SAG** *Nov. 23–Dec. 21*
♑ Capricorn, knees . . **CAP** *Dec. 22–Jan. 19*
♒ Aquarius, legs . . . . **AQU** *Jan. 20–Feb. 19*
♓ Pisces, feet . . . . **PSC** *Feb. 20–Mar. 20*

Astrology vs. Astronomy

■ **Astrology** is a tool we use to plan events according to the astrological placements of the Sun, the Moon, and eight planets in the 12 signs of the zodiac. The planetary movements do not cause events; rather, they explain the path, or "flow," that events tend to follow. **Astronomy** is the study of the actual placement of the known planets and constellations. *(The placement of the planets in the signs of the zodiac is not the same astrologically and astronomically.)* The Moon's astrological place is given on **page 227**; its astronomical place is given in the **Left-Hand Calendar Pages, 106–132.**

The dates in the **Best Times table, page 230,** are based on the astrological passage of the Moon. However, consider all indicators before making any major decisions.

When Mercury Is Retrograde

■ Sometimes the other planets appear to be traveling backward through the zodiac; this is an illusion. We call this illusion *retrograde motion.*

Mercury's retrograde periods can cause our plans to go awry. However, this is an excellent time to reflect on the past. Intuition is high during these periods and coincidences can be extraordinary. **(See page 228.)**

When Mercury is retrograde, remain flexible, allow extra time for travel, and avoid signing contracts. Review projects and plans at these times, but wait until Mercury is direct again to make any final decisions.

In 2007, Mercury will be retrograde from February 14–March 8, June 15–July 10, and October 12–November 2. *–Celeste Longacre*

Gardening by the Moon's Sign

Use the chart opposite to find the best dates for the following garden tasks:

■ **Plant, transplant, and graft:** Cancer, Scorpio, and Pisces. Taurus, Virgo, and Capricorn are good second choices.

■ **Control insect pests, plow, and weed:** Aries, Gemini, Leo, Sagittarius, or Aquarius.

■ **Prune:** Aries, Leo, or Sagittarius. During a waxing Moon, pruning encourages growth; during a waning Moon, it discourages growth.

■ **Build/fix fences or garden beds:** Capricorn.

■ **Clean out the garden shed:** Virgo.

Setting Eggs by the Moon's Sign

■ Chicks take about 21 days to hatch. Those born under a waxing Moon, in the fruitful signs of Cancer, Scorpio, and Pisces, are healthier and mature faster. To ensure that chicks are born during these times, determine the best days to "set eggs" (to place eggs in an incubator or under a hen). To calculate, find the three fruitful birth signs on the chart below. Use the **Left-Hand Calendar Pages, 106–132,** to find the dates of the new and full Moon. Using only the fruitful dates

between the new and full Moon, count back 21 days to find the best days to set eggs.

E X A M P L E :

In June, the Moon is new on June 14 and full on June 30. Between these dates, the Moon is in the sign of Cancer from June 15 to 17. To have chicks born on June 16, count back 21 days; set eggs on May 26.

Moon's Astrological Place, 2006–07

	Nov.	Dec.	Jan.	Feb.	Mar.	Apr.	May	June	July	Aug.	Sept.	Oct.	Nov.	Dec.
1	PSC	ARI	GEM	LEO	LEO	LIB	SCO	SAG	CAP	PSC	TAU	GEM	LEO	VIR
2	PSC	TAU	CAN	LEO	LEO	LIB	SCO	CAP	AQU	PSC	TAU	CAN	LEO	VIR
3	ARI	TAU	CAN	VIR	VIR	LIB	SCO	CAP	AQU	ARI	GEM	CAN	VIR	LIB
4	ARI	GEM	CAN	VIR	VIR	SCO	SAG	CAP	PSC	ARI	GEM	CAN	VIR	LIB
5	TAU	GEM	LEO	VIR	LIB	SCO	SAG	AQU	PSC	TAU	CAN	LEO	VIR	LIB
6	TAU	CAN	LEO	LIB	LIB	SAG	CAP	AQU	ARI	TAU	CAN	LEO	LIB	SCO
7	GEM	CAN	VIR	LIB	LIB	SAG	CAP	PSC	ARI	GEM	LEO	VIR	LIB	SCO
8	GEM	LEO	VIR	SCO	SCO	SAG	CAP	PSC	ARI	GEM	LEO	VIR	SCO	SAG
9	CAN	LEO	VIR	SCO	SCO	CAP	AQU	ARI	TAU	CAN	LEO	VIR	SCO	SAG
10	CAN	LEO	LIB	SCO	SAG	CAP	AQU	ARI	TAU	CAN	VIR	LIB	SCO	SAG
11	LEO	VIR	LIB	SAG	SAG	AQU	PSC	TAU	GEM	LEO	VIR	LIB	SAG	CAP
12	LEO	VIR	SCO	SAG	SAG	AQU	PSC	TAU	GEM	LEO	LIB	SCO	SAG	CAP
13	VIR	LIB	SCO	CAP	CAP	PSC	ARI	GEM	CAN	LEO	LIB	SCO	CAP	AQU
14	VIR	LIB	SCO	CAP	CAP	PSC	ARI	GEM	CAN	VIR	LIB	SCO	CAP	AQU
15	VIR	LIB	SAG	AQU	AQU	ARI	TAU	CAN	LEO	VIR	SCO	SAG	CAP	PSC
16	LIB	SCO	SAG	AQU	AQU	ARI	TAU	CAN	LEO	LIB	SCO	SAG	AQU	PSC
17	LIB	SCO	CAP	AQU	PSC	TAU	GEM	CAN	VIR	LIB	SAG	CAP	AQU	PSC
18	SCO	SAG	CAP	PSC	PSC	TAU	GEM	LEO	VIR	SCO	SAG	CAP	PSC	ARI
19	SCO	SAG	AQU	PSC	ARI	GEM	CAN	LEO	VIR	SCO	SAG	AQU	PSC	ARI
20	SCO	SAG	AQU	ARI	ARI	GEM	CAN	VIR	LIB	SCO	CAP	AQU	ARI	TAU
21	SAG	CAP	PSC	ARI	TAU	GEM	LEO	VIR	LIB	SAG	CAP	AQU	ARI	TAU
22	SAG	CAP	PSC	TAU	TAU	CAN	LEO	LIB	SCO	SAG	AQU	PSC	TAU	GEM
23	CAP	AQU	ARI	TAU	GEM	CAN	VIR	LIB	SCO	CAP	AQU	PSC	TAU	GEM
24	CAP	AQU	ARI	GEM	GEM	LEO	VIR	LIB	SCO	CAP	PSC	ARI	GEM	CAN
25	CAP	PSC	TAU	GEM	CAN	LEO	VIR	SCO	SAG	CAP	PSC	ARI	GEM	CAN
26	AQU	PSC	TAU	CAN	CAN	VIR	LIB	SCO	SAG	AQU	ARI	TAU	CAN	LEO
27	AQU	ARI	GEM	CAN	LEO	VIR	LIB	SAG	CAP	AQU	ARI	TAU	CAN	LEO
28	PSC	ARI	GEM	LEO	LEO	VIR	SCO	SAG	CAP	PSC	TAU	GEM	LEO	VIR
29	PSC	TAU	GEM	—	LEO	LIB	SCO	SAG	AQU	PSC	TAU	GEM	LEO	VIR
30	ARI	TAU	CAN	—	VIR	LIB	SCO	CAP	AQU	ARI	GEM	CAN	LEO	LIB
31	—	GEM	CAN	—	VIR	—	SAG	—	AQU	ARI	—	CAN	—	LIB

Mercury and You

BY ISABELLE GHANEH

There is a time to let things happen and a time to make things happen.

–Hugh Prather, American writer (b. 1938)

We are all influenced when Mercury is in retrograde. The type of influence depends on which of the 12 zodiac signs the planet is in when it goes retrograde. Here is a brief look at what to expect:

RETROGRADE DATES

October 28 to November 18, 2006: *Mercury turns retrograde in Scorpio.*

February 14 to March 8, 2007: *Mercury turns retrograde in Pisces/Aquarius.*

June 15 to July 10, 2007: *Mercury turns retrograde in Cancer.*

October 12 to November 2, 2007: *Mercury turns retrograde in Scorpio/Libra.*

IN ARIES: Expect to be frustrated and frazzled. Assertive, impulsive Aries wants to move ahead, and all of the energy is  going backward. Watch what you say and how you say it. Pay attention to what people say to you; you might be pleasantly surprised.

IN TAURUS: Take time to formulate your thoughts. Taurus, an unhurried sign, slows down the mental processes. He also governs banking, so delay money matters. Review  financial matters, and position yourself for growth.

IN GEMINI: Because Gemini rules communications, be prepared for miscommunications when Mercury is in this sign. Expect lots of phone calls or none, and lost or misplaced mail. You may not articulate clearly, and gossip abounds. Old friends may reconnect.

IN CANCER: Expect annoyances at home with baking, gardening, and household duties under domesticated Cancer. Complete repair projects that weren't finished or done correctly.

IN LEO: Avoid speculative investments. It is not a good time to buy and sell or do any trading. Instead, analyze your investment  portfolio. Use your know-how and advisory skills to help friends and associates.

IN VIRGO: Challenging situations arise, especially in the workplace. Expect product delays and equipment breakdowns,  as well as crankiness among coworkers under finicky, detail-oriented Virgo. Double-check your work before you call it finished.

IN LIBRA: Accept your physical attributes; do not have a make-over. Indecision reigns, so limit purchases—or risk returning  them. Libra, representing beauty, grace, charm, and diplomacy, is out of balance. Refresh, relax, and rejuvenate.

IN SCORPIO: Emotions rule— not common sense—so beware. Avoid affairs of the heart. Pas-sionate Scorpio is also secretive,  and your secrets may seep out. Keep them in a diary.

IN SAGITTARIUS: It is not a time to travel, so reschedule or expect delays, lines, and lost directions. Instead, take care of local affairs.  Patience and a sense of humor are needed.

IN CAPRICORN: Avoid buying, selling, or renting real estate un-der Capricorn, the sign that gov-erns property matters. Expect  problems with paperwork, packing, and movers. Re-unite with family or vacation at home.

IN AQUARIUS: With Mercury ret-rograde in Aquarius, the sign that governs relationships, friendships are put at risk. Petty  squabbles, misunderstandings, and miscommunica-tions abound. Know who your friends are.

IN PISCES: Foggy thinking, daydreams, and escapism are the norm; day-to-day realities confound otherwise clear heads  when Mercury, the planet that rules logic, is in Pisces, which governs illusion. Practice creative pursuits— writing, dancing, photography, film, or painting.

A MAN WITH A MESSAGE

Mercury comes from the Latin word *merx,* or *mercator,* which means merchant. Mercury is the name given by the ancient Romans to the Greek mytholog-ical god Her-mes. Mercury is depicted as a male figure hav-ing winged sandals and a winged hat, indicating the abil-ity to travel quickly. He was the official messenger of the gods and goddesses and, as such, governed communications. In 1782, Mercury became the first symbol of the United States' fledgling postal service. Today, he is recognized as the icon of an international floral delivery service as well as the official symbol of the postal service of Greece.

All of the planet's astrolog-ical attributes are rooted in ancient Greek and Roman mythology. In that context, Mercury is the god of travelers, literature, poetry, merchants, and thieves. He is cunning and clever and witty at a moment's notice. But he is also recog-nized as a trickster and thief, prone to misbehavior. □ □

Astrologer **Isabelle Ghaneh** finds that the best way to survive Mercury retrograde is to expect the unexpected.

Best Times

The following month-by-month chart is based on the Moon's sign and shows the best days each month for certain activities. *–Celeste Longacre*

	JAN.	FEB.	MAR.	APR.	MAY	JUNE	JULY	AUG.	SEPT.	OCT.	NOV.	DEC.
Quit Smoking	6, 11	7, 17	7, 16	3, 13	10, 14	6, 10	3, 8	4, 31	9, 28	6, 10	2, 7, 30	4, 27, 31
Begin diet to lose weight	6, 11	7, 17	7, 16	3, 13	10, 14	6, 10	3, 8	4, 31	9, 28	6, 10	2, 7, 30	4, 27, 31
Begin diet to gain weight	20, 24	21	21, 30	25, 30	23, 28	19, 24	16, 21	13, 17	14, 24	21, 25	17, 21	14, 19
Cut hair to discourage growth	5, 6, 10, 11	6, 7	6, 7	2, 3	11, 12	11, 12	9, 10	5, 6	1, 2, 29	5, 6, 26, 27	6, 7	3, 4
Cut hair to encourage growth	26, 27	22, 23	28, 29	29, 30	27, 28	22, 23, 24	20, 21	16, 17	12, 13, 14	21, 22	22, 23	20, 21
Have dental care	7, 8	4, 5	3, 4, 30, 31	26, 27, 28	24, 25	20, 21	17, 18	14, 15	10, 11	7, 8, 9	4, 5	1, 2, 28, 29
Start projects	20	18	20	18	17	16	15	15	12	12	10	10
End projects	18	16	18	16	15	14	13	13	10	10	8	8
Entertain	5, 6	1, 2, 28	1, 2, 28, 29	24, 25	21, 22	18, 19	15, 16	11, 12	8, 9	5, 6	1, 2, 29, 30	26, 27
Go camping	15, 16	11, 12	10, 11, 12	7, 8	4, 5	1, 28, 29	25, 26	21, 22	18, 19	15, 16	11, 12	8, 9
Plant aboveground crops	21, 22, 30, 31	18, 19, 26, 27	25, 26	22, 23	19, 20, 29, 30	16, 17, 25, 26	22, 23, 24	19, 20	15, 16	12, 13, 22, 23	10, 18, 19	15, 16
Plant belowground crops	3, 4, 12, 13	9, 10	8, 9	4, 5, 14	11, 12	7, 8	4, 5, 13	1, 8, 9	5, 6	3, 4, 30, 31	26, 27	6, 7, 25
Destroy pests and weeds	23, 24	20, 21	19, 20	15, 16	13, 14	9, 10	6, 7	3, 4, 30, 31	26, 27	24, 25	20, 21	18, 19
Graft or pollinate	3, 4, 30, 31	26, 27	25, 26	22, 23	19, 20	15, 16	13, 14	9, 10	5, 6	3, 4, 30, 31	26, 27	24, 25
Prune to encourage growth	23, 24	20, 21	20, 28, 29	24, 25	21, 22	18, 19	25, 26	21, 22	18, 19	15, 16	20, 21	18, 19
Prune to discourage growth	15, 16	11, 12	10, 11, 12	7, 8	13, 14	9, 10	6, 7	3, 4, 30, 31	8, 9, 27	5, 6	1, 2, 29	8, 26, 27
Harvest above-ground crops	26, 27	22, 23	21, 22	26, 27	24, 25	20, 21	17, 18	14, 15	20, 21	17, 18	14, 15, 23	11, 12
Harvest below-ground crops	7, 8	4, 5, 13, 14	3, 4	9, 10	6, 7	11, 12	9, 10	5, 6	1, 2, 10	7, 8	4, 5	1, 2, 28, 29
Cut hay	23, 24	20, 21	19, 20	15, 16	13, 14	9, 10	6, 7	3, 4, 30, 31	26, 27	24, 25	20, 21	18, 19
Begin logging	17, 18	13, 14	13, 14	9, 10	6, 7	3, 4, 30	1, 27, 28	24, 25	20, 21	17, 18	14, 15	11, 12
Set posts or pour concrete	17, 18	13, 14	13, 14	9, 10	6, 7	3, 4, 30	1, 27, 28	24, 25	20, 21	17, 18	14, 15	11, 12
Breed	12, 13	9, 10	8, 9	4, 5	1, 2, 3, 29, 30	25, 26	22, 23, 24	19, 20	15, 16	12, 13	9, 10	6, 7
Wean	6, 11	7, 17	7, 16	3, 13	10, 14	6, 10	3, 8	4, 31	9, 28	6, 10	2, 7, 30	4, 27, 31
Castrate animals	19, 20	15, 16	15, 16	11, 12	9, 10	5, 6	2, 3, 29, 30	26, 27	22, 23	20, 21	16, 17	13, 14
Slaughter livestock	12, 13	9, 10	8, 9	4, 5	1, 2, 3, 29, 30	25, 26	22, 23, 24	19, 20	15, 16	12, 13	9, 10	6, 7

Visit our Astrology Forum at Almanac.com/forum.

Frosts and Growing Seasons

■ Dates given are normal averages for a light freeze; local weather and topography may cause considerable variations. The possibility of frost occurring after the spring dates and before the fall dates is 50 percent. The classification of freeze temperatures is usually based on their effect on plants. **Light freeze:** 29° to 32°F—tender plants killed. **Moderate freeze:** 25° to 28°F—widely destructive effect on most vegetation. **Severe freeze:** 24°F and colder—heavy damage to most plants.

–courtesy of National Climatic Data Center

State	City	Growing Season (days)	Last Spring Frost	First Fall Frost	State	City	Growing Season (days)	Last Spring Frost	First Fall Frost
AK	Juneau	133	May 16	Sept. 26	ND	Bismarck	129	May 14	Sept. 20
AL	Mobile	272	Feb. 27	Nov. 26	NE	Blair	165	Apr. 27	Oct. 10
AR	Pine Bluff	234	Mar. 19	Nov. 8	NE	North Platte	136	May 11	Sept. 24
AZ	Phoenix	308	Feb. 5	Dec. 15	NH	Concord	121	May 23	Sept. 22
AZ	Tucson	273	Feb. 28	Nov. 29	NJ	Newark	219	Apr. 4	Nov. 10
CA	Eureka	324	Jan. 30	Dec. 15	NM	Carlsbad	223	Mar. 29	Nov. 7
CA	Sacramento	289	Feb. 14	Dec. 1	NM	Los Alamos	157	May 8	Oct. 13
CA	San Francisco	*	*	*	NV	Las Vegas	259	Mar. 7	Nov. 21
CO	Denver	157	May 3	Oct. 8	NY	Albany	144	May 7	Sept. 29
CT	Hartford	167	Apr. 25	Oct. 10	NY	Syracuse	170	Apr. 28	Oct. 16
DE	Wilmington	198	Apr. 13	Oct. 29	OH	Akron	168	May 3	Oct. 18
FL	Miami	*	*	*	OH	Cincinnati	195	Apr. 14	Oct. 27
FL	Tampa	338	Jan. 28	Jan. 3	OK	Lawton	217	Apr. 1	Nov. 5
GA	Athens	224	Mar. 28	Nov. 8	OK	Tulsa	218	Mar. 30	Nov. 4
GA	Savannah	250	Mar. 10	Nov. 15	OR	Pendleton	188	Apr. 15	Oct. 21
IA	Atlantic	141	May 9	Sept. 28	OR	Portland	217	Apr. 3	Nov. 7
IA	Cedar Rapids	161	Apr. 29	Oct. 7	PA	Carlisle	182	Apr. 20	Oct. 20
ID	Boise	153	May 8	Oct. 9	PA	Williamsport	168	Apr. 29	Oct. 15
IL	Chicago	187	Apr. 22	Oct. 26	RI	Kingston	144	May 8	Sept. 30
IL	Springfield	185	Apr. 17	Oct. 19	SC	Charleston	253	Mar. 11	Nov. 20
IN	Indianapolis	180	Apr. 22	Oct. 20	SC	Columbia	211	Apr. 4	Nov. 2
IN	South Bend	169	May 1	Oct. 18	SD	Rapid City	145	May 7	Sept. 29
KS	Topeka	175	Apr. 21	Oct. 14	TN	Memphis	228	Mar. 23	Nov. 7
KY	Lexington	190	Apr. 17	Oct. 25	TN	Nashville	207	Apr. 5	Oct. 29
LA	Monroe	242	Mar. 9	Nov. 7	TX	Amarillo	197	Apr. 14	Oct. 29
LA	New Orleans	288	Feb. 20	Dec. 5	TX	Denton	231	Mar. 25	Nov. 12
MA	Worcester	172	Apr. 27	Oct. 17	TX	San Antonio	265	Mar. 3	Nov. 24
MD	Baltimore	231	Mar. 26	Nov. 13	UT	Cedar City	134	May 20	Oct. 2
ME	Portland	143	May 10	Sept. 30	UT	Spanish Fork	156	May 8	Oct. 12
MI	Lansing	140	May 13	Sept. 30	VA	Norfolk	239	Mar. 23	Nov. 17
MI	Marquette	159	May 12	Oct. 19	VA	Richmond	198	Apr. 10	Oct. 26
MN	Duluth	122	May 21	Sept. 21	VT	Burlington	142	May 11	Oct. 1
MN	Willmar	152	May 4	Oct. 4	WA	Seattle	232	Mar. 24	Nov. 11
MO	Jefferson City	173	Apr. 26	Oct. 16	WA	Spokane	153	May 4	Oct. 5
MS	Columbus	215	Mar. 27	Oct. 29	WI	Green Bay	143	May 12	Oct. 2
MS	Vicksburg	250	Mar. 13	Nov. 18	WI	Janesville	164	Apr. 28	Oct. 10
MT	Fort Peck	146	May 5	Sept. 28	WV	Parkersburg	175	Apr. 25	Oct. 18
MT	Helena	122	May 18	Sept. 18	WY	Casper	123	May 22	Sept. 22
NC	Fayetteville	212	Apr. 2	Oct. 31		*Frosts do not occur every year.*			

Outdoor Planting Table

■ The best time to plant flowers and vegetables that bear crops *above ground* is during the *light* of the Moon; that is, from the day the Moon is new to the day it is full. Flowering bulbs and vegetables that bear crops *below ground* should be planted during the *dark* of the Moon; that is, from the day after it is full to the day before it is new again. The Moon Favorable columns at right give these days, which are based on the Moon's phases for 2007 and the safe periods for planting in areas that receive frost. Consult **page 231** for dates of frosts and lengths of growing seasons. See the **Left-Hand Calendar Pages, 106–132,** for the exact days of the new and full Moons.

■ **Aboveground crops are marked *.**

■ **(E) means early; (L) means late.**

■ **Map shades correspond to shades of date columns.**

* Barley	
* Beans	(E)
	(L)
Beets	(E)
	(L)
* Broccoli plants	(E)
	(L)
* Brussels sprouts	
* Cabbage plants	
Carrots	(E)
	(L)
* Cauliflower plants	(E)
	(L)
* Celery plants	(E)
	(L)
* Collards	(E)
	(L)
* Corn, sweet	(E)
	(L)
* Cucumbers	
* Eggplant plants	
* Endive	(E)
	(L)
* Kale	(E)
	(L)
Leek plants	
* Lettuce	
* Muskmelons	
* Okra	
Onion sets	
* Parsley	
Parsnips	
* Peas	(E)
	(L)
* Pepper plants	
Potatoes	
* Pumpkins	
Radishes	(E)
	(L)
* Spinach	(E)
	(L)
* Squashes	
Sweet potatoes	
* Swiss chard	
* Tomato plants	
Turnips	(E)
	(L)
* Watermelons	
* Wheat, spring	
* Wheat, winter	

Get growing at Almanac.com/garden.

Planting Dates	Moon Favorable	Planting Dates	Moon Favorable	Planting Dates	Moon Favorable	Planting Dates	Moon Favorable
2/15–3/7	2/17–3/3	3/15–4/7	3/18–4/2	5/15–6/21	5/16–31, 6/14–21	6/1–30	6/14–30
3/15–4/7	3/18–4/2	4/15–30	4/17–30	5/7–6/21	5/16–31, 6/14–21	5/30–6/15	5/30–31, 6/14–15
8/7–31	8/12–28	7/1–21	7/14–21	6/15–7/15	6/15–30, 7/14–15	–	–
2/7–28	2/7–16	3/15–4/3	3/15–17, 4/3	5/1–15	5/3–15	5/25–6/10	6/1–10
9/1–30	9/1–10, 9/27–30	8/15–31	8/29–31	7/15–8/15	7/30–8/11	6/15–7/8	7/1–8
2/15–3/15	2/17–3/3	3/7–31	3/18–31	5/15–31	5/16–31	6/1–25	6/14–25
9/7–30	9/11–26	8/1–20	8/12–20	6/15–7/7	6/15–30	–	–
2/11–3/20	2/17–3/3, 3/18–20	3/7–4/15	3/18–4/2	5/15–31	5/16–31	6/1–25	6/14–25
2/11–3/20	2/17–3/3, 3/18–20	3/7–4/15	3/18–4/2	5/15–31	5/16–31	6/1–25	6/14–25
2/15–3/7	2/15–16, 3/4–7	3/7–31	3/7–17	5/15–31	5/15	5/25–6/10	6/1–10
8/1–9/7	8/1–11, 8/29–9/7	7/7–31	7/7–13, 7/30–31	6/15–7/21	7/1–13	6/15–7/8	7/1–8
2/15–3/7	2/17–3/3	3/15–4/7	3/18–4/2	5/15–31	5/16–31	6/1–25	6/14–25
8/7–31	8/12–28	7/1–8/7	7/14–29	6/15–7/21	6/15–30, 7/14–21	–	–
2/15–28	2/17–28	3/7–31	3/18–31	5/15–6/30	5/16–31, 6/14–30	6/1–30	6/14–30
9/15–30	9/15–26	8/15–9/7	8/15–28	7/15–8/15	7/15–29, 8/12–15	–	–
2/11–3/20	2/17–3/3, 3/18–20	3/7–4/7	3/18–4/2	5/15–31	5/16–31	6/1–25	6/14–25
9/7–30	9/11–26	8/15–31	8/15–28	7/1–8/7	7/14–29	–	–
3/15–31	3/18–31	4/1–17	4/1–2, 4/17	5/10–6/15	5/16–31, 6/14–15	5/30–6/20	5/30–31, 6/14–20
8/7–31	8/12–28	7/7–21	7/14–21	6/15–30	6/15–30	–	–
3/7–4/15	3/18–4/2	4/7–5/15	4/17–5/2	5/7–6/20	5/16–31, 6/14–20	5/30–6/15	5/30–31, 6/14–15
3/7–4/15	3/18–4/2	4/7–5/15	4/17–5/2	6/1–30	6/14–30	6/15–30	6/15–30
2/15–3/20	2/17–3/3, 3/18–20	4/7–5/15	4/17–5/2	5/15–31	5/16–31	6/1–25	6/14–25
8/15–9/7	8/15–28	7/15–8/15	7/15–29, 8/12–15	6/7–30	6/14–30	–	–
2/11–3/20	2/17–3/3, 3/18–20	3/7–4/7	3/18–4/2	5/15–31	5/16–31	6/1–15	6/14–15
9/7–30	9/11–26	8/15–31	8/15–28	7/1–8/7	7/14–29	6/25–7/15	6/25–30, 7/14–15
2/15–4/15	2/15–16, 3/4–17, 4/3–15	3/7–4/7	3/7–17, 4/3–7	5/15–31	5/15	6/1–25	6/1–13
2/15–3/7	2/17–3/3	3/1–31	3/1–3, 3/18–31	5/15–6/30	5/16–31, 6/14–30	6/1–30	6/14–30
3/15–4/7	3/18–4/2	4/15–5/7	4/17–5/2	5/15–6/30	5/16–31, 6/14–30	6/1–30	6/14–30
4/15–6/1	4/17–5/2, 5/16–31	5/25–6/15	5/25–31, 6/14–15	6/15–7/10	6/15–30	6/25–7/7	6/25–30
2/1–28	2/3–16	3/1–31	3/4–17	5/15–6/7	5/15, 6/1–7	6/1–25	6/1–13
2/20–3/15	2/20–3/3	3/1–31	3/1–3, 3/18–31	5/15–31	5/16–31	6/1–15	6/14–15
1/15–2/4	1/15–17, 2/3–4	3/7–31	3/7–17	4/1–30	4/3–16	5/10–31	5/10–15
1/15–2/7	1/18–2/2	3/7–31	3/18–31	4/15–5/7	4/17–5/2	5/15–31	5/16–31
9/15–30	9/15–26	8/7–31	8/12–28	7/15–31	7/15–29	7/10–25	7/14–25
3/1–20	3/1–3, 3/18–20	4/1–30	4/1–2, 4/17–30	5/15–6/30	5/16–31, 6/14–30	6/1–30	6/14–30
2/10–28	2/10–16	4/1–30	4/3–16	5/1–31	5/3–15	6/1–25	6/1–13
3/7–20	3/18–20	4/23–5/15	4/23–5/2	5/15–31	5/16–31	6/1–30	6/14–30
1/21–3/1	2/3–16	3/7–31	3/7–17	4/15–30	4/15–16	5/15–6/5	5/15, 6/1–5
10/1–21	10/1–10	9/7–30	9/7–10, 9/27–30	8/15–31	8/29–31	7/10–31	7/10–13, 7/30–31
2/7–3/15	2/17–3/3	3/15–4/20	3/18–4/2, 4/17–20	5/15–31	5/16–31	6/1–25	6/14–25
10/1–21	10/11–21	8/1–9/15	8/12–28, 9/11–15	7/17–9/7	7/17–29, 8/12–28	7/20–8/5	7/20–29
3/15–4/15	3/18–4/2	4/15–30	4/17–30	5/15–6/15	5/16–31, 6/14–15	6/1–30	6/14–30
3/23–4/6	4/3–6	4/21–5/9	5/3–9	5/15–6/15	5/15, 6/1–13	6/1–30	6/1–13
2/7–3/15	2/17–3/3	3/15–4/15	3/18–4/2	5/1–31	5/1–2, 5/16–31	5/15–31	5/16–31
3/7–20	3/18–20	4/7–30	4/17–30	5/15–31	5/16–31	6/1–15	6/14–15
1/20–2/15	2/3–15	3/15–31	3/15–17	4/7–30	4/7–16	5/10–31	5/10–15
9/1–10/15	9/1–10, 9/27–10/10	8/1–20	8/1–11	7/1–8/15	7/1–13, 7/30–8/11	–	–
3/15–4/7	3/18–4/2	4/15–5/7	4/17–5/2	5/15–6/30	5/16–31, 6/14–30	6/1–30	6/14–30
2/15–28	2/17–28	3/1–20	3/1–3, 3/18–20	4/7–30	4/17–30	5/15–6/10	5/16–31
10/15–12/7	10/15–26, 11/9–24	9/15–10/20	9/15–26, 10/11–20	8/11–9/15	8/12–28, 9/11–15	8/5–30	8/12–28

Tide Corrections

■ Many factors affect the times and heights of the tides: the coastal configuration, the time of the Moon's southing (crossing the meridian), and the Moon's phase. The High Tide column on the **Left-Hand Calendar Pages, 106–132,** lists the times of high tide at Commonwealth Pier in Boston Harbor. The heights of some of these tides, reckoned from Mean Lower Low Water, are given on the **Right-Hand Calendar Pages, 107–133.** Use the table below to calculate the approximate times and heights of high tide at the places shown. Apply the time difference to the times of high tide at Boston and the height difference to the heights at Boston.

E X A M P L E :

■ The conversion of the times and heights of the tides at Boston to those at Cape Fear, North Carolina, is given below:

High tide at Boston	11:45 A.M.
Correction for Cape Fear	−3 55 hrs.
High tide at Cape Fear	7:50 A.M.
Tide height at Boston	11.6 ft.
Correction for Cape Fear	−5.0 ft.
Tide height at Cape Fear	6.6 ft.

Estimations derived from this table are *not* meant to be used for navigation. *The Old Farmer's Almanac* accepts no responsibility for errors or any consequences ensuing from the use of this table.

Coastal Site	Difference: Time (h. m.)	Height (ft.)
Canada		
Alberton, PE	*−5 45	−7.5
Charlottetown, PE	*−0 45	−3.5
Halifax, NS.	−3 23	−4.5
North Sydney, NS.	−3 15	−6.5
Saint John, NB	+0 30	+15.0
St. John's, NL	−4 00	−6.5
Yarmouth, NS	−0 40	+3.0
Maine		
Bar Harbor	−0 34	+0.9
Belfast.	−0 20	+0.4
Boothbay Harbor	−0 18	−0.8
Chebeague Island	−0 16	−0.6
Eastport.	−0 28	+8.4
Kennebunkport	+0 04	−1.0
Machias.	−0 28	+2.8
Monhegan Island	−0 25	−0.8
Old Orchard	0 00	−0.8
Portland.	−0 12	−0.6
Rockland.	−0 28	+0.1
Stonington.	−0 30	+0.1
York.	−0 09	−1.0
New Hampshire		
Hampton	+0 02	−1.3
Portsmouth	+0 11	−1.5
Rye Beach	−0 09	−0.9
Massachusetts		
Annisquam	−0 02	−1.1
Beverly Farms.	0 00	−0.5
Boston	0 00	0.0

Coastal Site	Difference: Time (h. m.)	Height (ft.)
Cape Cod Canal		
East Entrance	−0 01	−0.8
West Entrance	−2 16	−5.9
Chatham Outer Coast . .	+0 30	−2.8
Inside	+1 54	**0.4
Cohasset	+0 02	−0.07
Cotuit Highlands.	+1 15	**0.3
Dennis Port	+1 01	**0.4
Duxbury–Gurnet Point . .	+0 02	−0.3
Fall River	−3 03	−5.0
Gloucester.	−0 03	−0.8
Hingham	+0 07	0.0
Hull	+0 03	−0.2
Hyannis Port	+1 01	**0.3
Magnolia–Manchester . .	−0 02	−0.7
Marblehead	−0 02	−0.4
Marion.	−3 22	−5.4
Monument Beach	−3 08	−5.4
Nahant.	−0 01	−0.5
Nantasket	+0 04	−0.1
Nantucket	+0 56	**0.3
Nauset Beach	+0 30	**0.6
New Bedford.	−3 24	−5.7
Newburyport.	+0 19	−1.8
Oak Bluffs.	+0 30	**0.2
Onset–R.R. Bridge	−2 16	−5.9
Plymouth.	+0 05	0.0
Provincetown	+0 14	−0.4
Revere Beach	−0 01	−0.3
Rockport	−0 08	−1.0
Salem.	0 00	−0.5

Coastal Site	Difference: Time (h. m.)	Height (ft.)	Coastal Site	Difference: Time (h. m.)	Height (ft.)
Scituate	−0 05	−0.7	Rehoboth Beach	−3 37	−5.7
Wareham	−3 09	−5.3	Wilmington	+1 56	−3.8
Wellfleet	+0 12	+0.5	**Maryland**		
West Falmouth	−3 10	−5.4	Annapolis	+6 23	−8.5
Westport Harbor	−3 22	−6.4	Baltimore	+7 59	−8.3
Woods Hole			Cambridge.	+5 05	−7.8
Little Harbor	−2 50	**0.2	Havre de Grace	+11 21	−7.7
Oceanographic Institute	−3 07	**0.2	Point No Point.	+2 28	−8.1
Rhode Island			Prince Frederick		
Bristol	−3 24	−5.3	Plum Point	+4 25	−8.5
Narragansett Pier	−3 42	−6.2	**Virginia**		
Newport.	−3 34	−5.9	Cape Charles.	−2 20	−7.0
Point Judith	−3 41	−6.3	Hampton Roads	−2 02	−6.9
Providence	−3 20	−4.8	Norfolk	−2 06	−6.6
Sakonnet	−3 44	−5.6	Virginia Beach	−4 00	−6.0
Watch Hill	−2 50	−6.8	Yorktown.	−2 13	−7.0
Connecticut			**North Carolina**		
Bridgeport.	+0 01	−2.6	Cape Fear	−3 55	−5.0
Madison.	−0 22	−2.3	Cape Lookout	−4 28	−5.7
New Haven	−0 11	−3.2	Currituck	−4 10	−5.8
New London	−1 54	−6.7	Hatteras		
Norwalk.	+0 01	−2.2	Inlet.	−4 03	−7.4
Old Lyme			Kitty Hawk	−4 14	−6.2
Highway Bridge.	−0 30	−6.2	Ocean	−4 26	−6.0
Stamford	+0 01	−2.2	**South Carolina**		
Stonington.	−2 27	−6.6	Charleston.	−3 22	−4.3
New York			Georgetown.	−1 48	**0.36
Coney Island	−3 33	−4.9	Hilton Head.	−3 22	−2.9
Fire Island Light	−2 43	**0.1	Myrtle Beach	−3 49	−4.4
Long Beach	−3 11	−5.7	St. Helena		
Montauk Harbor	−2 19	−7.4	Harbor Entrance.	−3 15	−3.4
New York City–Battery. .	−2 43	−5.0	**Georgia**		
Oyster Bay	+0 04	−1.8	Jekyll Island	−3 46	−2.9
Port Chester	−0 09	−2.2	St. Simon's Island.	−2 50	−2.9
Port Washington	−0 01	−2.1	Savannah Beach		
Sag Harbor	−0 55	−6.8	River Entrance	−3 14	−5.5
Southampton			Tybee Light	−3 22	−2.7
Shinnecock Inlet	−4 20	**0.2	**Florida**		
Willets Point	0 00	−2.3	Cape Canaveral.	−3 59	−6.0
New Jersey			Daytona Beach	−3 28	−5.3
Asbury Park	−4 04	−5.3	Fort Lauderdale	−2 50	−7.2
Atlantic City	−3 56	−5.5	Fort Pierce Inlet	−3 32	−6.9
Bay Head–Sea Girt . . .	−4 04	−5.3	Jacksonville		
Beach Haven.	−1 43	**0.24	Railroad Bridge	−6 55	**0.1
Cape May	−3 28	−5.3	Miami Harbor Entrance	−3 18	−7.0
Ocean City	−3 06	−5.9	St. Augustine.	−2 55	−4.9
Sandy Hook.	−3 30	−5.0			
Seaside Park	−4 03	−5.4			
Pennsylvania					
Philadelphia	+2 40	−3.5			
Delaware					
Cape Henlopen	−2 48	−5.3			

*Varies widely; accurate within only 1½ hours. Consult local tide tables for precise times and heights.

**Where the difference in the Height column is so marked, the height at Boston should be multiplied by this ratio.

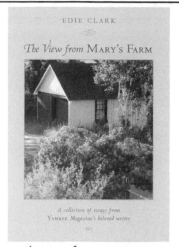

Tidal Glossary

Apogean Tide: A monthly tide of decreased range that occurs when the Moon is at apogee (farthest from Earth).

Diurnal Tide: A tide with one high water and one low water in a tidal day of approximately 24 hours.

Mean Lower Low Water: The arithmetic mean of the lesser of a daily pair of low waters, observed over a specific 19-year cycle called the National Tidal Datum Epoch.

Neap Tide: A tide of decreased range that occurs twice a month, when the Moon is in quadrature (during its first and last quarters, when the Sun and the Moon are at right angles to each other relative to Earth).

Perigean Tide: A monthly tide of increased range that occurs when the Moon is at perigee (closest to Earth).

Semidiurnal Tide: A tide with one high water and one low water every half day. East Coast tides, for example, are semidiurnal, with two highs and two lows during a tidal day of approximately 24 hours.

Spring Tide: A tide of increased range that occurs at times of syzygy each month. Named not for the season of spring but from the German *springen* ("to leap up"), a spring tide also brings a lower low water.

Syzygy: The nearly straight-line configuration that occurs twice a month, when the Sun and the Moon are in conjunction (on the same side of Earth at the new Moon) and when they are in opposition (on opposite sides of Earth at the full Moon). In both cases, the gravitational effects of the Sun and the Moon reinforce each other, and tidal range is increased.

Vanishing Tide: A mixed tide of considerable inequality in the two highs and two lows, so that the lower high (or higher low) may become indistinct or appear to vanish.

Time Corrections

■ Times for Sun and Moon rise and set, bright star transits, and planetary observations are given for Boston on **pages 106–132, 92,** and **94–95,** respectively. Use the Key Letter shown to the right of each time on those pages with this table to find the number of minutes (adjusted for location and time zone) that you must add to or subtract from Boston time to get the correct time for your city. (Because of complex calculations for different locales, times may not be precise to the minute.) If your city is not listed, use the figures for the city closest to you in latitude and longitude. Boston's latitude is 42°22' and its longitude is 71°03'. Selected Canadian cities are at the end of the table. For more information on use of Key Letters and this table, see **How to Use This Almanac, page 102.**

TIME ZONES: Codes represent *standard time*. Atlantic is −1, Eastern is 0, Central is 1, Mountain is 2, Pacific is 3, Alaska is 4, and Hawaii-Aleutian is 5.

State	City	North Latitude °	'	West Longitude °	'	Time Zone Code	A (min.)	B (min.)	Key Letters C (min.)	D (min.)	E (min.)
AK	Anchorage	61	10	149	59	4	−46	+27	+71	+122	+171
AK	Cordova	60	33	145	45	4	−55	+13	+55	+103	+149
AK	Fairbanks	64	48	147	51	4	−127	+ 2	+61	+131	+205
AK	Juneau	58	18	134	25	4	−76	−23	+10	+49	+86
AK	Ketchikan	55	21	131	39	4	−62	−25	0	+29	+56
AK	Kodiak	57	47	152	24	4	0	+49	+82	+120	+154
AL	Birmingham	33	31	86	49	1	+30	+15	+3	−10	−20
AL	Decatur	34	36	86	59	1	+27	+14	+4	−7	−17
AL	Mobile	30	42	88	3	1	+42	+23	+8	−8	−22
AL	Montgomery	32	23	86	19	1	+31	+14	+1	−13	−25
AR	Fort Smith	35	23	94	25	1	+55	+43	+33	+22	+14
AR	Little Rock	34	45	92	17	1	+48	+35	+25	+13	+4
AR	Texarkana	33	26	94	3	1	+59	+44	+32	+18	+8
AZ	Flagstaff	35	12	111	39	2	+64	+52	+42	+31	+22
AZ	Phoenix	33	27	112	4	2	+71	+56	+44	+30	+20
AZ	Tucson	32	13	110	58	2	+70	+53	+40	+24	+12
AZ	Yuma	32	43	114	37	2	+83	+67	+54	+40	+28
CA	Bakersfield	35	23	119	1	3	+33	+21	+12	+1	−7
CA	Barstow	34	54	117	1	3	+27	+14	+4	−7	−16
CA	Fresno	36	44	119	47	3	+32	+22	+15	+6	0
CA	Los Angeles–Pasadena– Santa Monica	34	3	118	14	3	+34	+20	+9	−3	−13
CA	Palm Springs	33	49	116	32	3	+28	+13	+1	−12	−22
CA	Redding	40	35	122	24	3	+31	+27	+25	+22	+19
CA	Sacramento	38	35	121	30	3	+34	+27	+21	+15	+10
CA	San Diego	32	43	117	9	3	+33	+17	+4	−9	−21
CA	San Francisco–Oakland– San Jose	37	47	122	25	3	+40	+31	+25	+18	+12
CO	Craig	40	31	107	33	2	+32	+28	+25	+22	+20
CO	Denver–Boulder	39	44	104	59	2	+24	+19	+15	+11	+7
CO	Grand Junction	39	4	108	33	2	+40	+34	+29	+24	+20
CO	Pueblo	38	16	104	37	2	+27	+20	+14	+7	+2
CO	Trinidad	37	10	104	31	2	+30	+21	+13	+5	0
CT	Bridgeport	41	11	73	11	0	+12	+10	+8	+6	+4
CT	Hartford–New Britain	41	46	72	41	0	+8	+7	+6	+5	+4
CT	New Haven	41	18	72	56	0	+11	+8	+7	+5	+4
CT	New London	41	22	72	6	0	+7	+5	+4	+2	+1
CT	Norwalk–Stamford	41	7	73	22	0	+13	+10	+9	+7	+5
CT	Waterbury–Meriden	41	33	73	3	0	+10	+9	+7	+6	+5
DC	Washington	38	54	77	1	0	+35	+28	+23	+18	+13
DE	Wilmington	39	45	75	33	0	+26	+21	+18	+13	+10

State	City	North Latitude °	North Latitude '	West Longitude °	West Longitude '	Time Zone Code	Key Letters A (min.)	B (min.)	C (min.)	D (min.)	E (min.)
FL	Fort Myers	26	38	81	52	0	+87	+63	+44	+21	+4
FL	Jacksonville	30	20	81	40	0	+77	+58	+43	+25	+11
FL	Miami	25	47	80	12	0	+88	+57	+37	+14	−3
FL	Orlando	28	32	81	22	0	+80	+59	+42	+22	+6
FL	Pensacola	30	25	87	13	1	+39	+20	+5	−12	−26
FL	St. Petersburg	27	46	82	39	0	+87	+65	+47	+26	+10
FL	Tallahassee	30	27	84	17	0	+87	+68	+53	+35	+22
FL	Tampa	27	57	82	27	0	+86	+64	+46	+25	+9
FL	West Palm Beach	26	43	80	3	0	+79	+55	+36	+14	−2
GA	Atlanta	33	45	84	24	0	+79	+65	+53	+40	+30
GA	Augusta	33	28	81	58	0	+70	+55	+44	+30	+19
GA	Macon	32	50	83	38	0	+79	+63	+50	+36	+24
GA	Savannah	32	5	81	6	0	+70	+54	+40	+25	+13
HI	Hilo	19	44	155	5	5	+94	+62	+37	+7	−15
HI	Honolulu	21	18	157	52	5	+102	+72	+48	+19	−1
HI	Lanai City	20	50	156	55	5	+99	+69	+44	+15	−6
HI	Lihue	21	59	159	23	5	+107	+77	+54	+26	+5
IA	Davenport	41	32	90	35	1	+20	+19	+17	+16	+15
IA	Des Moines	41	35	93	37	1	+32	+31	+30	+28	+27
IA	Dubuque	42	30	90	41	1	+17	+18	+18	+18	+18
IA	Waterloo	42	30	92	20	1	+24	+24	+24	+25	+25
ID	Boise	43	37	116	12	2	+55	+58	+60	+62	+64
ID	Lewiston	46	25	117	1	3	−12	−3	+2	+10	+17
ID	Pocatello	42	52	112	27	2	+43	+44	+45	+46	+46
IL	Cairo	37	0	89	11	1	+29	+20	+12	+4	−2
IL	Chicago–Oak Park	41	52	87	38	1	+7	+6	+6	+5	+4
IL	Danville	40	8	87	37	1	+13	+9	+6	+2	0
IL	Decatur	39	51	88	57	1	+19	+15	+11	+7	+4
IL	Peoria	40	42	89	36	1	+19	+16	+14	+11	+9
IL	Springfield	39	48	89	39	1	+22	+18	+14	+10	+6
IN	Fort Wayne	41	4	85	9	0	+60	+58	+56	+54	+52
IN	Gary	41	36	87	20	1	+7	+6	+4	+3	+2
IN	Indianapolis	39	46	86	10	0	+69	+64	+60	+56	+52
IN	Muncie	40	12	85	23	0	+64	+60	+57	+53	+50
IN	South Bend	41	41	86	15	0	+62	+61	+60	+59	+58
IN	Terre Haute	39	28	87	24	0	+74	+69	+65	+60	+56
KS	Fort Scott	37	50	94	42	1	+49	+41	+34	+27	+21
KS	Liberal	37	3	100	55	1	+76	+66	+59	+51	+44
KS	Oakley	39	8	100	51	1	+69	+63	+59	+53	+49
KS	Salina	38	50	97	37	1	+57	+51	+46	+40	+35
KS	Topeka	39	3	95	40	1	+49	+43	+38	+32	+28
KS	Wichita	37	42	97	20	1	+60	+51	+45	+37	+31
KY	Lexington–Frankfort	38	3	84	30	0	+67	+59	+53	+46	+41
KY	Louisville	38	15	85	46	0	+72	+64	+58	+52	+46
LA	Alexandria	31	18	92	27	1	+58	+40	+26	+9	−3
LA	Baton Rouge	30	27	91	11	1	+55	+36	+21	+3	−10
LA	Lake Charles	30	14	93	13	1	+64	+44	+29	+11	−2
LA	Monroe	32	30	92	7	1	+53	+37	+24	+9	−1
LA	New Orleans	29	57	90	4	1	+52	+32	+16	−1	−15
LA	Shreveport	32	31	93	45	1	+60	+44	+31	+16	+4
MA	Brockton	42	5	71	1	0	0	0	0	0	−1
MA	Fall River–New Bedford	41	42	71	9	0	+2	+1	0	0	−1
MA	Lawrence–Lowell	42	42	71	10	0	0	0	0	0	+1
MA	Pittsfield	42	27	73	15	0	+8	+8	+8	+8	+8
MA	Springfield–Holyoke	42	6	72	36	0	+6	+6	+6	+5	+5
MA	Worcester	42	16	71	48	0	+3	+2	+2	+2	+2
MD	Baltimore	39	17	76	37	0	+32	+26	+22	+17	+13

State	City	North Latitude °	North Latitude '	West Longitude °	West Longitude '	Time Zone Code	A (min.)	B (min.)	Key Letters C (min.)	D (min.)	E (min.)
MD	Hagerstown	39	39	77	43	0	+35	+30	+26	+22	+18
MD	Salisbury	38	22	75	36	0	+31	+23	+18	+11	+6
ME	Augusta	44	19	69	46	0	−12	−8	−5	−1	0
ME	Bangor	44	48	68	46	0	−18	−13	−9	−5	−1
ME	Eastport	44	54	67	0	0	−26	−20	−16	−11	−8
ME	Ellsworth	44	33	68	25	0	−18	−14	−10	−6	−3
ME	Portland	43	40	70	15	0	−8	−5	−3	−1	0
ME	Presque Isle	46	41	68	1	0	−29	−19	−12	−4	+2
MI	Cheboygan	45	39	84	29	0	+40	+47	+53	+59	+64
MI	Detroit–Dearborn	42	20	83	3	0	+47	+47	+47	+47	+47
MI	Flint	43	1	83	41	0	+47	+49	+50	+51	+52
MI	Ironwood	46	27	90	9	1	0	+9	+15	+23	+29
MI	Jackson	42	15	84	24	0	+53	+53	+53	+52	+52
MI	Kalamazoo	42	17	85	35	0	+58	+57	+57	+57	+57
MI	Lansing	42	44	84	33	0	+52	+53	+53	+54	+54
MI	St. Joseph	42	5	86	26	0	+61	+61	+60	+60	+59
MI	Traverse City	44	46	85	38	0	+49	+54	+57	+62	+65
MN	Albert Lea	43	39	93	22	1	+24	+26	+28	+31	+33
MN	Bemidji	47	28	94	53	1	+14	+26	+34	+44	+52
MN	Duluth	46	47	92	6	1	+6	+16	+23	+31	+38
MN	Minneapolis–St. Paul	44	59	93	16	1	+18	+24	+28	+33	+37
MN	Ortonville	45	19	96	27	1	+30	+36	+40	+46	+51
MO	Jefferson City	38	34	92	10	1	+36	+29	+24	+18	+13
MO	Joplin	37	6	94	30	1	+50	+41	+33	+25	+18
MO	Kansas City	39	1	94	20	1	+44	+37	+33	+27	+23
MO	Poplar Bluff	36	46	90	24	1	+35	+25	+17	+8	+1
MO	St. Joseph	39	46	94	50	1	+43	+38	+35	+30	+27
MO	St. Louis	38	37	90	12	1	+28	+21	+16	+10	+5
MO	Springfield	37	13	93	18	1	+45	+36	+29	+20	+14
MS	Biloxi	30	24	88	53	1	+46	+27	+11	−5	−19
MS	Jackson	32	18	90	11	1	+46	+30	+17	+1	−10
MS	Meridian	32	22	88	42	1	+40	+24	+11	−4	−15
MS	Tupelo	34	16	88	34	1	+35	+21	+10	−2	−11
MT	Billings	45	47	108	30	2	+16	+23	+29	+35	+40
MT	Butte	46	1	112	32	2	+31	+39	+45	+52	+57
MT	Glasgow	48	12	106	38	2	−1	+11	+21	+32	+42
MT	Great Falls	47	30	111	17	2	+20	+31	+39	+49	+58
MT	Helena	46	36	112	2	2	+27	+36	+43	+51	+57
MT	Miles City	46	25	105	51	2	+3	+11	+18	+26	+32
NC	Asheville	35	36	82	33	0	+67	+55	+46	+35	+27
NC	Charlotte	35	14	80	51	0	+61	+49	+39	+28	+19
NC	Durham	36	0	78	55	0	+51	+40	+31	+21	+13
NC	Greensboro	36	4	79	47	0	+54	+43	+35	+25	+17
NC	Raleigh	35	47	78	38	0	+51	+39	+30	+20	+12
NC	Wilmington	34	14	77	55	0	+52	+38	+27	+15	+5
ND	Bismarck	46	48	100	47	1	+41	+50	+58	+66	+73
ND	Fargo	46	53	96	47	1	+24	+34	+42	+50	+57
ND	Grand Forks	47	55	97	3	1	+21	+33	+43	+53	+62
ND	Minot	48	14	101	18	1	+36	+50	+59	+71	+81
ND	Williston	48	9	103	37	1	+46	+59	+69	+80	+90
NE	Grand Island	40	55	98	21	1	+53	+51	+49	+46	+44
NE	Lincoln	40	49	96	41	1	+47	+44	+42	+39	+37
NE	North Platte	41	8	100	46	1	+62	+60	+58	+56	+54
NE	Omaha	41	16	95	56	1	+43	+40	+39	+37	+36
NH	Berlin	44	28	71	11	0	−7	−3	0	+3	+7
NH	Keene	42	56	72	17	0	+2	+3	+4	+5	+6
NH	Manchester–Concord	42	59	71	28	0	0	0	+1	+2	+3

State	City	North Latitude °	'	West Longitude °	'	Time Zone Code	A (min.)	B (min.)	Key Letters C (min.)	D (min.)	E (min.)
NH	Portsmouth...........	43	5	70	45	0	−4	−2	−1	0	0
NJ	Atlantic City..........	39	22	74	26	0	+23	+17	+13	+8	+4
NJ	Camden	39	57	75	7	0	+24	+19	+16	+12	+9
NJ	Cape May	38	56	74	56	0	+26	+20	+15	+9	+5
NJ	Newark–East Orange...	40	44	74	10	0	+17	+14	+12	+9	+7
NJ	Paterson	40	55	74	10	0	+17	+14	+12	+9	+7
NJ	Trenton...............	40	13	74	46	0	+21	+17	+14	+11	+8
NM	Albuquerque	35	5	106	39	2	+45	+32	+22	+11	+2
NM	Gallup..............	35	32	108	45	2	+52	+40	+31	+20	+11
NM	Las Cruces	32	19	106	47	2	+53	+36	+23	+8	−3
NM	Roswell.............	33	24	104	32	2	+41	+26	+14	0	−10
NM	Santa Fe	35	41	105	56	2	+40	+28	+19	+9	0
NV	Carson City–Reno	39	10	119	46	3	+25	+19	+14	+9	+5
NV	Elko	40	50	115	46	3	+3	0	−1	−3	−5
NV	Las Vegas	36	10	115	9	3	+16	+4	−3	−13	−20
NY	Albany	42	39	73	45	0	+9	+10	+10	+11	+11
NY	Binghamton	42	6	75	55	0	+20	+19	+19	+18	+18
NY	Buffalo..............	42	53	78	52	0	+29	+30	+30	+31	+32
NY	New York	40	45	74	0	0	+17	+14	+11	+9	+6
NY	Ogdensburg	44	42	75	30	0	+8	+13	+17	+21	+25
NY	Syracuse.............	43	3	76	9	0	+17	+19	+20	+21	+22
OH	Akron	41	5	81	31	0	+46	+43	+41	+39	+37
OH	Canton	40	48	81	23	0	+46	+43	+41	+38	+36
OH	Cincinnati–Hamilton...	39	6	84	31	0	+64	+58	+53	+48	+44
OH	Cleveland–Lakewood ..	41	30	81	42	0	+45	+43	+42	+40	+39
OH	Columbus............	39	57	83	1	0	+55	+51	+47	+43	+40
OH	Dayton	39	45	84	10	0	+61	+56	+52	+48	+44
OH	Toledo...............	41	39	83	33	0	+52	+50	+49	+48	+47
OH	Youngstown	41	6	80	39	0	+42	+40	+38	+36	+34
OK	Oklahoma City........	35	28	97	31	1	+67	+55	+46	+35	+26
OK	Tulsa................	36	9	95	60	1	+59	+48	+40	+30	+22
OR	Eugene	44	3	123	6	3	+21	+24	+27	+30	+33
OR	Pendleton	45	40	118	47	3	−1	+4	+10	+16	+21
OR	Portland	45	31	122	41	3	+14	+20	+25	+31	+36
OR	Salem	44	57	123	1	3	+17	+23	+27	+31	+35
PA	Allentown–Bethlehem ..	40	36	75	28	0	+23	+20	+17	+14	+12
PA	Erie.................	42	7	80	5	0	+36	+36	+35	+35	+35
PA	Harrisburg	40	16	76	53	0	+30	+26	+23	+19	+16
PA	Lancaster	40	2	76	18	0	+28	+24	+20	+17	+13
PA	Philadelphia–Chester...	39	57	75	9	0	+24	+19	+16	+12	+9
PA	Pittsburgh–McKeesport	40	26	80	0	0	+42	+38	+35	+32	+29
PA	Reading	40	20	75	56	0	+26	+22	+19	+16	+13
PA	Scranton–Wilkes-Barre..	41	25	75	40	0	+21	+19	+18	+16	+15
PA	York	39	58	76	43	0	+30	+26	+22	+18	+15
RI	Providence	41	50	71	25	0	+3	+2	+1	0	0
SC	Charleston	32	47	79	56	0	+64	+48	+36	+21	+10
SC	Columbia	34	0	81	2	0	+65	+51	+40	+27	+17
SC	Spartanburg	34	56	81	57	0	+66	+53	+43	+32	+23
SD	Aberdeen	45	28	98	29	1	+37	+44	+49	+54	+59
SD	Pierre	44	22	100	21	1	+49	+53	+56	+60	+63
SD	Rapid City	44	5	103	14	2	+2	+5	+8	+11	+13
SD	Sioux Falls...........	43	33	96	44	1	+38	+40	+42	+44	+46
TN	Chattanooga..........	35	3	85	19	0	+79	+67	+57	+45	+36
TN	Knoxville	35	58	83	55	0	+71	+60	+51	+41	+33
TN	Memphis.............	35	9	90	3	1	+38	+26	+16	+5	−3
TN	Nashville	36	10	86	47	1	+22	+11	+3	−6	−14
TX	Amarillo.............	35	12	101	50	1	+85	+73	+63	+52	+43

Get local rise, set, and tide times at Almanac.com/astronomy.

State/ Province	City	North Latitude °	North Latitude ′	West Longitude °	West Longitude ′	Time Zone Code	A (min.)	B (min.)	Key Letters C (min.)	D (min.)	E (min.)
TX	Austin...............	30	16	97	45	1	+82	+62	+47	+29	+15
TX	Beaumont............	30	5	94	6	1	+67	+48	+32	+14	0
TX	Brownsville	25	54	97	30	1	+91	+66	+46	+23	+5
TX	Corpus Christi	27	48	97	24	1	+86	+64	+46	+25	+9
TX	Dallas–Fort Worth.....	32	47	96	48	1	+71	+55	+43	+28	+17
TX	El Paso	31	45	106	29	2	+53	+35	+22	6	−6
TX	Galveston............	29	18	94	48	1	+72	+52	+35	+16	+1
TX	Houston	29	45	95	22	1	+73	+53	+37	+19	+5
TX	McAllen.............	26	12	98	14	1	+93	+69	+49	+26	+9
TX	San Antonio	29	25	98	30	1	+87	+66	+50	+31	+16
UT	Kanab...............	37	3	112	32	2	+62	+53	+46	+37	+30
UT	Moab................	38	35	109	33	2	+46	+39	+33	+27	+22
UT	Ogden...............	41	13	111	58	2	+47	+45	+43	+41	+40
UT	Salt Lake City	40	45	111	53	2	+48	+45	+43	+40	+38
UT	Vernal..............	40	27	109	32	2	+40	+36	+33	+30	+28
VA	Charlottesville	38	2	78	30	0	+43	+35	+29	+22	+17
VA	Danville	36	36	79	23	0	+51	+41	+33	+24	+17
VA	Norfolk..............	36	51	76	17	0	+38	+28	+21	+12	+5
VA	Richmond............	37	32	77	26	0	+41	+32	+25	+17	+11
VA	Roanoke.............	37	16	79	57	0	+51	+42	+35	+27	+21
VA	Winchester...........	39	11	78	10	0	+38	+33	+28	+23	+19
VT	Brattleboro	42	51	72	34	0	+4	+5	+5	+6	+7
VT	Burlington	44	29	73	13	0	0	+4	+8	+12	+15
VT	Rutland..............	43	37	72	58	0	+2	+5	+7	+9	+11
VT	St. Johnsbury	44	25	72	1	0	−4	0	+3	+7	+10
WA	Bellingham...........	48	45	122	29	3	0	+13	+24	+37	+47
WA	Seattle–Tacoma– Olympia	47	37	122	20	3	+3	+15	+24	+34	+42
WA	Spokane	47	40	117	24	3	−16	−4	+4	+14	+23
WA	Walla Walla	46	4	118	20	3	−5	+2	+8	+15	+21
WI	Eau Claire............	44	49	91	30	1	+12	+17	+21	+25	+29
WI	Green Bay	44	31	88	0	1	0	+3	+7	+11	+14
WI	La Crosse	43	48	91	15	1	+15	+18	+20	+22	+25
WI	Madison	43	4	89	23	1	+10	+11	+12	+14	+15
WI	Milwaukee...........	43	2	87	54	1	+4	+6	+7	+8	+9
WI	Oshkosh	44	1	88	33	1	+3	+6	+9	+12	+15
WI	Wausau..............	44	58	89	38	1	+4	+9	+13	+18	+22
WV	Charleston	38	21	81	38	0	+55	+48	+42	+35	+30
WV	Parkersburg	39	16	81	34	0	+52	+46	+42	+36	+32
WY	Casper...............	42	51	106	19	2	+19	+19	+20	+21	+22
WY	Cheyenne	41	8	104	49	2	+19	+16	+14	+12	+11
WY	Sheridan.............	44	48	106	58	2	+14	+19	+23	+27	+31

CANADA

State/ Province	City	North Latitude °	North Latitude ′	West Longitude °	West Longitude ′	Time Zone Code	A (min.)	B (min.)	Key Letters C (min.)	D (min.)	E (min.)
AB	Calgary..............	51	5	114	5	2	+13	+35	+50	+68	+84
AB	Edmonton............	53	34	113	25	2	−3	+26	+47	+72	+93
BC	Vancouver	49	13	123	6	3	0	+15	+26	+40	+52
MB	Winnipeg	49	53	97	10	1	+12	+30	+43	+58	+71
NB	Saint John............	45	16	66	3	−1	+28	+34	+39	+44	+49
NS	Halifax	44	38	63	35	−1	+21	+26	+29	+33	+37
NS	Sydney	46	10	60	10	−1	+1	+9	+15	+23	+28
ON	Ottawa	45	25	75	43	0	+6	+13	+18	+23	+28
ON	Peterborough	44	18	78	19	0	+21	+25	+28	+32	+35
ON	Thunder Bay..........	48	27	89	12	0	+47	+61	+71	+83	+93
ON	Toronto	43	39	79	23	0	+28	+30	+32	+35	+37
QC	Montreal.............	45	28	73	39	0	−1	+4	+9	+15	+20
SK	Saskatoon............	52	10	106	40	1	+37	+63	+80	+101	+119

Mind-Manglers

Answers appear on page 251.

1 WHO WAS THE OLDEST?

Al, Bill, Chris, and Doug were all born on May 12, but in 1964, 1965, 1966, and 1967, respectively. Who was oldest on his 21st birthday?

2 WHICH BIRD IS THE FASTEST?

Three birds race 3,000 miles south to their wintering grounds.

A mallard leaves on November 1 and flies at 25 mph for 10 hours per day, stopping for three days of rest along the way.

A Canada goose leaves the next day and flies at 30 mph for 10 hours per day, stopping for just one day of rest.

A common loon leaves three days after the mallard and flies at 40 mph for 10 hours per day, stopping for two days of rest.

Which bird will arrive first?

3 HORSE CENTS

A man offered to sell his horse in return for a certain price for the nails in the horse's shoes. He was to have a half-cent for the first nail, and the amount was to be doubled for each succeeding nail. There were seven nails in each shoe. What was the price of the horse?

4 FOUR BY FOUR

Place the numbers 1 through 16 into a 4-by-4 grid so that the numbers will add up to 34 vertically, horizontally, and diagonally.

–Maurice Labossiere, Bathurst, New Brunswick

5 MANGLED MAXIMS

Read the new versions below and try to guess the original proverbs.

1. Tenants of vitreous abodes ought to hurl no lithoidal fragments.

2. Insufficient instruction to an aged canine will not result in its ability to undertake fresh stratagems.

3. Labor to the exclusion of frolic renders a lackluster soul.

4. The individual of the class Aves, arriving before an appointed time, seizes the invertebrate animal of the class Oligochaeta.

5. A painting has greater value than a vocabulary of ten times 100.

6. Double gray matter encasements are superior to a single such item.

7. What counts is not triumph or defeat but the process of the competition.

8. At no time, under any circumstances, say the words "at no time under any circumstances."

9. Tolerate it with a particle of NaCl.

10. It is not proper for mendicants to be indicative of preference.

–Esther Braslow, Ocean, New Jersey

☐ ☐

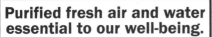

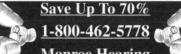
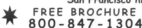

General Store Classifieds

ART

NORMAN ROCKWELL prints, posters, collectibles, calendars. Annual Christmas tree ball and ornament, etc. Rockwell Gallery Collection. 215-969-5619. www.rockwellsite.com

ASTROLOGY/OCCULT

LOVE? CAREER? HAPPINESS? Call Psychic Source now for new guidance and insight into your life. 1-866-447-5712. Low new-member rates. www.PsychicSource.com ent. only 18+.

ASTROLOGY: FREE CATALOG. Books, tapes, tarot, spirituality. 800-500-0453 or 714-255-9218. Church of Light, www.light.org

FREE OCCULT CATALOG! AzureGreen, 48-OFA Chester Rd., Middlefield MA 01243. 413-623-2155. www.azuregreen.com

UNLUCKY, UNWANTED, UNLOVED? Psychic Sabrina, 20 years' experience. Solves all problems. Guaranteed. Free consultation. 832-578-9929.

MRS. KING, spiritual reader, advisor, helps in matters of life where others have failed. Call 912-283-0635.

FREE LUCKY NUMBERS. Send birth date, self-addressed, stamped envelope. Mystic, Box 2009-R, Jamestown NC 27282.

OCCULT CATALOG: Hard-to-find witchcraft, voodoo supplies. $3. Power Products, PO Box 442F, Mars Hill NC 28754. Visit Web site: www.joanteresapowerproducts.com

PSYCHIC VERONICA. Solves the impossible problems immediately. Reunites Lovers. Restores Passion. Removes Darkness. Worry no more. 214-473-9699.

PSYCHIC JANIE. Are you having any problem with the past, future, love, marriage, business, lawsuits, or health? Call 1-706-215-0998.

READINGS BY ROSE FRANKLIN. There is hope for everyone. Lousy love, help, divorce. Rose can help through all problems of life. 972-788-2760.

FREE READING. Powerful love specialist. Psychic Olivia retores Love, Marriage, Business, Health. Reunites Lovers. Troubled, need answers? Call 214-902-0045.

AUGUSTINE'S SPIRITUAL GOODS, Lucky Mojo Bags. Free Catalog. 803 S. Lincoln Drive, Hancock MI 49930. Call 906-482-5323. www.augustinespiritualgoods.com

ABIGAIL, 100% accurate. Specializing in all problems of life. Amazing results! Toll-free 1-888-212-4778 or 210-224-5425.

FREE SPIRITUAL CATALOG—Luck, money, and love can be yours. Huge spiritual catalog with over 1,500 items. Church Goods Co., Dept. OFA, PO Box 718, Glenview IL 60025. www.theluckshop.com

MRS. RAINBOW. 45 years of experience. Reunites lovers. Removes evil influences. Tells your past, present, and future. Call 1-626-806-1630.

PSYCHIC READING BY MIA. Specializing in reuniting loved ones. Guaranteed results in six hours. Call 864-809-2470.

$1.95 PSYCHIC READING. 10-minute reading for $1.95. Get answers: Love, Money, Career, Resolve Problems. 800-561-7488. 18+. www.truereading.com

EUROPEAN PSYCHIC READER and advisor guarantees help with all problems. Call Sylvia for one free reading. 864-583-5776.

SPIRITUAL ADVICE. Help for all problems: relationships, nature, money, jobs. See results in 3 days. Call Dewberry, 800-989-1059 or 912-264-3259.

PSYCHIC SIERRA solves all problems. Reunites Lovers Fast! Removes Bad Luck. Reveals Enemies. Immediate results. 210-735-3947.

GIFTED HEALER. Solves all problems, troubles, unusual sickness, bad luck, love, life. Removes evil influences, nature problems, brings back lovers to stay, good luck, money. Uncle Doc Shedrickrack, Hwy. 48, 7905 Bluff Rd., Gadsden SC 29052. Call 803-353-0659.

MADAM PEBBLES helps in Relationships—Sickness—Lost Nature—Money—Luck and Love. 100% Satisfaction. 706-536-7983.

PSYCHIC READINGS BY MARTHA. Solves all problems. Reunites lovers. Immediate results! One free question. 214-363-4740.

MASTER PSYCHICS: Crystal, 1-866-571-1111; Laura, 1-877-852-8255; Eve, 1-888-237-2263. Daily Horoscope: Text "signs" to 45555, $4.99/week.

FREE MAGIC SPELL! Tell us exactly what you need! 909-473-7470. EKSES, PO Box 9315(B), San Bernardino CA 92427-9315. www.ekses.com

99¢ PSYCHIC LOVE READING. Truly Powerful. Get amazing answers for Love, Passion, Relationships, Destiny, Problems. 800-699-7088.

BEER & WINE MAKING

FREE ILLUSTRATED CATALOG. Fast service. Since 1967. Kraus, PO Box 7850-YB, Independence MO 64054. Phone: 800-841-7404. Web site: www.eckraus.com/offers/fd.asp

BOOKS/PUBLICATIONS/CATALOGS

FREE BOOKLETS: Life, death, soul, resurrection, hell, Judgment Day, restitution. Bible Standard (OF), 1156 St. Matthews Rd., Chester Springs PA 19425. www.biblestandard.com

BECOME A PUBLISHED AUTHOR. Publisher with 85-year tradition. "Author's Guide to Subsidy Publishing." 1-800-695-9599.

BUILDING A NEW HOME? Hiring a contractor? New Home Builders Survival Guide. $5.00 includes P&H. Guide, 206 CR 29, Canton NY 13617.

BUILDING SUPPLIES

BUILD UNDERGROUND Houses/Shelters/ Greenhouses dirt-cheap! Live protected. Slash energy costs. "Brilliant breakthrough thinking"—Countryside Magazine. Featured on HGTV. 1-800-328-8790. www.undergroundhousing.com

BUSINESS OPPORTUNITIES

WATKINS PRODUCTS. Buy retail or wholesale or start your own Watkins business. 800-215-2743 or www.cbbirch.com

$400 WEEKLY ASSEMBLING PRODUCTS from home. For free information, send SASE to Home Assembly-FA, PO Box 216, New Britain CT 06050-0216.

$1,000's WEEKLY mailing beautiful rose catalogs! Free supplies/postage! RBM-FA, Box 759, Lake Zurich IL 60047-0759.

FREE REPORT! Reveals how you can earn $4,280 a month. At Home. In Spare Time. Write Zaken Corp., Suite 50949FA, 20700 Plummer St., Chatsworth CA 91311.

ENVIRONMENTALLY FRIENDLY PRODUCTS

ATTENTION, ALL ENVIRONMENTALISTS: The world cannot be saved without first visiting EarthSunMoon.com (or call us at 888-458-1687). Mention Code OFA0906D10 and receive 10% off.

FARM & GARDEN

NEPTUNE'S HARVEST ORGANIC FERTILIZERS: Extremely effective. Commercially proven. Outperform chemicals. Wholesale/retail/farm. Catalog. Phone: 800-259-4769. Visit our Web site: www.neptunesharvest.com

FINANCIAL/LOANS BY MAIL

FREE GRANT MONEY! Immediate approval. No repayment. Debts, personal needs, business. Rush SASE: Grants-FA, PO Box 458, New Britain CT 06050-0458.

LET THE GOVERNMENT and Foundations Pay Your Bills, Taxes, Home Repair, New Home, Rent, Business! Blessings, Box 14590, Springfield MO 65814.

FOOD & RECIPES

TOTALLY NUTS brand peanuts and cashews. Call us at 1-888-489-6887 or visit our Web site at www.totallynuts.biz

GARDENING

CANNING SUPPLIES. Extensive selection. Stainless-steel canning rack, labels, canners, jars, pectin. FREE catalog. 1-800-776-0575. Web site: www.KitchenKrafts.com

GREENHOUSES

EXTEND YOUR GROWING SEASON 3–4 Months! Easy-to-assemble Greenhouse Kits starting at $299. Free catalog or see everything online. Hoop House, Mashpee, MA. 1-800-760-5192. www.hoophouse.com

HEALTH

NATURAL MUSCLE RELAXANT. Chronic Pain? Spasms? Formula 303 Natural Relaxant. Order Today for Pain Relief Tomorrow. Web site: www.NaturallyComplete.com

HEALTH & BEAUTY

LIKE GRAMMA'S RELIABLE OLD SALVE! Amish-made. Wonder Balm, absolute must! Price/Brochure: 888-452-4968. Web site: www.mysticwondersinc.com

STEM CELL THERAPY NOW. New product supports the release of Adult Stem Cells. Start regenerating today! www.StemCellsHeal.com

DETOX FOOT PATCHES. On your feet all day? A must! Sample one! 888-452-4968. Web site: www.mysticwondersinc.com

MACULAR DEGENERATION. There is Hope. Natural therapies from an MD that can help your eyes regenerate. 888-838-3937. www.BetterEyeHealth.com

HOME PRODUCTS

LESS/NO CHEMICALS using Earth-Friendly Wonder Laundry Ball and Dryerballs. Brochure, Info pack + $10.00 coupon. Phone: 888-452-4968. www.mysticwondersinc.com

HYPNOSIS

VISUALIZE DESIRED RESULTS: Create a successful future. Request information. Farrar's, Box 210562, Normandy MO 63121.

INSTRUCTION/EDUCATION

HIGH SCHOOL AT HOME—ACCREDITED. Diploma Awarded. Low Tuition. Call 1-800-531-9268 or write American School®, Dept. #348, 2200 E. 170th St., Lansing IL 60438.

DISCOVER how extraordinary you really are. www.rosicrucian.org

CANCER PREVENTION educator will provide individualized consultation. Sliding fee scale. donaldhassig@cancerpreventionnow.com

INVENTORS/INVENTIONS/PATENTS

AMERICA'S LEADING INVENTION COMPANY helps try to submit ideas/inventions to industry. Patent services. 1-888-439-IDEA.

MEDICAL

OXYGEN USERS: Enjoy freedom to travel! Oxlife's lightweight, American-made oxygen concentrators produce 3–6 LPM continuously. For home, car, even overseas. 1-800-780-2616. www.oxlifeinc.com

NURSERY STOCK

TREE/SHRUB SEEDLINGS direct from grower. Plants for landscaping, wildlife food and cover, timber, and Christmas tree production. Free color catalog. Carino Nurseries, PO Box 538AL, Indiana PA 15701. 800-223-7075. www.carinonurseries.com

HOME GARDEN FRUIT TREES. Disease-resistant & Heirloom. Berries, grapes, & unusual fruit. Supplies. Free catalog! Phone: 888-276-3187. www.johnsonnursery.com

OF INTEREST TO ALL

WIN AN EDUCATIONAL Wildlife T-shirt! You may, if you are smart and fast. Visit our Web site: www.athinkersdailychallenge.com

"YOU ARE WELCOME," cookbooklet of simple, nutritious, delicious recipes. Make check payable to Cancer Action NY, Inc., a not-for-profit. $20 includes P&H. CANY, 206 CR 29, Canton NY 13617.

PERSONALS

ASIAN BEAUTIES! Romance, love, marriage! Overseas. Free details, photos! Box 4601-FA, Thousand Oaks CA 91362. 805-492-8040.

MEET LATIN WOMEN seeking marriage. All ages. Free brochures and Singles Vacations DVD. TLC, 713-896-9993 or www.tlcworldwide.com

IT'S FREE! Ladies talk to local guys. It's new, fun, and exciting! Call 800-485-4047. 18+.

DIAL-A-MATE LIVE TALK and voice personals. 10,000 singles call every day! Try it free! 800-234-5558. 18+.

POULTRY

GOSLINGS, DUCKLINGS, GUINEAS, chicks, turkeys, bantams, game birds. Books and equipment. 1-717-365-3694. Hoffman Hatchery, PO Box 129P, Gratz PA 17030. Visit www.hoffmanhatchery.com

FREE CATALOG. Baby chicks, ducks, geese, turkeys, game birds, Canadian honkers, wood ducks. Eggs to incubators. Books and supplies. Stromberg's, Pine River 45, MN 56474-0400. Web site: www.strombergschickens.com

REAL ESTATE

CLAIM GOVERNMENT LAND. 320 acres/person now available. www.usgovernmentinformation.com Free recorded message: 707-448-1887. (4KE1)

LET THE GOVERNMENT PAY for your new or existing home. www.usgovernmentinformation.com 100+ programs. Free information: 707-448-3210. (8KE1)

SEEDS & PLANTS

LIVE HERB PLANTS for Culinary, Medicinal, and Aromatheraphy. Gourmet Vegetables, Plants, Bath Salts, and Bird Houses. Phone: 724-735-4700. www.AlwaysSummerHerbs.com

GROW YOUR OWN tobacco, medicinal plants & herbs, tropicals, heirloom veggies, and more. Free catalog. E.O.N.S., Dept. FA, PO Box 4604, Hallandale FL 33008. 954-455-0229. www.eonseed.com

SPIRITUAL ADVICE

WORLD-RENOWNED READER. Are you unhappy? Unlucky? Health, love, business. Removes bad luck. Free reading. 903-923-8980.

SPIRITUAL HEALER and advisor. Guaranteed help in all problems. Call for your Free reading. Phone: 817-613-0509.

MISS LISA, astrology reader and advisor. Extraordinary powers. Call for help with all problems. Waycross, GA. 912-283-3206.

CHRISTINA specializes in reuniting lovers, helps with all problems. Guaranteed immediate results. Free reading. 423-614-0902.

PSYCHIC READING BY ANDREA. Resolves all problems. Specializes in returning lovers. Immediate results in hours. Free Reading. 214-366-3103.

BEWARE OF DECEIVERS! Honest Psychic chosen by God to help you. Returns true love, heals unhappiness. Guaranteed. Free consultation, call anytime. 210-641-1153.

REMOVES EVIL SPELLS, court cases. Where others fail, I guarantee results in 24 hours. Mrs. Jackson, 334-281-1116. 35 years of experience.

READINGS BY NORA. Specializing in reuniting lovers, helps in all problems. Free reading. 817-461-2683.

ATTENTION: SISTER LIGHT, Spartanburg, South Carolina. One free reading when you call. I will help in all problems. 864-576-9397.

MOTHER DOROTHY tells past, present, and future. Gifted Healer. Phone: 404-755-1301. 1214 Ralph D. Abernathy Blvd., Atlanta GA 30310. Write or call.

SPIRITUAL HEALERS

REVEREND GINGER—Indian healer—works miracles, guaranteed in hours. Specializing in reuniting the separated. Call 504-463-3358.

SPIRITUAL HEALER GABRIELLE will solve your problems immediately. Returns lovers, stops breakups, infidelity, and divorce. Removes bad luck, fear. Worry no longer. Gabrielle guarantees results. 469-241-1192.

REV. NOAH GIBSON, NEW ORLEANS, LA. Powerful and gifted healer. Free spiritual reading. 1-334-651-1782.

REVEREND DOCTOR MILLER. Do you have bad luck? Are you sick? Need help? Reverend Miller reunites lovers. Stops divorce. Removes unnatural illness and curses. Guaranteed results. Phone: 912-876-4895.

MIRACLE HELP in two hours, not two days! Call 334-281-1116.

DOCTOR SAMUELS. Solves impossible problems. Love—lost nature—sickness—bad luck—evil spells—overweight—lucky bags. Call: 843-338-6269.

SPIRITUALISTS

MRS. RUTH, Southern-born spiritualist. Removes evil, bad luck. Helps all problems. Free sample reading. 334-616-6363.

SISTER HELEN. Spiritualist solves all problems. Love, money, marriage, bad luck, evil influences. Guaranteed results. Call for help. 678-472-5920.

GIFTED SPIRITUALIST. Helps with all problems in life. Will give you solutions that you never thought or dreamed of. Please write to: Miss Hart, 2146 Celanese Rd., Rock Hill SC 29732. Phone: 803-242-9973.

NEED GOOD LUCK? Want Good Karma? Psychic Trinity, Powerful Spiritualist: Aura Cleansings, Readings. Stop repeating your past! Go forward in life! Fast results. 817-731-0915.

SUPPLIES

PORTABLE BANDSAW MILLS: 18"–$3,000.00; 28"–$3,599.00; 30"–$4599.00; 36"–$6,250.00. Plus shipping. Free Catalog. Log Home Resource Center. 1-800-441-1564. www.loghomeresources.com

TRAVEL/MAINE RESORTS

BAR HARBOR AND ACADIA National Park. 150 oceanview rooms. Atlantic-Oakes-by-the-Sea. Open year-round. 800-33-MAINE (62463) or reserve online. Indoor Pool and Outdoor pool. Exercise Room and Tennis Courts. Wi-Fi available. www.barharbor.com

ATLANTIC EYRIE LODGE, Bar Harbor, Maine. Acadia National Park. 55 Oceanview rooms. Call 800-HabaVue. Online reservations available. E-mail: info@AtlanticEyrieLodge.com Fax: 207-288-8500. www.AtlanticEyrieLodge.com

INTIMATE OCEANFRONT HOTEL, townhomes, and house. The Bayview, 111 Eden Street, Bar Harbor, Maine. Call 800-356-3585 or visit us and book online at www.thebayviewbarharbor.com

TREES & SHRUBS

EVERGREEN SEEDLINGS for Christmas trees, reforestation, windbreaks, wildlife. Free catalog. Flickinger's Nursery, Box 245, Sagamore PA 16250. 800-368-7381. www.flicknursery.com

ANTIQUE APPLE TREES. 100+ varieties! Catalog, $3.00. Urban Homestead, 818-B Cumberland St., Bristol VA 24201. www.OldVaApples.com

WANTED TO BUY

CASH FOR 78-RPM RECORDS! Send $2 (refundable) for illustrated booklet identifying collectible labels, numbers, with actual prices I pay. Docks, Box 691035(FA), San Antonio TX 78269-1035.

WEATHER INFORMATION

CANADIAN WEATHER. For current real-time information, charts, analysis, and discussion, visit www.canadianweather.org online today.

The Old Farmer's Almanac classified rates (15-word min.): $21.50 per word. Payment required with order: MC, Visa, AmEx, and Discover/NOVUS accepted. For ad rates, Web classifieds, or ad information, contact Bernie Gallagher at OFAads@aol.com, phone 203-263-7171, or fax 203-263-7174. Write to: Gallagher Group, PO Box 959, Woodbury CT 06798. *The 2008 Old Farmer's Almanac* closing date is 05/10/07.

Index to Advertisers

19 OPEI Education & Research Foundation, opei.org/foundation
148 Optigen, Inc. Home Diabetes Supply Co., 800-491-0557
29 Pacific Yurts, 800-944-0240, yurts.com
244 Palmer Industries, 800-847-1304, palmerind.com
67 Penn Foster College/Penn Foster Career School, 800-572-1685, ext. 5348, pennfoster.edu, ID# AA2S96T
88 Powerbilt Steel Buildings, Inc., 800-547-8335
27 Premier Bathrooms, Inc., 800-578-2899, code 53017
243 Psychic Source, 866-690-6221, psychicsource.com
3 Rainhandler, 800-942-3004, rainhandler.com
60 RainWise Inc., 800-762-5723, rainwise.com
70 Regency Cap & Gown Co., 800-826-8612, rcgown.com
46 Research Products, 800-527-5551, incinolet.com
244 Rev. Doctor Adams, 770-622-9191
22 Rug Factory Store, 401-724-6840, rugfactorystore.com
61 Rush Industries, Inc., 516-741-0346, rushindustries.com
23 Sandwich Lantern Works, 888-741-0714, sandwichlantern.com
244 J. Savage, 401-272-1400, ext. 3029, jsavage@shlawri.com
33 Seltzer's, 800-353-2244, seltzersbologna.com
53 Shaker Workshops, 800-840-9121, shakerworkshops.com/fa
23 Shuttercraft, 203-245-2608, shuttercraft.com
81 Sinclair Pharmacal Co., Inc., 800-649-4372, boroleum.com
245 Sister Roberts, 770-994-1466
59 SkinZinc, 800-507-2971
245 Small Farmer's Journal, 800-876-2893, smallfarmersjournal.com
22 Snow Country Lifestyles, 800-715-8711, snowcountrylifestyles.com
43 Stannah Stairlift, 800-877-8247, ext. 166, stannah.com
88 Sun-Mar, 800-461-2461, sun-mar.com
33 Sunnyland Farms, Inc., 800-999-2488, sunnylandfarms.com
51 SunPorch Structures Inc., 203-557-2569, ext. OFA, sunporch.com, Promo code: OFA
23 Table Top Covers, 603-876-4006, tabletopcovers.com
61 Taylor Manufacturing Co., Inc., 800-985-5445, peasheller.com
21 Tempur-Pedic, Inc., 888-702-8557
56 ThyssenKrupp, 800-829-9760, tkaccess.com
245 TimberKing Inc., 800-942-4406, ext. FA7, timberking.com
22 Timberwolf, 800-340-4386, timberwolfcorp.com
139 Total Research, Inc.
9, 11, 13 Tractor Supply Co., myTSCstore.com
243 Watkins, 800-928-5467, WatkinsOnline.com
243 Wood-Mizer, 800-553-0182, woodmizer.com
53 Woodstock Soapstone Co., Inc., 888-664-8188, woodstove.com
43 Yesteryear Toys & Books, Inc., 800-481-1353, yesteryeartoys.com
245 Yourbreed Clothing Co., 888-772-8799, yourbreed.com
145 Zidrep Corporation, 800-457-8144, zidrep.com

ANSWERS TO
Maddening Mind-Manglers

FROM PAGE 242

1. WHO WAS THE OLDEST? Doug was oldest on his 21st birthday by one extra leap year day (February 29). He had six leap-year days. Al, Bill, and Chris had only five.

2. WHICH BIRD IS THE FASTEST? The Canada goose. It took the goose 11 days to make the trip. It arrived one-half day before the loon.

3. HORSE CENTS $\$1,342,177.275 = \frac{1}{2}$ cent for the first nail + 1 cent + 2 cents + 4 cents + 8 cents + 16 cents + 32 cents, etc., for 28 nails. The 28th nail costs $\$671,088.64$. Add the cost for all 28 nails to get the answer.

4. FOUR BY FOUR

1	15	14	4
8	10	11	5
12	6	7	9
13	3	2	16

5. MANGLED MAXIMS
1. People in glass houses shouldn't throw stones. 2. You can't teach an old dog new tricks. 3. All work, no play makes one a dull person. 4. The early bird catches the worm. 5. A picture is worth a thousand words. 6. Two heads are better than one. 7. It's not whether you win or lose, but how you play the game. 8. Never say never. 9. Take it with a grain of salt. 10. Beggars can't be choosers.

MANGLE OUR MINDS
Got a mind-bending math or word puzzle? Send it to us! We may use it in the Almanac. E-mail your puzzle (subject: Mind-Manglers) to almanac@yankeepub .com or send via regular mail to Mind-Manglers, The Old Farmer's Almanac, P.O. Box 520, Dublin, NH 03444. Include the solution clearly stated. All submittals become the property of Yankee Publishing Inc., which reserves the rights to the material. ☐ ☐

Anecdotes & Pleasantries

A sampling from the hundreds of letters, clippings, and e-mails sent to us by Almanac readers from all over the United States and Canada during the past year.

Flash! The Results of Six Brand-New Studies Now Available to Mankind!

All were conducted over the past 18 months by scientific researchers (who, one might surmise, have had a fair amount of time on their hands).

1 REDHEADS FEEL MORE PAIN. Dr. Daniel Sessler of the University of Louisville and his colleagues recently administered electric shocks to ten volunteer redheads and ten volunteer brunettes, along with a measurable numbing anesthetic. They discovered that to lower the pain to a certain measurable level, the redheads required a 20 percent greater dose of the anesthetic. (For reasons not disclosed by the university, blondes were not included in this research project.)

–courtesy of B.T.W., Toronto, Ontario

2 HOW BEST TO SKIP A STONE ACROSS WATER. After exhaustive testing at a local pond, researchers from the Tohoku University Department of Physics in Japan have determined that the best way to skip a stone across water (i.e., get more skips per throw) is for the thrower to tilt said stone precisely 20 degrees to the lake's surface. (This confirmed the results of French experiments conducted a few years ago.)

–courtesy of R.T.L., Dallas, Texas

3 OLD PEOPLE ARE NOT GRUMPY. Two studies conducted by the University of Michigan—one involving more than 1,000 people of various ages—have resulted in the conclusion that older people have less negative emotion and behave less aggressively than younger people. "When [older people] feel upset," reported one of the researchers, "they're more likely to wait to see if things improve rather than yell or argue."

–courtesy of S.M.A., Louisville, Kentucky, who credits Nicholas Bakalar of The New York Times

4 THE COLOR RED IS FOR WINNERS

(MAYBE). British researchers at the University of Durham, after a year-long study, have concluded that wearing red increases the chance of victory in sporting events. (On the other hand, a representative of William Hill, a leading betting company in England, called the study "absolute rubbish.")

–courtesy of H. B., Atlanta, Georgia, who credits John Schwartz of The New York Times

5 THERE'S A NOSE SPRAY THAT MAKES PEOPLE GIVE AWAY MONEY.

As reported by CBC News, researchers at the University of Zurich, Switzerland, sprayed the noses of 178 male volunteers who were playing an investment game with real money. Some were dosed with a substance containing the hormone oxytocin; the others, with a placebo. Directly afterward, it was found that those whose noses had been sprayed with oxytocin were far more trusting and willing to give away their money than they were before the spraying and also far more trusting and willing to give away their money than those sprayed with the placebo.

–courtesy of F.W.P., West Caldwell, New Jersey

6 BEWARE OF A MAN'S INDEX FINGER.

After measuring the fingers of 298 men and women, researchers at the University of Alberta, Canada, concluded that the shorter a man's index finger as compared to his ring finger, the more physically aggressive he is likely to be. (Female finger-length ratios showed no correlation with any of the measures used.)

–courtesy of C.T.R., Seattle, Washington, who credits Nicholas Bakalar of The New York Times

Guess What? In California, It's Not Illegal for Certain Chickens to Cross the Road.

In March 2005, a chicken belonging to Linc and Helena Moore crossed the road near their home in Johannesburg, California. (Reportedly, the purpose of the crossing was to get to the other side.) The Moores were then issued a ticket by Kern County Sheriff's Deputy J. Nicholson, who pointed out that it's illegal for livestock to be on highways. The fine of $54 was eventually thrown out of court, however, when the Moores pointed out to the judge that this particular chicken was not livestock but rather a domesticated chicken. Under California law, it's okay for domesticated chickens to cross the road—for whatever reason. (The case has been widely acclaimed as a victory for chickens everywhere.)

–courtesy of D.F.H., Chicago, Illinois

(continued)

An Elderly Indiana Farmer's Best Advice

1 Don't corner somethin' that you know is meaner'n you.

2 Lettin' the cat outta the bag is a whole lot easier than puttin' it back in.

3 Most of the stuff that people worry about ain't never gonna happen anyway.

4 Timin' has a lot to do with the outcome of a rain dance.

5 Life is simpler when you plow around the stump.

6 Remember that silence is sometimes the best answer.

7 Words that soak into your ears are whispered . . . not yelled.

8 Always drink upstream from the herd.

9 The biggest troublemaker you'll probably ever have to deal with watches you from the mirror every mornin'.

10 Don't interfere with somethin' that ain't botherin' you none.

–courtesy of F.W.P., West Caldwell, New Jersey

We Are What We Eat (If It's Pizza)

Dr. Alan Hirsch, director of the Smell and Taste Treatment and Research Foundation in Chicago, has found that personalities can be revealed by choices of pizza toppings.

PEOPLE WHO PREFER . . .	ARE . . .
Nontraditional toppings, such as pineapple	Aggressive, achievement-oriented, natural leaders who do not suffer fools easily
One meat	Irritable, argumentative, procrastinators who frequently conveniently "forget" obligations at work and home
Several meats	Dramatic, seductive, extroverts who thrive as the center of attention, crave novelty, and are impeccably groomed
One vegetable	Empathetic, understanding, well-adjusted, easygoing— the ideal parents
Several vegetables	Trustworthy, loyal, dependable, humble, introverted, and function best in a group environment
Extra cheese	Well, everyone likes extra cheese.

–courtesy of M. M., Newport, Rhode Island

Electricity Was Discovered by Rubbing Two Cats Together Backwards

For the real "story" in history, we need go no further than these excerpts collected from schoolchildren's essays:

■ "Moses led the Hebrew slaves to the Red Sea, where they made unleavened bread, which is bread made without any ingredients. Moses went up on Mount Cyanide to get the ten commandments. He died before he ever reached Canada."

■ "Solomon had 300 wives and 700 porcupines."

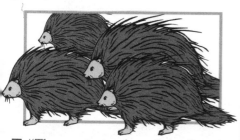

■ "The greatest writer of the Renaissance was William Shakespeare. He was born in the year 1564, supposedly on his birthday. He never made much money and is famous only because of his plays. He wrote tragedies, comedies, and hysterectomies, all in Islamic pentameter. Romeo and Juliet are an example of a heroic couple. Romeo's last wish was to be laid by Juliet."

[Editor's Note: We are certain that this young writer meant "laid to rest."]

■ "Writing at the same time as Shakespeare was Miguel Cervantes. He wrote Donkey Hote."

■ "Thomas Jefferson, a Virgin, and Benjamin Franklin were two singers of the Declaration of Independence. Franklin discovered electricity by rubbing two cats together backwards and declared, 'A horse divided against itself can not stand.' Franklin died in 1790 and is still dead."

–courtesy of M. K., Woodbury, Connecticut

50 Legendary Songs Of The Old West

WAGON WHEELS

From out of the Golden West we bring you a giant memory-stirring treasury of unforgettable cowboy favorites. Here are America's beloved singing cowboys with all the romantic western songs that helped build the legends of the Old West. It's a goldmine of musical memories...every one a timeless all-time favorite. *This treasury is not sold in stores so be sure to order yours today!*

The Cowboy Music Treasury That's Sweeping America On TV!

I'M BACK IN THE SADDLE AGAIN
Gene Autry

TUMBLING TUMBLEWEEDS
Sons Of The Pioneers

CATTLE CALL
Eddy Arnold

THE LAST ROUNDUP
Rex Allen

COOL WATER
Sons Of The Pioneers

RIDERS IN THE SKY
Vaughn Monroe

HIGH NOON
Tex Ritter

MULE TRAIN
Frankie Laine

HOME ON THE RANGE
Gene Autry

NEW SAN ANTONIO ROSE
Bob Wills

BURY ME NOT ON THE LONE PRAIRIE
Tex Ritter

TWILIGHT ON THE TRAIL
Sons Of The Pioneers

MEXICALI ROSE
Jim Reeves

SOMEDAY YOU'LL WANT ME TO WANT YOU
Elton Britt

I'M AN OLD COWHAND
Patsy Montana

THE SHIFTING WHISPERING SANDS
Jim Reeves

WHOOPIE TI YI YO (GET ALONG LITTLE DOGGIE)
Sons Of The Pioneers

WHEN IT'S SPRINGTIME IN THE ROCKIES
Montana Slim

NOBODY'S DARLIN' BUT MINE
Jimmie Davis

TAKE ME BACK TO MY BOOTS AND SADDLE
Jimmy Wakely

THE STREETS OF LAREDO
Marty Robbins

WAGON WHEELS
Sons Of The Pioneers

EMPTY SADDLES
Sons Of The Pioneers

MY LITTLE CHEROKEE MAIDEN
Bob Wills

DOWN IN THE VALLEY
Slim Whitman

EL RANCHO GRANDE
Gene Autry

SOUTH OF THE BORDER
Patsy Cline

OLD SHEP
Red Foley

I'M THINKING TONIGHT OF MY BLUE EYES
The Carter Family

THE PRISONER'S SONG
Vernon Dalhart

YOU ARE MY SUNSHINE
Jimmie Davis

PISTOL PACKIN' MAMA
Al Dexter

DON'T FENCE ME IN
Bing Crosby

GOODNIGHT IRENE
Ernest Tubb & Red Foley

DEEP IN THE HEART OF TEXAS
Bob Wills

ALONG THE NAVAJO TRAIL
Sons Of The Pioneers

SIOUX CITY SUE
Bing Crosby

RED RIVER VALLEY
Slim Whitman

HAPPY TRAILS
Roy Rogers & Dale Evans

AND MANY MORE...
50 IN ALL!

The Beautiful Music Company, Dept. CW-269
320 Main Street, Northport, NY 11768
Please rush my *WAGON WHEELS Treasury* on your unconditional money-back guarantee.
❏ I enclose $19.98. Send 2 Cassettes.
❏ I enclose $24.98. Send 2 Compact Discs.

WE SHIP FREE!
No Postage Or Handling Fees!

Or Charge To: ❏ VISA ❏ MasterCard ❏ American Express ❏ Discover

Card No._____ Exp. Date_____

Name _____

Address_____

City_____ State_____ Zip_____

A Reference Compendium

compiled by Mare-Anne Jarvela

Weather

Calendar

The Garden

Household

Lasting Words

REFERENCE

A Table Foretelling the Weather Through All the Lunations of Each Year, or Forever

This table is the result of many years of actual observation and shows what sort of weather will probably follow the Moon's entrance into any of its quarters. For example, the table shows that the week following January 11, 2007, will be stormy, because the Moon enters the last quarter that day at 7:45 A.M. EST. (See the **Left-Hand Calendar Pages, 106–132**, for 2007 Moon phases.)

Editor's note: Although the data in this table is taken into consideration in the yearlong process of compiling the annual long-range weather forecasts for *The Old Farmer's Almanac*, we rely far more on our projections of solar activity.

Time of Change	Summer	Winter
Midnight to 2 A.M.	Fair	Hard frost, unless wind is south or west
2 A.M. to 4 A.M.	Cold, with frequent showers	Snow and stormy
4 A.M. to 6 A.M.	Rain	Rain
6 A.M. to 8 A.M.	Wind and rain	Stormy
8 A.M. to 10 A.M.	Changeable	Cold rain if wind is west; snow, if east
10 A.M. to noon	Frequent showers	Cold with high winds
Noon to 2 P.M.	Very rainy	Snow or rain
2 P.M. to 4 P.M.	Changeable	Fair and mild
4 P.M. to 6 P.M.	Fair	Fair
6 P.M. to 10 P.M.	Fair if wind is northwest; rain if wind is south or southwest	Fair and frosty if wind is north or northeast; rain or snow if wind is south or southwest
10 P.M. to midnight	Fair	Fair and frosty

This table was created about 175 years ago by Dr. Herschell for the Boston Courier; *it first appeared in* The Old Farmer's Almanac *in 1834.*

Safe Ice Thickness*

Ice Thickness	Permissible Load	Ice Thickness	Permissible Load
3 inches	Single person on foot	12 inches	Heavy truck (8-ton gross)
4 inches	Group in single file	15 inches	10 tons
7½ inches	Passenger car (2-ton gross)	20 inches	25 tons
8 inches	Light truck (2½-ton gross)	30 inches	70 tons
10 inches	Medium truck (3½-ton gross)	36 inches	110 tons

*Solid, clear, blue/black pond and lake ice

Slush ice has only half the strength of blue ice. The strength value of river ice is 15 percent less.

Snowflakes

S nowflakes are made up of six-sided crystals. If you look carefully at the snowflakes during the next snowstorm, you might be able to find some of the crystal types below. The basic shape of a crystal is determined by the temperature at which it forms. Sometimes a snowflake is a combination of more than one type of crystal.

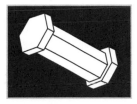

CAPPED COLUMNS
(also called tsuzumi crystals) occur when the temperature is 25°F or less.

NEEDLES
(long and thin but still six-sided crystals) occur when the temperature is 21° to 25°F.

SPATIAL DENDRITES
(irregular and feathery crystals) occur in high-moisture clouds at 3° to 10°F.

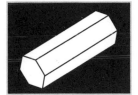

COLUMNS
(dense crystals, act like prisms) occur when the temperature is 25°F or less.

PLATES
(mirrorlike crystals) occur under special weather conditions.

STELLAR CRYSTALS
(beautiful, delicate crystals) occur under special weather conditions.

Weather Phobias

Name of Fear	Object Feared
Ancraophobia	Wind
Anemophobia	Wind
Antlophobia	Floods
Astraphobia	Lightning, thunder
Auroraphobia	Northern lights, southern lights
Brontophobia	Lightning, thunder
Ceraunophobia	Thunder
Cheimatophobia	Cold
Chionophobia	Snow
Cryophobia	Extreme cold, frost, ice
Frigophobia	Cold
Heliophobia	Sun, sunshine

Name of Fear	Object Feared
Homichlophobia	Fog
Hygrophobia	Dampness, moisture
Keraunophobia	Lightning, thunder
Lilapsophobia	Hurricanes, tornadoes
Nebulaphobia	Fog
Nephophobia	Clouds
Ombrophobia	Rain
Pagophobia	Frost, ice
Phengophobia	Daylight, sunshine
Pluviophobia	Rain
Psychrophobia	Cold
Thermophobia	Heat
Tonitrophobia	Thunder

REFERENCE

The UV Index for Measuring Ultraviolet Radiation Risk

The U.S. National Weather Service daily forecasts of ultraviolet levels use these numbers for various exposure levels:

UV Index Number	Exposure Level	Time to Burn	Actions to Take
0, 1, 2	Minimal	60 minutes	Apply SPF 15 sunscreen
3, 4	Low	45 minutes	Apply SPF 15 sunscreen; wear a hat
5, 6	Moderate	30 minutes	Apply SPF 15 sunscreen; wear a hat
7, 8, 9	High	15–25 minutes	Apply SPF 15 to 30 sunscreen; wear a hat and sunglasses
10 or higher	Very high	10 minutes	Apply SPF 30 sunscreen; wear a hat, sunglasses, and protective clothing

"Time to Burn" and "Actions to Take" apply to people with fair skin that sometimes tans but usually burns. People with lighter skin need to be more cautious. People with darker skin may be able to tolerate more exposure.

What Are Cooling/Heating Degree Days?

■ Each degree of a day's average temperature above 65°F is considered one cooling degree day, an attempt to measure the need for air-conditioning. If the average of the day's high and low temperatures is 75°, that's ten cooling degree days.

Similarly, each degree of a day's average temperature below 65°F is considered one heating degree and is an attempt to measure the need for fuel consumption. For example, a day with temperatures ranging from 60°F to 40°F results in an average of 50°, or 15 degrees less than 65°. Hence, that day would be credited as 15 heating degree days.

Richter Scale for Measuring Earthquakes

Magnitude	Possible Effects
1	Detectable only by instruments
2	Barely detectable, even near the epicenter
3	Felt indoors
4	Felt by most people; slight damage
5	Felt by all; minor to moderate damage
6	Moderate destruction
7	Major damage
8	Total and major damage

–devised by American geologist Charles W. Richter in 1935 to measure the magnitude of an earthquake

Psychrometric Table

To determine relative humidity, take the temperature with both a dry-bulb and a wet-bulb thermometer. Find the difference between the two measurements, and then see where the numbers intersect on the chart below.

Temperature on a Dry-Bulb Thermometer (°F)	Temperature Difference Between Dry-Bulb and Wet-Bulb Thermometers (°F)								
	4	**5**	**6**	**7**	**8**	**9**	**10**	**11**	**12**
	Relative Humidity (%)								
40	68	60	52	45	37	29	22	15	7
50	74	67	61	55	49	43	38	32	27
60	78	73	68	63	58	53	48	43	39
70	81	77	72	68	64	59	55	51	48
80	83	79	75	72	68	64	61	57	54
90	85	81	78	74	71	68	65	61	58

Example: When the dry-bulb temperature is 70°F and the wet-bulb temperature is 65°F (a difference of 5 degrees), the relative humidity is 77 percent. For a Celsius version of the Psychrometric Table, visit Almanac.com/weathercharts.

Atlantic Tropical (and Subtropical) Storm Names for 2007

Andrea	Gabrielle	Melissa	Tanya
Barry	Humberto	Noel	Van
Chantal	Ingrid	Olga	Wendy
Dean	Jerry	Pablo	
Erin	Karen	Rebekah	
Felix	Lorenzo	Sebastien	

Eastern North-Pacific Tropical (and Subtropical) Storm Names for 2007

Alvin	Gil	Manuel	Tico
Barbara	Henriette	Narda	Velma
Cosme	Ivo	Octave	Wallis
Dalila	Juliette	Priscilla	Xina
Erick	Kiko	Raymond	York
Flossie	Lorena	Sonia	Zelda

Retired Atlantic Hurricane Names

These storms have been some of the most destructive and costly; as a result, their names have been retired from the six-year rotating list of names.

NAME	YEAR	NAME	YEAR	NAME	YEAR
Frederic	1979	Bob	1991	Isabel	2003
Allen	1980	Andrew	1992	Charley	2004
Alicia	1983	Opal	1995	Frances	2004
Elena	1985	Roxanne	1995	Ivan	2004
Gloria	1985	Fran	1996	Dennis	2005
Gilbert	1988	Mitch	1998	Katrina	2005
Joan	1988	Floyd	1999	Rita	2005
Hugo	1989	Keith	2000	Stan	2005
Diana	1990	Lili	2002	Wilma	2005
Klaus	1990	Fabian	2003		

Wind/Barometer Table

Barometer (Reduced to Sea Level)	Wind Direction	Character of Weather Indicated
30.00 to 30.20, and steady	westerly	Fair, with slight changes in temperature, for one to two days.
30.00 to 30.20, and rising rapidly	westerly	Fair, followed within two days by warmer and rain.
30.00 to 30.20, and falling rapidly	south to east	Warmer, and rain within 24 hours.
30.20 or above, and falling rapidly	south to east	Warmer, and rain within 36 hours.
30.20 or above, and falling rapidly	west to north	Cold and clear, quickly followed by warmer and rain.
30.20 or above, and steady	variable	No early change.
30.00 or below, and falling slowly	south to east	Rain within 18 hours that will continue a day or two.
30.00 or below, and falling rapidly	southeast to northeast	Rain, with high wind, followed within two days by clearing, colder.
30.00 or below, and rising	south to west	Clearing and colder within 12 hours.
29.80 or below, and falling rapidly	south to east	Severe storm of wind and rain imminent. In winter, snow or cold wave within 24 hours.
29.80 or below, and falling rapidly	east to north	Severe northeast gales and heavy rain or snow, followed in winter by cold wave.
29.80 or below, and rising rapidly	going to west	Clearing and colder.

Note: A barometer should be adjusted to show equivalent sea-level pressure for the altitude at which it is to be used. A change of 100 feet in elevation will cause a decrease of $\frac{1}{10}$ inch in the reading.

The Volcanic Explosivity Index (VEI) for Measuring Volcanic Eruptions

VEI/Description	Plume Height	Volume	Classification	Frequency
0 Nonexplosive	<100 m	1,000 m³	Hawaiian	Daily
1 Gentle	100–1,000 m	10,000 m³	Hawaiian/Strombolian	Daily
2 Explosive	1–5 km	1,000,000 m³	Strombolian/Vulcanian	Weekly
3 Severe	3–15 km	10,000,000 m³	Vulcanian	Yearly
4 Cataclysmic	10–25 km	100,000,000 m³	Vulcanian/Plinian	10 years
5 Paroxysmal	>25 km	1 km³	Plinian	100 years
6 Colossal	>25 km	10 km³	Plinian/Ultra-Plinian	100 years
7 Supercolossal	>25 km	100 km³	Ultra-Plinian	1,000 years
8 Megacolossal	>25 km	1,000 km³	Ultra-Plinian	10,000 years

Weather Lore Calendar

For centuries, farmers and sailors—people whose livelihoods depended on the weather—relied on lore to forecast the weather. They quickly connected changes in nature with rhythms or patterns of the weather. Here is a collection of proverbs relating to months, weeks, and days.

January

Fog in January brings a wet spring.

[14th] St. Hilary, the coldest day of the year.

[22nd] If the Sun shine on St. Vincent, there shall be much wind.

February

There is always one fine week in February.

If bees get out in February, the next day will be windy and rainy.

Fogs in February mean frosts in May.

Winter's back breaks about the middle of February.

March

When March has April weather, April will have March weather.

Thunder in March betokens a fruitful year.

Dust in March brings grass and foliage.

A March Sun sticks like a lock of wool.

April

If it thunders on All Fools' Day, it brings good crops of corn and hay.

Moist April, clear June.

Cloudy April, dewy May.

Snow in April is manure.

May

Hoar frost on May 1st indicates a good harvest.

A swarm of bees in May is worth a load of hay.

In the middle of May comes the tail of winter.

June

A good leak in June, sets all in tune.

When it is hottest in June, it will be coldest in the corresponding days of the next February.

[24th] Rain on St. John's Day, and we may expect a wet harvest.

July

If the 1st of July be rainy weather, it will rain more or less for three weeks together.

Ne'er trust a July sky.

[3rd] Dog days bright and clear, indicate a happy year.

August

If the first week in August is unusually warm, the winter will be white and long.

[24th] Thunderstorms after St. Bartholomew are mostly violent.

When it rains in August, it rains honey and wine.

September

Fair on September 1st, fair for the month.

Heavy September rains bring drought.

If on September 19th there is a storm from the south, a mild winter may be expected.

[29th] If St. Michael's brings many acorns, Christmas will cover the fields with snow.

October

Much rain in October, much wind in December.

For every fog in October, a snow in the winter.

Full Moon in October without frost, no frost till full Moon in November.

November

A heavy November snow will last till April.

Thunder in November, a fertile year to come.

Flowers in bloom late in autumn indicate a bad winter.

December

Thunder in December presages fine weather.

A green Christmas, a white Easter.

As the days lengthen, so the cold strengthens.

If it rains much during the twelve days after Christmas, it will be a wet year.

PHASES OF THE MOON

New

First Quarter

Full

Last Quarter

New

WAXING

WANING

REFERENCE

Origin of Full-Moon Names

Historically, the Native Americans who lived in the area that is now the northern and eastern United States kept track of the seasons by giving a distinctive name to each recurring full Moon. This name was applied to the entire month in which it occurred. These names, and some variations, were used by the Algonquin tribes from New England to Lake Superior.

Name	Month	Variations
Full Wolf Moon	January	Full Old Moon
Full Snow Moon	February	Full Hunger Moon
Full Worm Moon	March	Full Crow Moon Full Crust Moon Full Sugar Moon Full Sap Moon
Full Pink Moon	April	Full Sprouting Grass Moon Full Egg Moon Full Fish Moon
Full Flower Moon	May	Full Corn Planting Moon Full Milk Moon
Full Strawberry Moon	June	Full Rose Moon Full Hot Moon
Full Buck Moon	July	Full Thunder Moon Full Hay Moon
Full Sturgeon Moon	August	Full Red Moon Full Green Corn Moon
Full Harvest Moon*	September	Full Corn Moon Full Barley Moon
Full Hunter's Moon	October	Full Travel Moon Full Dying Grass Moon
Full Beaver Moon	November	Full Frost Moon
Full Cold Moon	December	Full Long Nights Moon

The Harvest Moon is always the full Moon closest to the autumnal equinox. If the Harvest Moon occurs in October, the September full Moon is usually called the Corn Moon.

When Will the Moon Rise Today?

A lunar puzzle involves the timing of moonrise. If you enjoy the out-of-doors and the wonders of nature, you may wish to commit to memory the following gem:

 The new Moon always rises at sunrise

 And the first quarter at noon.

 The full Moon always rises at sunset

 And the last quarter at midnight.

■ Moonrise occurs about 50 minutes later each day.

■ The new Moon is invisible because its illuminated side faces away from Earth, which occurs when the Moon lines up between Earth and the Sun.

■ One or two days after the date of the new Moon, you can see a thin crescent setting just after sunset in the western sky as the lunar cycle continues. (See **pages 106–132** for exact **moonrise times.**)

Origin of Month Names

January Named for the Roman god Janus, protector of gates and doorways. Janus is depicted with two faces, one looking into the past, the other into the future.

February From the Latin word *februa,* "to cleanse." The Roman Februalia was a month of purification and atonement.

March Named for the Roman god of war, Mars. This was the time of year to resume military campaigns that had been interrupted by winter.

April From the Latin word *aperio,* "to open (bud)," because plants begin to grow in this month.

May Named for the Roman goddess Maia, who oversaw the growth of plants. Also from the Latin word *maiores,* "elders," who were celebrated during this month.

June Named for the Roman goddess Juno, patroness of marriage and the well-being of women. Also from the Latin word *juvenis,* "young people."

July Named to honor Roman dictator Julius Caesar (100 B.C.–44 B.C.). In 46 B.C., Julius Caesar made one of his greatest contributions to history: With the help of Sosigenes, he developed the Julian calendar, the precursor to the Gregorian calendar we use today.

August Named to honor the first Roman emperor (and grandnephew of Julius Caesar), Augustus Caesar (63 B.C.–A.D. 14).

September From the Latin word *septem,* "seven," because this had been the seventh month of the early Roman calendar.

October From the Latin word *octo,* "eight," because this had been the eighth month of the early Roman calendar.

November From the Latin word *novem,* "nine," because this had been the ninth month of the early Roman calendar.

December From the Latin word *decem,* "ten," because this had been the tenth month of the early Roman calendar.

REFERENCE

Origin of Day Names

The days of the week were named by the Romans with the Latin words for the Sun, the Moon, and the five known planets. These names have survived in European languages, but English names also reflect an Anglo-Saxon influence.

English	Latin	French	Italian	Spanish	Saxon
SUNDAY	Solis (Sun)	dimanche	domenica	domingo	Sun
MONDAY	Lunae (Moon)	lundi	lunedì	lunes	Moon
TUESDAY	Martis (Mars)	mardi	martedì	martes	Tiw (the Anglo-Saxon god of war, the equivalent of the Norse Tyr or the Roman Mars)
WEDNESDAY	Mercurii (Mercury)	mercredi	mercoledì	miércoles	Woden (the Anglo-Saxon equivalent of the Norse Odin or the Roman Mercury)
THURSDAY	Jovis (Jupiter)	jeudi	giovedì	jueves	Thor (the Norse god of thunder, the equivalent of the Roman Jupiter)
FRIDAY	Veneris (Venus)	vendredi	venerdì	viernes	Frigg (the Norse god of love and fertility, the equivalent of the Roman Venus)
SATURDAY	Saturni (Saturn)	samedi	sabato	sábado	Saterne (Saturn, the Roman god of agriculture)

Best Planetary Encounters of the 21st Century

Me = Mercury   V = Venus   Mn = Moon   Ma = Mars   J = Jupiter   S = Saturn

In all of these cases, face west between twilight and 10 P.M. to see the conjunction.

DATE	OBJECTS	DATE	OBJECTS	DATE	OBJECTS
June 30, 2007	V, S	March 7, 2047	V, J	November 15, 2080	Ma, J, S
December 1, 2008	V, Mn, J	May 13, 2066	V, Ma		
February 20, 2015	V, Mn, Ma	July 1, 2066	V, S	November 17, 2080	Mn, Ma, J, S
June 30–July 1, 2015	V, J	March 14, 2071	V, J		
July 18, 2015	V, Mn, J	June 21, 2074	V, J	December 24, 2080	V, J
December 20, 2020	J, S	June 27, 2074	V, Mn, J	March 6, 2082	V, J
March 1, 2023	V, J	June 28, 2076	Ma, J	April 28, 2085	Mn, Ma, J
December 1–2, 2033	Ma, J	October 31, 2076	Mn, Ma, S	June 13, 2085	Me, V, J
February 23, 2047	V, Ma	February 27, 2079	V, Ma	May 15, 2098	V, Ma
		November 7, 2080	Ma, J, S	June 29, 2098	V, J

Love calendar lore? Find more at Almanac.com.

REFERENCE

How to Find the Day of the Week for Any Given Date

To compute the day of the week for any given date as far back as the mid–18th century, proceed as follows:

■ Add the last two digits of the year to one-quarter of the last two digits (discard any remainder), the day of the month, and the month key from the key box below. Divide the sum by 7; the remainder is the day of the week (1 is Sunday, 2 is Monday, and so on). If there is no remainder, the day is Saturday. If you're searching for a weekday prior to 1900, add 2 to the sum before dividing; prior to 1800, add 4. The formula doesn't work for days prior to 1753. From 2000 to 2099, subtract 1 from the sum before dividing.

Example:
The Dayton Flood was on March 25, 1913.

Last two digits of year:	13
One-quarter of these two digits:	3
Given day of month:	25
Key number for March:	4
Sum:	45

45 ÷ 7 = 6, with a remainder of 3. The flood took place on Tuesday, the third day of the week.

KEY

January	1
leap year	0
February	4
leap year	3
March	4
April	0
May	2
June	5
July	0
August	3
September.	6
October.	1
November	4
December	6

Easter Dates (2007–11)

■ Christian churches that follow the Gregorian calendar celebrate Easter on the first Sunday after the full Moon that occurs on or just after the vernal equinox.

YEAR	EASTER
2007.	April 8
2008.	March 23
2009.	April 12
2010.	April 4
2011.	April 24

■ Eastern Orthodox churches follow the Julian calendar.

YEAR	EASTER
2007.	April 8
2008.	April 27
2009.	April 19
2010.	April 4
2011.	April 24

Triskaidekaphobia Trivia

Here are a few facts about Friday the 13th:

■ In the 14 possible configurations for the annual calendar (see any perpetual calendar), the occurrence of Friday the 13th is this:

6 of 14 years have one Friday the 13th.
6 of 14 years have two Fridays the 13th.
2 of 14 years have three Fridays the 13th.

■ There is no year without one Friday the 13th, and no year with more than three.

■ There are two Fridays the 13th in 2007. The next year to have three Fridays the 13th is 2009.

■ The reason we say "Fridays the 13th" is that no one can pronounce "Friday the 13ths."

The Animal Signs of the Chinese Zodiac

The animal designations of the Chinese zodiac follow a 12-year cycle and are always used in the same sequence. The Chinese year of 354 days begins three to seven weeks into the western 365-day year, so the animal designation changes at that time, rather than on January 1. See **page 105** for the exact date of the start of the Chinese New Year.

RAT
Ambitious and sincere, you can be generous with your money. Compatible with the dragon and the monkey. Your opposite is the horse.

1900	1936	1984
1912	1948	1996
1924	1960	2008
	1972	

DRAGON
Robust and passionate, your life is filled with complexity. Compatible with the monkey and the rat. Your opposite is the dog.

1904	1940	1988
1916	1952	2000
1928	1964	2012
	1976	

MONKEY
Persuasive, skillful, and intelligent, you strive to excel. Compatible with the dragon and the rat. Your opposite is the tiger.

1908	1944	1992
1920	1956	2004
1932	1968	2016
	1980	

OX OR BUFFALO
A leader, you are bright, patient, and cheerful. Compatible with the snake and the rooster. Your opposite is the sheep.

1901	1937	1985
1913	1949	1997
1925	1961	2009
	1973	

SNAKE
Strong-willed and intense, you display great wisdom. Compatible with the rooster and the ox. Your opposite is the pig.

1905	1941	1989
1917	1953	2001
1929	1965	2013
	1977	

ROOSTER OR COCK
Seeking wisdom and truth, you have a pioneering spirit. Compatible with the snake and the ox. Your opposite is the rabbit.

1909	1945	1993
1921	1957	2005
1933	1969	2017
	1981	

TIGER
Forthright and sensitive, you possess great courage. Compatible with the horse and the dog. Your opposite is the monkey.

1902	1938	1986
1914	1950	1998
1926	1962	2010
	1974	

HORSE
Physically attractive and popular, you like the company of others. Compatible with the tiger and the dog. Your opposite is the rat.

1906	1942	1990
1918	1954	2002
1930	1966	2014
	1978	

DOG
Generous and loyal, you have the ability to work well with others. Compatible with the horse and the tiger. Your opposite is the dragon.

1910	1946	1994
1922	1958	2006
1934	1970	2018
	1982	

RABBIT OR HARE
Talented and affectionate, you are a seeker of tranquility. Compatible with the sheep and the pig. Your opposite is the rooster.

1903	1939	1987
1915	1951	1999
1927	1963	2011
	1975	

SHEEP OR GOAT
Aesthetic and stylish, you enjoy being a private person. Compatible with the pig and the rabbit. Your opposite is the ox.

1907	1943	1991
1919	1955	2003
1931	1967	2015
	1979	

PIG OR BOAR
Gallant and noble, your friends will remain at your side. Compatible with the rabbit and the sheep. Your opposite is the snake.

1911	1947	1995
1923	1959	2007
1935	1971	2019
	1983	

REFERENCE

Sowing Vegetable Seeds

Sow or plant in cool weather	Beets, broccoli, brussels sprouts, cabbage, lettuce, onions, parsley, peas, radishes, spinach, Swiss chard, turnips
Sow or plant in warm weather	Beans, carrots, corn, cucumbers, eggplant, melons, okra, peppers, squash, tomatoes
Sow or plant for one crop per season	Corn, eggplant, leeks, melons, peppers, potatoes, spinach (New Zealand), squash, tomatoes
Resow for additional crops	Beans, beets, cabbage, carrots, kohlrabi, lettuce, radishes, rutabagas, spinach, turnips

A Beginner's Vegetable Garden

A good size for a beginner's vegetable garden is 10x16 feet. It should have crops that are easy to grow. A plot this size, planted as suggested below, can feed a family of four for one summer, with a little extra for canning and freezing (or giving away).

Make 11 rows, 10 feet long, with 6 inches between them. Ideally, the rows should run north and south to take full advantage of the sunlight. Plant the following:

ROW	
1	Zucchini (4 plants)
2	Tomatoes (5 plants, staked)
3	Peppers (6 plants)
4	Cabbage

ROW	
5	Bush beans
6	Lettuce
7	Beets
8	Carrots
9	Chard
10	Radishes
11	Marigolds (to discourage rabbits!)

Traditional Planting Times

■ Plant **corn** when elm leaves are the size of a squirrel's ear, when oak leaves are the size of a mouse's ear, when apple blossoms begin to fall, or when the dogwoods are in full bloom.

■ Plant **lettuce, spinach, peas,** and other cool-weather vegetables when the lilacs show their first leaves or when daffodils begin to bloom.

■ Plant **tomatoes, early corn,** and **peppers** when dogwoods are in peak bloom or when daylilies start to bloom.

■ Plant **cucumbers** and **squashes** when lilac flowers fade.

■ Plant **perennials** when maple leaves begin to unfurl.

■ Plant **morning glories** when maple trees have full-size leaves.

■ Plant **pansies, snapdragons,** and other hardy annuals after the aspen and chokecherry trees leaf out.

■ Plant **beets** and **carrots** when dandelions are blooming.

Growing Vegetables

VEGETABLE	START SEEDS INDOORS (weeks before last spring frost)	START SEEDS OUTDOORS (weeks before or after last spring frost)	MINIMUM SOIL TEMPERATURE TO TO GERMINATE (°F)	COLD HARDINESS
Beans		Anytime after	48–50	Tender
Beets		4 before to 4 after	39–41	Half-hardy
Broccoli	6–8	4 before	55–75	Hardy
Brussels sprouts	6–8		55–75	Hardy
Cabbage	6–8	Anytime after	38–40	Hardy
Carrots		4–6 before	39–41	Half-hardy
Cauliflower	6–8	4 before	65–75	Half-hardy
Celery	6–8		60–70	Tender
Corn		2 after	46–50	Tender
Cucumbers	3–4	1–2 after	65–70	Very tender
Lettuce	4–6	2–3 after	40–75	Half-hardy
Melons	3–4	2 after	55–60	Very tender
Onion sets		4 before	34–36	Hardy
Parsnips		2–4 before	55–70	Hardy
Peas		4–6 before	34–36	Hardy
Peppers	8–10		70–80	Very tender
Potato tubers		2–4 before	55–70	Half-hardy
Pumpkins	3–4	1 after	55–60	Tender
Radishes		4–6 before	39–41	Hardy
Spinach		4–6 before	55–65	Hardy
Squash, summer	3–4	1 after	55–60	Very tender
Squash, winter	3–4	1 after	55–60	Tender
Tomatoes	6–8		50–55	Tender

REFERENCE

WHEN TO FERTILIZE	WHEN TO WATER
After heavy bloom and set of pods	Regularly, from start of pod to set
At time of planting	Only during drought conditions
Three weeks after transplanting	Only during drought conditions
Three weeks after transplanting	At transplanting
Three weeks after transplanting	Two to three weeks before harvest
Preferably in the fall for the following spring	Only during drought conditions
Three weeks after transplanting	Once, three weeks before harvest
At time of transplanting	Once a week
When eight to ten inches tall, and again when first silk appears	When tassels appear and cobs start to swell
One week after bloom, and again three weeks later	Frequently, especially when fruits form
Two to three weeks after transplanting	Once a week
One week after bloom, and again three weeks later	Once a week
When bulbs begin to swell, and again when plants are one foot tall	Only during drought conditions
One year before planting	Only during drought conditions
After heavy bloom and set of pods	Regularly, from start of pod to set
After first fruit-set	Once a week
At bloom time or time of second hilling	Regularly, when tubers start to form
Just before vines start to run, when plants are about one foot tall	Only during drought conditions
Before spring planting	Once a week
When plants are one-third grown	Once a week
Just before vines start to run, when plants are about one foot tall	Only during drought conditions
Just before vines start to run, when plants are about one foot tall	Only during drought conditions
Two weeks before, and after first picking	Twice a week

R
E
F
E
R
E
N
C
E

Vegetable Gardening in Containers

Lack of yard space is no excuse for not gardening, because many vegetables can be readily grown in containers. In addition to providing five hours or more of full sun, you must give attention to choosing the proper container, using a good soil mix, observing planting and spacing requirements, fertilizing, watering, and selecting appropriate varieties. Here are some suggestions:

Vegetable	Type of Container	Recommended Varieties
Beans, snap	5-gallon window box	Bush 'Blue Lake', Bush 'Romano', 'Tender Crop'
Broccoli	1 plant/5-gallon pot 3 plants/15-gallon tub	'DeCicco', 'Green Comet'
Carrots	5-gallon window box at least 12 inches deep	'Danvers Half Long', 'Short 'n Sweet', 'Tiny Sweet'
Cucumbers	1 plant/1-gallon pot	'Patio Pik', 'Pot Luck', 'Spacemaster'
Eggplant	5-gallon pot	'Black Beauty', 'Ichiban', 'Slim Jim'
Lettuce	5-gallon window box	'Ruby', 'Salad Bowl'
Onions	5-gallon window box	'White Sweet Spanish', 'Yellow Sweet Spanish'
Peppers	1 plant/2-gallon pot 5 plants/15-gallon tub	'Cayenne', 'Long Red', 'Sweet Banana', 'Wonder', 'Yolo'
Radishes	5-gallon window box	'Cherry Belle', 'Icicle'
Tomatoes	Bushel basket	'Early Girl', 'Patio', 'Small Fry', 'Sweet 100', 'Tiny Tim'

TIPS

■ Clay pots are usually more attractive than plastic ones, but plastic pots retain moisture better. To get the best of both, slip a plastic pot into a slightly larger clay pot.

■ Avoid small containers. They often can't store enough water to get through hot days.

■ Add about one inch of coarse gravel in the bottom of the container to improve drainage.

■ Vegetables that can be easily transplanted are best suited for containers. Transplants can be purchased from local nurseries or started at home.

■ Feed container plants at least twice a month with liquid fertilizer, following the instructions on the label.

■ An occasional application of fish emulsion or compost will add trace elements to container soil.

■ Place containers where they will receive maximum sunlight and good ventilation. Watch for and control insect pests.

REFERENCE

Fertilizer Formulas

Fertilizers are labeled to show the percentages by weight of nitrogen (N), phosphorus (P), and potassium (K). Nitrogen is needed for leaf growth. Phosphorus is associated with root growth and fruit production. Potassium helps the plant fight off diseases. A 100-pound bag of 10-5-10 contains 10 pounds of nitrogen, 5 pounds of phosphorus, and 10 pounds of potassium. The rest is filler.

Manure Guide

PRIMARY NUTRIENTS (pounds per ton)

Type of Manure	Water Content	Nitrogen	Phosphorus	Potassium
Cow, horse	60%–80%	12–14	5–9	9–12
Sheep, pig, goat	65%–75%	10–21	7	13–19
Chicken:				
Wet, sticky, and caked	75%	30	20	10
Moist, crumbly to sticky	50%	40	40	20
Crumbly	30%	60	55	30
Dry	15%	90	70	40
Ashed	None	None	135	100

TYPE OF GARDEN	BEST TYPE OF MANURE	BEST TIME TO APPLY
Flowers	Cow, horse	Early spring
Vegetables	Chicken, cow, horse	Fall, spring
Potatoes or root crops	Cow, horse	Fall
Acid-loving plants (blueberries, azaleas, mountain laurels, rhododendrons)	Cow, horse	Early fall or not at all

Soil Fixes

If you have . . .

CLAY SOIL: Add coarse sand (not beach sand) and compost.

SILT SOIL: Add coarse sand (not beach sand) or gravel and compost, or well-rotted horse manure mixed with fresh straw.

SANDY SOIL: Add humus or aged manure, or sawdust with some extra nitrogen. Heavy, clay-rich soil can also be added.

Soil Amendments

To improve soil, add . . .

BARK, GROUND: Made from various tree barks; improves soil structure.

COMPOST: Excellent conditioner.

LEAF MOLD: Decomposed leaves; adds nutrients and structure to soil.

LIME: Raises the pH of acidic soil; helps loosen clay soil.

MANURE: Best if composted; a good conditioner.

SAND: Improves drainage in clay soil.

TOPSOIL: Usually used with another amendment; replaces existing soil.

R E F E R E N C E

pH Preferences of Trees, Shrubs, Vegetables, and Flowers

An accurate soil test will tell you where your pH currently stands and will specify the amount of lime or sulfur that is needed to bring it up or down to the appropriate level. A pH of 6.5 is just about right for most home gardens, since most plants thrive in the 6.0 to 7.0 (slightly acidic to neutral) range. Some plants (blueberries, azaleas) prefer more strongly acidic soil, while a few (ferns, asparagus) do best in soil that is neutral to slightly alkaline. Acidic (sour) soil is counteracted by applying finely ground limestone, and alkaline (sweet) soil is treated with gypsum (calcium sulfate) or ground sulfur.

Common Name	Optimum pH Range	Common Name	Optimum pH Range	Common Name	Optimum pH Range
TREES AND SHRUBS		Spruce	5.0–6.0	Canna	6.0–8.0
Apple	5.0–6.5	Walnut, black	6.0–8.0	Carnation	6.0–7.0
Ash	6.0–7.5	Willow	6.0–8.0	Chrysanthemum	6.0–7.5
Azalea	4.5–6.0			Clematis	5.5–7.0
Basswood	6.0–7.5	**VEGETABLES**		Coleus	6.0–7.0
Beautybush	6.0–7.5	Asparagus	6.0–8.0	Coneflower, purple	5.0–7.5
Birch	5.0–6.5	Bean, pole	6.0–7.5	Cosmos	5.0–8.0
Blackberry	5.0–6.0	Beet	6.0–7.5	Crocus	6.0–8.0
Blueberry	4.0–6.0	Broccoli	6.0–7.0	Daffodil	6.0–6.5
Boxwood	6.0–7.5	Brussels sprout	6.0–7.5	Dahlia	6.0–7.5
Cherry, sour	6.0–7.0	Carrot	5.5–7.0	Daisy, Shasta	6.0–8.0
Chestnut	5.0–6.5	Cauliflower	5.5–7.5	Daylily	6.0–8.0
Crab apple	6.0–7.5	Celery	5.8–7.0	Delphinium	6.0–7.5
Dogwood	5.0–7.0	Chive	6.0–7.0	Foxglove	6.0–7.5
Elder, box	6.0–8.0	Cucumber	5.5–7.0	Geranium	6.0–8.0
Fir, balsam	5.0–6.0	Garlic	5.5–8.0	Gladiolus	5.0–7.0
Fir, Douglas	6.0–7.0	Kale	6.0–7.5	Hibiscus	6.0–8.0
Hemlock	5.0–6.0	Lettuce	6.0–7.0	Hollyhock	6.0–8.0
Hydrangea, blue-flowered	4.0–5.0	Pea, sweet	6.0–7.5	Hyacinth	6.5–7.5
Hydrangea, pink-flowered	6.0–7.0	Pepper, sweet	5.5–7.0	Iris, blue flag	5.0–7.5
Juniper	5.0–6.0	Potato	4.8–6.5	Lily-of-the-valley	4.5–6.0
Laurel, mountain	4.5–6.0	Pumpkin	5.5–7.5	Lupine	5.0–6.5
Lemon	6.0–7.5	Radish	6.0–7.0	Marigold	5.5–7.5
Lilac	6.0–7.5	Spinach	6.0–7.5	Morning glory	6.0–7.5
Maple, sugar	6.0–7.5	Squash, crookneck	6.0–7.5	Narcissus, trumpet	5.5–6.5
Oak, white	5.0–6.5	Squash, Hubbard	5.5–7.0	Nasturtium	5.5–7.5
Orange	6.0–7.5	Tomato	5.5–7.5	Pansy	5.5–6.5
Peach	6.0–7.0			Peony	6.0–7.5
Pear	6.0–7.5	**FLOWERS**		Petunia	6.0–7.5
Pecan	6.4–8.0	Alyssum	6.0–7.5	Phlox, summer	6.0–8.0
Pine, red	5.0–6.0	Aster, New England	6.0–8.0	Poppy, oriental	6.0–7.5
Pine, white	4.5–6.0	Baby's breath	6.0–7.0	Rose, hybrid tea	5.5–7.0
Plum	6.0–8.0	Bachelor's button	6.0–7.5	Rose, rugosa	6.0–7.0
Raspberry, red	5.5–7.0	Bee balm	6.0–7.5	Snapdragon	5.5–7.0
Rhododendron	4.5–6.0	Begonia	5.5–7.0	Sunflower	6.0–7.5
		Black-eyed Susan	5.5–7.0	Tulip	6.0–7.0
		Bleeding heart	6.0–7.5	Zinnia	5.5–7.0

R
E
F
E
R
E
N
C
E

274

Lawn-Growing Tips

Test your soil: The pH balance should be 7.0 or more; 6.2 to 6.7 puts your lawn at risk for fungal diseases. If the pH is too low, correct it with liming, best done in the fall.

The best time to apply fertilizer is just before it rains.

If you put lime and fertilizer on your lawn, spread half of it as you walk north to south, the other half as you walk east to west to cut down on missed areas.

Any feeding of lawns in the fall should be done with a low-nitrogen, slow-acting fertilizer.

In areas of your lawn where tree roots compete with the grass, apply some extra fertilizer to benefit both.

Moss and sorrel in lawns usually means poor soil, poor aeration or drainage, or excessive acidity.

Control weeds by promoting healthy lawn growth with natural fertilizers in spring and early fall.

Raise the level of your lawn-mower blades during the hot summer days. Taller grass resists drought better than short.

You can reduce mowing time by redesigning your lawn, reducing sharp corners and adding sweeping curves.

During a drought, let the grass grow longer between mowings, and reduce fertilizer.

Water your lawn early in the morning or in the evening.

Herbs to Plant in Lawns

Choose plants that suit your soil and your climate. All these can withstand mowing and considerable foot traffic.

Ajuga or bugleweed *(Ajuga reptans)*

Corsican mint *(Mentha requienii)*

Dwarf cinquefoil *(Potentilla tabernaemontani)*

English pennyroyal *(Mentha pulegium)*

Green Irish moss *(Sagina subulata)*

Pearly everlasting *(Anaphalis margaritacea)*

Roman chamomile *(Chamaemelum nobile)*

Rupturewort *(Herniaria glabra)*

Speedwell *(Veronica officinalis)*

Stonecrop *(Sedum ternatum)*

Sweet violets *(Viola odorata* or *V. tricolor)*

Thyme *(Thymus serpyllum)*

White clover *(Trifolium repens)*

Wild strawberries *(Fragaria virginiana)*

Wintergreen or partridgeberry *(Mitchella repens)*

A Gardener's Worst Phobias

Name of Fear	Object Feared
Alliumphobia	Garlic
Anthophobia	Flowers
Apiphobia	Bees
Arachnophobia	Spiders
Batonophobia	Plants
Bufonophobia	Toads
Dendrophobia	Trees
Entomophobia	Insects
Lachanophobia	Vegetables
Melissophobia	Bees
Mottephobia	Moths
Myrmecophobia	Ants
Ornithophobia	Birds
Ranidaphobia	Frogs
Rupophobia	Dirt
Scoleciphobia	Worms
Spheksophobia	Wasps

REFERENCE

Growing Herbs

HERB	PROPAGATION METHOD	START SEEDS INDOORS (weeks before last spring frost)	START SEEDS OUTDOORS (weeks before or after last spring frost)	MINIMUM SOIL TEMPERATURE TO GERMINATE (°F)	HEIGHT (inches)
Basil	Seeds, transplants	6–8	Anytime after	70	12–24
Borage	Seeds, division, cuttings	Not recommended	Anytime after	70	12–36
Chervil	Seeds	Not recommended	3–4 before	55	12–24
Chives	Seeds, division	8–10	3–4 before	60–70	12–18
Cilantro/ coriander	Seeds	Not recommended	Anytime after	60	12–36
Dill	Seeds	Not recommended	4–5 before	60–70	36–48
Fennel	Seeds	4–6	Anytime after	60–70	48–80
Lavender, English	Seeds, cuttings	8–12	1–2 before	70–75	18–36
Lavender, French	Transplants	Not recommended	Not recommended	—	18–36
Lemon balm	Seeds, division, cuttings	6–10	2–3 before	70	12–24
Lovage	Seeds, division	6–8	2–3 before	70	36–72
Oregano	Seeds, division, cuttings	6–10	Anytime after	70	12–24
Parsley	Seeds	10–12	3–4 before	70	18–24
Rosemary	Seeds, division, cuttings	8–10	Anytime after	70	48–72
Sage	Seeds, division, cuttings	6–10	1–2 before	60–70	12–48
Sorrel	Seeds, division	6–10	2–3 after	60–70	20–48
Spearmint	Division, cuttings	Not recommended	Not recommended	—	12–24
Summer savory	Seeds	4–6	Anytime after	60–70	4–15
Sweet cicely	Seeds, division	6–8	2–3 after	60–70	36–72
Tarragon, French	Cuttings, transplants	Not recommended	Not recommended	—	24–36
Thyme, common	Seeds, division, cuttings	6–10	2–3 before	70	2–12

REFERENCE

SPREAD (inches)	BLOOMING SEASON	USES	SOIL	LIGHT*	GROWTH TYPE
12	Midsummer	Culinary	Rich, moist	◯	Annual
12	Early to midsummer	Culinary	Rich, well-drained, dry	◯	Annual, biennial
8	Early to midsummer	Culinary	Rich, moist	◑	Annual, biennial
18	Early summer	Culinary	Rich, moist	◯	Perennial
4	Midsummer	Culinary	Light	◯◑	Annual
12	Early summer	Culinary	Rich	◯	Annual
18	Mid- to late summer	Culinary	Rich	◯	Annual
24	Early to late summer	Ornamental, medicinal	Moderately fertile, well-drained	◯	Perennial
24	Early to late summer	Ornamental, medicinal	Moderately fertile, well-drained	◯	Tender perennial
18	Midsummer to early fall	Culinary, ornamental	Rich, well-drained	◯◑	Perennial
36	Early to late summer	Culinary	Fertile, sandy	◯◑	Perennial
18	Mid- to late summer	Culinary	Poor	◯	Tender perennial
6–8	Mid- to late summer	Culinary	Medium-rich	◑	Biennial
48	Early summer	Culinary	Not too acid	◯	Tender perennial
30	Early to late summer	Culinary, ornamental	Well-drained	◯	Perennial
12–14	Late spring to early summer	Culinary, medicinal	Rich, organic	◯	Perennial
18	Early to midsummer	Culinary, medicinal, ornamental	Rich, moist	◑	Perennial
6	Early summer	Culinary	Medium rich	◯	Annual
36	Late spring	Culinary	Moderately fertile, well-drained	◯◑	Perennial
12	Late summer	Culinary, medicinal	Well-drained	◯◑	Perennial
7–12	Early to midsummer	Culinary	Fertile, well-drained	◯◑	Perennial

REFERENCE

Two Seasons of Bulb Basics

COMMON NAME	LATIN NAME	HARDINESS ZONE	SOIL	SUN/ SHADE*	SPACING (inches)
Allium	Allium	3–10	Well-drained/moist	○	12
Begonia, tuberous	Begonia	10–11	Well-drained/moist	○●	12–15
Blazing star/ gayfeather	Liatris	7–10	Well-drained	○	6
Caladium	Caladium	10–11	Well-drained/moist	○●	8–12
Calla lily	Zantedeschia	8–10	Well-drained/moist	○◐	8–24
Canna	Canna	8–11	Well-drained/moist	○	12–24
Cyclamen	Cyclamen	7–9	Well-drained/moist	◐	4
Dahlia	Dahlia	9–11	Well-drained/fertile	○	12–36
Daylily	Hemerocallis	3–10	Adaptable to most soils	○◐	12–24
Freesia	Freesia	9–11	Well-drained/moist/sandy	○◐	2–4
Garden gloxinia	Incarvillea	4–8	Well-drained/moist	○	12
Gladiolus	Gladiolus	4–11	Well-drained/fertile	○◐	4–9
Iris	Iris	3–10	Well-drained/sandy	○	3–6
Lily, Asiatic/Oriental	Lilium	3–8	Well-drained	○◐	8–12
Peacock flower	Tigridia	8–10	Well-drained	○	5–6
Shamrock/sorrel	Oxalis	5–9	Well-drained	○◐	4–6
Windflower	Anemone	3–9	Well-drained/moist	○◐	3–6
Bluebell	Hyacinthoides	4–9	Well-drained/fertile	○◐	4
Christmas rose/ hellebore	Helleborus	4–8	Neutral–alkaline	○◐	18
Crocus	Crocus	3–8	Well-drained/moist/fertile	○◐	4
Daffodil	Narcissus	3–10	Well-drained/moist/fertile	○◐	6
Fritillary	Fritillaria	3–9	Well-drained/sandy	○◐	3
Glory of the snow	Chionodoxa	3–9	Well-drained/moist	○◐	3
Grape hyacinth	Muscari	4–10	Well-drained/moist/fertile	○◐	3–4
"Iris, bearded"	Iris	3–9	Well-drained	○◐	4
"Iris, Siberian"	Iris	4–9	Well-drained	○◐	4
Ornamental onion	Allium	3–10	Well-drained/moist/fertile	○	12
Snowdrop	Galanthus	3–9	Well-drained/moist/fertile	○◐	3
Snowflake	Leucojum	5–9	Well-drained/moist/sandy	○◐	4
Spring starflower	Ipheion uniflorum	6–9	Well-drained loam	○◐	3–6
Star of Bethlehem	Ornithogalum	5–10	Well-drained/moist	○◐	2–5
Striped squill	Puschkinia scilloides	3–9	Well-drained	○◐	6
Tulip	Tulipa	4–8	Well-drained/fertile	○◐	3–6
Winter aconite	Eranthis	4–9	Well-drained/moist/fertile	○◐	3

Side labels: SPRING-PLANTED BULBS; FALL-PLANTED BULBS

DEPTH (inches)	BLOOMING SEASON	HEIGHT (inches)	NOTES
3–4	Spring to summer	6–60	Usually pest-free; a great cut flower
1–2	Summer to fall	8–18	North of Zone 10, lift in fall
4	Summer to fall	8–20	An excellent flower for drying; north of Zone 7, plant in spring, lift in fall
2	Summer	8–24	North of Zone 10, plant in spring, lift in fall
1–4	Summer	24–36	Fragrant; north of Zone 8, plant in spring, lift in fall
Level	Summer	18–60	North of Zone 8, plant in spring, lift in fall
1–2	Spring to fall	3–12	Naturalizes well in warm areas; north of Zone 7, lift in fall
4-6	Late summer	12–60	North of Zone 9, lift in fall
2	Summer	12–36	Mulch in winter in Zones 3 to 6
2	Summer	12–24	Fragrant; can be grown outdoors in warm climates
3–4	Summer	6–20	Does well in woodland settings
3–6	Early summer to early fall	12–80	North of Zone 10, lift in fall
4	Spring to late summer	3–72	Divide and replant rhizomes every two to five years
4–6	Early summer	36	Fragrant; self-sows; requires excellent drainage
4	Summer	18–24	North of Zone 8, lift in fall
2	Summer	2–12	Plant in confined area to control
2	Early summer	3–18	North of Zone 6, lift in fall
3–4	Spring	8–20	Excellent for borders, rock gardens and naturalizing
1–2	Spring	12	Hardy, but requires shelter from strong, cold winds
3	Early spring	5	Naturalizes well in grass
6	Early spring	14–24	Plant under shrubs or in a border
3	Midspring	6–30	Different species can be planted in rock gardens, woodland gardens, or borders
3	Spring	4–10	Self-sows easily; plant in rock gardens, raised beds, or under shrubs
2–3	Late winter to spring	6–12	Use as a border plant or in wildflower and rock gardens; self-sows easily
4	Early spring to early summer	3–48	Naturalizes well; good cut flower
4	Early spring to midsummer	18–48	An excellent cut flower
3–4	Late spring to early summer	6–60	Usually pest-free; a great cut flower
3	Spring	6–12	Best when clustered and planted in an area that will not dry out in summer
4	Spring	6–18	Naturalizes well
3	Spring	4–6	Fragrant; naturalizes easily
4	Spring to summer	6–24	North of Zone 5, plant in spring, lift in fall
3	Spring	4–6	Naturalizes easily; makes an attractive edging
4–6	Early to late spring	8–30	Excellent for borders, rock gardens, and naturalizing
2–3	Late winter to spring	2–4	Self-sows and naturalizes easily

REFERENCE

Flowers and Herbs That Attract Butterflies

Allium. . . . . *Allium*
Aster . . . . *Aster*
Bee balm. . . . . *Monarda*
Butterfly bush . . . . *Buddleia*
Catmint . . . . *Nepeta*
Clove pink. . . . . *Dianthus*
Cornflower . . . . *Centaurea*
Creeping thyme . . . . . *Thymus serpyllum*
Daylily . . . . *Hemerocallis*
Dill. . . . . *Anethum graveolens*
False indigo . . . . *Baptisia*
Fleabane . . . . *Erigeron*
Floss flower . . . . *Ageratum*
Globe thistle . . . . *Echinops*
Goldenrod . . . . *Solidago*
Helen's flower . . . . *Helenium*
Hollyhock. . . . . *Alcea*
Honeysuckle . . . . *Lonicera*
Lavender. . . . . *Lavendula*
Lilac . . . . *Syringa*
Lupine. . . . . *Lupinus*
Lychnis . . . . *Lychnis*

Mallow . . . . *Malva*
Mealycup sage . . . . *Salvia farinacea*
Milkweed . . . . *Asclepias*
Mint . . . . *Mentha*
Oregano. . . . . *Origanum vulgare*
Pansy. . . . . *Viola*
Parsley. . . . . *Petroselinum crispum*
Phlox . . . . *Phlox*
Privet. . . . . *Ligustrum*
Purple coneflower. . *Echinacea purpurea*
Purple loosestrife. . . . . *Lythrum*
Rock cress. . . . . *Arabis*
Sea holly . . . . *Eryngium*
Shasta daisy . . . . *Leucanthemum*
Snapdragon . . . . *Antirrhinum*
Stonecrop . . . . *Sedum*
Sweet alyssum . . . . *Lobularia*
Sweet marjoram. . . *Origanum majorana*
Sweet rocket . . . . *Hesperis*
Tickseed . . . . *Coreopsis*
Zinnia . . . . *Zinnia*

Flowers* That Attract Hummingbirds

Beard tongue . . . . *Penstemon*
Bee balm. . . . . *Monarda*
Butterfly bush . . . . *Buddleia*
Catmint. . . . . *Nepeta*
Clove pink. . . . . *Dianthus*
Columbine . . . . *Aquilegia*
Coral bells . . . . *Heuchera*
Daylily . . . . *Hemerocallis*
Desert candle . . . . *Yucca*
Flag iris . . . . *Iris*
Flowering tobacco. . . . . *Nicotiana alata*
Foxglove . . . . *Digitalis*
Larkspur . . . . *Delphinium*

Lily . . . . *Lilium*
Lupine. . . . . *Lupinus*
Petunia. . . . . *Petunia*
Pincushion flower . . . . *Scabiosa*
Red-hot poker . . . . *Kniphofia*
Scarlet sage . . . . *Salvia splendens*
Soapwort . . . . *Saponaria*
Summer phlox . . . . . . *Phlox paniculata*
Trumpet honeysuckle . . . . *Lonicera sempervirens*
Verbena . . . . *Verbena*
Weigela. . . . . *Weigela*

* Note: Choose varieties in red and orange shades.

Plant Resources

Bulbs

American Daffodil Society
4126 Winfield Rd., Columbus, OH 43220
www.daffodilusa.org

American Dahlia Society
1 Rock Falls Ct., Rockville, MD 20854
www.dahlia.org

American Iris Society
P.O. Box 28, Cedar Hill, MO 63016
www.irises.org

International Bulb Society
P.O. Box 336, Sanger, CA 93657
www.bulbsociety.org

Netherlands Flower Bulb Information Center
www.bulb.com

Ferns

American Fern Society
Missouri Botanical Garden
P.O. Box 299, St. Louis, MO 63166
http://amerfernsoc.org

The Hardy Fern Foundation
P.O. Box 166, Medina, WA 98036
www.hardyferns.org

Flowers

American Peony Society
www.americanpeonysociety.org

American Rhododendron Society
P.O. Box 525, Niagra Falls, NY 14304
416-424-1942 • www.rhododendron.org

American Rose Society
P.O. Box 30,000, Shreveport, LA 71119
318-938-5402 • www.ars.org

Hardy Plant Society/Mid-Atlantic Group
1549 Clayton Rd., West Chester, PA 19382
www.hardyplant.org

International Waterlily and Water Gardening Society
6828 26th St. W., Bradenton, FL 34207
www.iwgs.org

Lady Bird Johnson Wildflower Center
4801 La Crosse Ave., Austin, TX 78739
512-292-4100 • www.wildflower.org

Perennial Plant Association
3383 Schirtzinger Rd., Hilliard, OH 43026
614-771-8431 • www.perennialplant.org

Fruits

California Rare Fruit Growers
The Fullerton Arboretum-CSUF
P.O. Box 6850, Fullerton, CA 92834
www.crfg.org

Home Orchard Society
P.O. Box 230192, Tigard, OR 97281
www.homeorchardsociety.org

North American Fruit Explorers
1716 Apples Rd., Chapin, IL 62628
www.nafex.org

Herbs

American Herb Association
P.O. Box 1673, Nevada City, CA 95959
530-265-9552 • www.ahaherb.com

The Flower and Herb Exchange
3094 North Winn Rd., Decorah, IA 52101
563-382-5990 • www.seedsavers.org

Herb Research Foundation
4140 15th St., Boulder, CO 80304
303-449-2265 • www.herbs.org

The Herb Society of America
9019 Kirtland Chardon Rd.,
Kirtland, OH 44094
440-256-0514 • www.herbsociety.org

R
E
F
E
R
E
N
C
E

Cooperative Extension Services

Contact your local state cooperative extension Web site to get help with tricky insect problems, best varieties to plant in your area, or general maintenance of your garden.

Alabama
www.aces.edu

Alaska
www.uaf.edu/coop-ext

Arizona
www.ag.arizona.edu/
extension

Arkansas
www.uaex.edu

California
www.ucanr.org

Colorado
www.ext.colostate.edu

Connecticut
www.canr.uconn.edu/ces

Delaware
http://ag.udel.edu/
extension

Florida
www.ifas.ufl.edu/
extension/ces.htm

Georgia
www.caes.uga.edu/extension

Hawaii
www2.ctahr.hawaii.edu/
extout/extout.asp

Idaho
www.uidaho.edu/ag/
extension

Illinois
web.extension.uiuc.edu/
state/index.html/

Indiana
www.ces.purdue.edu

Iowa
www.extension.iastate.edu

Kansas
www.oznet.ksu.edu

Kentucky
www.ca.uky.edu

Louisiana
www.lsuagcenter.com

Maine
www.umext.maine.edu

Maryland
www.agnr.umd.edu/mce/
index.cfm

Massachusetts
www.umassextension.org

Michigan
www.msue.msu.edu/home

Minnesota
www.extension.umn.edu

Mississippi
www.msucares.com

Missouri
www.extension.missouri.edu

Montana
http://extn.msu.montana.edu

Nebraska
www.extension.unl.edu

Nevada
www.unce.unr.edu

New Hampshire
www.ceinfo.unh.edu

New Jersey
www.rce.rutgers.edu

New Mexico
www.cahe.nmsu.edu/ces

New York
www.cce.cornell.edu

North Carolina
www.ces.ncsu.edu

North Dakota
www.ext.nodak.edu

Ohio
http://extension.osu.edu

Oklahoma
www.dasnr.okstate.edu/oces

Oregon
www.osu.orst.edu/extension

Pennsylvania
www.extension.psu.edu

Rhode Island
www.edc.uri.edu

South Carolina
www.clemson.edu/
extension

South Dakota
http://sdces.sdstate.edu

Tennessee
www.utextension.utk.edu

Texas
http://texasextension.tamu
.edu

Utah
www.extension.usu.edu

Vermont
www.uvm.edu/~uvmext

Virginia
www.ext.vt.edu

Washington
http://ext.wsu.edu

West Virginia
www.wvu.edu/~exten

Wisconsin
www.uwex.edu/ces

Wyoming
http://uwadmnweb.uwyo
.edu/uwces

Makeshift Measurers

When you don't have a measuring stick or tape, use what is at hand. To this list, add other items that you always (or nearly always) have handy.

Credit card . . . . 3⅜" x 2⅛"	Your foot/shoe: _____
Business card (standard). . . . . . 3½" x 2"	Your outstretched arms, fingertip
Floor tile . . . . 12" square	to fingertip: _____
Dollar bill . . . . 6⅛" x 2⅝"	Your shoelace: _____
Quarter (diameter) . . . . 1"	Your necktie: _____
Penny (diameter) . . . . ¾"	Your belt: _____
Sheet of paper. . . . . 8½" x 11"	
(legal size: 8½" x 14")	

If you don't have a scale or a measuring spoon handy, try these for size:
A piece of meat the size of your hand or a deck of cards = 3 to 4 ounces.
A piece of meat or cheese the size of a golf ball = about 1 ounce.
From the tip of your smallest finger to the first joint = about 1 teaspoon.
The tip of your thumb = about 1 tablespoon.

The idea of using available materials to measure is not new.
1 foot = the length of a person's foot.
1 yard = the distance from a person's nose to the fingertip of an outstretched arm.
1 acre = the amount of land an ox can plow in a day.

Hand Thermometer for Outdoor Cooking

■ Hold your palm close to where the food will be cooking: over the coals or in front of a reflector oven. Count "one-and-one, two-and-two," and so on (each pair is roughly equivalent to one second), for as many seconds as you can hold your hand still.

Seconds Counted	Heat	Temperature
6–8	Slow	250°–350°F
4–5	Moderate	350°–400°F
2–3	Hot	400°–450°F
1 or less	Very hot	450°–500°F

Miscellaneous Length Measures

ASTRONOMICAL UNIT (A.U.): 93,000,000 miles; the average distance from Earth to the Sun

BOLT: 40 yards; used for measuring cloth

CHAIN: 66 feet; one mile is equal to 80 chains; used in surveying

CUBIT: 18 inches; derived from the distance between elbow and tip of middle finger

HAND: 4 inches; derived from the width of the hand

LEAGUE: usually estimated at 3 miles

LIGHT-YEAR: 5,880,000,000,000 miles; the distance light travels in a vacuum in a year at the rate of 186,281.7 miles per second

PICA: about ⅙ inch; used in printing for measuring column width, etc.

SPAN: 9 inches; derived from the distance between the end of the thumb and the end of the little finger when both are outstretched

R
E
F
E
R
E
N
C
E

Body Mass Index (BMI) Formula

Here's an easy formula to figure your Body Mass Index (BMI), thought to be a fairly accurate indicator of relative body size. **W** is your weight in pounds and **H** is your height in inches.

$$BMI = \left(\frac{W}{H^2}\right) \times 703$$

■ If the result is 18.5 to 24.9, you are within a healthy weight range.

■ If it's below 18.5, you are too thin.

■ From 25 to 29.9, you are overweight and at increased risk for health problems.

■ At 30 and above, you are considered obese and at a dramatically increased risk for serious health problems.

There are exceptions to the above, including children, expectant mothers, and the elderly. Very muscular people with a high BMI generally have nothing to worry about, and extreme skinniness is generally a symptom of some other health problem, not the cause.

Tape-Measure Method

■ Here's another way to see if you are dangerously overweight. Measure your waistline. A waist measurement of more than 35 inches in women and more than 40 inches in men, regardless of height, suggests a serious risk of weight-related health problems.

Calorie-Burning Comparisons

If you hustle through your chores to get to the fitness center, relax. You're getting a great workout already. The left-hand column lists "chore" exercises, the middle column shows the number of calories burned per minute per pound of body weight, and the right-hand column lists comparable "recreational" exercises. For example, a 150-pound person forking straw bales burns 9.45 calories per minute, the same workout he or she would get playing basketball.

Chore	Calories	Recreational
Chopping with an ax, fast	0.135	Skiing, cross-country, uphill
Climbing hills, with 44-pound load	0.066	Swimming, crawl, fast
Digging trenches	0.065	Skiing, cross-country, steady walk
Forking straw bales	0.063	Basketball
Chopping down trees	0.060	Football
Climbing hills, with 9-pound load	0.058	Swimming, crawl, slow
Sawing by hand	0.055	Skiing, cross-country, moderate
Mowing lawns	0.051	Horseback riding, trotting
Scrubbing floors	0.049	Tennis
Shoveling coal	0.049	Aerobic dance, medium
Hoeing	0.041	Weight training, circuit training
Stacking firewood	0.040	Weight lifting, free weights
Shoveling grain	0.038	Golf
Painting houses	0.035	Walking, normal pace, asphalt road
Weeding	0.033	Table tennis
Shopping for food	0.028	Cycling, 5.5 mph
Mopping floors	0.028	Fishing
Washing windows	0.026	Croquet
Raking	0.025	Dancing, ballroom
Driving a tractor	0.016	Drawing, standing position

Tile and Vinyl Flooring

Make a scale drawing of your room with all measurements clearly marked, and take it with you when you shop for tile flooring. Ask the salespeople to help you calculate your needs if you have rooms that feature bay windows, unusual jogs or turns, or if you plan to use special floor patterns or tiles with designs.

Ceramic Tile

■ Ceramic tiles for floors and walls come in a range of sizes, from 1x1-inch mosaics up to 12x12-inch (or larger) squares. The most popular size is the 4¼-inch-square tile, but there is a trend toward larger tiles (8x8s, 10x10s, 12x12s). Installing these larger tiles can be a challenge because the underlayment must be absolutely even and level.

■ Small, one-inch mosaic tiles are usually joined together in 12x12-inch or 12x24-inch sheets to make them easier to install. You can have a custom pattern made, or you can mix different-color tiles to create your own mosaic borders, patterns, and pictures.

Sheet Vinyl

■ Sheet vinyl typically comes in 6- and 12-foot widths. If your floor requires two or more pieces, your estimate must include enough overlap to allow you to match the pattern.

Vinyl Tile

■ Vinyl tiles generally come in 9- and 12-inch squares. To find the number of 12-inch tiles you need, just multiply the length of the room (in feet) by the width (rounding fractions up to the next foot) to get the number of tiles you need. Add 5 percent extra for cutting and waste. Measure any obstructions on the floor that you will be tiling around (such as appliances and cabinets), and subtract

that square footage from the total. To calculate the number of 9-inch tiles, divide the room's length (in inches) by 9, then divide the room's width by 9. Multiply those two numbers together to get the number of tiles you need, and then add 5 percent extra for cutting and waste.

Wallpaper

Before choosing your wallpaper, keep in mind that wallpaper with little or no pattern to match at the seams and the ceiling will be the easiest to apply, thus resulting in the least amount of wasted wallpaper. If you choose a patterned wallpaper, a small repeating pattern will result in less waste than a large repeating pattern. And a pattern that is aligned horizontally (matching on each column of paper) will waste less than one that drops or alternates its pattern (matching on every other column).

To determine the amount of wall space you're covering:

■ Measure the length of each wall, add these figures together, and multiply by the height of the walls to get the area (square footage) of the room's walls.

■ Calculate the square footage of each door, window, and other opening in the room. Add these figures together and subtract the total from the area of the room's walls.

■ Take that figure and multiply by 1.15, to account for a waste rate of about 15 percent in your wallpaper project. You'll end up with a target amount to purchase when you shop.

■ Wallpaper is sold in single, double, and triple rolls. Coverage can vary, so be sure to refer to the roll's label for the proper square footage. (The average coverage for a double roll, for example, is 56 square feet.) After choosing a paper, divide the coverage figure (from the label) into the total square footage of the walls of the room you're papering. Round the answer up to the nearest whole number. This is the number of rolls you need to buy.

■ Save leftover wallpaper rolls, carefully wrapped to keep clean.

HOW MUCH DO YOU NEED?
Interior Paint

Estimate your room size and paint needs before you go to the store. Running out of a custom color halfway through the job could mean disaster. For the sake of the following exercise, assume that you have a 10x15-foot room with an 8-foot ceiling. The room has two doors and two windows.

For Walls

■ Measure the total distance (perimeter) around the room:

(10 ft. + 15 ft.) x 2 = 50 ft.

■ Multiply the perimeter by the ceiling height to get the total wall area:

50 ft. x 8 ft. = 400 sq. ft.

■ Doors are usually 21 square feet (there are two in this exercise):

21 sq. ft. x 2 = 42 sq. ft.

■ Windows average 15 square feet (there are two in this exercise):

15 sq. ft. x 2 = 30 sq. ft.

■ Take the total wall area and subtract the area for the doors and windows to get the wall surface to be painted:

400 sq. ft. (wall area)
− 42 sq. ft. (doors)
− 30 sq. ft. (windows)
328 sq. ft.

■ As a rule of thumb, one gallon of quality paint will usually cover 400 square feet. One quart will cover 100 square feet. Because you need to cover 328 square feet in this example, one gallon will be adequate to give one coat of paint to the walls. (Coverage will be affected by the porosity and texture of the surface. In addition, bright colors may require a minimum of two coats.)

For Ceilings

■ Using the rule of thumb for coverage above, you can calculate the quantity of paint needed for the ceiling by multiplying the width by the length:

10 ft. x 15 ft. = 150 sq. ft.

This ceiling will require approximately two quarts of paint. (A flat finish is recommended to minimize surface imperfections.)

For Doors, Windows, and Trim

■ The area for the doors and windows has been calculated above. (The windowpane area that does not get painted should allow for enough paint for any trim around doors and windows.) Determine the baseboard trim by taking the perimeter of the room, less 3 feet per door (3 ft. x 2 = 6 ft.), and multiplying this by the average trim width of your baseboard, which in this example is 6 inches (or 0.5 feet).

50 ft. (perimeter) − 6 ft. = 44 ft.
44 ft. x 0.5 ft. = 22 sq. ft.

■ Add the area for doors, windows, and baseboard trim.

42 sq. ft. (doors)
+30 sq. ft. (windows)
+22 sq. ft. (baseboard trim)
94 sq. ft.

One quart will be sufficient to cover the doors, windows, and trim in this example.

−courtesy M.A.B. Paints